DIGITAL GENERATIONS

*Children, Young People,
and New Media*

DIGITAL GENERATIONS

Children, Young People, and New Media

Edited by

David Buckingham
Rebekah Willett
Institute of Education, University of London

LEA Lawrence Erlbaum Associates
Taylor & Francis Group

New York London

Lawrence Erlbaum Associates, Inc., Publishers
10 Industrial Avenue
Mahwah, New Jersey 07430
www.erlbaum.com

Cover design by Kathryn Houghtaling Lacey

Library of Congress Cataloging-in-Publication Data

Digital generations : children, young people, and new media / edited by
    David Buckingham and Rebekah Willett.
        p.   cm.
    Includes bibliographical references and index.
    ISBN 0-8058-5980-2 (alk. paper) — ISBN 0-8058-5862-8 (case)
    1. Internet and children.   2. Internet and teenagers.   3. Electronic games—Social
aspects.   4. Digital media—Social aspects.   I. Buckingham, David, 1954–
II. Willett, Rebekah.

HQ784.I58D53   2006
303.48′33083—dc22   2005043509
                                                                          CIP

Books published by Lawrence Erlbaum Associates are printed on acid-free paper,
and their bindings are chosen for strength and durability.

Printed in the United States of America
10 9 8 7 6 5 4 3 2

Contents

II THE INTERNET

III IDENTITIES AND ONLINE COMMUNITIES

IV LEARNING AND EDUCATION

Preface

Computer games, the internet, and other new communications media are often seen to pose threats and dangers to young people; but they also provide new opportunities for creativity and self-determination. This book draws on papers presented at a successful international conference held at the Institute of Education, London University, in July 2004. Of the more than 130 papers presented at the conference, we selected 17 of the best, seeking to produce a comprehensive and coherent account of the field. The collection brings together researchers from a range of academic disciplines—including media and cultural studies, anthropology, sociology, psychology, and education—and is aimed at a wide audience of researchers, practitioners in digital media, and educators. Several of the authors are well known internationally, while others are promising younger scholars.

The book is organized in terms of four key themes. In Part I, "Play and Gaming," chapters address debates around the negative effects and educational potential of computer games, approaches to analyzing gaming experiences, and the multimedia nature of young people's fan productions. Part II, "The Internet," presents research on parents' regulation of the internet in the home, uses of the internet for political communication and its role in promoting civic participation, and the political economy of internet regulation. In Part III, "Identities and Online Communities," four chapters address the experience of girls, gay and lesbian youth, blogging, and informal learning in online communities. Part IV, "Learning and Education," presents research on the use of new technologies in youth and community projects and schools, and discussions of the role of education with respect to the digital divide. The book is prefaced by an overview chapter exploring and questioning the concept of the *digital generation*, and each part is prefaced by a brief introduction outlining the following chapters.

We would like to thank the sponsors of the conference for providing financial support and bursaries for conference delegates: the British Academy, the Next Generation Foundation, Eduserv, and Ofcom. Thanks also to Liza Chan and Tim Neumann for support with the editorial work, to Emily Wilkinson and Bonita d' Amil at Lawrence Erlbaum Associates for their patience and support, and to our contributors for meeting their deadlines in good time.

List of Contributors

Liesbeth de Block, Institute of Education, University of London, UK
Magdalena Bober, London School of Economics and Political Science, UK
David Buckingham, Institute of Education, University of London, UK
Andrew Burn, Institute of Education, University of London, UK
Julia Davies, University of Sheffield, UK
Susan Driver, Wilfrid Laurier University, Canada
James Durran, Parkside Community College, Cambridge, UK
Ed Figueroa, Hopeworks, Camden, New Jersey, USA
Julie Frechette, Worcester State College, USA
Barbara Gottlieb-Robles, American University, USA
Bill Holderness, UPE, South Africa
Mizuko Ito, University of Southern California, USA
Henry Jenkins, Massachusetts Institute of Technology, USA
Sonia Livingstone, London School of Economics and Political Science, UK
Margaret Mackey, University of Alberta, Canada
Kathryn Montgomery, American University, USA
Martin Oliver, Institute of Education, University of London, UK
Tobias Olsson, Lund University, Sweden
Caroline Pelletier, Institute of Education, University of London, UK
Michele Polak, Miami University, USA
Jeff Putthoff, Hopeworks, Camden, New Jersey, USA

Ingegerd Rydin, Halmstad University, Sweden

Lois Ann Scheidt, Indiana University, USA

Carol C. Thompson, University of Pennsylvania, USA

Rebekah Willett, Institute of Education, University of London, UK

Chapter 1

Is There a Digital Generation?

David Buckingham
University of London

The title of this book reflects a kind of generational rhetoric that often characterizes discussions of the use and impact of so-called *new media*. Young people are frequently described as a *digital generation*—a generation defined in and through its experience of digital computer technology. This rhetoric can be found in popular commentary in fields as diverse as commerce, government, education, and youth activism. Thus, the electronics company Panasonic is currently advertising its new e.wear MP3 players as providing "digital music for a digital generation"; the U.S. Department of Commerce speaks about "preparing the digital generation for the age of innovation" (Mehlman, 2003); the educationalist Papert (1996) writes of the "digital generation gap" between parents and children; and the journalist Lasica (2002) seeks to defend young people from what he sees as "Hollywood's war against the digital generation." Elsewhere, we encounter "the Nintendo generation" (Green & Bigum, 1993), "the Playstation generation" (Blair, 2004), and the "net generation" (Tapscott, 1998), as well as related constructions such as "cyberkids" (Holloway & Valentine, 2003), "bionic children" ("Bionic Kids," 2003), and even "cyborg babies" (Davis-Floyd & Dumit, 1998). Meanwhile in Japan, there has been considerable discussion of the "thumb generation"—young people who have apparently developed a new dexterity in their thumbs as a result of their use of game consoles and mobile phones (Brooke, 2002).

Of course the notion of a "generation gap" has been around for decades, if not centuries. It typically emerges as a consequence of adults' fears about

1

the escalating pace of social change and their anxieties about a loss of continuity with the past. The idea of a digital generation merely connects these fears and anxieties to technology: It suggests that something has fundamentally and irrevocably changed, and that this change is somehow produced by technology. In this opening chapter, I suggest that we should approach these issues with a degree of skepticism. Rather than falling back on easy rhetoric, there are several fundamental questions we need to address. Is there indeed a digital generation—or even digital generations, in the plural? If there is, how do we define it, does it matter, and in what ways?

THE SOCIAL HISTORY OF GENERATIONS

In their book *Generations, Culture, and Society,* Edmunds and Turner (2002) provide the basis for a sociological and historical theory of generations. They define a *generation* as "an age cohort that comes to have social significance by virtue of constituting itself as a cultural identity" (p. 7). As this implies, generations are defined both historically and culturally. Most simply, a generation is a cohort of individuals born within a particular time frame, although, as Edmunds and Turner suggest, a generation may also be defined by its relationship to a particular traumatic event, such as a world war, the Great Depression, or the rise of fascism. (It may be that the attack on the U.S. World Trade Center in 2001, and the ensuing reconfiguration of world politics, will come to be seen as a similarly defining moment.) However, this process of definition is also a cultural issue; it is a matter of how the potential members of a generation constitute themselves as having a shared identity. It is possible, following this argument, that some generations may be more self-conscious or self-reflexive than others, and hence come to claim greater social significance: The "1960s generation" (at least in Western countries) might be seen in this way. More subjectively, this argument also implies that individuals' generational identifications are malleable and fluid, and so we may identify with a generation of which we are not strictly members in terms of biological age.

This theory of the construction of generations raises broader questions about structure and agency that are central to social theory. Mannheim (1952/1979), for example, argues that the definition of generations is partly a matter of the particular life chances that are available to people by virtue of when they happened to be born; but it is also a question of how people respond to those life chances, how they interpret their given historical circumstances, and the shared meanings they attribute to their position. Mannheim argues that different units within a given generation are likely to define their situation—and hence to behave as members of a generation (to "act their age," perhaps)—in different ways. Interestingly, he also notes that, as the pace of social change accelerates, the boundaries between generations are likely to become blurred. Similarly, Bourdieu (1993) argues that generations are socially and culturally defined and produced. Different generations will have different tastes, orientations, beliefs, and dispositions (or habitus). Although these are partly a result of the historical and economic circumstances in which people were born, they also emerge through struggles between generations over cultural and economic resources. As this implies, generations are naturally occurring phenomena, which emerge simply as a result of the passing of time. But generations also produce themselves, as their members (and, presumably, nonmembers too) define the *meanings* of generational membership.

These ideas find many echoes in recent work on the sociology of childhood and youth. Alanen (2001) uses the notion of *generationing* to describe the ways in which children and adults assert and jointly construct their differences on grounds of age. Defining who is an adult and who is a child (or a young person) occurs partly through a continual othering—and indeed policing—of those who are older or younger. This kind of social constructionist view is often criticized for failing to pay enough attention to biological or developmental differences, but it does reflect the ways in which the generational order is constantly being renegotiated. Likewise, in youth research, researchers are now inclined to conceive of socialization not merely as something that adults do to young people, but as a process in which young people are also active participants. The notion of *self-socialization*, which has become prominent in youth studies in Germany (e.g., Fromme et al., 1999), implies that socialization is something that young people work to achieve for themselves, among the peer group. Meanwhile others have discussed the notion of *reverse socialization* (Hoikkala, 2004)—the possibility that young people may socialize their parents to adapt to social change, not least around technology. Both these ideas reflect a broader rejection of the notion that the social or generational order is something fixed and is simply imposed on passive individuals. In both cases also, the media and consumer culture have been seen to play a central role in this defining and redefining of generational differences and identities (e.g., see Arnett, 1995; Johansson, 2004).

Nevertheless, just as in discussions of gender, the study of generational differences inevitably runs the risk of essentializing those differences. It is worth recalling here Mannheim's notion of *generational units* and his argument that a generation is not necessarily uniform, but that members attribute meaning to generational experiences in quite different ways. It is also difficult to know where the distinctions between generations are to be drawn. For example, if we explore the construction of a popular category such as *Generation X*, there is considerable disagreement about its historical parameters, let alone whether the term actually means anything to the people who are allegedly members of this generation (Ulrich & Harris, 2003). Which experiences, dispositions, or characteristics do we take to be representative of a generation? Who are the spokespersons of their generation, and how is their authority established? How do we actually identify the boundaries—or even the shared consciousness—of a generation?

These kinds of questions are often at the heart of academic controversies about the nature of social change. For example, there has been considerable debate within sociology between Ronald Inglehardt and others about the notion of a postmaterialist generation (Brechin & Kempton, 1994; Inglehardt, 1990; Reimer, 1989). Essentially, Inglehardt argues that there has been a generational shift from materialist to postmaterialist values in the postwar period; yet his analysis raises difficult theoretical and methodological questions about how we measure and identify values, and about the relationship between the values that people might proclaim or sign up to in a questionnaire and their actual behavior. Both within the academy and popular debate, therefore, the concept of *generation* is complex and contested, and how we define, characterize, and study generations is highly problematic.

ACCOUNTING FOR MEDIA AND TECHNOLOGY

This issue becomes even more complicated when we take account of the potential role of media and technology in the construction and self-construction of generations. Within media and cultural studies, age has (somewhat belatedly) come to join class, ethnicity, and gender as a key dimension of social identity. In attempting to escape the limitations of normative psychological accounts, there has been a growing emphasis on how the media—and the ways in which the media are used—participate in defining the meanings of age differences (Buckingham, 2000; Jenkins, 1998). As I noted, sociologists like Edmunds and Turner (2002) sometimes point to the role of traumatic defining events—such as wars—in defining generations. It is possible, at least in principle, that radical shifts in technology or media might also play a role in this respect. The Australian cultural theorist Wark (1993), for example, argues that: "Generations are not defined by war or depression any more. They are defined by media culture" (p. 75).

What is the evidence for such a claim? On one level, we might draw attention to the role of taste cultures among children and young people that serve precisely to exclude adults, and thereby to assert their own generational distinctiveness. This is most apparent in the case of specialized areas of popular music and fashion (Bennett, 1999), but it also occurs around more mainstream media such as TV (Davies et al., 2000). We might also point to the phenomenon of retro culture—the periodic revivals of particular musical or fashion styles, or enthusiasms for cult TV shows of earlier decades, which often combine nostalgia and irony. As these examples imply, media can be used self-reflexively, as signifiers of generational affiliation.

Of course the media industries are also busily defining and reconfiguring generational categories for the purposes of maximizing profit. Thus, it is possible to trace the historical emergence of age-based categories within marketing discourse and practice. The category of the *teenager* is often seen as a phenomenon of the postwar consumer boom, which came to prominence in market research during the 1950s (Abrams, 1959). Cook's (2004) history of the children's clothing industry in the United States identifies the gradual emergence of age-based distinctions, and the construction of new age-defined categories such as the *toddler* during the 1930s. In more recent years, we have seen the construction of the *tween* consumer (Willett, 2005), as well as a proliferation of new age-based marketing categories such as *kidults*, *middle youth*, *adultescents*, and so on. As in the case of *Generation X*, it is possible to show that, even if these categories were not invented by marketers, they are very quickly taken up by them as a means of describing and hoping to control what they perceive as a volatile and unpredictable market.

Beyond this, it could be argued that *youth* has become a symbolic value that can be marketed to a wide range of audiences—to children aspiring to escape from the constraints of childhood (as in the marketing of girls' fashion products and makeup), and to adults aspiring to recover lost values of youthful energy and rebellion (as in the marketing of much contemporary rock music). In the increasingly competitive environment of contemporary media, such distinctions have a growing commercial significance. The term *youth* in particular invokes a set of symbolic meanings that can refer to fantasy identities as much as to material possibilities. How old you are—or how old you imagine yourself to be—is increasingly defined by what you consume, by your relationship to specific brands and commodities; and youth culture, it would seem, is no longer just for young people.

Social theorists have suggested that, in recent decades, chronological age has become decoupled from people's actual life situations, and that the normative biography—or the steady progress of the life course—has become decentered (Ziehe, 2005). Even so, children and young people are not passive victims of this process: They are actively involved in sustaining the distinctions and boundaries between the generations even as they may aspire to challenge them. In exploring the changing meanings of such age-based, generational categories, therefore, we need to understand how they are actually used by young people—and indeed, whether they recognize them at all—as well as how they work to regulate and define the meanings of age differences. We need to recall that such categories are not merely discursive, imaginary fictions: They also have real material consequences.

Despite these qualifications (and others to be considered in due course), Wark's assertion that generations are "defined by media culture" does raise some interesting empirical questions. Do young people who are growing up with digital media in fact have a different orientation to the world, a different set of dispositions or characteristics—or in Bourdieu's terms, a different habitus? It should be possible to ask this question without assuming a simple before-and-after sequence—not least because the dissemination of technology is bound to be gradual and incremental. It should be possible to address it without necessarily assuming a form of technological determinism—and to take account of the fact that technology may reinforce changes that would be happening in any case. It should be possible to answer it without having to reduce everything to age—to acknowledge that there may indeed be differences (e.g., to do with gender, culture, and social class) *within* a given generation. At least in principle, therefore, it should be possible to posit the existence of a digital generation without recourse to teleology, determinism, or essentialism.

THE GENERATIONAL HYPOTHESIS

Tapscott's (1998) book, *Growing Up Digital: The Rise of the Net Generation,* is one of the best-known and most ambitious arguments in favor of the idea of the digital generation. Tapscott's account is based on two sets of binary oppositions—between technologies (TV vs. the internet) and between generations (the Baby Boomers vs. the net generation). He draws clear lines between the generations, based primarily on birth-rate statistics: The Boomers were born between 1946 and 1964, followed by the Bust (1965–1976) and the Boom Echo (1977–1997). According to Tapscott, the Boomers are the "TV generation," who are defined by their relationship with that medium, just as the children of the Boom Echo are the net generation.

Tapscott's oppositions between these technologies are stark and absolute. Television is a passive medium, whereas the Net is active; TV "dumbs down" its users, whereas the Net raises their intelligence; TV broadcasts a singular view of the world, whereas the Net is democratic and interactive; TV isolates, whereas the Net builds communities; and so on. Just as TV is the antithesis of the Net, so the TV generation is the antithesis of the net generation. Like the technology they now control, the values of the TV generation are increasingly conservative, hierarchical, inflexible, and centralized. By contrast, the N-Geners are "hungry for expression, discovery and their own self-development": They are savvy, self-reliant, analytical, articulate, creative, inquisitive, accepting of diversity, and socially conscious. These generational differences are seen to be *produced* by technology, rather than being a result of other social, historical, or cultural forces. Unlike their parents, who are portrayed as incompetent technophobes, children are seen to possess an intuitive, spontaneous relationship with digital technology. "For many kids," Tapscott (1998) argued, "using the new technology is as natural as breathing" (p. 40). Technology is the means of their empowerment, and it will ultimately lead to a "generational explosion."

Growing Up Digital takes the reader through a series of areas—cognition, play, learning, family, consumption, and work. In each case, the argument is essentially the same: Technology offers a new form of empowerment for young people and is producing a generation gap as the habits and preferences of the older generation are coming to be superseded. From an academic vantage point, it is perhaps rather easy to mock these kinds of arguments: They lack scholarly caution and qualification, and the evidence on which they are based is unrepresentative and often anecdotal. Tapscott is a management consultant, entrepreneur, and motivational speaker; as such, academic virtues are likely only to dilute his appeal. Yet in fact many of his arguments come quite close to the kinds of ideas that circulate in the discourse of policymakers—and, I would suggest, in the academy as well. For this reason, it is worth exploring his claims more closely.

Tapscott argues that technology produces a wide range of social, psychological, and even political changes. Five key claims are particularly relevant to our concerns here:

1. First, technology is seen to create new styles of communication and interaction. Among the 10 themes that Tapscott sees as characteristic of Web-based communication, he included independence and autonomy, emotional and intellectual openness, innovation, free expression, immediacy, and an investigative approach. The internet provides new means for constructing community: It is an active and participatory medium, which is about many-to-many, distributed communication. These new communities are inclusive and require the creation of new kinds of trust. They are about breaking down walls, and they allow the creation of new kinds of relationships, both in the form of friendships and new family lifestyles: The internet, Tapscott argued, will give rise to "a new kind of open family" characterized by equality, dialogue, and mutual trust.

2. Second, the internet also produces new styles of playful learning. Unlike the TV generation, the net generation is inquisitive and self-directed in learning. It is more skeptical and analytical, more inclined toward critical thinking, and more likely to challenge and question established authorities than previous generations. Net-based learning is interactive, rather than a matter of transmission. Where old-style education was teacher-dominated

and authoritarian, digitally based education is nonlinear and learner-centered, based on discovery rather than the delivery of information. The net transforms the teacher into a facilitator, whose input has to be customized to learners' needs. Above all, learning via the internet is "fun": Learning is play and play is learning, and so "the net is a place where kids can be kids." However, this new style of learning is also particularly appropriate to the so-called *knowledge economy* and to the new kinds of employment that are emerging there. In this new world, the old knowledge hierarchies no longer apply, and the working environment is one of personal networking, innovation, and openness.

3. These new conditions of education, work, and social life also require new competencies or new forms of "literacy." This is apparent to some degree in the innovative, informal styles of language that are emerging on the internet—emoticons and so on—and in the changing conventions of language use (or netiquette). More broadly, however, internet communication is seen to require and produce new intellectual powers and even more complex brain structures: It results in a kind of accelerated development, and young people who do not have access to it will be "developmentally disadvantaged." The net generation not only has different skills in terms of accessing and navigating through information, it also processes and evaluates information in a radically different way from the TV generation. This new orientation toward information is natural and spontaneous, rather than learned: It somehow connects with the inherent condition of childhood.

4. At each of these levels, technology is implicitly seen to have direct psychological effects. Yet it also has consequences at a more psychic level: It provides new ways of forming identity, and hence new forms of personhood. For all the reasons identified earlier, the net generation is high in self-esteem: The use of digital media imparts an enhanced sense of efficacy and self-worth—not only for young people with disabilities, but for all. In the digital world, the child is the actor. Via the medium of chat, the internet provides opportunities for experimentation and play with identity, and for the adoption or construction of multiple selves. By offering communication with different aspects of the self, it enables young people to relate to the world and to others in more powerful ways.

5. Finally, the internet is also seen to be leading to the emergence of a new kind of politics. The net is distributed and democratic: It is a collectively shared, nonhierarchical delivery system that serves as "a medium for social awakening." Its effects on offline behavior are also inherently democratizing. According to Tapscott, the net generation is more tolerant, more globally oriented, more inclined to exercise social and civic responsibility, and more inclined to respect the environment. Technology is radicalizing them, just as TV ultimately led the Baby Boomers to accept the status quo.

ANOTHER STORY

In many ways, these are familiar arguments. To a greater or lesser extent, they are shared by many popular and academic commentators on the impact of digital media. They place a generational spin on what has come to be called the *Californian ideology*—the form of cyberlibertarianism favored not just by Internet activists, but also (perhaps paradoxically) by many marketing gurus (Barbrook & Cameron, 1996). Despite the evident pleasures of wishful thinking, it is important to restate some of the fundamental limitations of such arguments.

Tapscott's approach is clearly based on a form of technological determinism. From this perspective, technology is seen to emerge from a neutral process of scientific research and development, rather than from the interplay of complex social, economic, and political forces. It is then seen to have effects—to bring about social, psychological, and political changes— irrespective of the ways in which it is used, and of the social contexts and processes into which it enters. Technology is regarded as an autonomous force that is somehow independent of human society and acts on it from outside. This view connects with a familiar rhetoric about the information society (or the knowledge economy), which similarly appears to attribute a determining power to some disembodied force (information). This perspective has been widely challenged. Williams (1974), for example, criticized the reductionism of this approach and its tendency to reify technology, as if it existed independently of human activity, although he also challenged the opposite view—that technology is entirely shaped by preexisting social, economic, and political forces (see also Chandler, 1995; Webster, 1995). Meanwhile, the notion of the *information society* also seems to neglect the role of human agency, and the complex, gradual processes through which technologies are integrated within existing social activities and arrangements (May, 2002).

These kinds of ideas carry a particular emotional charge when it comes to the discussion of childhood. The combination of childhood and technology serves as a powerful focus for much broader hopes and fears about social change: For all those who believe, like Tapscott, that technology is liberating and empowering children, there are many others who see it as destroying or betraying the essence of childhood (e.g., Cordes & Miller, 2002; Postman, 1983). Yet the fundamental question here is how we understand the causal relationships that are at stake. As I have argued elsewhere (Buckingham, 2000, 2005), contemporary developments in technology do present new risks and opportunities for children. But these developments can only be adequately understood in the light of other changes—for example, in the political economy of children's culture, the sociocultural policies and practices that regulate and define childhood, and the everyday social realities of children's lives. These latter changes can also be overstated, and frequently are; but in any case, it makes little sense to consider them in isolation from each other.

This technologically determinist stance means that there are many issues and phenomena that Tapscott and other such technology boosters are bound to ignore. He neglects the fundamental continuities and interdependencies between new media and the old media (such as TV) that he so despises—continuities that exist at the level of form and content, as well as in terms of economics. A longer historical view clearly shows that old and new technologies often come to co-exist: Particularly in the area of media, the advent of a new technology may change the functions or uses of old technologies, but it rarely completely displaces them. Tapscott's approach is also bound to ignore what one can only call the *banality* of much new media use. Recent studies (e.g., Facer et al., 2003; Holloway & Valentine, 2003; Livingstone & Bober, 2005) suggest that most children's everyday uses of the internet are characterized not by spectacular forms of innovation and creativity, but by relatively mundane forms of information retrieval. What most children are doing on the internet is visiting fan web sites, downloading music and movies, e-mailing or chatting with friends, and shopping (or at least window shopping). Technology offers them different ways of communicating with each other or pursuing specialist hobbies and interests, as compared with offline methods, but the differences can easily be overstated.

Given his relentless optimism, Tapscott inevitably ignores the downside of the internet—the undemocratic tendencies of many online communities, the limited nature of much so-called *digital learning*, and the grinding tedium of much technologically driven work. One of the most troubling issues here is the continuing digital divide—the gap between the technology rich and the technology poor, both within and between societies. In common with other technology enthusiasts, Tapscott believed that this is a temporary phenomenon, and that the technology poor will eventually catch up, although this is obviously to assume that the early adopters will stay where they are. It is also to assume—as Tapscott very clearly does—that the market is a neutral mechanism that functions simply by giving individuals what they need. The possibility that technology might be used to exploit young people economically (see Center for Media Education, 1997), or indeed that the market might not provide equally for all, does not enter the picture. The complacency of this argument is at least compounded by the view that children growing up without access to such technology—for example, in developing countries—are likely to be "developmentally disadvantaged."

The technologically empowered cyberkids of the popular imagination may indeed exist. But even if they do, they are in a minority, and they are untypical of young people in general. One could even argue that, for most young people, technology is a relatively marginal concern. Very few are interested in technology in its own right, and most are simply concerned about what they can use it for. But like other forms of marketing rhetoric, the discourse of the digital generation is precisely an attempt to construct the object of which it purports to speak. It represents not a description of what children or young people actually are, but a set of imperatives about what they should be or what they need to become.

CONCLUSION

So is there a digital generation? I would argue that, to a greater or lesser extent, technological change affects us all, adults included. Yet the consequences of technology depend crucially on how we use technology and what we use it for, and these things are subject to a considerable degree of social variation within age groups as well as between them. There may indeed be broad systematic differences between what adults do with technology and what young people do with it. However, it is important to note that the meanings and uses of technology are variable: We need some fine distinctions to capture what is happening here. For example, computer games are frequently identified as a children's or young people's medium, but in fact research suggests that the average age of game players is now 30 (Entertainment Software Association, 2005). Of course young people may well be playing different types of games from adults, or even playing the same games in different ways. But in exploring this phenomenon in any detail, we will almost certainly need to jettison any essentialist assumptions about the differences between children and adults.

My aim in this introductory chapter has been to puncture some of the rhetoric and hype that typically surrounds discussions of young people's relationships with digital technology. This is, frankly, a fairly easy task. What is more difficult is to conduct and analyze the research that will genuinely further our understanding of these issues—and that is something I leave to the diverse chapters that follow. Even so, I hope this discussion has raised some important caveats and questions that will inform your reading of the book as a whole. As I have suggested, the notion of a *generation* is more complex than it might appear at first sight. To identify a generation, set boundaries around it, and characterize or define it is far from being a straightforward matter—particularly if we wish to avoid undue generalization and acknowledge the significance of other social differences. The notion of a *digital generation*—a generation defined through its relationship with a particular technology or medium—clearly runs the risk of attributing an all-powerful role to technology. This is not to imply that, on the contrary, technology is merely an outcome or function of other social processes; but it is to suggest that it needs to be seen in the context of other social, economic, and political developments. From this perspective, it also becomes easier to avoid the rhetoric of fundamental and irreversible change that often characterizes the discussion of children and technology.

The chapters that follow take different stances on these issues and address quite diverse concerns. Some of the cross-cutting themes are drawn out in our introductory remarks at the start of each part of the book. However, all the contributors share a commitment to rigorous empirical investigation—and it is this commitment that needs to come to the fore in future debates about the role of digital technology in children's lives.

REFERENCES

Abrams, M. (1959). *The teenage consumer.* London: London Press Exchange.

Alanen, L. (2001). Explorations in generational analysis. In L. Alanen & B. Mayall (Eds.), *Conceptualizing child–adult relations* (pp. 11–22). London: Routledge Falmer.

Arnett, J. (1995). Adolescents' uses of media for self-socialisation. *Journal of Youth and Adolescence, 25,* 519–534.

Barbrook, R., & Cameron, A. (1996). *The Californian ideology.* Available at http://www.hrc.wmin.ac.uk/theory-californianideology.html

Bennett, A. (1999). Subcultures or neo-tribes? Rethinking the relationship between youth, style and musical taste. *Sociology, 33*(3), 599–617.

Bionic kids: How technology is altering the next generation of humans. (2003, August 25–September 1). *Newsweek.*

Blair, A. (2004). *Playstation generation could be alone for life.* Retrieved November 14, 2005, from http://www.timesonline.co.uk/article/0,7947-1335635,00.html

Bourdieu, P. (1993). "Youth" is just a word. In P. Bourdieu (Ed.), *Sociology in question* (pp. 94–102). London: Sage.

Brechin, S., & Kempton, W. (1994). Global environmentalism: A challenge for the postmaterialist thesis? *Social Science Quarterly, 75*(2), 245–269.

Brooke, J. (2002). *Youth let their thumbs do the talking in Japan.* Retrieved November 14, 2005, from http://www2.gol.com/users/coynerhm/youthlettheirthumbsdothetalking.htm

Buckingham, D. (2000). *After the death of childhood: Growing up in the age of electronic media.* Cambridge: Polity.

Buckingham, D. (2005). Children and new media. In L. Lievrouw & S. Livingstone (Eds.), *Handbook of new media* (2nd ed.). London: Sage.

Center for Media Education. (1997). *Web of deception: Threats to children from online marketing.* Washington, DC: Author.

Chandler, D. (1995). *Technological or media determinism.* Available at http://www.aber.ac.uk/media/Documents/tecdet/tecdet.html

Cook, D. T. (2004). *The commodification of childhood.* Durham, NC: Duke University Press.

Cordes, C., & Miller, E. (Eds.). (2002). *Fool's gold: A critical look at computers and childhood.* Available at http://www.allianceforchildhood.net/projects/computers/computers_reports_fools_gold_download.htm

Davies, H., Buckingham, D., & Kelley, P. (2000). In the worst possible taste: Children, television and cultural value. *European Journal of Cultural Studies, 3*(1), 5–25.

Davis-Floyd, R., & Dumit, J. (Eds.). (1998). *Cyborg babies: From techno-sex to techno-tots.* New York: Routledge.

Edmunds, J., & Turner, B. (2002). *Generations, culture and society.* Buckingham: Open University Press.

Entertainment Software Association. (2005). *Essential facts about the computer and video game industry.* Available at www.theesa.com

Facer, K., Furlong, J., Furlong, R., & Sutherland, R. (2003). *Screenplay: Children and computing in the home.* London: Routledge.

Fromme, J., Kommer, S., Mansel, J., & Treumann, K. (Eds.). (1999). *Selbstsozialisation, Kinderkultur und Mediennutzung* [Self-socialization, children's culture and media use]. Opladen: Leske & Budrich.

Green, B., & Bigum, C. (1993). Aliens in the classroom. *Australian Journal of Education, 37*(2), 119–141.

Hoikkala, T. (2004, April). *Global youth media as new forms of socialization.* Presentation at United Nations Workshop on Global Youth Culture, New York.

Holloway, S., & Valentine, G. (2003). *Cyberkids: Children in the information age.* London: Routledge Falmer.

Inglehardt, R. (1990). *Culture shift in advanced industrial society.* Princeton, NJ: Princeton University Press.

Jenkins, H. (Ed.). (1998). *The children's culture reader.* New York: New York University Press.

Johansson, B. (2004). *Generationing in consumer contexts.* Göteborg University, Center for Consumer Science. Available at www.ckf.gu.se

Lasica, J. D. (2002). *Darknet: Hollywood's war against the digital generation.* London: Wiley.

Livingstone, S., & Bober, M. (2005). *UK children go online: Listening to young people's experiences.* London: London School of Economics and Political Science.

Mannheim, K. (1952/1979). The problem of generations. In *Collected works of Karl Mannheim* (Vol. 5, pp. 276–320). London: Routledge.

May, C. (2002). *The information society: A skeptical view.* Cambridge: Polity.

Mehlman, B. (2003, January 24). *ICT literacy: Preparing the digital generation for the age of innovation.* Presentation at ICT Literacy Summit, Washington, DC. Available at http://www.technology.gov/Speeches/BPM_030124-DigGen.htm

Papert, S. (1996). *The connected family: Bridging the digital generation gap.* Atlanta, GA: Longstreet.

Postman, N. (1983). *The disappearance of childhood.* London: W. H. Allen.

Reimer, B. (1989). Postmodern structures of feeling: Values and lifestyle in the postmodern age. In J. Gibbins (Ed.), *Contemporary political culture* (pp. 110–126). London: Sage.

Tapscott, D. (1998). *Growing up digital: The rise of the net generation.* New York: McGraw-Hill.

Ulrich, J., & Harris, S. (Eds.). (2003). *Genxegesis: Essays on alternative youth (sub)culture.* Madison: University of Wisconsin Press.

Wark, M. (1993, December). Planet of noise: So who are generation X and why are they saying these terrible things about us? *Juice,* pp. 74–78.

Webster, F. (1995). *Theories of the information society.* London: Routledge.

Willett, R. (2005). Constructing the digital tween: Market forces, adult concerns and girls interests. In C. Mitchell & J. Reid Walsh (Eds.), *Seven going on seventeen: Tween culture in girlhood studies* (pp. 278–293). Oxford: Peter Lang.

Williams, R. (1974). *Television, technology and cultural form.* Glasgow: Fontana.

Ziehe, T. (2005, June). *Post-detraditionalization: Reflections on a changed life attitude of today's youth.* Plenary presentation at Childhoods 2005 conference, University of Oslo.

Part I

PLAY AND GAMING

Play has often been regarded as the business of childhood. Therefore, it is hardly surprising that play with digital games should be seen as one of the defining experiences of the digital generation. In Part I of the book, we bring together four chapters that focus on different aspects of young people's playful engagements with digital culture. Collectively, these chapters move beyond narrow preoccupations with the psychological effects of computer games, paying close attention to how the meanings of play are established in and through young people's social interactions and relationships around technology. In the process, they also raise challenging questions about how the cultures of digital play and gaming should be analyzed and understood.

Henry Jenkins' chapter (chap. 2, this volume) tackles the debate about the effects of video games head-on and with characteristic clarity. He contrasts long-standing concerns about the effects of video game violence on young players with an account of emerging research on the pedagogical potential of games. He begins with a discussion of a major U.S. court case that initially found that video games did not constitute a meaningful medium of expression—a decision that was subsequently overturned, not least as a result of the intervention of media scholars. He exposes the pedagogical assumptions made by critics of video games and those who have sought to defend the medium. He then moves on to a consideration of the ways in which creative design and educational intervention are encouraging players to reflect on and debate the meanings of *violence*. He suggests that the developers of educational games might learn a great deal by revisiting the debate about media violence—but also that the new research on games and education offers a new and challenging perspective on these perennial questions of media effects.

In her chapter "Digital Games and the Narrative Gap," Margaret Mackey (chap. 3, this volume) shifts the focus to look more directly at the experience of game players. In line with her earlier work in this field, this analysis situates computer games within a broader account of the literacies that young people acquire and develop through their encounters with a whole range of media. In this case, she focuses specifically on the narrative elements of games and the differences and similarities between games and literary narratives. The chapter provides an exploration of the computer game *Black & White* from the perspectives of nine players who were recorded as they played and subsequently interviewed. Drawing on rapidly expanding theories of digital narrative and game play, Mackey explores the different ways in which players mobilized and interpreted a common set of potentials. She offers a taxonomy of different styles of play and analyzes the implications of these interpretive approaches in the light of broader questions concerning games, simulations, and stories. She considers the relationship between players' immersion within the world of the story and their engagement with the larger construction of the game, pulling out implications for a broader understanding of the nature of narrative games.

In chapter 4 (this volume), Mizuko Ito offers a broader take on the issue of children's play within digital culture. She looks at the different forms of amateur fan production that have arisen around Japanese animation, computer games, and comics since the 1980s, and that are now widely popular around the world. She focuses on the diverse activities of highly engaged fan groups who produce their own media works by poaching from professionally produced content—works that include fan comics, novels, computer games, character goods, and costumes. She traces how, in the late 1990s, these groups took up the internet and lower cost digital authoring tools to expand their repertoire of activities and media forms. Now, Japanimation-related *otaku* communities of technical and cultural poachers are a transnational phenomenon. Ito describes some of the practices of these fan communities and relates them to broader trends in digital culture, including the transnationalization of Japanese media cultures, the growth of amateur cultural production in networked environments, and the emergent culture of digital remix and appropriation. These trends are related, in turn, to a contemporary model of media literacy that goes beyond traditional notions of critical viewing to include participation in networked systems of exchange.

Finally, Martin Oliver and Caroline Pelletier (chap. 5, this volume) outline and apply a methodology for analyzing the detailed encounters between players and games. Their approach uses activity theory in an attempt to strike a balance between the structure of the game text and the agency of the player. They seek to clarify the educational dimension of game playing—that is, how players learn to play games—in terms of a social, rather than a psychological, theory of learning. By analyzing short transcripts of a single player's engagement with a popular game, they show how specific problems with play can be brought to light with user testing, and how in-game tasks can be analyzed in terms of the operations they require. They expose some of the assumptions that are made within the game system about the player's learning and how contradictions can be intentionally designed into games to create opportunities for learning—for example, through structured training missions in which new challenges must be overcome. Although their primary aim is to illustrate the application of this analytical methodology, their account also has implications in terms of the principles of game design and the debate about the value of games in education.

These chapters raise several broader issues that are also taken up in subsequent contributions. The issue of learning, addressed in broad terms by Jenkins and Ito, and in close detail by Oliver and Pelletier, cuts across several of the later chapters and is addressed most directly in Part IV. Mackey's account of the different orientations of game players alerts us to the diversity of young people's engagements with digital culture, which is exemplified in many of the contributions that follow. Meanwhile, questions about the agency of players and fans, raised here by Ito and by Oliver and Pelletier, are explored in a different way by several of the contributions in Part III, which looks at identity in online culture.

Chapter 2

The War Between Effects and Meaning: Rethinking the Video Game Violence Debate

Henry Jenkins
Massachusetts Institute of Technology

Suppose a federal judge was asked to determine whether books were protected by the First Amendment. Instead of seeking expert testimony, examining the novel's historical evolution, or surveying the range of the local bookstore, the judge chooses four books, all within the same genre, to stand for the entire medium. Teachers and librarians would rise up in outrage. So, where were you when they tried to take the games away?

On April 19, 2002, U.S. District Judge Stephen N. Limbaugh, Sr. ruled that video games have "no conveyance of ideas, expression or anything else that could possibly amount to speech," and thus enjoy no constitutional protection. Limbaugh had been asked to evaluate the constitutionality of a Saint Louis law that restricted youth access to violent or sexually explicit content. Constitutional status has historically rested on a medium's highest potential, not its worst excesses. Limbaugh essentially reversed this logic, saying that unless all games expressed ideas, then no game should be protected.

The judge did not look hard for meaning in games, having already decided (again, contrary to well-established legal practice) that works whose primary purpose was to entertain could not constitute artistic or political expression. Saint Louis County had presented the judge with videotaped excerpts from four games, all within a narrow range of genres and all the subject of previous controversy.

Gamers have expressed bafflement over how Limbaugh can simultaneously claim that video games do not express ideas and that they represent a dangerous influence on American youth. Reformers, in turn, are perplexed that the defenders of games can argue that they have no direct consequences for the people who consume them and yet warrant constitutional protection. To understand this paradox, we have to recognize a distinction between *effects* and *meanings*. Limbaugh and company see games as having social and psychological effects (or, in some formulations, as constituting risk factors that increase the likelihood of violent and antisocial conduct). Their critics argue that gamers produce meanings through game play and related activities. Effects are seen as emerging more or less spontaneously, with little conscious effort, and are not accessible to self-examination. Meanings emerge through an active process of interpretation—they reflect our conscious engagement, they can be articulated into words, and they can be critically examined. New meanings take shape around what we already know and what we already think, and thus each player will come away from a game with a different experience and interpretation. Often reformers in the effects tradition argue that children are particularly susceptible to confusions between fantasy and reality. A focus on meaning, however, would emphasize the knowledge and competencies possessed by game players, starting with their mastery over the aesthetic conventions that distinguish games from real-world experience.

I do not come at this debate between the effects and meanings models as a neutral observer. Based on my research into the place of video games in boy culture, I testified before the U.S. Senate Commerce Committee about "marketing violent entertainment to youth." I went around the country speaking at high schools and listening to what students, parents, and teachers had to say about the place of violent entertainment in their lives. I conducted a series of creative leaders workshops at trade shows and individual companies designed to foster innovation, diversity, and artistic responsibility within the games industry. I helped to found a major research initiative, The Education Arcade (www.educationarcade.org), which seeks to examine games' educational potential and foster media literacy training. I was 1 of more than 30 scholars from different disciplines who filed an amicus brief contesting and helping to overturn the Limbaugh decision. So, in many ways, this chapter is a report from the front lines.

The Limbaugh decision was reversed by higher courts, and the Saint Louis ordinance seems to be dead for the moment. Yet similar city and state regulations are being proposed and contested. We have not heard the end of this debate. Often these policy discussions filter down into decisions being made in our schools, such as how to draft digital policies (which may allow or exclude the use of games in computer labs or dorm rooms) or whether game playing constitutes a warning sign of antisocial personalities.

The educational significance—and potential value—of games is partly a consequence of their growing importance in young people's lives. The Pew

Internet and American Life Center (2003) reported the results of a survey of more than 1,000 undergraduates from 27 American colleges and universities. One hundred percent of respondents had played computer games; 65% described themselves as regular or occasional gamers. Regardless of whether you know it, experiences in game playing are thus an increasingly important part of what students are bringing with them into the classroom. In this chapter, I want to first consider the claims about education that are being made in the public policy debates about video games. Both sides talk about games as "teaching machines," but what they mean by learning, education, and teaching differs dramatically. Second, I want to describe some contemporary efforts to use games as a springboard for discussing and learning about the place of violence within our culture.

THE EFFECTS MODEL

Grossman (2000), a retired military psychologist and West Point instructor, argued that video games are teaching kids to kill in more or less the same ways that the military trains soldiers. He identified "brutalization, classical conditioning, operant conditioning, and role modeling" as the basic mechanisms by which boot camps prepare raw recruits for the battlefield. Each of these methods, he suggested, have their parallels in the ways players interact with computer games. Kids are "brutalized" by overexposure to representations of violence at an age when they cannot yet distinguish between representation and reality. They are "conditioned" by being consistently rewarded for in-game violence. Soldiers in boot camp rehearse what they are going to do on the battlefield until it becomes second nature. Similarly, Grossman claimed, "Every time a child plays an interactive point-and-shoot video game, he is learning the exact same conditioned reflex and motor skills" (n.p.). According to Grossman, such "practice" helped prepare school shooters for the real-world violence they would commit:

> This young man did exactly what he was conditioned to do: he reflexively pulled the trigger, shooting accurately just like all those times he played video games. This process is extraordinarily powerful and frightening. The result is ever more homemade pseudo-sociopaths who kill reflexively and show no remorse. Our children are learning to kill and learning to like it. (n.p.)

Finally, Grossman argued, soldiers learn by mimicking powerful role models, and players learn by imitating the behaviors they see modeled on the screen. Indeed, given the first-person framing of such games, they are pulling the trigger from the minute the game starts.

So, where is meaning, interpretation, evaluation, or expression in Grossman's model? Grossman assumed almost no conscious cognitive activity on the part of the gamers, who have all of the self-consciousness of Pavlov's dogs. He reverted to a behaviorist model of education that has long been discredited among schooling experts. Grossman saw games as shaping our reflexes, impulses, and emotions almost without regard to our previous knowledge and experience. It is precisely because such conditioning escapes any conscious policing that Grossman believed games represent such a powerful mechanism for reshaping our behavior. Educational psychologist Provenzo (2001) adopted a similar position:

> The computer or video game is a teaching machine. Here is the logic: highly skilled players learn the lessons of the game through practice. As a result, they learn the lesson of the machine and its software—and thus achieve a higher score. They are behaviorally reinforced as they play the game and thus they are being taught. (n.p.)

Again, the model is one of stimulus–response, not conscious reflection.

Grossman reaffirmed the distaste many educators feel for the contents of popular culture and cagily exploited liberal discomfort with the military mindset. Many teachers feel angry that time spent playing games often comes at the expense of what they would see as more educationally or culturally beneficial activities. Yet if we think critically about the claims Grossman made, they would seem to be at odds with our own classroom experiences and with what we know about how education works.

As a teacher, I may fantasize about being able to decide exactly what I want my students to know and transmit that information to them with sufficient skill and precision that every student in the room learns exactly what I want. But real-world education does not work that way. Each student pays attention to some parts of the lesson and ignores or forgets others. Each has his or her own motivations for learning. Previous understandings and experience color how they interpret my words. Some students may disregard my words altogether. There is a huge difference between education and indoctrination.

Add to that the fact that consumers do not sit down in front of their game consoles to learn a lesson. Their attention is even more fragmented; their goals are even more personal; they are not really going to be tested on what they learn. They tend to dismiss anything they encounter in fantasy or entertainment that is not consistent with what they believe to be true about the real world. The military uses the games as part of a specific curriculum with clearly defined goals, in a context where students actively want to learn and have a clear need for the information and skills being transmitted. Soldiers have signed up to defend their country with their lives, so there are clear consequences for not mastering those skills. Grossman's model only works if we assume that players are not capable of rational thought, ignore critical differences in how and why people play games, and remove training or education from any meaningful cultural context.

THE MEANINGS MODEL

Humanistic researchers have also made the case that games can be powerful teaching tools. In his recent book, *What Video Games Have to Teach Us About Learning and Literacy*, Gee (2003) described game players as active problem solvers who see mistakes as opportunities for learning and reflection and who are constantly searching for newer, better solutions to obstacles and challenges. Players are encouraged to constantly form and test hypotheses about the game world. Players are pushed to the outer limits of their abilities, but rarely in a good game beyond them. Increasingly, games are designed to be played successfully by players with very different goals and skill sets.

For Gee, the most powerful dimension of game playing is what he called *projective identity*, which refers to the way that role-playing enables us to experience the world from alternative perspectives. Terminology here is key: Identity is projected (chosen or at least accepted by the player, actively constructed through game play), rather than imposed. Gee, for example, discussed *Ethnic Cleansing*, a game designed by Aryan Nation to foster White supremacy. For many students, he noted, playing the game will encourage critical thinking about the roots of racism and reaffirm their own commitments to social justice, rather than provoking race hatred. Whether the game's ideas are persuasive depends on the players' backgrounds, experiences, and previous commitments. Games, like other media, are most powerful when they reinforce our existing beliefs and least effective when they challenge our values.

Although Provenzo worries about players being forced to conform to machine logic, Gee suggested that our active participation enables us to map our own goals and agendas into the game space. To some degree, they are talking about games of different technological generations—the simple early games, which amount to little more than digital shooting galleries, versus the more robust and expansive universes created by more recent game genres. But they are also adopting very different models of the kinds of learning that occurs through games.

Another humanistic researcher, Squire (2004), has been studying what kinds of things game players might learn about social studies through playing *Civilization III* (the third game in Sid Meier's best-selling *Civilization* series) in classroom environments. His work provides a vivid account of how game-based learning builds on players' existing beliefs and takes shape within a cultural context. Students can win the game several different ways, roughly lining up with political, scientific, military, cultural, or economic victories. Players seek out geographical resources, manage economies, plan the growth of their civilization, and engage in diplomacy with other nation-states. Squire's research has focused on students performing well below grade-level expectations. They largely hated social studies, which they saw as propaganda. Several minority students were not interested in playing the game—until they realized that it was possible to win the game playing as an African or Native American civilization. These kids took great joy in study-ing hypothetical history, exploring the conditions under which colonial conquests might have played out differently. Squire's study showed that teachers played an important role in learning, directing students' atten-tion, shaping questions, and helping them interpret events. An important part of the teacher's role was to set the tone of the activity—to frame game play as an investigation into alternative history as opposed to just learning directly from the game.

Squire asked what meanings these students take from playing games and what factors—in the game, in the player, and in the classroom environ-ment—shape the interpretations they form. These kids are taught to ex-plore their environment, make connections between distinct develop-ments, form interpretations based on making choices and playing out their consequences, and map those lessons onto their understanding of the real world. Might something similar be occurring when players engage with vio-lent video games? Might they be setting their own goals, working through their own emotional questions, forming their own interpretations, talking about them with their friends, and testing them against their observations of the real world?

As we move games into the classroom, teachers can play a vital role in helping students to become more conscious about the assumptions shaping their simulations. Yet such issues crop up spontaneously online where gamers gather to talk strategy or share game-playing experiences. Just as classroom culture plays a key role in shaping how learning occurs, the social interactions between players, what we call meta-gaming, is a central factor shaping the meanings they ascribe to the represented actions. Almost 60% of frequent video game players play with friends, 33% play with siblings, and 25% play with spouses or parents (Entertainment Software Association, 2003). As Friedman (1999) noted in regard to *Civilization*, players need to know how the game thinks (and the blind spots in its assumptions) to beat it. This means that as players discuss how to win games, they are also think-ing about the assumptions underlying rule systems and simulations.

Sociologist Wright (2002) logged many hours observing how online com-munities interact with violent video games, concluding that meta-gaming provides a context for thinking about rules and rule breaking. There are really two games taking place simultaneously—one, the explicit conflict and combat on the screen, the other, the implicit cooperation and comradeship between the players. Two players may be fighting to death on screen and growing closer as friends off screen. Within the magic circle (Salen & Zimmerman, 2003), then, we can let go of one set of constraints on our actions because we have bought into another set of constraints—the rules of society give way to the rules of the game. Social expectations are reaffirmed through the social contract governing play even as they are symbolically cast aside within the transgressive fantasies represented within the games.

Comparative Media Studies graduate student Li (2003) researched the online communities that grew up around *America's Army*, an online game developed as part of the U.S. Military's recruitment efforts. Li even interviewed players as the first bombs were being dropped on Baghdad. Veterans and current GIs were often critical of the casual and playful attitudes with which nonmilitary people play the game. For the veterans, playing the game represented a place to come together and talk about the way that war had impacted their lives. Many discussions surrounded the design choices the military made to promote official standards of behavior, such as preventing players from *fragging* teammates in the back or rewarding them for ethical and valorous behavior. The military had built the game to get young people excited about military service. They had created something more— a place where civilians and service folk could discuss the serious experience of real-life war.

Games do represent powerful tools for learning—if we understand learning in a more active, meaning-driven sense. The problem comes when we make too easy an assumption about what is being learned just by looking at the surface features of the games. As Jones (2002) noted in his book, *Killing Monsters*, media reformers tend to be incredibly literal minded in reading game images, whereas players are not. He wrote, "in focusing so intently on the literal, we overlook the emotional meaning of stories and images. . . . Young people who reject violence, guns, and bigotry in every form can sift through the literal contents of a movie, game, or song and still embrace the emotional power at its heart" (p. 11).

MEANINGFUL VIOLENCE?

Not every gamer thinks deeply about his or her play experiences, nor does every designer reflect on the meanings attached to violence in his or her work. Most contemporary games do little to encourage players to reflect and converse about the nature of violence. If anything, the assumption that game play is meaningless discourages rather than fosters such reflection.

Media reformers often fail to make even the most basic distinctions about different kinds of representations of violence (Heins, 2002). For example, The American Academy of Pediatrics (2001) reported that 100% of all animated feature films produced in the United States between 1937 and 1999 portrayed violence. For this statistic to be true, the researcher must define *violence* so broadly as to be meaningless. Does violence that occurs when hunters shoot Bambi's mother mean the same thing as the violence that occurs when giant robots smash each other in a Japanese anime movie, for example? What percentage of books taught in English classes would be deemed violent by these same criteria? The reform groups are battling a monolith, media violence, rather than helping our culture to make meaningful distinctions between different ways of representing violence.

In its 2002 decision striking down an Indianapolis law regulating youth access to violent games, the Federal Court of Appeals (Pozner, 2001) noted:

> Violence has always been and remains a central interest of humankind and a recurrent, even obsessive theme of culture both high and low. It engages the interest of children from an early age, as anyone familiar with the classic fairy tales collected by Grimm, Andersen, and Perrault are aware. To shield children right up to the age of 18 from exposure to violent descriptions and images would not only be quixotic, but deforming; it would leave them unequipped to cope with the world as we know it. (n.p.)

Historically, cultures have used stories to make sense of the senseless acts of violence. Telling stories about violence can, in effect, remove some of its sting and help us comprehend acts that shatter our normal frames of meaning. When culture warriors and media reformers cite examples of violent entertainment, they are almost always drawn to works that are explicitly struggling with the meaning of violence—works that have won critical acclaim or cult status in part because they break with the formulas through which our culture normally employs violence. They rarely cite banal, formulaic, or aesthetically uninteresting works, although such works abound in the marketplace. It is as if the reformers are responding to the work's own invitations to struggle with the costs and consequences of violence, yet their literal-minded critiques suggest an unwillingness to deal with those works with any degree of nuance. These works are condemned for what they depict, not examined for what they have to say.

Like all developing media, the earliest games relied on fairly simple-minded and formulaic representations of violence. Many games were little more than shooting galleries where players were encouraged to blast everything that moves. As game designers have discovered and mastered their medium, they have become increasingly reflective about the player's experience of violent fantasy. Many current games are designed to be ethical testing grounds; the discussions around such games provide a context for reflection on the nature of violence.

The Columbine shootings and their aftermath provoked soul searching within the games industry—more than might meet the eye to someone watching shifts in games content from the outside. As game designers grappled with their own ethical responsibilities, they have increasingly struggled to find ways to introduce some moral framework or some notion of consequence into their work. Because these designers work within industrial constraints and well-defined genres, these changes are subtle, not necessarily the kinds of changes that generate headlines or win the approval of reform groups. Yet they impact on the game play and have sparked debate among designers, critics, and players.

TOWARD MORE REFLECTIVE GAME DESIGN

Games, according to *Sims* designer Will Wright (personal interview), are perhaps the only medium that allows us to experience guilt over the actions of fictional characters. In a movie, because we do not control what occurs, we can always pull back and condemn the character or artist when he or she crosses social taboos, but in playing a game we choose what happens to the characters. In the right circumstances, we can be encouraged to examine our own values by seeing what we are willing to do within virtual space. Wright's own contribution has been to introduce a rhetoric of mourning into the video game. In *The Sims*, if a character dies, the surviving characters grieve over their loss. Such images are powerful reminders that death has human costs.

Wright has compared *The Sims* to a dollhouse within which we can reenact domestic rituals and dramas. As such, he evokes a much older tradition of doll play. In the 19th century (Formanek-Brunnell, 1998), doll funerals were a recognized part of the culture of doll play—a way children worked through their anxieties about infant mortality or, later, the massive deaths caused by the Civil War. Today, players use *The Sims* as a psychological workshop, testing the limits of the simulation (often by acting out violent fantasies among the residents), but also using the simulation to imitate real-world social interactions. As *The Sims* has moved online, it has become a social space where players debate alternative understandings of everyday life. Some see the fantasy world as freeing them from constraints and consequences. Others see the online game as a social community that must define and preserve a social contract. These issues have come to a head as some players have banded together into organized crime families seeking to rule territories, while others have become law enforcers trying to protect their fledgling communities.

The representations and simulations of games become more sophisticated, enabling players to set their own goals within richly detailed and highly responsive environments, and the opportunities for ethical reflection have grown. *Morrowind*, a fantasy role-playing game, gives characters memories across their family line. Christopher Weaver (personal interview), founder of Bethesda Softworks, which produced the game, explains that he wanted to show the "interconnectedness of lives" in a society governed by strong loyalties to families or clans: "The underlying social message being that one may not know the effect of their actions upon the future, but one must guide their present actions with an awareness of such potential ramifications."

Grand Theft Auto 3 is one of the most controversial games on the market today because of its vivid representations of violence (Jenkins, 2002). Yet it also represents a technical breakthrough in game design, which may lead toward more meaningful representations of violence in games. The protagonist has escaped from prison. What kind of life is he going to build for himself? The player interacts with more than 60 distinctive characters and must choose between a range of possible alliances with various gangs and crime syndicates. Every object responds as it would in the real world; the player can exercise enormous flexibility in where they can go and what they can do in this environment. Certain plot devices cue possible missions, which include expectations of violence, but nothing stops the player from stealing an ambulance and racing injured people to the hospital, grabbing a fire truck and putting out blazes, or simply walking around town. Some of what happens is outrageous and offensive, but this open-ended structure puts the burden on the user to make choices and explore their consequences. If you choose to use force, you are going to attract the police. The more force, the more cops. Pretty soon you are going down. Every risk you take comes with a price. Violence leaves physical marks. Early on, players act out, seeing how much damage and mayhem they can inflict, but more experienced players tell me they often see how long they can go without breaking any laws, viewing this as a harder and more interesting challenge. A richer game might offer a broader range of options, including allowing the player to go straight, get a job, and settle into the community.

Peter Molyneux designs games that encourage ethical reflection. In *Black and White*, the player functions as a god-like entity, controlling the fates of smaller creatures. Your moral decisions to help or abuse your creatures map themselves directly onto the game world: Malicious actions make the environment darker and more gnarly, whereas virtuous actions make the world flower and glisten. Most players find it hard to be purely good or purely evil; most enter into ethical gray areas and, in so doing, start to ask some core philosophical and theological questions. His newest game, *Fable*, takes its protagonist from adolescence to old age, and every choice along the way has consequences in terms of the kind of person you will become and the kind of world you will inhabit. If you work out, you will grow muscles. If you pig out, you will get fat. If you carve your initials in a tree, the tree remains scarred as it grows. If you trample your seedlings, the trees will not grow. By living an accelerated lifetime within the game world, teens get to see the long-term impact of their choices on their own lives and those of people around them.

FOSTERING GAMES LITERACY

If design innovations are producing games that support more reflection and discussion, media literacy efforts can expand the frameworks and vocabulary players bring to those discussions. Around the country, people are beginning to experiment with both classroom and after-school programs designed to foster games literacy. The best such programs combine critical analysis of existing commercial games with media production projects that allow students to re-imagine and re-invent game content. What kids learn is that current commercial games tell a remarkably narrow range of stories and adopt an even narrower range of perspectives on the depicted events. Rethinking game genres can encourage greater diversity and, in doing so, introduce new contexts for thinking about game violence.

OnRampArts, a Los Angeles-based nonprofit arts organization, conducted an after-school violence-prevention workshop for students at Belmont High School, a 90% Latino public school in downtown Los Angeles. Students critiqued existing games, trying to develop a vocabulary for talking about the ways they represented the world. Students created digital superhero characters (like a rock-playing guerilla fighter, a man who transforms into a low-rider, or a peace-loving mermaid) that reflected their own cultural identities and built digital models of their homes and communities as a means of thinking about game space. Students studied their family histories and turned immigration stories into game missions, puzzles, and systems. In other words, they imagined games that might more fully express their own perspectives and experiences.

In the second phase, students, teachers, and local artists worked together to create a web game, *Tropical America*. Because so many of the kids working on the project were first- or second-generation immigrants, the project increasingly came to focus on the conquest and colonization of the Americas. Jessica Irish, one of the project's directors, said that the greatest debate centered around what kind of role the protagonist should play. Through resolving that question, students came away with a more powerful understanding of the meaning and motivation of violence in games.

In *Tropical America*, the player assumes the role of the sole survivor of a 1981 massacre in El Salvador, attempting to investigate what happened to this village and why. In the process, you explore some 500 years of the history of the colonization of Latin America, examining issues of racial genocide, cultural dominance, and the erasure of history. Winners of the game become Heroes of the Americas and, in the process, uncover the name of another victim of the actual slaughter. Students had to master the history, distilling it down to core events and concepts, and determine what images or activities might best express the essence of those ideas. They enhanced the game play with an encyclopedia that allowed players to learn more about the historical references and provided a space where meta-gaming could occur. Rather than romanticizing violence, the kids dealt with the political violence and human suffering that led their parents to flee from Latin America.

CONCLUSION

Rethinking the debates about media violence in terms of meanings rather than effects has pushed us in two important directions. On the one hand, it has helped us see how game designers and players are rethinking the consequences of violence within existing commercial games. These shifts in thinking may be invisible as long as the debate is framed in terms of the presence or absence of violence, rather than in terms of what the violence means and what features of the game shape our responses to it. On the other hand, a focus on meaning rather than effects has helped us identify some pedagogical interventions that can help our students develop the skills and vocabulary needed to think more deeply about the violence they encounter in the culture around them. Through media literacy efforts like OnRampArts' *Tropical America* project, teachers, students, and local artists are working together to envision alternative ways to represent violence in games and, in the process, to critique the limitations of current commercial games. Students are encouraged to think about the media from the inside out, assuming the role of media makers and thinking about their own ethical choices.

Such educational interventions are still few and far between. They are underfunded and underpublicized. They often occur in isolation. One of the goals of the newly launched Education Arcade is to explore the potential educational uses of games. Our focus includes the development of new games specifically designed for classroom use, the development of curricular and teacher training materials to support the use of existing commercial games for pedagogical purposes, the building of shared resources that teachers can draw on to build their own games, the management of an online forum where teachers and designers can share notes, and the effort to consolidate and publicize best practices in the emerging field of games literacy education. My hope is that this discussion has offered a new framework for thinking about the challenge of game violence and, beyond that, has helped educators realize why game playing can be a meaningful activity.

REFERENCES

American Academy of Pediatrics. (2001). *Committee on Public Education, Policy Statement on Media Violence.* Available at http://aappolicy.aappublications.org/cgi/content/full/pediatrics;108/5/1222

Entertainment Software Association. (2003). *Top ten industry facts.* Available at http://www.theesa.com/pressroom.html

Formanek-Brunnell, M. (1998). The politics of dollhood in 19th century America. In H. Jenkins (Ed.), *The children's culture reader* (pp. 363–381). New York: New York University Press.

Friedman, T. (1999). Civilization and its discontents: Simulation, subjectivity and space. In G. M. Smith (Ed.), *On a silver platter: CD-ROMs and the promises of a new technology* (pp. 132–150). New York: New York University Press. Available at http://www.duke.edu/~tlove/civ.htm

Gee, J. (2003). *What video games have to teach us about learning and literacy.* New York: Palgrave.

Grossman, D. (2000). *Teaching kids to kill. Phi Kappa Phi "National Forum."* Available at http://www.killology.org/article_teachkid.htm

Heins, M. (2002). *Brief amica curiae of thirty media scholars.* Submitted to the U.S. Court of Appeals, Eight Circuit, Interactive Digital Software Association et al. vs. St. Louis County et al. Available at http://www.fepproject.org/courtbriefs/stlouissummary.html

Jenkins, H. (2002). *Coming up next: Ambushed on "Donahue."* Available at http://www.salon.com/tech/feature/2002/08/20/jenkins_on_donahue/

Jones, G. (2002). *Killing monsters: Why children need fantasy, super heroes, and make-believe violence.* New York: Basic.

Li, Z. (2003). *The potential of America's army: The video game as civilian–military public sphere.* Unpublished master's thesis, Comparative Media Studies Program, MIT.

Pozner, R. (2001). U.S. Court of Appeals, AMERICAN AMUSEMENT MACHINE ASS'N, et al., Plaintiffs—Appellants, v. TERI KENDRICK, et al. as quoted at http://www.fepproject.org/courtbriefs/kendricksummary.html

Provenzo, E. (2001). *Children and hyperreality: The loss of the real in contemporary childhood and adolescence.* Draft presented at University of Chicago Cultural Policy Center conference, available at http://culturalpolicy.uchicago.edu/conf2001/papers/provenzo.html

Salen, K., & Zimmerman, E. (2003). *Rules of play: Game design fundamentals.* Cambridge: MIT Press.

Squire, K. (2004). *Replaying history: Learning world history through playing* Civilization III. Unpublished doctoral dissertation, Indiana University School of Education, Bloomington, IN.

Wright, T. (2002, December). Creative player actions in FPS online video games: Playing *Counter-Strike. Game Studies.* Available at http://www.gamestudies.org/0202/wright/

Chapter 3

Digital Games and the Narrative Gap

Margaret Mackey
University of Alberta

Theorists of narrativity and digital games all struggle with the question of if and/or how an interactive text such as a computer game represents a narrative. Adults who work with digitally sophisticated young people struggle with the question of how to understand new forms of story-making and world-building. In this chapter, I address two gaps: that between theory and the actuality of the game world, and that between gamers and the uncomprehending adults who try to make sense of a new world. It sounds like two topics, but I propose a way to address these questions that actually makes room for a considerable amount of overlap.

For the sake of simplicity, I make an arbitrary and crass terminological distinction between *game insiders* (by which I mean those, of any age, who are comfortable with digital games of various kinds) and *outside adult observers* (by which I mean those who have not grown up with these digital texts, but now find themselves in positions of trying to support young people from arrears, from a position of not comprehending the new skills and behaviors—many teachers, librarians, and parents fall into this category). I am well aware that this distinction is an outrageous oversimplification, but some quick-and-dirty vocabulary makes it easier to pursue my main line of argument. *Inside* and *outside* in this lexicon is just a way of labeling digital capacities and understandings. My argument is as follows: If we can find useful ways to describe games in terms of narrative, it may help adult observers to understand the new in relation to (and/or in contrast to) the familiar.

Outside adult observers are very comfortable with concepts of reading narrative; they understand (intuitively, if not explicitly) how the process works. When they look at games, however, they cannot begin to make any kind of serious meaning out of what they see. Heppell (1993), writing when the population of game outsiders was even larger, supplies a useful description of how a surplus of data can interfere with the making of meaning:

> When we adults observe children playing computer games, what we see is colored by our own experience. Our experience does not usually include computer games in any depth. We find a cacophony of sound, an anarchic blur of vision and action. We see children reacting to this, absorbed in their activity, but we under-value what is happening because we don't see what they see. They see sophisticated cues and clues. They see categories of visual information. They have expectations about the behavior of objects of the screen, and within this environment they see challenges and solve problems that their parents and teachers are not even aware of. (p. 3)

In the years since Heppell made this observation, many adults have learned to see more than cacophony and anarchy on the screen of a game, but misunderstanding still runs very deep. This misunderstanding manifests itself in large-scale public generalizations and in small local blindnesses.

In the summer of 2004, for example, the National Endowment for the Arts produced a report lamenting the decline of literary reading in the United States. In the introduction, Gioia (2004) presented a prejudice about computer games that is still very common:

> Reading a book requires a degree of active attention and engagement. Indeed, reading itself is a progressive skill that depends on years of education and practice. By contrast, most electronic media, such as television, recordings, and radio make fewer demands on their audiences, and indeed often require no more than passive participation. *Even interactive electronic media, such as video games and the Internet, foster shorter attention spans and accelerated gratification.* (p. vii; italics added)

Gioia offered a deficit model of media use that is still relatively commonplace, even today, but it is striking that the attitude toward video games is not simply pejorative, but also demonstrably wrong. Video games may or may not be lacking in many qualities, but large numbers of them actively foster very extended attention spans indeed, and gratification is delayed for hours and days at a time as players master the different demands of a new game. In many cases, the time lag between initial investment and returns of satisfaction and engagement is much more extensive than it is in a wide range of reading experiences. Gioia's dismissal of games in these terms suggests an absence of experience—not just of playing games, but even of paying any attention to other people's playing. In such terms, the gap between game insiders and outsiders (who cannot even be called observers in this case) is reified and calcified.

It is not just significant members of the literary establishment who belittle these games or express ignorance and indifference concerning the broad variety of digital pleasures that young people take in their stride. Nor is it strictly a generational issue. I conducted a small local survey of about 50 preservice primary school teachers taking a compulsory course in teaching English language arts in my western Canadian university. My intention was to explore their comfort levels with contemporary media formats, so the students completed a questionnaire indicating a range of responses from *complete comfort* to *complete unfamiliarity* with a long list of media formats. I rather expected to find a generational divide, but, somewhat to my surprise, it turned out that about half of even the youngest cohort (those below age 25, about half of the total population of this little survey) were not at all at home with digital games played on consoles (such as PlayStation) or hand-held equipment (such as GameBoy). Two thirds were comfortable with computer games, but that group includes those who play only *Solitaire* or *Tetris*, games with no narrative content. Gender perhaps plays a role here; the group was substantially female. Whatever the root cause, this little survey represents a straw in the wind to indicate that the gap between many students and their teachers may not close in the immediate future.

HOW TO SEE WHEN YOU DO NOT KNOW
WHAT TO WATCH

Gioia's very public example of misunderstanding and the uneasiness about digital games expressed by the student teachers in my survey both highlight some of the difficulties of communicating across a gap of comprehension. Adult outside observers know about reading and story-making, but fail to see how they can make a connection to the bewildering and noisy data overload on the game screen. Without categories to focus their perception, they do not even know how to watch. Such lack of comprehension is perfectly reasonable until it morphs into a value judgment. "I don't understand it" turns readily into "I don't like it" and then, unfortunately, all too often into "Which proves it's not worth understanding or liking." Games are castigated for mindlessness, violence, misogyny, crudeness, and antisocial tendencies—the classic deficit model of media dismissal.

However, if we apply a more constructive asset model approach (Mackey, 2002a; Robinson & Mackey, 2003; Tyner, 1998) and ask what kinds of understanding the playing of games may foster and contribute to people's overall interpretive skills, we reach very different answers. To accomplish such a positive transformation, outside adult observers (among whom I definitely class myself) need to look for help. In this chapter, I present two forms of such help. The first form of assistance is the guidance to the world of digital gaming that was offered to me by nine participants in a research project, who worked intensively with me between 2001 and 2003. The second form of help comes from theoretical and practical accounts of game playing written by people who are *expert* insiders.

NINE PLAYERS

Before turning to the theoretical accounts of digital gaming, I briefly describe my study and the participants who, ages 19 to 36, were certainly adults in their own right and were also all game insiders as a result of growing up with computer technology. Although I did not select them just for their gaming capabilities, every one of them was competent with at least one form of digital game. The nine participants, selected to take part in this study through largely opportunistic means, represent a reasonably broad range of backgrounds for such a small sample.

The Participants

The participants more or less fit into the 18 to 34 demographic that is so appealing to advertisers, although it is noticeable in this list how few of them occupy a position of economic security.

Jeremy (19)	a university undergraduate, considering history as a major
Ben (21)	a student in a one-year computer network course, working in a pizza parlor to fund his studies
Denise (23)	a recent graduate in microbiology, studying to be a qualified massage therapist in the absence of work related to her university degree
Damian (24)	a college student taking undergraduate courses and a Reserve in the Canadian Armed Forces
Courtney (26)	a new mother at home with her baby and a graduate in education who has had very little work as a teacher
Drew (27)	a new father with training in computer network management who was looking for satisfying work and doing part-time work on a computer helpline at the time of the sessions
Seth (28)	a nurse
Jocelyn (31)	a mid-level manager in a local shopping mall
Isaac (36)	a substitute teacher with occasional day work

The Project

Each of these participants spent five 2-hour sessions with me; these sessions were audio- and videorecorded. During this time, participants looked at a broad range of materials: books, short stories, a picture book, and graphic novels; an e-book and a PDA with downloaded samples of extended text; two hypertext novels and an online poem; a variety of internet sites; DVDs of film and TV; and a range of computer and console games. In the last session, each of them engaged in some extended play of the computer game *Black & White* (2001). Their play of this game was recorded in the same way as the other sessions of this project (audio- and videotaped from two angles), and the tapes and transcripts were loaded onto the software Transana (a program that permits the mounting of video records and transcripts on the same screen, with a variety of coding options for analysis, freely available at http://www2.wcer.wisc.edu/Transana).

ONE GAME

Black & White is a role-playing game where the role *you* as game player take on is that of god of the screen universe. You are able to choose whether to treat your people well or badly. You have a Creature to do your bidding, raised and trained by you to do good or evil. You have an island world to explore, a busy kingdom to administer.

Although there are many potential twists and turns to this game that could easily be described as narrative—and although the game starts with a video cut scene that sets up a narrative situation as you are declared to be a god as a result of rescuing a village child from drowning—players have so many choices to make that the plural entity of *Black & White* is hard to describe as a story. Certainly it is not a singular story, although all instantiations of the game through playing it have a certain amount in common. In its emphasis on exploring and mastering the space of the island that you now rule, this game exemplifies Fuller and Jenkins' (1995) category of "forms of narrative that privilege space over characterization or plot development" (p. 71).

My relationship to the game of *Black & White* is certainly that of an outside adult observer. My own physical responses with the mouse are clumsy and slow, and my understanding of game conventions is laborious and faulty. When I play the game, I resemble nothing so much as the child learning to read, who is famous for "barking at print" (as some teachers put it), rather than smoothly making meaning. When I play, it is a kind of barking at commitment to the game world; I am so busy monitoring all my actions and suppositions that I cannot get beyond the surface of game control at any point.

However, I would not ask a child in the early stages of "barking at print" to reach judgment on the plot or literary qualities of the story being attempted. I would certainly not want to evaluate *Black & White* (let alone games in general) on the basis of my own clumsy experience of it. A child initially learns about the pleasures of print by being read to; similarly, in this project and elsewhere, I turned to other players to help me interpret this game.

Before analyzing my video and transcript records of the nine played versions of the game, I set out to see what guidance could be offered from some of the theorists of aesthetic form and game narrativity. I discovered a rapidly expanding field of study, but in this chapter I focus on one aspect of narrativity and format—the issue of verb tense and mood as a central aspect of telling. To confine even a short discussion to this restricted territory is to oversimplify, but I hope that the implications of this exploration suggest new ways of thinking about a complex question. At the end of this chapter, I broaden the discussion to consider the potential value of looking at the verbs involved in reading and playing.

THE TENSE OF THE TEXT: TWO THEORETICAL PERSPECTIVES ON TEXT FORM

As a kind of ground-clearing exercise, I turned to a philosopher of aesthetics from the 1940s and 1950s. Langer (1953), in her *tour-de-force* exploration of form, *Feeling and Form*, offered some distinctions between different kinds of literature using verb tense as a distinguishing agent. Novels, she said, always represent a virtual past: The story has always happened *before* the moment of telling; the telling represents a backward look at the events. Lyric poetry, she suggested, represents a virtual present: We are invited to stand in the poet's world at the moment the poet meets that world. For a virtual future, she turned to drama: With the actors working out the story in front of us, she said, drama represents destiny rather than memory.

Jesper Juul (2001) is a game theorist who also used the idea of tense to explore how a story world is created, although he did not refer to Langer's work. Juul referred to the distinctions among the time of the story events, the time of the telling, and the time of the reading, listening, viewing, or playing. He suggested that games are a special category because, in an action-based digital game, the time of the narration and the time of the events told merge with the time of the playing. He said,

> It is clear that the events represented cannot be *past* or *prior*, since we as players can influence them. By pressing the CTRL key, we fire the current

weapon, which influences the game world. In this way, the game constructs the story time as *synchronous* with narrative time and reading/viewing time: the story time is *now*. Now, not just in the sense that the viewer witnesses events now, but in the sense that the events are *happening* now, and that what comes next is not yet determined. (n.p.)

Juul's *now* in a game like *Black & White* is an interesting hybrid; it is the real-time *now* of players' game-playing experience and affects the game events in real time, as Juul observed. Yet there is still a quality of the virtual *now* that Bruner (1986) described as the subjunctive of the story, "trafficking in human possibilities rather than in settled certainties" (p. 26). It is a *now* in which you have just rescued a drowning child and been hailed as a god. As the players moved through the game, they were both in this as-if world of the subjunctive and *also* in an open-ended present tense where their own particular actions would affect what ensued in genuinely unpredetermined ways. Children's games of make believe occupy a similarly hybrid zone, located on a kind of fault line between fictional and real time. We have similar terminological difficulties with make-believe games; they are certainly fictional, but they are not exactly stories.

Games combine a present-tense narrative structure with a reliance on the capacity of players to get things right at tactile and strategic levels. Even in a genre where the hero conventionally does not die, the gamer knows it is possible for the *player* to fail the hero. Death is indeed much more common in games than in other media versions of the same story and is often caused simply by player clumsiness (Atkins, 2003).

Nevertheless, the range of possibilities open to my nine players, although enormously large and freighted with significant consequences of possible failure, was not limitless. Elsaesser (1998) helpfully reminded us that participants' choices in such a situation are not completely open-ended:

> While the ideology of a self-selected narrative and open-ended storyline suggest freedom and choice ... the user colludes with being a "player" whose freedom can be summed up as: "you can go wherever you like as long as I was there before you"—which is of course precisely the strategy of the "conventional" story-teller. (p. 217)

As they played, my nine participants were aware that some options were foreclosed by the allowances established in the game. Courtney, for example, dropped a crucial stone and spent a long time searching for it. Asked whether this kind of process frustrated her, she said, "No, I just think that's just the way it is. You know, I have some appreciation for the difficulty of programming." Later she said, "I don't mind having a really set scenario. To have lots of different options is—it's nice but it's not a necessity." Seth also dropped the same important stone and acknowledged that he might not be able to progress in the game. Unlike Courtney, however, he began to experiment with ways of sabotaging the game, throwing sheep instead of rocks and badgering the inhabitants of his kingdom. His game continued, but his game play ceased to be focused on the forward progression of the story. He registered that breakdown by turning his back on the limits of his narrative progress.

TIME AND STORY PROGRESS

Distinctively, game play collapses event time, narration time, and reception time. Grodal (2003) offered some interesting observations on whether such a collapse is a *reduction*; he suggested that it is not:

> Films based on novels may often in some dimensions be simpler than the novels because the richness of the perceptual presentation and the pressure of experiential time are in conflict with other dimensions of complexity that may characterize the printed medium. Similarly, the complexity of the active control of story development in video games is in conflict with other dimensions of complexity. Playing video games demands a detailed richness and specificity in cognitive maps of spaces and opposing agents, of causal inferences that do not only have to be vague premonitions as in films or novels in which the author/director is in control, but precise ideas in order to work. The perceptions have to be fast and precise, the motor control coordinated with the perceptions, and thus the computer story demands the acquisition of a series of procedural schemas. From another point of view, therefore, video games are not imploded stories, but on the contrary the full, basic story that the retelling has to omit, including its perceptual and muscular realization. Video games are based on learning processes and rehearsals and are therefore stories *in the making*, sketches of different stories, different coping strategies. (pp. 147–148)

The participants in this study responded differently to the perceptual and muscular demands of their story building. One example of game play in *Black & White* exemplifies some of the narrative and temporal dimensions of the kinesthetic qualities of the game, including its capacity to suspend the present tense of game progress. Early in *Black & White*, players are invited to practice throwing rocks against a tree. It is not immediately clear how this activity furthers the story in any meaningful way; in terms of tense, it represents a kind of ongoing present participle, with little apparent potential for forward narrative movement. The participants in this study responded variously to the skill-testing challenge of this diversion. Damian was prepared to be patient over an extended period of time. Drew was more easily frustrated, but keen to get it right. Ben commented on the need to practice and returned to the site to throw more rocks during a narrative delay in his main story, keeping his rock throwing suspended among other elements of the game.

In contrast to these participants, Jeremy had played the game before, and his fine muscle control over the rock throwing was much better. He succeeded in hitting the tree, which caused some small narrative development. Awarded a prize from a chest of trophies for his prowess, he selected a beach ball for his Creature to play with. But Jeremy's narrative progression was very short-lived in its consequences. Laughing heartily, he reported, "Oh no, he ate his toy! He just ate the beach ball. Oh and it looks like he didn't like it either." In terms of the overall narrative trajectory toward the end of the game, at the level of macroplay, Jeremy's game thus did not vary all that greatly from the others—his Creature ate the prize so quickly it had very little impact on the broad shape of the story. At the microplay level, in terms of developing muscular control and earning a short-term story payoff that struck him as very funny, he had a more satisfying experience that offered a modest plot development, even if it was short-lived. Of course, developing the precise muscular finesse required by this game allowed him to focus more smoothly on the narrative elements, rather than being forced to pay most attention to the surface requirements of his game controls.

Jenkins (2004) talked about *enacted* narrative elements. With Drew, Damian, and Ben throwing rocks in vain, the process of enactment seems to suspend the ongoing present tense of the narrative. There is a *time out* from the story devoted to the refinement of the tactile connections with the motor impetus of the story. This opportunity to finesse the physical controls of the game offered, at best, a small return in terms of story shaping, but the players were determined to improve their skills as part of the development of the game. The hiatus in narrative progress caused by the need to practice annoyed some of them more than others, but everybody recognized the need to tune their reactions to the physical demands of the game. What transpired was a "perceptual and muscular realization" of the story that slowed down the narrative progress, but immersed the players in the fictional world of the game at a kinesthetic level.

GAME AS OPEN STORY

Exploring the idea that a game operates on a different kind of organizational framework helped me, as an outside observer, to consider the very open-ended nature of the specific games played by the participants. A different kind of theory offered me another way of looking at the significance of what the players bring to the game.

The stance and expectations of the print reader play a significant role in how written story is understood. If I am reading a novel, I respond differently to the beautiful girl who is introduced in chapter 1 according to whether I think the book is a romance or a mystery. My expectations provide me with a certain stance toward this character and her likely fate. The open-ended nature of a digital game may mean that the stance of the player may contribute even more significantly to how the game is put together. Richard Bartle, a game developer and theorist, worked intensively with players in a multi-user dungeon (MUD) game (an online world created by the words of the players, who type entries describing setting, characters, and plot events and work collaboratively to create an ongoing universe). Created by its users, a MUD is much more open ended than a CD-ROM game like *Black & White*. Nevertheless, Bartle's observations are suggestive.

Bartle (1996) surveyed a number of MUD users about the satisfactions they received from the format and discovered that stance had a strong impact on the way they played. He raised the question of the open nature of the MUD and asked:

Are MUDs:

- games? Like Chess, tennis, AD&D [*Advanced Dungeons and Dragons*, a role-playing game]?
- pastimes? Like reading, gardening, cooking?
- sports? Like huntin', shootin', fishin'?
- entertainments? Like nightclubs, TV, concerts? (n.p.)

Pursuing this category question, Bartle established some relatively robust subgroups among his MUDders. Continuing his online discussion of the issue, he offered online gamers the chance to comment on his categories and found they made sense to the gamers as well.

Bartle (1996) established four stances toward the game, labeled with somewhat stereotypical headings:

- Some players are *achievers*. They "give themselves game-related goals and vigorously set out to achieve them" (n.p.).
- Some players are *explorers* who "try to find out as much as they can about the virtual world" (n.p.).
- Some players are *socialisers*, who "use the games communicative facilities, and apply the role-playing that these engender, as context in which to converse (and otherwise interact) with their fellow players" (n.p.).

- Some players are *killers*, who like to impose on others; they "use the tools provided by the game to cause distress to (or, in rare circumstances, to help) other players" (n.p.).

Bartle (1996) returned to his opening questions with a set of interesting and differentiated answers.

Are MUDs:

- games? Like chess, tennis, D&D?
  - Yes—to *achievers*
- pastimes? Like reading, gardening, cooking?
  - Yes—to *explorers*
- sports? Like huntin', shootin', fishin'?
  - Yes—to *killers*
- entertainments? Like nightclubs, TV, concerts?
  - Yes—to *socialisers* (n.p.; italics added)

THE IMPLICATIONS OF DIVERSIFICATION

Bartle's typology of game players clearly offers scope for differing stances toward the text. I was interested to see whether his list of possibilities provided any useful lens on the game-playing participants in my own project. Before I turn to that issue, however, I want to address an element that appears to be completely absent from his list: the potential for narrative or story-making. Bartle did not make room for storytellers in his set of possibilities. Possibly this absence is a consequence of the test matrix of MUDs from which he developed his list; a MUD is ongoing, with a strong emphasis on setting and character, less emphasis on plot, and very little scope for closure. A predilection for story-making might not flourish in such an environment.

Black & White offers more story potential, perhaps, although none of my participants played it long enough to catch even a glimpse of the possibility of closure. Nevertheless, I was interested to see whether Bartle's list of categories would help me explore the responses of my participants, and whether it would cast any light on the question of narrative and story-making.

At first I found the categories simplistic and thought they might be too restrictive to be of use. As I analyzed the transcripts, however, I found the categories rather more robust than I had suspected. With the partial exception of Denise, who was the least experienced gamer of the group (apart from many hours spent on GameBoys on childhood car journeys), all my participants could readily be categorized under one heading or another. As Bartle pointed out, no stance is permanent, and all of these headings are porous to some extent, but most players show a predilection for one category above all the others. So I found it with the participants in my study. Three of the categories were fairly clear cut and can be illustrated with a few sample quotes from the transcripts. In each case, many more quotes expressing a similar approach could be located, and I offer only a small specimen.

The category of *explorers* was represented by Courtney, who manifested little concern when she found it difficult to achieve any immediate end.

- "Exploration is pretty important. It's nice just to appreciate all the work that went into it, even seeing all the little birds flying around—you know, the waves that lap on the shore—and you can hear it and you can see it and it's really interesting. It gives you a better appreciation for the game itself."

Jeremy represented the *socializers* and, of all the participants in my study, adhered most whole-heartedly to one single approach to his play. He constantly made reference to his online friends and game buddies:

- "There are gaming groups that play with each other and you get to know these people quite well and they will readily help you out."
- "It's a lot easier to learn from other people rather than figure it out on your own."

The *killer* category was represented by Damian, whose game was peppered with exhortations:

- "Squish him, squish him!"
- "Let's get to this fighting."
- "Better start smiting soon!"

The *achievers* were somewhat more differentiated, and I offer three examples of different approaches to the end of achievement. For example, Drew was keen to get his community to work:

- "I am giving the people something to do—all this chilling out is just not cool. Production, production, production!"
- "Hey—fishing! How do you fish?"

Jocelyn was more interested in other aspects of the game:

- "It is cool that you can be nice to people and it's kind of cool that you get to pick which you want to do."

- "I *really* like the cow [her selected Creature]."
- "I just like things like that little white dude [the 'good' conscience who acts as a guide, along with an 'evil' peer]."

Isaac was committed to different ideas again:

- "Now doing the evil-influenced stuff is kind of like, more, it's not what you're expecting, it's not the norm, it's not complacent. I don't want to play a game that's just all complacent."
- "The Creature should be trained to be evil so there would be something that's creating havoc."

I would argue that these three players were playing to achieve, but to achieve different ends. Drew wanted to achieve control; of these three players, he is closest to Bartle's account of achievers. Jocelyn, however, was much more committed to the idea of achieving some form of emotional connection; she saw this relationship as something to be *accomplished*, and her emphasis and energies lay in the creation of this emotional link to the story. Of the nine players, in my view, Isaac was most interested in achieving the creation of some kind of story out of his game. In his observations about the importance of mayhem, he was talking about a need for plot. The role of evil in his scenario seems not to be dedicated particularly to smiting or other forms of killer behavior. The role of evil is to give the game something to build a story around—the classic disturbance of the status quo that kicks off the plot development.

IF NOT MAKING STORIES, THEN WHAT?

Bartle's taxonomy makes no explicit allowance for the creation of story as one stance toward the playing of games. Of my nine players, only one develops the category of achieving to include the making of some kind of plot. Narrative is not ruled out of court by this analysis, but it does not seem to be a prime trigger of play. Small wonder that an outside adult observer, attempting to follow the development of potential plot ingredients, may be confused, discouraged, and inclined to think that games simply do not make sense.

Nevertheless, it is clear that some of the ingredients of story are in play in a game such as *Black & White*. There is a fictional universe with its own history and geography, there are characters who take actions that have consequences, and there is something of a sequence of events, although not necessarily linear. Is there any kind of overlap between this game world and the narrative worlds of print so familiar to many of us?

It may perhaps seem a glib conclusion to say that the outside observer trying to make sense of a digital game will make better progress by paying attention to the verbs of playing, rather than the nouns of achievement. Nevertheless, I think that such amateur observers will make better progress in understanding game playing if they consider the processes rather than the products. The imaginative endeavors of creating a mental world have more in common in both gaming and reading than might seem obvious at first glance.

Building fictional meaning is a complex mental and emotional process. To look to a digital game for the same kind of product or outcome as is offered by a print story is to ignore a more useful point of contact or overlap, the cognitive acts that develop and sustain a fictional world from a set of pre-arranged and/or arrangeable symbolic resources. In other words, the outside adult observer may conduct more useful observations by saying, "What is that player doing to create a story world?" than by saying, "I see no outcome that I can recognize as a story." The notion of the tense of the text may seem specialist, or even obscure, yet it conveys some sense of how the different formats diverge and how closure and coherence are differently composed and assessed in fictions of print and of digital game. Therefore, the interpretive processes that lead to the *building* of a fiction provide an interesting and productive place to begin observing.

It is also important to remember that a reader of print is "doing" too; that a reading is not some invisible structure imported ready-made into the reader's mind, but something that is created over time, involving flow of attention and mental world building in ways that are more comparable to game playing than a cursory outside glance at both activities would suggest. To pay attention to the verbs of game playing is instructive, but to attend to reading in useful ways also involves paying heed to the performative verbs. One helpful account of reading (Rabinowitz, 1987) talks about how readers *notice,* how they *discern the significance* of what they notice, how they *organize a mental order of events* that makes sense, and how they *consider the overall coherence* of a fiction. These verbs of reading can be transferred usefully to observations of game play (Mackey, 2002b, 2005). They serve as a reminder that building a fictional world in the subjunctive mode of human possibilities is an activity that happens purposefully over time, making use of the symbolic resources to hand—whether these involve the powers of make believe, the affordances of a print fiction, or the potential of a digital game.

We may also learn more about how reading works if we consider the various stances and their impact on readers' abilities to create a mental map of the changing situation of the fictional world. It would also be interesting to see how far Bartle's categories might stretch into the world of media other than MUDs. Jeremy, to take a clear-cut example, talked as a socializer in relation to books and movies as well as to games. Jocelyn was always interested in achieving an emotional connection to whatever text was given to her. In the broader work of this research project, I found some overlap with other media behaviors, but I did not have the question in mind when I began the work. In general, the data of this study do not support an extensive analysis of this taxonomy. The utility of Bartle's categories as more general descriptors of how people approach fiction remains an intriguing question for further research.

CONCLUSIONS

A serious contemporary risk is that the gap between insiders and outsiders in the digital revolution will turn into a kind of no-man's-land. Those who can only bark at digital play need to find guides to show them how things work when an insider takes charge. They should explore the possibility that interpretive processes they do not understand may actually serve as an asset, rather than instantly writing them off as a deficit.

The videotapes and transcripts of my project allowed me to look at game playing in something akin to slow motion, and they enabled me to explore how different players took differing stances toward the same game. The theoretical perspectives on tense and format gave me a way to consider what had previously seemed inexplicable to me as an outsider. Not everybody has the luxury of time and equipment to explore these games so densely. However, asking a game insider to explain the processes of a particular game is not nearly so demanding. Listening respectfully to the answers to that request is a simple way of beginning to understand how the pleasures of fiction may be expressed as past, present, or future possible worlds.

REFERENCES

Atkins, B. (2003). *More than a game: The computer game as fictional form.* Manchester, England: Manchester University Press.

Bartle, R. (1996). *Hearts, clubs, diamonds, spades: Players who suit MUDs.* Retrieved January 26, 2004, from http://www.mud.co.uk/richard/hcds.htm

Black & White [CD-ROM]. (2001). Redwood City, CA: Lionhead Studios/EA Games.

Bruner, J. (1986). *Actual minds, possible worlds.* Cambridge, MA: Harvard University Press.

Elsaesser, T. (1998). Digital cinema: Delivery, event, time. In T. Elsaesser & K. Hoffman (Eds.), *Cinema futures: Cain, Abel or cable? The screen arts in the digital age* (pp. 201–222). Amsterdam: Amsterdam University Press.

Fuller, M., & Jenkins, H. (1995). Nintendo® and new world travel writing: A dialogue. In S. G. Jones (Ed.), *CyberSociety: Computer-mediated communication and community* (pp. 57–72). London: Sage.

Gioia, D. (2004, July). *Introduction. Reading at risk: A study of literary reading in America* (Research Division Report No. 46). Washington, DC: National Endowment for the Arts.

Grodal, T. (2003). Stories for eye, ear, and muscles: Video games, media, and embodied experiences. In M. J. P. Wolf & B. Perron (Eds.), *The video game theory reader* (pp. 129–155). New York: Routledge.

Heppell, S. (1993, June 18). Hog in the limelight. *The Times Educational Supplement,* Computer Updates Section, pp. 3–4.

Jenkins, H. (2004). Game design as narrative architecture. In N. Wardrip-Fruin & P. Harrigan (Eds.), *First person: New media as story, performance, and game* (pp. 118–130). Cambridge, MA: MIT Press.

Juul, J. (2001, July). Games telling stories?—A brief note on games and narratives. *Game Studies, 1*(1). Retrieved February 3, 2004, from http://www.gamestudies.org/0101/juul-gts/

Langer, S. K. (1953). *Feeling and form: A theory of art developed from philosophy in a new key.* New York: Charles Scribner's Sons.

Mackey, M. (2002a). An asset model of new literacies: A conceptual and strategic approach to change. In B. R. C. Barrell & R. F. Hammett (Eds.), *Digital expressions: Media literacy and English language arts* (pp. 199–217). Calgary: Detselig.

Mackey, M. (2002b). *Literacies across media: Playing the text.* London: Routledge Falmer.

Mackey, M. (2005). Children reading and interpreting stories in print, film, and computer games. In J. Evans (Ed.), *Literacy moves on: Popular culture, new technologies, and critical literacy in the elementary classroom* (pp. 50–62). Portsmouth, NH: Heinemann.

Rabinowitz, P. J. (1987). *Before reading: Narrative conventions and the politics of interpretation.* Ithaca, NY: Cornell University Press.

Robinson, M., & Mackey, M. (2003). Film and television. In N. Hall, J. Larson, & J. A. Marsh (Eds.), *Handbook of early childhood literacy* (pp. 126–141). London: Paul Chapman/Sage.

Tyner, K. (1998). *Literacy in a digital world: Teaching and learning in the age of information.* Mahwah, NJ: Lawrence Erlbaum Associates.

Chapter 4

Japanese Media Mixes and Amateur Cultural Exchange

Mizuko Ito
University of Southern California

In research about young people's relationship to media, there is growing recognition that children are capable of active and critical engagement and interpretation, rather than uncritical and passive viewing of mass media messages. For example, in his introduction to his reader on children's culture, Jenkins (1998) argues against the view of children as innocent victims "in favor of works that recognize and respect their social and political agency" (p. 3). Similarly, Kinder (1999) suggests that "children's reactions to media culture tend to be more active, variable, and negotiated than is usually realized" (p. 19). When translated to educational practice, this recognition has led to what Buckingham (2003) calls a "new paradigm" in media education that seeks less to protect children from the harmful effects of media than to promote understanding and participation in media cultures. These new approaches to media education take children's existing knowledge of and pleasures in media culture as a starting point, with the aim of developing critical practices of reflection and active media production. Buckingham also suggests that "the participatory potential of new technologies—and particularly of the internet—has made it much more possible for young people to undertake creative media production" (p. 14).

Digital technologies enter the conversation about children, media, and media literacy in the context of offering new tools and environments for children to author their own perspectives in media worlds. Although it is crucial to question hyperbole and technical determinist rhetorics when evaluating the promises of these new technologies, it is also important for research to grasp foundational changes to children's lives that are accompanying their growing engagement with digital media. As Valentine and Holloway (2001) suggest, there are problems with both those who are exclusively boosters and the debunkers of new technologies (see also Buckingham, 2000). My own perspective is that digital media broaden the base of participation in certain long-standing forms of media engagement. This includes the growing accessibility to tools of media production, as well as more diverse Internet-enabled means for communicating about and trafficking in cultural content. In this chapter, I focus on the latter, the peer-to-peer exchange surrounding a particular genre of new media: Japanese animation media mixes that rely on a combination of various analog and digital media forms. I argue that children's engagement with these media mixes provides evidence that they are capable not only of critical engagement and creative production, but also of entrepreneurial *participation* in the exchange systems and economies that they have developed around media mix content.

I describe two cases from my fieldwork in Tokyo from 1998 to 2000, where I tracked young people's engagement with current media mixes. I focus on media engagement that involves new forms of peer-to-peer participation and exchange to highlight young people's political and economic entrepreneurism. After first describing my conceptual framework for understanding media fandom and participatory media cultures, I describe the cultural and historical backdrop to the Japanese media *otaku* as an example of particularly activist forms of media engagement. My two ethnographic cases are, first, the creation, collection, and exchange of Yugioh cards, and, second, amateur girls' comics.

PARTICIPATORY MEDIA CULTURES

Studies of fan groups have provided ample fodder for understanding media engagement that involves not only active and negotiated interpretation, but also rich social exchange and alternative cultural production. Even before the advent of digital authoring tools and internet exchange, fans appropriated mainstream cultural icons and narratives to organize communities of shared interest and create their own fan fictions, music videos, and music (Bacon-Smith, 1991; Jenkins, 1992; Penley, 1997; Tulloch & Jenkins, 1995). In other words, fans invoke what Jenkins (1992) calls a *participatory* media culture that blurs the distinction between production and consumption. Fans not only consume professionally produced media, but also produce their own meanings and media products. Jenkins' model of participatory culture includes this productive activity, as well as the ongoing social exchange that is at the core of robust fan activities—fans will develop interpretations and alternative readings of shows in group viewing situations and, historically, exchange fan-produced art, zines, videos, and audiotapes in conventions and through the mail.

Fan-level peer-to-peer organization has expanded in tandem with technological changes. VCR and photocopier technologies enabled alternative production and reproduction, stimulating the fan cultures of the 1970s and 1980s, the fan zines, filk (folk) songs, and remixed music videos that the first wave of fan researchers documented in their ground-breaking studies. Now the internet has emerged as a privileged technology of social organization and exchange as fans communicate over blogs and bulletin boards, share media over file-sharing sites, and sell amateur works over auction sites such as eBay. This lateral, peer-to-peer social organization represents both an evolution of existing fan groups, as well as an expansion of fanlike cultural activity to a broader demographic. In many ways, fan groups epitomize the kinds of niche communities of interest that are thriving on the internet and, in turn, have driven the evolution of new forms of internet technology and social organization.

Historically, this kind of organized fan activity has been a subcultural and marginalized cultural domain and, in the United States, mostly comprised of adults. Although audience and reader studies have documented how even relatively casual engagement involves active and negotiated interpretive positions in relation to media texts (e.g., Ang, 1996; Morley, 1992; Radway, 1991), fan studies have been distinctive in documenting a more activist and productive stance toward the content of mainstream media. Casual consumers generally see this stance as obsessive, infantilized, and cut off from normative realities. Although this tension between casual/mainstream and participatory/fan media cultures is resilient, there is also clearly a growing cadre of consumers who are crossing the line toward more activist forms of engagement. Even a quick search on the internet for any popular media content will reveal dozens of fan-oriented discussion groups and informational sites with hundreds of participants of varying ages. Ethnographies of fandoms in the pre-internet era document a higher threshold for participation, where people had to travel to conventions or develop local interpersonal networks to engage in this participatory media culture. Now having an internet-connected computer enables easy access to a rich archive of fan communication and content. This accessibility is particularly significant in the case of children and youth, who are generally not able to travel to local gatherings and national conventions but may have online access.

The point is *not* that the new technology of the internet has somehow created a burgeoning network of participatory media cultures. Rather, these networks have expanded over the internet because existing fan cultures and activities have driven and taken up new technological capabilities. In other words, the new technologies of internet communication and exchange are produced by old fan activity as much as they are productive of new forms of social and cultural practice. In this approach, I draw from social studies of the technology that see the internet as growing out of existing social contexts as well as producing new ones (e.g., Hine, 2000; Lessig, 1999; Miller & Slater, 2000). This relationship between emergent technologies and existing media cultures and practices is particularly evident within a subset of international media fandoms—those associated with Japanorigin manga, anime, and games. Although these types of fandoms have only recently become internationally visible as part of Japan's newfound "gross national cool" (McGray, 2002), they are grounded in a much older tradition of media connoisseurship associated with Japan's *otaku* cultures. After providing an introduction to *otaku* culture, I describe in more detail two cases of children and youth participatory media cultures that are evidence of the spread of *otaku*-like media culture across different age groups and countries.

MEDIA MIXES, *OTAKU* CULTURES, AND MEDIA LITERACY

Although English-language research literature on Japanese manga and anime-related fandom is just beginning to emerge (Kinsella, 2000; McLelland, 2001; Napier, 2000), these types of media have been a significant force in both Japan and abroad for over three decades. Outside of Japan, *Pokémon* forced the recognition of Japanese anime into the mainstream in the 1990s (Tobin, 2004), providing a popular counterpoint to the longer term growth of adult anime fandom in other parts of Asia, the United States, and Europe. In Japan, vibrant manga (comics) and anime (animation) cultures originated in the 1960s as child- and youth-identified media and have grown into a multigenerational and transnational phenomenon. My primary reference point for this chapter is Japanese *otaku* cultures and my research in Japan. But in keeping with the transnational spread of these cultures, I also include some observations from my U.S.-based research on media engagement of American children and online fan communication.

Japan-origin manga, anime, and game content are heterogeneous, spanning multiple media types and genres, yet still recognized as a cluster of linked cultural forms. Because of the absence of a single overarching media type or genre, I use the native industry term *media mix* to describe the linked character-based media types of games, anime, and manga. Manga are generally (but not always) the primary texts of these media forms. They were the first component of the contemporary mix to emerge in the postwar period in the 1960s and 1970s, eventually providing the characters and narratives that go on to populate games, anime, and merchandise. Although electronic gaming was in a somewhat separate domain through the 1980s, by the 1990s, it was well integrated with the overall media mix of manga and anime characters, aided by the popularity of game-origin characters such as Mario and Pikachu. In this chapter, my focus is on this overall media mixed ecology and the ways in which digital media are amplifying certain dimensions of the mix. In other words, I see the move toward new media as an interaction between long-standing and emergent media forms, rather than a shift from old analog to new digital media. I spend most of my time discussing the low-tech media of trading cards and comic books, but I hope to make clear how these analog media forms are being newly inflected through digitally enabled sociality.

The same period of rapid economic growth and cultural renewal that gave birth to Japan's contemporary media mix also gave birth to youth cultures that responded to the new material affluence and media culture. During the 1960s, young people flocked to manga as a new form of culture that fit their generational identity. Kinsella (1998) writes, "By spending hours with their noses buried in children's manga books obtuse students demonstrated their hatred of the university system, of adults, and of society as a whole" (p. 291). Young people developed new sensibilities that responded to consumer brands, rich media environments, and new urban street cultures that were not available to the wartime generation of their parents. Soon they were labeled as *shinjinrui* or *the new breed*. A subset of these young media consumers went on to create distinctive participatory fan cultures. In the 1980s, the term *otaku* was coined and popularized to describe these media-obsessed youth who took manga and anime as their primary cultural referents.

According to *otaku* scholar and apologist Okada (2000), the term originated in the beginning of the 1980s as a polite term of address between upper crust college students who were fans of emergent anime cultures. The term was transformed into a label for a social group by columnist Akio Nakamori, who published a column on "*Otaku* Research" in a manga magazine in 1983. In 1989, a full-blown moral panic (Cohen, 1972) about *otaku* arose after the arrest of Miyazaki Tsutomu. He had abducted, murdered, and mutilated four girls, and *otaku* media were blamed for providing the inspiration for his sociopathic acts. Photos and footage of his bedroom, crammed with manga and videotapes, many of the Lolita-complex and pornographic variety, flooded the popular press, and Miyazaki became the posterboy of the *otaku* subculture. After this, the term came to be used and recognized by the mainstream as a stigmatizing label for somebody who is obsessed with media mix content and out of touch with everyday social reality.

Mainstream perception of *otaku* bears at least a family resemblance to how Trekkies have been stereotyped in the United States (Jenkins, 1992).

An important difference, however, between English-language terms such as *fan* or *Trekkie* and the term *otaku* is that the Japanese term invokes a broader set of cultural connotations not restricted to a particular social group, set of activities, or media type, genre, or artist. *Otaku-kei* or *otaku*-variety cultural style is part of a general palette of Japanese popular cultural reference. A publication or an anime series might be described as *otaku-kei* even if it is in mainstream distribution. Similarly, people can engage with a wide variety of cultural activities in an *otaku*-like way. Colloquially, the term gets used to describe a specific subculture of youth who are fans of media mixes, but also as a general term for collection and connoisseurship. For example, one might call somebody a *wine otaku* or a *fishing otaku*. In this, the term is probably closer to *geek* or *nerd* than to *fan*. It is a term that has come to connote a general sociocultural logic or gestalt, which takes as its core a sense of connoisseurship, attention to esoterica, media mixing, and amateur cultural production.

Okada (2000) argues against the stigmatizing use of the term *otaku* and offers a counterdefinition: "I believe *otaku* are a new breed born in the 20th century 'visual culture era.' In other words, *otaku* are people with a viewpoint based on an extremely evolved sensitivity toward images" (p. 14). Further, he argues that the uses of the term in such labels as *fishing otaku* or *anime otaku* are fundamentally incorrect, and that one defining feature of the *otaku* sensibility is that they do not obsess over a single media genre or type, but rather read across genres and media forms.

> Anime are certainly the home ground for *otaku*-ism. But games, special effects, Western films, and manga also include works which rank high on the *otaku* scale. And actually, these works influence one another. The *otaku* sensibility comes from recognizing and enjoying these as genre cross-overs. (p. 43)

In the 1990s, the term started to be taken up with mostly positive valences overseas to refer to enthusiasts of Japanese media mixes, particularly anime. In its premier 1993 issue, *Wired* magazine featured an article on *otaku* as "the incredibly strange mutant creatures who rule the universe of alienated Japanese zombie computer nerds." More recently, science fiction writer Gibson (2001) described *otaku* as "passionate obsessives," and English-language anime fan sites proudly adopt the term as a form of self-address.

I believe that Okada's approach and the recent transnational popularity of the term represents a valuable native view of *otaku* culture and is a useful corrective to the penumbra of connotations that resulted from the moral panics over the Miyazaki incident. At the same time, I would argue for a view of *otaku* that locates the subculture within a resilient set of cultural and social structural dynamics, rather than just the internal definitions that

Okada provides. Viewed anthropologically, the more stigmatizing meanings attached to *otaku* by the mainstream culture are not simply misunderstandings, but structurally determined outcomes of challenges that *otaku* represent to mainstream logics of cultural production, capitalism, gender, and age categories. As Okada suggests, the *otaku* sensibility has grown out of contemporary media cultures, pushing back at their dominant cultural logics and power dynamics. *Otaku* sensibilities were born from the specific sociocultural contexts of Japan, but have also proved to have appeal well beyond Japan's borders. Specifically, *otaku* culture destabilizes certain key sociocultural categories: the distinction between professional and amateur cultural production, the commodity form of media, age-based boundaries for media consumption, and normative forms of gender and sexuality. I return to these broader structural dynamics in the conclusion of my chapter after first turning to my two ethnographic cases.

THE *YUGIOH* KNOWLEDGE
AND CARD-TRADING ECONOMY

During the period of my fieldwork in Japan, the most popular forms of play among boys centered around *Yugioh*, a media mix series that rose from the ashes of *Pokémon* to become a major force both in Japan and overseas. Like *Pokémon*, *Yugioh* relies on cross-referencing among serialized manga, a TV anime series, a card game, video games, occasional movie releases, and a plethora of character merchandise. The series centers on a boy, Mutoh Yugi, a game master who gets involved in various adventures with a small cohort of friends and rivals. The narrative, first rendered in manga and then anime, focuses on long sequences of card game duels, stitched together by an adventure narrative. Yugi and his friends engage in a card game derivative of the U.S.-origin game *Magic the Gathering*, and the series is devoted to fantastic duels that function to explicate the detailed esoterica of the games, such as the strategies and rules of game play, the properties of the cards, and the fine points of card collecting and trading. Compared with *Pokémon*, where games were only loosely tied to the narrative media by character identification, with *Yugioh* the gaming comprises the central content of the narrative.

As part of my research, I talked to parents and played with children who engaged with *Yugioh* as part of their everyday local peer relations. I was also a regular at specialty card shops that hosted weekly *Yugioh* tournaments, and I was able to befriend an older group of *Yugioh* aficionados who engaged in more deeply *otaku*-like forms of engagement with *Yugioh*. Although these two groups of *Yugioh* players—children engaged in play at or near home, and older players congregating at specialty shops—represent different degrees of game expertise and knowledge networks, both groups exhibit similar types of enthusiasm and investments in both collecting cards and knowledge. In other words, across a spectrum of *Yugioh* players, all evidenced certain forms of *otaku*-like engagement in a participatory media culture. Both the "core" community of older *Yugioh* players and the larger mass of kid *Yugioh* players can be located on a shared cultural continuum.

In the case of a media mix such as *Yugioh*, the participatory dimensions of media culture lie at the core, rather than being something "poached" at the margins as is the case for most TV and cinema content (Jenkins, 1992). Building on the lessons of *Pokémon*, *Yugioh* card game play has been designed around the premise that learning will happen in a group social setting, rather than as a relation between child and machine or child and text. As Sefton-Green (2004) writes with respect to *Pokémon*, *Yugioh* play involves a "knowledge industry." It is nearly impossible to learn how to play the card game rules and strategy without the coaching of more experienced players. My research assistants and I spent several weeks with the *Yugioh* starter pack, poring through the rule book and the instructional videotape, trying to figure out how to play. It was only after several game sessions with some 9- to 10-year-olds, followed by some coaching from some of the more patient adults at the card shops, that we slowly began to understand the basic game play as well as some of the fine points of collection—how cards are acquired, valued, and traded.

Among children, this learning process is part of their everyday peer relations, as they congregate after school in homes and parks, showing off their cards, hooking up their Game Boys to play against one another, and trading cards and information. We found that children generally develop certain conventions of play among their local peer group, negotiating rules locally, often on a duel-by-duel basis. They will collectively monitor the weekly manga release in *Shonen Jump* magazine, often sharing copies among friends. In addition to the weekly manga about Yugi, the magazine also features information about upcoming card releases, tournaments, and tournament results. The issues featuring the winning decks of tournament duelists are often the most avidly studied. When children get together with their collections of *Yugioh* cards, there is a constant buzz of information exchange and deal-cutting, as children debate the merits of different cards and seek to augment both their play deck and their broader card collection. Players build a personalized relationship to the media mix content by collecting their own set of cards and virtual monsters and combining them into a deck or battle team that reflects a unique style of play. Buckingham and Sefton-Green (2004) write that with *Pokémon* "activity—or agency—is an indispensable part of the process rather than something that is exercised *post hoc*" (p. 19). *Yugioh* card game play similarly requires active participation as a precondition of media engagement.

In the case of the older *Yugioh* aficionados, the productive and participatory dimensions are even more pronounced, leading to the construction of alternative economies of knowledge and card exchange. *Yugioh otaku* are avid fans of *Yugioh* and rely on the mainstream media and toy industry to produce the content that is central to their activity. At the same time, they engage in tactics and entrepreneurial activities that push back at the dominant meanings of the narrative and game content, as well as at the structures of commodity capitalism. When a new series of cards is released, they are the first to purchase the whole series, posting the new cards in the series on their web sites and trying them out for playability. Any ambiguity in play dynamics and rules is immediately identified and reported to the company. On one of my evenings at a card shop, a group of gamers were talking about how they had telephoned the official Konami gamers line repeatedly to complain about the play dynamic of a particular card.

The buying, selling, and trading of postmarket single cards after the card pack has been opened are largely at the level of peer-to-peer exchange. The industries that produce *Yugioh* get no direct benefit from the millions of card trades and purchasing among children, at specialty card shops, and among card collectors on the internet and at conventions. Konami has been rumored to have tried unsuccessfully to pressure some card shops to stop the sale of single cards. Although by far the bulk of *Yugioh* card exchange is noncommercial, for serious Internet traders and specialty shops, the sale of single cards is a significant source of income. Card collectors scour the shelves of convenience stores on the night of a new series release, using special methods to identify packs with rare cards that they will add to their collections and auction on the internet. Although looked down on by all card *otaku* I spoke to, there is also a vibrant industry of counterfeit *Yugioh* cards that are often sold on street corners or at festivals, drawing throngs of appreciative children.

Although fan studies have documented the participatory dimensions of engagement with TV, film, and print media, media mixes are more consciously designed for player level customization, remix, and social interaction. The format of media mixes like *Yugioh* builds on the sensibilities of children who grew up with the interactive and layered formats of video games as a fact of life, bringing this subjectivity to bear on other media forms. *Pokémon* decisively inflected children's video game culture toward personalization and recombination, demonstrating that children can master highly esoteric content, customization, remixing, and a pantheon of hundreds of characters. These participatory dimensions—collecting, remixing, customizing, revaluing, and reframing within a social context of peer-to-peer exchange—are central to an *otaku*-like approach to media engagement.

DOUJINSHI AND *SHOJO* FAN CULTURES

Although gaming *otaku* cultures have been largely dominated by boys, girls have had a leadership role in the cultures of *doujinshi* (amateur manga), an arena of *otaku* practice that is in many ways more challenging to mainstream sensibilities than the peer-to-peer exchanges of *Yugioh* cards. Like the case of *Yugioh* card exchange, manga production by girls spans a range between casual engagement by young girls and average consumers and *otaku*-identified practices that are much more activist and entrepreneurial.

Manga have been a major source of subcultural cultural capital since the postwar period, particularly from the 1970s onward. The period of high-speed economic growth in Japan from the 1960s through the 1970s transformed existing graphical arts into modern mass cultural production industries. Through the course of the 1970s and 1980s, manga slowly became recognized as a legitimate cultural product that could take up difficult intellectual and political topics as well as provide light entertainment. The Japanese manga industry is unique in that it comprises about 38% of all print publications in Japan (Schodt, 1996) and spans a much wider range of genres and topics than in other countries. Topics taken up by manga include fictional and nonfictional topics that are generally not published in comic books elsewhere (e.g., adult-oriented pornography, stories of businessmen, childrearing, mah jong, sports, and historical fiction). Today, manga are enjoyed by all age groups in Japan and are generally the primary literacy experiences for children. Manga are such a central fixture of Japanese childhood that one editor asked me with puzzlement after our interview, "What do American children *do* without manga?"

As part of my fieldwork with children in Japan, I made regular visits to a public children's center that runs an afterschool program for elementary-school-age children. I spent most of my time in the arts and crafts room and the library on the second floor, foraying down to the first-floor gym only during the occasional Yugioh tournaments hosted there. The library had a substantial collection of novels and reference books, but also stocked the latest manga magazine for elementary-age boys and girls, as well as well-thumbed archives of popular series that are later released in paperback book format. In the library, there was always an array of children sprawled on the floor and on the sofas with manga in hand. In the arts and crafts room, they copied and traced their favorite manga characters from coloring books or drew them from memory in their notebooks. When there was not a structured activity in the arts and crafts room, small groups of girls would often be drawing their own pictures of characters from popular anime. *Pokémon* and *Hamtaro* characters were the most popular, and girls would often delight in showing me and other girls how skilled they were at drawing a particular *Pokémon* or hamster from the pantheon.

The children frequenting this center were mostly first and second grad-ers (6- to 8-year-olds) just beginning to use the visual culture of manga as part of their own form of personal expression. When I spoke to older girls and women in other contexts, many described how this early drawing prac-tice evolved into "pencil manga" or the drawing of manga frames and narra-tives in the late elementary through high school years. For those who came on to be more serious or fan-identified, they might aspire to become a pro-fessional manga artist or participate in the vibrant *doujinshi* scene. In this sense, there is a continuity between the informal and everyday practices of growing up in a manga-saturated childhood and the more hard-core or *otaku* practices of aspiring to be a manga artist. At the same time, the iden-tity shift from a girl who can draw manga characters to an *otaku* who aspires to writing her own manga is a shift from a normative to an alternative or subcultural identity. Just as in the case of *Yugioh* fandom, where *otaku* knowledge and card economies are bifurcated from mainstream econo-mies, "regular" girls do not participate beyond the reading of manga and casual drawing of favorite characters.

One event I attended traced the boundary zones between the subjectivity of manga readership, fandom, and production. In 2001, I attended a sum-mer festival organized by *Ribon* magazine, the most popular manga maga-zine for lower elementary school-age girls. Readers of the magazine applied with postcards to a lottery to be selected to attend the festival, and the large hall in central Tokyo was packed with girls and young women. The high-light of the event was a panel of four of the magazine's most popular artists. All four described how they had started drawing manga in elementary school, eventually moving to pencil manga, and had their first manga work published while they were in high school. The MC of the event said that the most common question that readers have for the artists is, "How did you get so good at drawing?" He introduced a prerecorded sequence of the most popular artists giving tips on drawing and character development. The au-dience was assumed to be young aspiring artists. In the back of all manga magazines are regular announcements inviting readers to submit their own manga to competitions designed to identify new talent. The successful works are published with fanfare together with the more established artists who run regular series in any given magazine. Although only the most dedi-cated of readers go on to submit their own manga to a competition of this sort, the magazines interpellate all readers as potential manga writers, si-multaneously citing and constructing the shared cultural frame that manga writing is a commonplace form of literacy and expression.

These types of events and competitions represent the officially sanc-tioned interface zones between mainstream publishing and the amateur and aspiring artist, but this is just the tip of the iceberg of the girls' amateur manga movement. In tandem with the growth of the manga industry, the *otaku* base of manga readership also grew. In the early 1970s, with the advent of photocopying and cheap offset printing, amateur manga and fan fiction became a viable medium for what came to be called "mini communications" or "minicomi," in contrast to mass communication (Kinsella, 2000). Aided by the relatively relaxed copyright regime of Japanese publishers, this amateur manga movement flourished in the late 1970s and 1980s. Comic Market, the premier convention for *doujinshi*, began in 1974, growing from a small annual gathering to become the largest convention of any kind in Japan. By the mid-1990s, up to 300,000 *doujinshi* aficionados would flock to the largest convention center in Tokyo for the now biannual meeting. In addition to Comic Market, numerous other smaller gatherings are organized regularly around the country focused on region or specific manga genre or title.

Historically, amateur manga contained a large number of original works and represented a way for an aspiring artist to break into mainstream publishing. With the broadening base of participation, however, works derivative of professional content became the overwhelming majority. *Doujinshi* written for women by women that depict romance between *bishounen* (beautiful boys) appropriated from mainstream manga represented the first major wave of popular *doushinshi* writing in the 1970s and 1980s. More recently, the *bishoujo* (beautiful girl) and *Lolicom* (Lolita complex comics) genres written by men for men have become popular. Both of these genres of *doujinshi* are scorned by the mainstream because of their often explicit and offbeat sexual content, the fact that the works are derivative, and because they generally lack any substantive narrative development (see Kinsella, 1998, 2000; McLelland, 2001).

After the arrest of Miyazaki in 1989, the ensuing moral panic engulfed the *doujinshi* scene. Kinsella (2000) writes, "Amateur manga culture was repeatedly linked to Miyazaki, creating what became a new public perception, that young people involved with amateur manga are dangerous, psychologically-disturbed perverts" (p. 128). By the early 1990s, *doujinshi* artists and purveyors became subject to police harassment, where bookshops were raided and artists were brought in for questioning. This public discourse was taken up by young people as well as the older generation (Kinsella, 2000). "Young people themselves, were persuaded that amateur manga subculture was a serious social problem, rather than a 'cool' youth activity that they might like to enter into" (Kinsella, 2000, p. 137). In my fieldwork in Japan, I found these attitudes alive and well over a decade after the Miyazaki incident. Although the young people staffing the booths at the Comic Market were quite happy to chat with me about their works, they balked at the idea of doing a follow-up interview. The operators of the Comic Market continue to be vigilant about negative press and publicizing participants' identities. Cameras and video cameras are banned on the

Comic Market floor. Others I spoke to involved with *doujinshi* or related activities often kept their activities hidden from their classmates and family, attesting to the continued social stigma attached to these subcultures.

With the spread of the Internet in the late 1990s, the dynamics of *doujinshi* exchange are changing substantially. As with the case of *Yugioh* card trafficking, *doujinshi* are ideal collectors' items to be exchanged via internet auction sites and homepages run by the artists. A quick search on popular Japanese auction sites will bring up thousands of *doujinshi* for sale, ranging from the equivalent of hundreds of U.S. dollars to just a few. This internet trafficking in *doujinshi* and related information has made these cultural products much more accessible to a broader demographic both within and outside Japan (McLelland, 2001). In the Comic Market convention catalog from summer 2000, one of the organizers editorializes about the "out of control boom in net auctions" (Unamu, 2000, p. 1314). Unlike professionalized and mass distributed comics, *doujinshi* were traditionally only available at conventions like the Comic Market or a handful of specialty shops in urban centers stocking only a fraction of the comics that you would see at a large-scale event. Now with net distribution, rare and niche publications can be easily bought and sold. The author of the Comic Market editorial ponders the pluses and minuses of having works sold on the net for much higher prices than sold on the Comic Market floor, the emergence of people who seem to be buying and selling *doujinshi* to make a living, people auctioning off their spots on the Comic Market floor, and the emergent grey zone of auctioneers who photocopy rare *doujinshi* and sell them on auction sites. He concludes:

> At the rate things are going, people are going to start auctioning their staff IDs and armbands. But for the generation who started going to Comic Market after it moved to the Ariake site, and were already contacting each other with mobile phones, this is just a normal state of affairs. Even if the older folks complain about a declining morality, there is nothing we can do. We need to look ahead and say this is the current state of affairs. Now how should we respond to it? (p. 1319)

The jury is still out as to the long-term prospects of the burgeoning *doujinshi* activities on the internet, but clearly the trend is toward moving more and more of the *doujinshi* traffic online. This is particularly true of foreign readers of Japanese *doujinshi* who gain access to these publications almost exclusively through internet sales (McLelland, 2001). Some of these sites even offer scanlations (scanned translations) into English. Due to the sexually explicit nature of many *doujinshi*, controversy continues to abound as to the appropriateness of the traffic in these publications, particularly among the teens who both produce and purchase these works. In

many ways, the internet has proved to be an ideal medium for bringing together marginal and niche communities of interest that are highly dispersed. At the same time, the net has become a vehicle for making these
subcultures visible and subject to scrutiny by an unsympathetic mainstream. At one U.S. anime fan convention I attended, a high school student lamented that she felt uncomfortable reading manga in front of her
friends because they assumed that she was reading pornography, even
though she was not interested in those genres of manga. Although only
one sector of an immense and diverse format of publication, the image of
manga as focusing on sex and violence has even been exported overseas as
a mainstream perception.

AMATEUR CULTURAL PRODUCTION

For my purposes here, the most significant aspects of *doujinshi* production
and exchange are not the particulars of how the communities have shifted
to online and transnational spaces. Rather, I am interested in how *doujinshi*
production and exchange, even in the pre-internet era, represent the activist participatory media cultures that are proliferating in tandem with the
spread of digital media. In a sense, they are prototypical of niche communities of disenfranchised youth who are mobilizing through the internet to
create communities of interest that challenge elite and adult sensibilities.
In her studies of *doujinshi* and "cute" girl culture central to much of manga
and anime, Kinsella (1995) suggests that these cultures operate from a position of disenfranchisement vis-à-vis the mainstream. *Doujinshi*, in particular,
have working-class origins, and Kinsella (2000) suggests that "this is one of
the very few cultural and social forums in Japan (or any other industrialized
country), which is not managed by privileged and highly educated classes
of society" (p. 110).

> It is possible that the intense emphasis placed, firstly, on educational achieve-
> ment, and secondly, on acquiring a sophisticated cultural taste, in Japan since
> the 1960s, has also stimulated the involvement of young people excluded
> from these officially recognized modes of achievement, with amateur manga
> subculture. (Kinsella, 2000, p. 111)

Although it is probably clear that I share with *otaku* cultures an appreciation for peer-based and bottom-up forms of media production and exchange, my view of these subcultures is not univocally celebratory. I have
questioned the implicit technical determinism in both cautionary and celebratory visions of the digital generation, and I acknowledge that contradic-

tory tendencies emerge from the heterogeneous uptake of diverse digital technologies. The profound unease that educated elites experience when confronted with the "junk culture" of *Yugioh* and *doujinshi* is evidence of the persistent tension between high-brow educational agendas and subaltern youth activism (see Seiter, 1993). We may celebrate the active nature of youth media engagement, but we may not be prepared to cede control or provide validation to bottom-up kid cultures interested in the esoterica of fantasy game play or Lolita porn. As an ethnographer interested in educational reform, my own stance has been that we need to first understand and appreciate the social and political dynamics represented by these expanding subaltern networks before we can arrive at principled interventions that do not simply reinscribe the distinctions between high and low, kid and adult cultures.

The cultural movements I have described—*otaku* media subcultures, card trafficking, and amateur manga—are all examples of participatory media cultures that predate the so-called "digital age." They grow out of resilient dynamics of stratification by age, gender, and class. At the same time, these practices are merging with new digital technologies of production and exchange to expand the range and possibilities of amateur cultural production. My goal in this chapter has been to describe a certain politics of engagement with media cultures that are not specific to media type, but have strong affinities with the recombinant and peer-to-peer forms of media and communication that have been increasingly supported by digital technologies. The broadening base of participation in *otaku* culture, as well as their transnational spread, are evidence of the synergistic relationship between these niche subcultures and the networked ecologies of the internet. In Japan, as elsewhere, those engaged in hard-core fan and *otaku* activities are a relatively small proportion of overall media consumers. At the same time, the communicative environment of the internet, interactive media formats, as well as the industry paradigm represented by Japanese media mixes encourage these types of practices and subjectivities among even casual readers and players. My effort, in other words, has been to highlight continuities as much as ruptures between new and old media and between marginal and mainstream consumers.

The cases I have described may seem irrelevant and exotic, but I would argue for their growing salience in the international media ecology. Although this is speculative, I feel that the transnational spread of Japanese-origin media mixes and the tropes of *otaku* culture are evidence of the resonance between *otaku* subjectivities and digital cultures. Clearly this spread has been uneven and restricted to technologically privileged and non-mainstream media consumers overseas. At the same time, the spread of a subculture of this sort from a cultural margin to Euro-American cultural centers is enough to have raised a wave of well-circulated writing about Japan's "gross national cool" and "soft" power (Faiola, 2003; McGray, 2002; Solomon, 2003). I am not suggesting an exclusively Japanese national original to *otaku* fandoms, but rather a new transnational cross-pollination among participatory media cultures of diverse national stripes. My cases are examples of the unique alchemy when marginal subcultures and subaltern groups combine with distributed and heterogeneous media networks and ecologies. Although the cultural identities of niche media cultures are diverse, they are probably part of a shared technocultural trend that challenges modern distinctions between production and consumption, and between child and adult subjectivity.

Given that stratification by class and age seem unlikely to disappear anytime soon, subaltern groups of amateur media producers will continue to thrive in the shadows of mainstream media production, pushing back at their dominant logics and narratives. For those shut out of dominant and professionalized adult subjectivities by factors such as age or class identity, these shadow exchanges and amateur reputation systems offer an alternative economy of value and productive participation. If we place these amateur practices along a global–local scale that contrasts large-scale cultural production and individual-scale cultural consumption, we can see that they lie in the intermediary zone that we might call a community scale of interaction. Cultural content is being exchanged and engaged with at a scale that is larger than intimate and personal communication, but not at the scale of mass media transmission. This is the scale of perhaps a dozen to several hundred people where there is some kind of named relation among participants, emergent leadership, and ongoing community exchange. Although lacking access to professional media networks, these amateur networks are viable subeconomies where young people gain a sense of expertise, deep knowledge, and validation from knowledgeable peers. In other words, these are expert communities, although not professionalized ones.

I would like to conclude with a question. Is it possible to legitimate amateur cultural production and exchange as a domain of learning and identity production for young people? Institutionally and culturally, amateurism is a marginalized domain, associated with volunteers, starving artists, and hobbyists. Yet it is clearly also an arena that supports vibrant learning communities and forms of productive activity that differ from the power dynamics of schooling. If we shift from the domain of entertainment to education, many of the distinctions between cultural producers and consumers also apply to knowledge producers and consumers, which in the academy we distinguish as faculty and students or teachers and learners. Amateur fan cultural production shares many structural similarities to community-level learning that has been the subject of ethnographic studies of apprenticeship and other small-scale learning communities. This is a layer of social organization that supports identities like the assistant, apprentice, or graduate student—people who do not occupy the professional identity category, but who still perform productive labor in that community, rather than being passive consumers of knowledge (see also Lave & Wenger, 1991). Although the roguish practices I have described may seem distant from our current ideas of media education, perhaps they provide some hints for supporting practices that are driven by the motivations of young people's participation in media and peer networks, complicating our long-standing distinctions between who are the producers and who are the consumers of knowledge and culture.

REFERENCES

Ang, I. (1996). *Living room wars: Rethinking media audiences in a postmodern world.* New York: Routledge.

Bacon-Smith, C. (1991). *Enterprising women: Television fandom and the creation of popular myth.* Philadelphia: University of Pennsylvania Press.

Buckingham, D. (2000). *After the death of childhood: Growing up in the age of electronic media.* Cambridge: Polity.

Buckingham, D. (2003). *Media education: Literacy, learning, and contemporary culture.* Cambridge: Polity.

Buckingham, D., & Sefton-Green, J. (2004). Structure, agency, and pedagogy in children's media culture. In J. Tobin (Ed.), *Pikachu's global adventure: The rise and fall of Pokémon* (pp. 12–33). Durham, NC: Duke University Press.

Cohen, S. (1972). *Folk devils and moral panics.* London: MacGibbon & Kee.

Faiola, A. (2003, December 27). Japan's empire of cool. *Washington Post,* p. A01.

Hine, C. (2000). *Virtual ethnography.* London: Sage.

Gibson, W. (2001, April 1). Modern boys and mobile girls. *The Observer.* Retrieved November 15, 2005, from http://observer.guardian.co.uk/life/story/0,6903,466391,00.html

Jenkins, H. (1992). *Textual poachers: Television fans and participatory culture.* New York: Routledge.

Jenkins, H. (1998). Introduction: Childhood innocence and other modern myths. In H. Jenkins (Ed.), *The children's culture reader* (pp. 1–37). New York: New York University Press.

Kinder, M. (1999). Kids' media culture: An introduction. In M. Kinder (Ed.), *Kids' media culture* (pp. 1–12). Durham, NC: Duke University Press.

Kinsella, S. (1995). Cuties in Japan. In L. Skov & B. Moeran (Eds.), *Women, media, and consumption in Japan* (pp. 220–254). Honolulu: University of Hawaii Press.

Kinsella, S. (1998). Japanese subculture in the 1980s: Otaku and the amateur manga movement. *Journal of Japanese Studies, 24,* 289–316.

Kinsella, S. (2000). *Adult manga: Culture and power in contemporary Japanese society.* Honolulu: University of Hawaii Press.

Lave, J., & Wenger, E. (1991). *Situated learning: Legitimate peripheral participation.* Cambridge: Cambridge University Press.

Lessig, L. (1999). *Code and other laws of cyberspace.* New York: Basic Books.

McGray, D. (2002, June/July). Japan's gross national cool. *Foreign Policy.* Retrieved July 13, 2005, from http://www.douglasmcgray.com/articles.html

McLelland, M. (2001). Local meanings in global space: A case study of women's "Boy Love" Web sites in Japanese and English. *Mots Pluriels, 19.* Retrieved July 13, 2005, from http://www.arts.uwa.edu.au/MotsPluriels/MP1901mcl.html

Miller, D., & Slater, D. (2000). *The Internet: An ethnographic approach.* New York: Berg.

Morley, D. (1992). *Television, audiences, and cultural studies.* New York: Routledge.

Napier, S. J. (2000). *Anime: From Akira to Princess Mononoke.* New York: Palgrave.

Okada, T. (2000). *Otaku-gaku Nyuumon* [Introduction to otaku studies]. Tokyo: Ohta Shuppan.

Penley, C. (1997). *Nasa/Trek: Popular science and sex in America.* New York: Verso.

Radway, J. A. (1991). *Reading the romance: Women, patriarchy, and popular literature.* Chapel Hill: University of North Carolina Press.

Schodt, F. L. (1996). *Dreamland Japan: Writings on modern manga.* Berkeley, CA: Stonebridge.

Sefton-Green, J. (2004). Initiation rites: A small boy in a Poké-World. In J. Tobin (Ed.), *Pikachu's global adventure: The rise and fall of Pokémon* (pp. 141–164). Durham, NC: Duke University Press.

Seiter, E. (1993). *Sold separately: Parents and children in consumer culture.* New Brunswick, NJ: Rutgers University Press.

Solomon, C. (2003, June 1). Inspired by the film they inspired. *Los Angeles Times,* p. E24.

Tobin, J. (Ed.). (2004). *Pikachu's global adventure: The rise and fall of Pokémon.* Durham, NC: Duke University Press.

Tulloch, J., & Jenkins, H. (1995). *Science fiction audiences: Watching Doctor Who and Star Trek.* New York: Routledge.

Unamu, H. (2000). Nazono Burokku-cho Misutaa S no Kachiku Yahoo [Mystery block chief Mister S domestic yahoo]. *Comic Market 58 Catalog* (pp. 1314–1319).

Valentine, S., & Holloway, G. (2001). *Cyberkids: Children in the information age.* New York: Routledge.

Chapter 5

Activity Theory and Learning From Digital Games: Developing an Analytical Methodology

Martin Oliver
Caroline Pelletier
University of London

In the last few years, there has been growing interest in the use of digital games for educational purposes. Researchers have explored a range of concerns such as the practical issues raised by using games as classroom resources (Egenfeldt-Nielsen, 2004), the possibility of using game-like interfaces and designs to make educational software more motivating and effective (Dawes & Dumbleton, 2001; Gander, 2000; Prensky, 2001), the social practices that develop around computer game play outside school (Williamson & Facer, 2003), and the kinds of multimodal literacies that games develop (Beavis, 1998; Burn & Parker, 2003). Two areas of research focus in particular on the relationship between the design of the game and the experience of the player during the game-playing process, examining how and what players learn through play and how games function as pedagogic texts or designs. In so doing, they raise questions regarding the balance between the text and the player in learning through game play.

The first of these areas concerns itself with the informational or factual content of games and adapts the kind of frameworks used in the evaluation of educational software. In the UK, the British Educational Technology Agency (BeCTA) and Teachers Evaluating Education Media (TEEM) reports into the educational benefits of computer games are the most prominent examples of this kind of research, examining the cognitive and social processes involved in playing a number of games (Dawes & Dumbleton, 2001; McFarlane et al., 2002). The BeCTA report, for example, argued that *The Sims* can teach the value of budgeting because it requires players to manage financial resources, whereas *Championship Manager*, which involves putting together football teams according to the strengths and weaknesses of different available players, can be used to teach database handling (Dawes & Dumbleton, 2001).

This kind of research defines the educational potential of games in terms of the opportunities for players to evaluate information, hypothesize and test out solutions, and work in groups. However, it does not comment on how such opportunities are taken up. The TEEM report, for example, reviewed the informational content of a number of digital games and included feedback collected through postplay focus groups and questionnaires. However, it does not observe the process of playing, nor does it include research on the nature and quality of moment-by-moment social and technological interactions and how these might relate to each other. Both the BeCTA and TEEM reports concluded that playing certain computer games, particularly 'realistic' simulations, involves learning of some kind. However, because they do not develop a theory for explaining how learning takes place, nor a method for investigating the learning process, their findings are largely inferential. This is not to criticize these reports, but to acknowledge a problem they both faced. The TEEM report, for example, concluded that computer games can enhance certain key but context-free skills, such as strategic thinking and problem solving. But the authors are not in a position to explain how students develop such skills through play, what might count as evidence for such skills within the context of playing a game, or whether there is transference to other contexts.

The second approach outlined here focuses on the learning principles that computer games demonstrate. This involves researching games both as a set of social practices as well as a type of text that functions according to specific design grammars. In his book, *What Video Games Have to Teach Us About Learning and Literacy*, Gee (2003) outlined the theory of learning embedded in computer game play. He argued that when people learn to play video games, they are learning a new literacy, which involves not only decoding the game as text, but also knowing various ways of acting, interacting, valuing, and feeling. Learning in games is defined not so much as an outcome, but as part of the process of playing, and relates not so much to the content of the game as to the complexity of its design. According to Gee, learning and playing are simultaneous and largely synonymous processes. The pleasures and frustrations of playing are akin to those of learning.

Gee's book theorizes how learning takes place in playing games and how learning and playing are related. However, it does not include a method for researching learning and playing in different contexts. For example, Gee argues that it is only 'good' games that involve complex learning processes—these are in effect distinguished from 'bad' games that presumably do not. His theory of how learning works in computer games is based on the analysis of 'good' games only. Therefore, it is a theory of the potential of well-designed games to bring about worthwhile learning. But he does not give criteria to establish how one can distinguish between a good and a bad game, or (except in the most general ways) how literacy in game playing relates to the nature of the game and the sociocultural dimension of playing. Although Gee extends the notion of literacy to games, his approach does not give researchers the methodological tools to investigate how different texts and contexts influence the development of literacy.

What is missing from both the approaches outlined earlier and from the literature on learning and digital games in general is a method that looks at the process and outcomes of play and how these relate to the design of the game text as well as the social and cultural aspect of play. This gap in the research is highlighted by Squire (2002), who argued in favor of naturalistic studies of game-playing experiences and the kind of practices people engage in while gaming:

> What's missing from contemporary debate on gaming and culture is any naturalistic study of what game-playing experiences are like, how gaming fits into people's lives, and the kinds of practices that people are engaged in while gaming. Few, if any researchers have studied how and why people play games, and what gaming environments are like. [. . .] Investigators might benefit by acknowledging the cultural contexts of gaming, and studying game-playing as a cultural practice. If nothing else, it highlights the importance of putting aside preconceptions and examining gamers on their own terms. (pp. 2–3)

His critique of research into learning from games is stronger still: "We know very little about what [people] are learning playing these games (if anything)" (p. 4). This chapter seeks to address this challenge, but first it is necessary to explore *how* people learn from games. In the next section, a research methodology is developed that can contribute to this aim.

METHODOLOGY

Theoretical Framework

Squire's (2002) review of computer game research suggests several theoretical frameworks that could provide a sociocultural insight into learning and games. One of the perspectives that is reviewed is activity theory. In this section, this suggested framework is outlined and then developed as a research methodology.

As Squire describes, activity theory emerged from Vygotsky's psychological research into learning, and specifically from his discussion of the mediating role of artefacts in cognition. Activity theory proposes a situated account of learning, in which individual actions are informed by a wider cultural and historical context (such as the way in which Tools are produced, individuals' actions are legitimated or sanctioned, how the production of resources is organized, etc.). It rejects previous theories such as behaviorism that fail to account for mental activity, and also perspectives such as cognitivism that (by seeking to re-introduce mental activity, but treating it as something additional to behavior) result in an irresolvable dualism between thought and action. In seeking to reconcile the mental and behavioral, activity theory takes intentional action as its basic unit of analysis. It focuses on how individuals appropriate concepts, practices, and tools. Thus, it focuses on individuals' internalization of external concepts and practices, which includes consideration of how people and institutions create, legitimate, and control such resources. It is also a theory that focuses on the analysis of the particular, rather than on the formation of generalized claims and hypotheses.

The initial formulation of activity theory (Vygotsky, 1978) involved the proposal that intentional human action is invariably mediated by a tool, although it is noted that the tool may be conceptual or symbolic (such as an idea or language), rather than necessarily being embodied (such as a hammer or computer). The basic unit of analysis under this theory, then, consisted of a system such as that shown in Fig. 5.1. Within this system, the person acting is referred to as the Subject, their intention (or objective) is referred to as the Object, and the mediating artifact is referred to as a Tool. For example, this could represent a person (Subject) using a hammer (Tool) to affix a wall hanging (Object) or a student (Subject) using a theory (Tool) to guide the interpretation of data (Object). Following the conventions of Kuutti (1996), the proposition that human activity is always mediated by Tool use is represented by the dashed arrow; this relationship is implied by the two other relationships (between Subject and Tool and between Tool and Object), rather than being a direct relationship.

This initial analytical framework was subsequently expanded to take the cultural and historical context of activities into account in a more explicit way (Engeström, 2001; Kuutti, 1996; Squire, 2002). This expansion

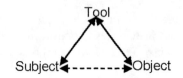

FIG. 5.1.   An activity system (initial triad).

involved adding another layer to the system to represent the Community within which the activity takes place, the Rules that hold within that Community, and the way in which work is organized to achieve its objective (its Division of Labor). As with the first iteration of the system, some relationships between elements of the system are implied. For example, the Community is related to the Subject only through Rules and likewise is related to the Object only through its Division of Labor. This expanded system is illustrated in Fig. 5.2. This might illustrate, for example, the way in which a student using a theory to guide the interpretation of data does so following the conventions for analysis (the Rules) introduced to him or her by his or her tutor as part of a research methods program (the Community), within which each student was given the same task as homework (Division of Labor).

Initial uses of this analytic framework focused on descriptions of children's learning and play. However, as use of activity theory developed, the idea of internal (secondary) contradictions within systems as a motivation for development grew in importance (Engeström, 2001). Contradictions are inconsistencies in the system. These are typically cases where conventional practice fails—for example, because of a technical breakdown, a disagreement between those involved in the activity, a confusion over who is responsible for a particular task, or a purpose (an Object) that is impossible, incoherent, or impractical. Such contradictions suggest that the system is somehow inadequate and needs to be improved through some kind of transformation or development.

Although this approach requires users to employ considerable conceptual clarity when describing problems, it does not propose solutions. Contradictions can be identified and analyzed, but an activity theoretic analysis does not directly suggest what to do to remedy the situation. Solutions must be inferred from knowledge of the cultural-historical context. In the context of analyzing learning, such solutions may well be left to the Subject to develop. Because of the importance of these moments in activity, identification and analysis of contradictions will form the primary analytical application of the approach developed here.

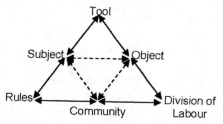

FIG. 5.2. An activity system (extended representation).

Analyzing Learning

As discussed earlier, the basic unit of analysis within activity theory is not the individual Subject or a Tool, but a system that considers intentional Tool use within a cultural context. The implication of this is that using activity theory to explain learning involves drawing conclusions at the level of the system. Engeström's (2001) notion of expansive learning (the current dominant explanation of learning within activity theory) describes how systems are reconceived in more inclusive ways in response to contradictions that arise in practice.

The restriction of learning to the level of the system means that, from a strict interpretation of this perspective, nothing can be said about the learner (i.e., the Subject as a person who learns). However, within this chapter, we intend to reclaim the use of the term *learning* to draw conclusions about the individual. This deviation from the dominant discourse within this tradition can be justified on two grounds.

First, there is an inherent epistemic bias within Activity Systems; Subjects have agency in a way that Tools, Rules, and arguably even Communities (conceived of in the abstract) do not (Nardi, 1996). If learning is to be conceived of as happening within any part of an Activity System, then it seems reasonable to conclude that it should be a property attributed to Subjects.

Second, within the context of learning from games, there may well be *some* situations in which it seems improbable that the other parts of the system could be expanded (in Engeström's sense). For example, in a system that represents a child playing a game on a console, attempting to complete a task devised by a Community of game designers, there is little possibility of feedback to enable the designers to change the Rules, Objects, Tools, and so on. Consequently, the only opportunity for expansion when contradictions arise will involve the Subject learning how to use the Tool better or developing a better understanding of the Rules devised by the developers. Roussou (2003) used this analysis to provide an account of children's learning from Virtual Reality exhibits designed for use in museums. This work suggests that resolved contradictions between the Subject and Tool indicate examples of skill development (understood as proficient use of a Tool), and that resolved contradictions between the Subject and Rules illustrate examples of learning socially accepted concepts or practices.

Another important consideration in this respect concerns the status of claims made about learning. Systems within activity theory are representations of activities; as such, these are *accounts* of practice. Alternative representations could be produced. At any moment, several Tools might be in use—for example, in gaming, a conceptual map of the weaknesses of a particular target, an on-screen map of the layout of a level, or the physical embodied Tool of the TV or controller. Similarly, if we consider Wenger's (1998) related discussion of communities of practice, we must recognize that people are simultaneously members of multiple communities. Which Community is chosen for a particular system depends on the purpose of the particular representation that is being created. Thus, what can be produced from these analyses are accounts of learning; they are subjective interpretations of observations, and their credibility will have to be judged on the basis of the quality of the data gathered and of the analysis. This might be demonstrated in a number of ways, such as presentation of data alongside an example of its analysis (a transcript or video excerpt in an online article), reports on interrater reliability (perhaps focusing on analyzing examples of disagreements), or triangulation with other research methods (such as interviews exploring the player's own interpretations, perhaps prompted by replaying a video of particular contradictions).

It is also useful to be explicit about the way in which the sociocultural elements of activity theory relate to this focus on the individual. As noted earlier, the kinds of contradictions that are the focus here concern players' uses of Tools and their improved understanding of Rules. These frame the moment-to-moment interaction in terms of wider cultural issues. The use of any Tool (console, game, controller, screen) implies a kind of consumption—not merely an economic consumption (although typically this can be assumed to have taken place), but a cultural one. The choice of Tool used positions the player in relation to existing social influences (publishers, producers, manufacturers, and other players). The player's learning of Rules similarly positions the player in relation to the game designers, the authors of game guides and walkthroughs, and so on. Whether the player is good, successful, noteworthy, or subversive depends on the way in which he or she understands, conforms to, rejects, or subverts sanctioned patterns of behavior.

Levels of System

Further refinement of activity theory has led to the development of three levels at which activity can be analyzed (Kuutti, 1996). The most general level is called the level of *activity*; this describes high-level plans (such as visiting a friend or building a house). The second level is more specific, focusing on the *actions* that contribute to the activity (such as driving along a particular route or building a wall). The third is more specific still, consisting of *operations* that contribute to each action (such as changing gears or laying a brick). Operations are usually routine or automatic, rarely being the focus of conscious attention unless something goes wrong (a contradiction arises). This model is illustrated in Fig. 5.3.

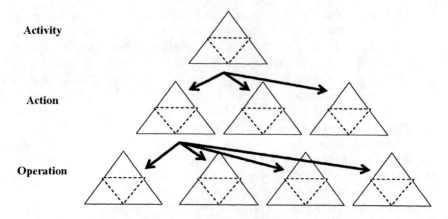

FIG. 5.3. Levels of activity systems.

This nested, hierarchical model of activity permits fine-grained analyses to be undertaken and integrated with broader, more general studies. Within the context of learning from games, this permits analysis at the strategic level of game objective (complete a level, beat a boss—analogous to activities), the tactical level (gather the remaining tokens, follow a particular pattern of movements—analogous to actions), or the operational level (move the avatar forward, press a particular button). It also permits these elements to be integrated.

The importance of this variation in the level of analysis is revisited in the discussion that follows the study. However, for the moment, it is sufficient to note that this permits a taxonomy of learning to be created from detailed studies of gaming from the near-trivial level of button presses to the more complex level of strategic knowledge. It is proposed that once such a taxonomy has been created, the relative *value* of things that have been learned can then be assessed in relation to some other framework (e.g., in terms of personal satisfaction, curriculum objectives, or skills development). The choice of the other framework—and thus the judgment of value—is *not* determined by this particular analytic perspective.

Operationalizing the Theory as a Method of Analysis

Having elaborated the important elements of activity theory in some detail, it is now possible to present a method for analysis that reflects the main points outlined earlier:

1. Activity theory requires representations of activities to be created in terms of the Subject, Tool, Object, Community, Rules, and Division of Labor.

2. The systems that are most important to focus on are those where contradictions exist.

3. The contradictions that are most likely to indicate individual learning are those that are resolved between an individual and the Tool and those between an individual and the Rules. Other resolved contradictions might represent development of the system in other ways (e.g., development of a better control device, a bug fix, creation of a cooperative mode of play or creation of particular challenges, such as completing a level in a set time among a group of friends).

4. Contradictions might occur at one of three levels: strategically, tactically, or operationally. Mapping incidents across all three levels provides a way to analyze how modest forms of learning contribute to more significant outcomes.

5. Mapping the learning that occurs at all three levels will provide a taxonomy of learning from game play. The elements of this can then be judged against some separate value framework to judge which, if any, are deemed important.

Again, it is important to emphasize that such representations are *accounts* of learning, and are therefore subjective interpretations to be judged according to their credibility or coherence, for example (Pope & Mays, 1999). One example of a data analysis tool that incorporates these features would be Table 5.1. Note that the number of actions and operations within each activity is purely illustrative.

TABLE 5.1
A Data Analysis Tool Based on an Activity Theoretic
Perspective of Learning From Games

Activity	*Action*	*Operation*	*Contradiction Between . . .*	*Rationale*	*Evidence of Learning (Resolution)*

THE STUDY

In the following sections of this chapter, we apply this framework to the analysis of data drawn from a broader research project exploring children's interaction with computer games. We focus in particular on a relatively short piece of data—a video recording of a 13-year-old playing the game *Harry Potter and the Philosopher's Stone.* She was filmed for 25 minutes as part of a lunch-time game-playing club at her school. This teenager was chosen for the study because she had played the same game consistently over several weeks and was highly motivated to progress through it. For the game play analyzed here, the researcher asked her to complete a level she had not played before, positioned a video camera behind her shoulder, and then left her to play. The video recording was analyzed using the tool presented in Table 5.1. Four separate kinds of learning were identified. Each is described in turn.

Learning to Use a Tool Skillfully

The first kind of learning that was observed addressed contradictions between the Subject and Tool; it was resolved by learning to use the Tool more effectively. This allowed the player to complete objectives that were previously too hard. An example of this kind of learning is illustrated in Table 5.2. Here we see the girl struggling to use the mouse to trace a gesture for a new spell. However, it should be noted that improvement was not linear or consistent; this is revisited in the discussion section. Note that, in the table, comments are provided in parentheses. The last—questioning whether this was luck or learning—is revisited in the discussion section.

Learning About the Properties of In-Game Objects

Although improved skill is a simple and obvious form of learning, it was not the dominant form within the game. The predominant kind of learning that was observed stemmed from the simple tactic of pointing and clicking on objects to learn how they responded to player interaction. (This was possible because interaction was context sensitive, rather than relying on the player to decide *how* she should interact with each object.) Table 5.3 provides an example of this.

However, this tactic was not universally appropriate. On several occasions, the player attempted to click on objects with which no interaction was possible, as we see in Table 5.4. This was because the player could not decide which objects were worth interacting with and which were not. Arguably, this was the result of the player's and designers' understanding of the unwritten Rules being different.

TABLE 5.2
An Example of Improved Tool Use

Time Index	Activity	Action	Operation	Contradiction Between . . .		Rationale	Evidence of Learning (Resolution)
05:28	Learning the gesture for a new spell	Using mouse to draw the gesture	Traces pattern	Subject	Tool	Mouse tracing not accurate enough	
			Observes feedback on success				
			Traces pattern	Subject	Tool	Mouse tracing not accurate enough	(Actually gets worse)
			Observes feedback on success				
			Traces pattern	Subject	Tool	Mouse tracing not accurate enough	(Gets even worse)
			Observes feedback on success				
			Traces pattern	Subject	Tool	Mouse tracing not accurate enough	(Slightly better score)
			Observes feedback on success				
			Traces pattern	Subject	Tool	Mouse tracing not accurate enough	Accuracy improves; nearly accurate enough
			Observes feedback on success				
			Traces pattern				Passes accuracy threshold (Did she learn it or just get lucky?)

TABLE 5.3
An Example of Pointing and Clicking to Learn the Properties of an Object

Time Index	Activity	Action	Operation	Contradiction Between . . .		Rationale	Evidence of Learning (Resolution)
00:23	Getting through the garden	Checking for beans/secrets in the garden	Looks at statue by lake				
			Aims at statue				
			Clicks mouse (no response)	Subject	Rule	Tries to elicit a response from a nonresponsive game object	
			Turns avatar				
			Moves toward second statue				
			Aims at statue				
			Clicks mouse (no response)	Subject	Rule	Tries to elicit a response from a nonresponsive game object	Changes behavior—ignores two more statues, having learned they are not responsive

TABLE 5.4
An Example of Failed Learning From Clicking

Time Index	Activity	Action	Operation	Contradiction Between . . .	Rationale	Evidence of Learning (Resolution)
01:17	Getting through the "garden" level	Checking for beans/secrets in the garden	Moves to face hanging vines Clicks mouse (no response)	Subject Rules	Tries to elicit a response from a nonresponsive game object (because a path leads to it and it is a distinctive section of a wall)	Moves away after one attempt, having decided this is not a responsive feature

Learning About Game Conventions

A more complex kind of learning involved interpreting situations within a game and developing an appropriate response. In effect, sections of the game could be seen as a limited repertoire of set pieces, each dressed differently depending on their location within a level. Some game conventions related to combinations of objects within a space. For example, whenever the player saw a block, she immediately looked for an object that might act as a switch that could be activated by magically levitating a block on top of it. Other situations entailed more complex behaviors, as is indicated (although not fully documented) in Table 5.5.

Learning About Spaces Within the Game

The last kind of learning that was observed concerned the use of space within the game. It was clear that the player sought to see every area that could be accessed (e.g., learning about the layout of the level and the objects each place contained). There were also examples of the player learning particular routes through levels, which included issues of timing (for getting past snapping plants) and placing (for managing jumps between platforms). Table 5.6 illustrates one such example of learning about the qualities of spaces within the game.

DISCUSSION

The study described in this chapter has raised issues in relation to two areas: methodology (process) and research into learning and games (outcomes). Each is discussed in turn.

Methodological Implications

The systematic approach to analyzing the video was generally successful, providing evidence that could substantiate claims about learning how to play (i.e., about the development of strategies that guide successful play). No modifications to the research tool were needed, and the process of documentation took between 3 and 4 hours, which seems reasonable for a close-detailed case analysis of this kind.

There were, however, a number of questions raised by this process. The first was that, as the analysis progressed, it became apparent that this was a process that might reveal new learning, but not what had been previously learned. Its focus on resolving contradictions, rather than on listing successful behaviors, means that it is essentially dynamic; it is about learning as a process. Claims can be made with confidence because evidence of learn-

TABLE 5.5
Two Examples of Learning a Response to Set Pieces in the Game

Time Index	Activity	Action	Operation	Contradiction Between . . .		Rationale	Evidence of Learning (Resolution)
02:15	Getting through the "garden" level	Exploring the garden	Moves toward a gate Waits at the gate	Subject	Rules	Trying to see if the gate opens; it doesn't	Realizes another strategy is needed—looks for a key to activate it
Clip 3, 2:16	Moving through herbology halls (still)	Activate sprinklers	Moves to exit; waits for it to open (it doesn't)	Subject	Rules	Door won't open until task completed	Realizes things still to be done; tries clicking on other features in room

TABLE 5.6
An Example of Learning About Spaces and Paths

Time Index	Activity	Action	Operation	Contradiction Between . . .		Rationale	Evidence of Learning (Resolution)
07:27	Moving through herbology halls	Get through the room with tree jumping and snapping plants	Moves around platform (and gets bitten by plant)	Subject	Rules	Doesn't realize that the plant can reach her	
			Climbs back up to a platform (gets bitten again until she falls back off)	Subject	Rules	Thinks there might be a path past (edging around the tree in the middle of the platform), when there isn't	Gives up seeking a safe path across this platform and tries another route through the room

ing is identified, but the method reveals only a subset of what the player knows; it does not necessarily reveal what she knew *before* the observed session. This means, for example, that there may be less to be found from observing skillful players than novices using this method.

The second concerns the interpretation and classification of observed behaviors, and in particular the assertion that a particular action did or did not work. Such claims are difficult to justify without assuming (rather than knowing) the intentions of the player. For example, when the player clicked on a statue, two interpretations are possible. The first is that the player is trying to make the statue respond, but it does not—which might be classed as a failed operation. The second is that the player is seeking to understand whether such statues are worth clicking—in which case the lack of a response is useful data: She may learn from this that statues of this kind are unresponsive and not bother to click on more of them in the future. In some cases, distinction between such options may be possible on the basis of future in-game action (such as ignoring more examples of the statue), but nevertheless this does highlight the complexity of interpretation.

The third is that some operations are hard to gather evidence about. Unless tools for eye motion tracking are introduced, for example, it is hard to observe when the player is reading the interface to spot a distinctive section of wall or assess the avatar's health. As well as being difficult to notice, such operations may prove hard to record in the table because they may be ongoing rather than discrete events. (For example, "View the screen" is an essential and almost ubiquitous operation—although there were examples of the player looking away—but these were not recorded alongside discrete actions such as button presses.)

The fourth is that for the category of learning to use Tools skillfully, there is no easy transition between unskilled and skilled performance. Rather than being binary states, there is a continuum of skillful performance (although the game does make a binary distinction between good enough and inadequate mouse use in sections such as drawing the spell with the mouse). This situation is complicated by luck. In Table 5.2, for example, it was hard to tell whether the improved performance would be sustained in future actions or was just a fluke.

Finally, it would be possible to provide a finer-grained reading of the action than was undertaken if each key press or mouse movement could be recorded. This would prove impractical for long sections of video, but could prove useful for detailed analysis of key incidents.

Research Implications

Although the main purpose of this chapter is to develop and test the methodology, the study with which it has been illustrated has also allowed some conclusions to be drawn about learning from games. Our main conclusion was that this was really a simple game. The majority of learning was of the same type—clicking on objects to determine their properties. This suggests a rather impoverished game-play experience.

Another issue that arose was the level of claims that were made about learning. Working at the level of operations, most of the instances of learning that were seen were low level, such as learning about properties of one object. We concluded that another step was needed. The tool outlined in Table 5.1 provides a sound mechanism for documenting learning, but further inference is required to fully analyze it. Reviewing the individual learning tactics (e.g., "Click on an object") recorded in the table, a series of learning strategies was then proposed, equating to learning-oriented actions in activity theory. This involved trying to provide reasons that could explain the observed instances of learning. For each, a rule was proposed and then the table reviewed so that it could be refined by testing its explanatory power with each appropriate observational instance. This process was repeated until a set of rules was developed that explained all of the observed behavior. This, we propose, constitutes the set of Rules (in the Activity Theoretic sense) followed by the player. Note that these Rules are a proposed explanation; they were not made explicit—and may not even be recognized—by the player or games designer. They also exclude the improvements in skill that were noted because this category relates to contradictions between Subject and Tool, not Subject and Rules. The set of Rules that the player developed are as follows:

1. "Spot unusual objects and click on them."
2. "If you can't progress (e.g., a door won't open), systematically explore the area until you find something you missed." (Note: This typically led to uses of Rule 1.)
3. "If you see a block, levitate it onto something."
4. "If you've run out of things to click on, move on to a new area."
5. "If you haven't explored an area, do so."
6. "If there is a threat, move past it carefully (beware of positioning and timing)."

Rule 1 was related on a one-to-one basis with the category of learning about the properties of objects. Rules 2 and 3 relate to learning game conventions. Rules 4 to 6 relate to learning about in-game spaces. Between them, these six simple rules motivate and justify every operation observed during the session.

This simple classification raises the question of transfer—something that Squire (2002) identified as important to understand if the educational value of games is to be established:

Unfortunately for educators looking to use games to support learning, this sceptical transfer limits what we hope players might learn from gaming. While pundits and theorists suggest that game-playing might be increasing kids' critical thinking or problem-solving skills [. . .], research on transfer gives very little reason to believe that players are developing skills that are useful in anything but very similar contexts. A skilled *Half-Life* player might develop skills that are useful in playing *Unreal Tournament* [. . .] but this does not mean that players necessarily develop generalizable "strategic thinking" or "planning" skills. (pp. 8–9)

Some of these Rules would, conceivably, transfer successfully to many other games (e.g., Rule 5, concerning exploration—see Gee, 2003). Others, however, might not transfer at all or be inappropriate (such as responding to the presence of blocks by trying to levitate them). Potentially, some of these Rules may not even transfer from one section of the game to another. This process cannot be fully understood by the data from this study; however, there may well be a better transfer between similar games. This suggests that an analysis of game play using this approach and leading to the identification of Rules might be a way of exploring the concept of game genres—a topic that is notoriously nebulous at present.

Some elements of the analysis have implications for game design. For example, the Rule prompting the player to learn the qualities of objects that seem unusual has implications for how objects are represented. Deviance in presentation (e.g., an unfamiliar kind of statue) was interpreted as significant. There were examples where this conclusion was unjustified (e.g., garden paths leading to dead ends or sections of wall where the presence of vines did not mask a hidden door). The implication is that if players are looking for such deviance to signify importance, designers may wish to use representation explicitly rather than implicitly (and, in this game, inconsistently) to structure the gaming experience.

Finally, the consequences of learning were inconsistent. Some arduous tasks—such as mastery of the mouse for copying the spell symbol—were irrelevant to the game except as a requirement for progression. Mundane operations—such as clicking on everything—produced great variation in the rewards provided to players (e.g., the number of game tokens—beans—that were awarded). Some simple errors had drastic consequences—like jumping from the wrong spot on a platform so that the avatar fell to its death and an entire section had to be replayed.

CONCLUSIONS

This chapter outlined the development of a methodology that could credibly answer Squire's (2002) challenge to identify what, if anything, people are learning by playing games. What they are learning, unsurprisingly, is how to play—represented here by the development of strategies that guide successful play. The questions of whether such strategies transfer to other contexts or are valued remain to be explored, however. Using activity theory as a framework for analysis has proved to be possible and productive, although some methodological issues (such as what can be observed and how things should be inferred) do remain. Nonetheless, this approach has been demonstrated as being a viable way of beginning to explore the process of learning from games within a social, cultural, and historical context, not least in terms of how individuals take up Tools (understood within activity theory as historically produced cultural artifacts) and conform to the Rules (socially sanctioned forms of acting and knowing) of specific communities—in this case, primarily, games and console designers. Inevitably, this small study has focused on one example of play, but the methodology could be applied to other situations such as game playing in the home. Additionally, because of our focus on learning to play, we have not explored other possible contextual issues such as changes to the Division of Labor (e.g., by considering children as game producers as well as consumers) or other Objectives (such as the production of particular subjectivities within a peer group).

The approach worked in terms of allowing us to analyze in fine detail a short excerpt of game play, illustrating how the player became more skillful and learned the rules of the game. This analysis serves to demonstrate how individuals develop cultural competences—in this instance, how they learn to take up and employ cultural resources (technologies, artifacts, concepts, etc.—examples of sociocultural Tools) and use them in ways that are sanctioned by individuals or institutions in society (i.e., in accordance with the Rules of the community). In this case, there is evidence of the player learning how to use a particular game, with its associated technologies, in ways that are sanctioned by the designers.

The study chosen to illustrate this method has also led to particular conclusions about learning from the *Harry Potter* game. Six strategic rules explain all of the player's actions. Indeed the majority of actions can be explained using only two or three of these. This illustrates the simplicity of the game. This is not a criticism—such simplicity may be appropriate for a game intended to engage people who are not experienced gamers. However, it illustrates that learning to play *Harry Potter* involved a relatively limited range of strategies and competencies.

The development of this method and the findings of this preliminary study suggest several further areas of work that may be productive. These might include, for example:

- Studying learning within more complex games, including the development of the rule sets that explain learning from play within them.

- Seeing whether players transfer rules—appropriately or otherwise—from one game to another, and whether this helps in formulating a coherent definition of game genres.
- Exploring whether designers (professionals or children) can use rule sets such as that identified here in the design of new games.
- Investigating how the process of learning is altered when a different Community—such as fellow players, co-present or otherwise—is involved.

Finally, it is worth identifying the implications of this study (and this approach) for games design. Identification of the strategies through which players learn to play games provides a new perspective for designers. Arguably, the presence of strategies that include clauses such as "identify unusual objects . . ." implies that designers should be conscious of the consistency with which objects are represented in the game world. They may consciously break this rule, of course, but an intentional break as part of a game's design may be desirable in a way that unintentional inconsistencies (as observed in this session) are not. Identification of such rules provides a rudimentary metric for assessing the complexity of games, which may be valuable to designers in its own right. More important, however, the potential to analyze play with prototype systems and gain insight from the analysis of learning strategies may be a valuable contribution to existing game design practice.

REFERENCES

Beavis, C. (1998). Computer games, culture and curriculum. In I. Snyder (Ed.), *Page to screen: Taking literacy into the electronic age* (pp. 234–255). London: Routledge.

Burn, A., & Parker, D. (2003). *Analysing multimodal texts.* London: Continuum.

Dawes, L., & Dumbleton, T. (2001). *Computer games in education project.* Retrieved July 15, 2004, from http://www.becta.org.uk/page_documents/research/cge/report.pdf

Egenfeldt-Nielsen, S. (2004). *Practical barriers in using educational computer games, work in progress.* Retrieved July 15, 2004, from http://www.it-c.dk/people/sen/papers/Practical%20barriers%20in%20using%20educational%20computer%20games_0.6.doc

Engeström, Y. (2001). Expansive learning at work: Towards an activity theoretical reconceptualization. *Journal of Education and Work, 14*(1), 133–156.

Gander, S. (2000). Does learning occur through gaming? *Electronic Journal of Instructional Science and Technology (E-JIST), 3*(2), 28–43.

Gee, J. (2003). *What video games have to teach us about learning and literacy.* New York: Palgrave Macmillan.

Kuutti, K. (1996). Activity theory as a potential framework for human computer interaction research. In B. A. Nardi (Ed.), *Context and consciousness: Activity theory and human–computer interaction* (pp. 17–44). Cambridge, MA: MIT Press.

Mays, N., & Pope, C. (2000). Quality in qualitative health research. In C. Pope & N. Mays (Eds.), *Qualitative research in health care* (pp. 65–74). Bristol: BMJ Books. Retrieved July 20, 2004, from http://www.bmjpg.com/qrhc/

McFarlane, A., Sparrowhawk, A., & Heald, Y. (2002). *Report on the educational use of games: An exploration by TEEM on the contribution which games can make to the educational process.* Cambridge: TEEM.

Nardi, B. A. (1996). Studying context: A comparison of activity theory, situated action models, and distributed cognition. In B. A. Nardi (Ed.), *Context and consciousness: Activity theory and human–computer interaction* (pp. 69–102). Cambridge, MA: MIT Press.

Prensky, M. (2001). *Digital game-based learning.* London: McGraw-Hill.

Roussou, M. (2003). *Interactivity and learning: Examining young learners' activity within interactive virtual environments.* Unpublished doctoral dissertation, University College London.

Squire, K. (2002). Cultural framing of computer/video games. *GameStudies, 2*(1). Retrieved July 20, 2004, from http://www.gamestudies.org/0102/squire/

Vygotsky, L. (1978). *Mind and society: The development of higher mental processes.* Cambridge, MA: Harvard University Press.

Wenger, E. (1998). *Communities of practice.* Cambridge: Cambridge University Press.

Williamson, B., & Facer, K. (2003). More than *"just a game": The implications for schools of children's computer games communities.* Draft articles, NESTA Futurelab. Retrieved July 15, 2004, from http://www.nestafuturelab.org/research/draft_articles.htm

Part II

THE INTERNET

The internet is often discussed, on the one hand, as offering unlimited educational resources, support networks, and creative outlets for young people, and, on the other hand, exposure to risky material, financial scams, and dangerous people. Part II picks apart this dichotomy by presenting four chapters that examine different aspects of internet use among children and families: parents' regulation of the internet in the home, uses of the internet for political communication and civic participation, and the political economy of web production.

The first chapter in this part (chap. 6), by Sonia Livingstone and Magdalena Bober, focuses on internet use and family life. The authors ask how the internet may be transforming—or may be shaped by—family life, peer networks and learning, formal and informal. Their study combines qualitative interviews and observations with a major national face-to-face survey of children (both users and nonusers) and their parents. New findings presented in this chapter analyze how the internet is proving challenging and often frustrating for both parents and children as they attempt to fit it into their lives and homes. As national regulation of domestic media environments is ever more difficult to sustain, there is increasing interest in building parental regulation of their chil-

dren's media use into national and international policy. The findings of
Livingstone and Bober's research project reveal how parents and children
are responding to this challenge. Findings in this chapter center on the tendency of parents to underestimate the risks their children are encountering
online, the tendency of children to underestimate the rules that their parents are attempting to implement regarding internet use, and some of the
issues that complicate parent–child negotiation of domestic regulation.

In chapter 7, Tobias Olsson examines the notion of young people as active media users through their political participation on the internet. The
chapter focuses on a specific set of media users/audiences—young citizens
(16–19 years of age) who are engaged in youth organizations affiliated with
the established political parties in Sweden. Olsson discusses the term *hyperactive audience* in relation to young people's media use in general, and their
use of the new ICTs in particular, referring to the calculated use of media
by these politically active citizens. The young people in Olsson's study invest time and energy in using media to learn skills and information that will
be useful for their political activities: learning how to conduct debates,
learning new arguments, and trying out and developing their own political
points of view. At the same time, they show an awareness of potential biases
of the media.

Continuing on the theme of civic participation, Kathryn Montgomery
and Barbara Gottlieb-Robles' chapter (chap. 8) reports findings from a research project that included content analysis of over 300 civic web sites, as
well as in-depth interviews with some of their designers. This research lays
the groundwork for providing youth with resources, including opportunities to participate in the production of civic content, that can help them develop into competent and responsible citizens. The chapter first maps the
landscape of the online youth civic sector, giving an overview of the kinds of
organizations and individuals involved in these efforts, their various goals
and missions, and the ways in which they seek to engage young people in
civic activities. It then examines the various ways this sector is taking advantage of the special features of the internet and digital communication, and
how these features might play a role in the larger goal of fostering civic engagement. The chapter goes on to identify key trends, the challenges con-
fronting the youth civic online community, and the key issues raised by
these efforts. The chapter concludes with a series of recommendations,
both for further study and for maximizing the use and effectiveness of the
wealth of civic content for youth that can be found online.

Content on the internet, however, needs close examination, so we end
this part with a chapter that raises questions about the regulation of online
content. In chapter 8, Julie Frechette argues that, although government
regulation of the internet has been decried as undercutting free speech,
the control of internet content through capitalist gateways—namely, profit-

driven software companies—has gone largely uncriticized. This chapter argues that this discursive trend manufactures consent through a hegemonic force while neglecting to confront the invasion of online advertising or marketing strategies directed at children. It suggests that inappropriate content (i.e., nudity, pornography, obscenity) constitutes a cultural currency through which concerns and responses to the internet have been articulated within the mainstream. By examining the rhetorical and financial investments of the telecommunications business sector, it contends that the rhetorical elements creating cybersafety concerns within the mainstream attempt to reach the consent of parents and educators by asking them to see some internet content as value-laden while disguising the interests and authority of profitable computer software and hardware industries. The chapter argues that we must explore the means through which technological access is deployed to discover what it means to be literate in the information age.

The four chapters in Part II move away from the polarized debates that often characterize discussions of children's internet use. By examining how families negotiate internet use and regulation, Livingstone and Bober provide us with a complicated picture as families try to maximize the benefits of the internet while minimizing the risks. Olsson provides us with an analysis that, although showing internet use as active, allows us to examine what we mean by active and calculated media use. Broadening the perspective, Montgomery and Gottlieb-Robles' examination of web sites provide us with information on how different organizations are utilizing features of the internet to engage with young people, again suggesting that active use of the internet is not automatic and needs to be examined closely. Finally, Frechette raises questions about internet content and points to the need to consider media literacy in relation to internet use. This part sets the scene for Part III, which looks at identities and online communities.

Chapter 6

Regulating the Internet at Home: Contrasting the Perspectives of Children and Parents

Sonia Livingstone
Magdalena Bober
London School of Economics and Political Science

OPPORTUNITIES AND RISKS AS CHILDREN GO ONLINE

Young people's access to the internet is steadily increasing. Three quarters of 9- to 19-year-olds in the UK had accessed the internet from a computer at home in spring 2004 (Livingstone & Bober, 2004), this figure being among the highest in Europe (Eurobarometer, 2004) and far higher than among UK adults generally (49% of UK households had internet access in December 2003; Office for National Statistics, 2004). The ways in which the internet is rapidly becoming embedded in everyday life are attracting widespread attention, raising questions about access and inequalities, the nature and quality of use, the implications for children's social and educational development, and the balance between online opportunities and risks for children and their families.

In academic and policy debates over the management of internet diffusion and appropriation, children and young people tend to be regarded with ambivalence, being seen both as the *digital generation*, pioneers in developing online competencies, yet also vulnerable and potentially at risk. Parents seem to share this ambivalence, especially given their children's apparently greater expertise with the internet. Thus, parents are keen to improve their children's educational prospects, but also concerned about online dangers (Facer et al., 2003; Livingstone, 2002; Turow & Nir, 2000). As locations and platforms for internet access diversify, domestic management and regulation of children's internet access and use is increasingly challenging. No longer can parents monitor a single computer in the living room. One fifth (19%) of 9- to 19-year-olds have internet access in their bedroom (particularly boys, middle-class children, and teenagers), and fewer than half of the computers online in homes with children are located in a public room (Livingstone & Bober, 2004).

The opportunities afforded by the internet are considerable, although to a fair extent still untapped at present. But media attention, and hence public concern, more often alerts the public to the potential risks and dangers, stimulating discussions of how to regulate or restrict children's internet access and use. These opportunities include creative/content production, civic/political expression and deliberation, community involvement and activism, gaining valued technological expertise, advancing careers or employment, obtaining personal/health/sexual advice, accessing educational/information resources, participating in specialist/identity/fan forums, and sharing a common culture. The risks, however, include exposure to illegal content, contact with pedophiles (e.g., via grooming in chatrooms), exposure to harmful or offensive content, encountering extreme (sexual) violence or racist/hate material, being open to commercial exploitation and manipulation or misinformation, invasions of privacy, and unwelcome contact (spam, viruses, etc.). Although many of these opportunities and risks are not new to society, they are, arguably, more immediate and widespread—especially for children—than was the case for previously new media (Flichy, 2002; Livingstone, 2002). In terms of media regulation, therefore, it may be that the stakes have never been higher as society seeks to strike a balance between the failure to minimize the dangers and the failure to maximize the opportunities.

This chapter examines the activities of parents and children in balancing these risks and opportunities as they seek ways to use the internet meaningfully within their daily lives. We caution, however, that researching issues of domestic regulation often pushes at the limits of research methodology because they relate to the private, often unnoticed, and sometimes secret or illicit practices of everyday life. This raises ethical challenges and measurement difficulties, risking answers that are more socially desirable than honest, more official than actual, and more context-dependent than universal (Greig & Taylor, 1999; Livingstone & Lemish, 2001). The research reported here, drawing on the *UK Children Go Online* (UKCGO) project, could only attempt to address this through sensitive questioning, cautious interpretation of answers, and triangulating multiple data sources while recognizing the complex nature of families' interpretations of everyday, sometimes contested, practices.

FRAMING POLICY-RELEVANT RESEARCH

As social institutions, activities, and services increasingly move online, the regulation of internet access and use is of growing concern across many domains, including education, consumer law, child protection, employment skills, crime, the arts, e-commerce, and policies for media literacy and social in/exclusion. Regulatory responsibilities for online risks and opportunities must be apportioned to stakeholders dispersed across government, industry, education, employers, police, child welfare services, parents, and children. Questions concern not only how to apportion such responsibilities, but also how to ensure coordination across them. Within this, a key point of contestation is how far to devolve responsibility from the state to the industry (via self-regulation) or to the individual citizen (here, mainly parents, although also children). In seeking to inform these deliberations and the policy tools and outcomes that result (e.g., government regulation, industry codes of practice, public education and awareness programs, media literacy training), a detailed empirical account of the emerging domestic practices of regulation is vital.

Empirical research suggests that the very breadth of activities and services supported by the internet gives rise to ambivalence among parents much more so than for other media. Parents worry that internet use may lead their children to become isolated from others, expose them to sexual and/or violent images, displace more worthwhile activities, and risk their privacy. At the same time, most believe that the internet can help their children do better at school and help them learn worthwhile things. Indeed, this is why they acquire domestic access in the first place (Buckingham, 2002; Livingstone & Bovill, 2001; Turow & Nir, 2000). So there is a perhaps unprecedented challenge for parents as they introduce into their homes a medium that offers such great benefits that they can hardly miss out and yet risks such great dangers that they can hardly give it house room. Although in the early days some ambivalence was also attached to television, the opportunities and risks online are rather more extreme. The technology is also much more difficult to manage, thereby adding to parents' burden. From the early research on domestic internet use, much of it primarily qualitative and small scale, a research agenda is emerging (Livingstone, 2003). Research questions include:

- How are children accessing and using the internet? Does their use fit with societal expectations?
- How are parents regulating their children's use? Does this parallel or differ from the regulation of previously new media?

- When and why do children's and parents' interests, practices, and understandings coincide or conflict in relation to the internet?
- What opportunities and risks are children encountering online? What challenges do parents face? What policies would support both children and parents?

In pursuing research that may inform policy, we do not mean to position ourselves simply on the administrative side of an administrative/critical opposition (Lazarsfeld, 1941). Rather, we hope to be reflexively self-critical regarding the possible uses of the research and to adopt an independent critical stance toward the policy agenda. We must leave it to the reader to judge whether we have achieved this.

DEVOLVING REGULATION TO PARENTS

As the research agenda moves forward, so too does the policy agenda. In the UK, an early struggle occurred over whether internet governance should rely on state regulation or self-regulation—and so whether it should be top-down or lighter-touch regulation, the latter winning out at least for the moment. As the draft Communications Bill (eventually, the Communications Act of 2003) was being debated, the UK government position seemed to be in support of the free market and against regulating internet content. When the new regulator, the Office for Communications (Ofcom), was created, the Secretary for State in the Department of Media, Culture and Sport, Tessa Jowell (2003), stated, "OFCOM must now deliver a new regulatory system that will be light touch and unobtrusive wherever possible, but decisive and robust wherever necessary." A couple of years on, the risks faced by young users of the internet are increasingly apparent to a concerned public, and the policy of not regulating content seems less straightforward (Currie, 2005). One policy response is to bring the issue under the rubric of "media literacy." Hence, Ofcom's consultation document on media literacy stated:

> With increasing complexity of technology and wider media choice people will have to take more responsibility for what they and their children see and hear on screen and online. . . . We will all become gatekeepers for content coming into our homes. (Ofcom, 2004)

Although it is as yet unclear whether individuals can or will bear this responsibility successfully, or even what *successfully* would mean in this context, the present approach—for a range of political, economic, and social reasons—is to build parental regulation into UK (and international) policy, in effect devolving the regulation of children's access and use onto parents. The reasons for this development are many and are worthy of critical analysis. They return us to some long-standing struggles, hardly new to the internet, of cultural protectionists versus civil libertarians, communitarians versus market liberals, technologists versus social reformers, commercial expansionism versus the ethic of public service, and nation states versus the emerging institutions of global governance. The uneasy alliance between the civil liberties lobby and the pornography industry complicates matters, as does the unwelcome turn of events by which child welfare activists find themselves coopted by the conservative forces of the moral majority. Meanwhile the state is subject to the buffeting of much bigger forces. By contrast with the normative and cultural contexts that shaped the regulatory institutions and norms for previous media (press, film, broadcasting, etc.), in the case of the internet, there is considerable pressure on governments to achieve near-universal access to the technology to support economic and social goals, together with the considerable challenge of managing national responses to a global technology and the difficulty of developing regulation for a technology that changes rapidly and flexibly, often precisely in response to regulatory initiatives.

Early moves to delegate responsibility and authority downward were evident in the European Commission's (1997) "Green Paper on the Convergence of Telecommunications, Media and Information Technology Sectors." This sought to instigate a shift from direct control by government to governance through "action at a distance" by regulating parents, for example, through discursively established norms of "good parenting" and "appropriate children's conduct" (Oswell, 1999, p. 52). It would seem that devolving responsibility to parents offers a policy solution for some otherwise intractable problems, avoiding the need for politically difficult intervention in the market while promoting a discourse of individual empowerment and consumer choice. Put positively, the result is an expectation that individual actors—parents, teachers, even children—will become informed through the dissemination of appropriate expertise and so empowered to regulate themselves and each other in their internet use. However, as Harden (2000) more caustically observed, "While anxieties about risk may be shaped by public discussion, it is as individuals that we cope with these uncertainties" (p. 46). Focusing then on the policy consequences for individuals, this chapter asks what it means for families that their once-private practices of using and managing media use in the home are increasingly a matter of public—and commercial—regulatory policy. We examine some of the ways in which parents and children are responding to this greater responsibility to take charge of the media entering their homes, and we identify some of the emerging difficulties for children, parents, and policymakers.

PARENTAL STRATEGIES OF DOMESTIC REGULATION

The internet is proving challenging, even frustrating, for parents and children as they attempt to fit it into their homes and lives. These challenges include practicalities (such as affordability, knowing what to buy, installing and upgrading), questions of use (involving social capital or social support), and, more subtly, cultural and cognitive issues relating to media or internet literacy (gaining the benefits and avoiding the risks, becoming a producer as well as a receiver of content, and critically evaluating the information accessed). Although parents' strategies for managing their children's use of the internet are emerging, so too are children's tactics for evading or resisting (de Certeau, 1984), this family game being further complicated by the fact that children often have more confidence and expertise with new media than do their parents.

Academic literature divides regulation into positive regulation (encouraging, facilitating, or requiring certain activities) and negative regulation (discouraging, impeding, or prohibiting certain activities). Research on parental mediation of children's use of media, conducted mainly in relation to TV, shows that parents tend to combine positive and negative strategies, from the relatively open, nondirectional strategy of parent–child coviewing or sharing the media experience to more restrictive or controlling strategies (Bybee et al., 1982; Dorr et al., 1989; Lin & Atkin, 1989; Van Der Bulck & Van Den Bergh, 2000). Parents may try to influence their child's reactions through discussion or by simply sharing media time with the child, and they may seek to control access to media and, hence, time spent on that activity. Clearly, these strategies vary in their aims. Some treat the media as, potentially, a positive influence on their children, whereas others are designed to protect children from possible media harms. In relation to TV, a variety of factors influence parental mediation of children's viewing, and such mediation has, in turn, been shown to have various consequences—for media use, media effects, consumer socialization, and media literacy (Abelman, 1985; Austin, 1993).

Critics of this research tradition argue that it takes an adult-centered approach, focused more on parents' concerns and practices than on children's interests or desires, often assuming that parents' and children's perspectives on domestic regulation will concur. By contrast, a child-centered approach makes no such assumption, instead including within the research design the possibility of adult–child divergence, particularly in relation to children's interests and concerns with their autonomy, privacy, play, and rights to self-expression (Corsaro, 1997; James et al., 1998; Livingstone, 1998). Hence, a child-centered approach regards children as active and interpretative (although not necessarily highly sophisticated or media savvy) agents who appropriate and shape the meanings and consequences of the new through a series of established and novel social semiotic practices. Other critics are concerned about the implicit agenda at stake, suggesting that this is motivated by moral panics about technology and the mass public, and that, in response, it constructs a false ideal of the innocent and vulnerable child, which then misleads research and policy (Buckingham, 2002; Drotner, 2000; Oswell, 2002).

THE CHALLENGE OF CONDUCTING A RISK ASSESSMENT

Let us turn to the empirical. Within the regulatory discourses of government and policymakers, it seems that, implicitly if not explicitly, advice to parents treats assessing the risks faced by a particular child as straightforward. Yet problematically, because parental and other regulation is based on a risk assessment, if parents underestimate children's risks, they may devote less effort to minimizing these risks than if their perceptions were veridical. Unfortunately, perhaps there is no veridical account to be obtained here. However, one of the main findings of our UKCGO survey is a considerable discrepancy between the accounts that parents and children give of children's experiences online. Although parents and children would not be expected to tell identical stories of childhood experiences, because many factors shape their differing perspective on everyday family life, these discrepancies are both systematic and substantial.

Strikingly, for a wide range of risky experiences, parents systematically underestimate the frequency with which their children encounter such risks (see Fig. 6.1). To put this rather more cautiously, because we cannot know the truth of the matter, children report considerably higher levels of problematic online experiences than do their parents. For example, nearly half (46%) of 9- to 19-year-olds who go online at least once a week say they have given out personal information, whereas only 5% of parents think their child has given out such information. Similarly, although 57% of these young people have come into contact with pornography on the Internet, only 16% of their parents believe this to have occurred. Again, although one in three say they have received nasty or sexual comments online, only 7% of parents think their child has received sexual comments, and only 4% think their child has been bullied online.

Possibly these differences are methodological, with parents and children applying different criteria to the definition of *pornography* or *hateful comments*, for example. Even if this is the whole explanation, the regulatory challenge as perceived by parents would not match that drawn out of children's own accounts. However, the scale and range of these discrepancies suggest that, in some key ways, parents are unaware of children's need for discussion, guidance, and, in some cases, restrictions on their internet use.

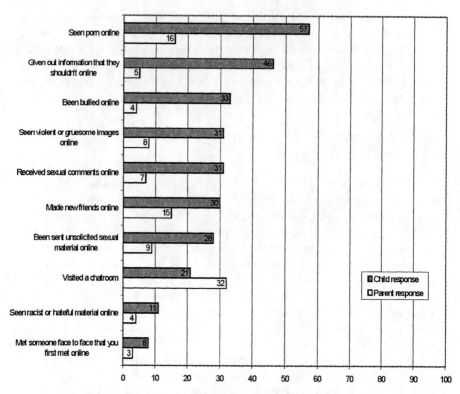

FIG. 6.1. Have you/has your child done these things on the internet? (Multiple response) Base: All 9- to 19-year-olds who use the internet at least once a week (N = 1,257); Parents of 9- to 17-year-olds (N = 906).

SETTING DOMESTIC RULES

Given these discrepancies in assessing the occurrence of problematic incidents, should one ask parents or children about the occurrence of equally subtle domestic practices? These practices occur in the privacy of the home, and they are not always welcomed or even recognized by children, yet parents do not always practice as they preach. Thus, although we have reasons to question the accounts of both children and parents, the UKCGO survey asked both 9- to 17-year-olds who use the internet at home at least once a week and their parents about, first, the rules of internet use and, second, the practices of internet use, again in the hope that, if their views did not coincide, the discrepancies would prove informative.

Restrictive forms of guidance appear a little more common than evaluative or conversational forms of guidance: 42% of children ages 9 to 17 who live with their parents say that they have to follow rules about for how long and 35% about when they can go online. Parents agree with their children—43% of parents claim to have set up rules for how much time their child can spend on the internet. The balance of rules overall reveals parental priorities, assuming that they set rules for those activities that concern them. Some internet uses are clearly considered worthwhile or, more likely, safe and so less in need of restrictive regulation (e.g., games, e-mail, instant messaging [IM]), whereas others that parents consider unsafe are regulated more (e.g., shopping, privacy, chat, some forms of interactivity).

When we pursued these rules in more detail, we found that not only do children perceive a higher incidence of risky problematic experiences online than do their parents, but, conversely, parents perceive a higher degree of domestic regulation than do their children. Figure 6.2 shows that parents claim a greater degree of domestic control than their children recognize. For example, 86% of parents do not allow their children to give out personal information online, but only 49% of children say this is the case; 20% of children claim they must not fill out forms online, compared with 57% of parents who do not allow this; 62% of parents forbid their children to use chatrooms, but only 40% of children acknowledge this rule.

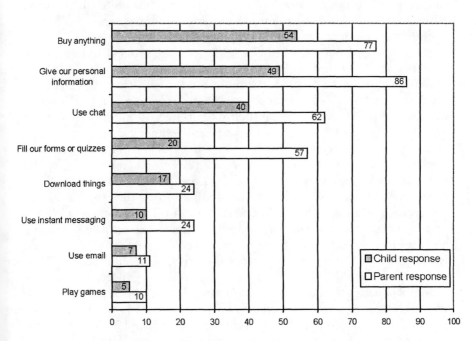

FIG. 6.2. Are there any things that you are (your child is) not allowed to do on the internet? (Multiple response) Base: 9- to 19-year-olds who use the internet at least once a week (*N* = 1,257); Parents of 9-to 19-year-olds whose child has home internet access (*N* = 677).

In short, asking parents and children the same questions about domestic regulation of the internet does not produce the same answers. Doubtless, the truth lies somewhere in between. We may conclude that parents are more complacent than is wise, assuming that rules are being followed when they are not and assuming that rules are not needed when they are. It is also likely that children and parents differ in their conception of rules, especially because rules are often implicit and may not be complied with. Parents may stress the general or official rule of the household, which holds even while exceptions are made. Children may instead reflect on actual circumstances, not identifying a rule if it is occasionally broken. Regardless of whether a greater degree of understanding between parents and children is desirable or achievable, regulatory discourses should not presume either to be the norm.

IMPLEMENTING DOMESTIC REGULATORY PRACTICES

Rules are one thing, practice is often different. In relation to the internet, parents may regulate through social and/or technical strategies. According to children, one third say that their parents play a direct social role in supporting their internet use—by helping (32%), suggesting web sites for the child to visit (32%), and generally sharing in the experience of using the internet by sitting at the computer with the child (31%). However, up to two thirds do not. One third of 9- to 17-year-olds also report a variety of indirect monitoring activities, saying that their parents know what they (the child) are doing online (31%), how to check what sites they have visited (30%), and how to access their (the child's) email (15%). However, only a fifth say that their parents stay in the same room (22%) or keep an eye on the screen (17%) when they are online, and few parents, they say, actually check up on their emails (4%) or history file of web sites visited (9%).

Parents give a somewhat different account of the social context of children's internet use. They are more likely to claim a direct role in sharing and supporting their child on the internet: 81% say they ask what the child is doing on the internet (compared with only 25% of children), 57% say they help the child online (compared with 32% of children), and 32% claim to sit with the child when online (and here children agree—31%). Parents also stress an indirect social monitoring role: 63% say they keep an eye on the screen (compared with 17% of children), and 50% say they stay in the same room when the child is online (compared with 22% of children). Parents less often claim technical monitoring, although they do this more than children realize: 41% of parents say they check the computer later to see what the child has been doing (compared with only 9% of chil-

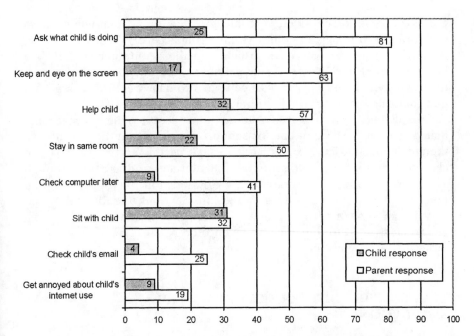

FIG. 6.3. What parents do when child is using the internet. (Multiple response) Base: 9- to 17-year-olds who live with parent(s) and use the internet at least once a week (*N* = 1,060); Parents of 9- to 17-year-olds whose child has home internet access (*N* = 677).

dren), and 25% claim to check their children's emails (only 4% of children seem aware of this; see Fig. 6.3).

Not all regulatory practices are socially managed, and considerable reliance is being placed by government and industry on technical forms of management—filtering, monitoring, rating, and so forth. Children can be positive about filtering, as Emma (10, from Hertfordshire) tells us: "It restricts the web sites that you can go on. My uncle set it up for me. And it stops people emailing you like nasty emails. . . . It deletes their email, so if like really bad people email you, it changes your email for you automatically." Other young people are more skeptical about the effectiveness of filtering, such as this group of 14- to 15-year-old boys from Essex:

Jim: Filtering, yeah, sometimes, yeah, it filters out what you don't want it to filter.

Sean: You type in bad language or something or something to do with pornography, and if you go to Google, and you want pictures of Essex—because it's got sex at the end, it won't let you on it. That's what happened with the school.

Moreover, we found considerable confusion regarding the implementation of filtering technology. In homes with internet access, 35% of children say that filtering software has been installed on their computer, and 46% of parents claim this. However, 23% of parents say they do not know whether a filter is installed, and only 15% of parents who have used the internet say that they know how to install a filter.

Overall, most parents whose child has home access to the internet claim that they directly share in and/or support their child on the internet, although their children are less likely to say that this occurs. Parents also claim to monitor their child's internet use indirectly or discreetly, although again children appear less aware of this. However, 1 in 10 (10%) say they do not know what their child does on the internet, and one fifth (18%) say they do not know how to help their child use the internet safely. This suggests a clear need to improve and extend the reach of awareness and internet literacy initiatives.

THE PRACTICAL DIFFICULTIES OF PARENTAL REGULATION

At least two difficulties undermine parents' attempts to regulate their children's internet use. The first is that although parents are responsible for their children's safety, they must also manage their children's growing independence and rights to privacy—something that children feel strongly about. The second is that, as parents and children agree, children are more often more expert on the internet than their parents.

On privacy, our qualitative work shows that children relish the opportunities the internet affords them for identity play, relationships, exploration, and communication, and they may not wish to share this experience with their parents. Despite government advice, it is not accidental that many computers are located in private rather than public spaces at home, making regulation more difficult and intrusive than it would be otherwise. Nor is it irrelevant that children can appear silly, naughty, or even deceitful in relation to rules of media use. As household members with comparatively little power, these and other tactics represent a means to a valued end—that of maintaining one's privacy (Livingstone, in press). Indeed the survey shows that wherever the computer is placed—in a private or public room—children seek to use the internet in privacy, with four fifths (79%) of those with home access mostly using the internet alone.

Although online privacy is more commonly discussed in relation to invasions of privacy from commercial organizations (Montgomery & Pasnik, 1996), children are more concerned about maintaining their privacy from people whom they know, unsurprisingly given the nature of at least some of their online communication. Amir (15, from London) explains, "My parents don't ask me, 'ooh, what did you go on?' because I wouldn't like it if I came from school, came home, and they search my pockets. I'd say, 'what are you doing—that's personal.' What if I had something I didn't want them to see? Just like I wouldn't search my mum's bag." Consider too the conversation among this group of 17-year-olds from Manchester:

Stuart:	Good thing about the internet at home is you're free to access anything you want.
Steve:	My mum says, as long as she doesn't get charged on the phone bill on top of the internet, she doesn't care what I go on.
Interviewer:	Does your mum sometimes check what you're doing?
Steve:	She'll check what I'm doing. But most of the time I'm just in chatrooms or doing e-mail.
Stuart:	Good thing about search engines, they can't actually trace what web site you've been on, if you actually learn to search for it.
Nina:	That's what I do.
Stuart:	'Cause my mum used to check what web sites I've been on, but she doesn't now, so like . . .
Interviewer:	What do you mean? You go to a web site through the search engine?
Stuart:	Yeah, you like, um, bring up the Ask Jeeves, shall we say, then you type in the web site you want to go on—say like Lycos—you type in Lycos in the actual bar, and that brings Lycos up. Do it that way, it's untraceable.
Nina:	You just like don't want your mum spying on you and knowing everything about you.
Steve:	Because you want your independence, really, you don't want your mum looking over your shoulder checking what you're doing all the time.

Young people's freedom and independence are here contrasted with parents who spy or check up on you. Within the peer group, young people share tactics to maintain their privacy, regardless of any justification parents may have for such a monitoring role.

Asked by the UKCGO survey which of a list of activities they mind their parents doing, two thirds (69%) of 9- to 17-year-olds who use the internet at least once a week say they mind their parents restricting or monitoring their internet use, including checking their e-mail (42%), blocking web sites (28%), checking their internet use without their knowledge (30%), or even checking with their knowledge (15%). The survey findings also confirm that parents and children can easily fall into a kind of tactical dance in which the more parents attempt to monitor or control their children's internet use, the more children are minded to evade such control. We asked 12- to 19-year-olds with home access who use the internet at least weekly if they had taken any actions to protect their privacy online and offline. Although 35% say they have not done this, two thirds have taken some action to protect their privacy online, both from outsiders and from those they know. Thus, 38% report having deleted e-mails so no one else could read them, 38% have minimized a window when someone else came into the room, 17% have deleted the history file, 17% have deleted unwanted cookies, 12% have hidden or mislabeled files to keep them private, and 12% have used someone else's password without their permission.

The result is that parents and children are positioned as opponents in a struggle rather than in cooperation to resolve an externally generated problem—a risky technology. When Amir (15, from London) points out that, "Talking to your parents about the internet is bad for you. They might try and think about taking the Internet off your computer, which isn't good for us," he makes it plain that the power of parents to restrict children's pleasures undermines the discussion necessary for a more cooperative and open style of regulation. In some cases, these struggles result in conflict: 19% of parents and 9% of children acknowledge that the internet occasions conflict or annoyance between parents and children.

This tactical dance is made more complicated by children's confidence and skills in internet use. The intriguing and even unusual way in which internet expertise reverses the traditional generation gap, positioning parents as naive and children as authorities, poses a second difficulty for parental regulation. Quite simply, many parents lack the expertise, especially by comparison with their children, to intervene in or mediate their internet use, whether technically (e.g., by installing a filter) or socially (by discussing contents or services with their child). Nina (17, from Manchester) speaks for many when she says, "My dad hasn't even got a clue. Can't even work the mouse . . . so I have to go on the internet for him."

In the UKCGO survey, we asked parents and children to rate their internet skills. Unsurprisingly, children usually consider themselves more expert than their parents. Even among internet users who go online daily or weekly, 19% of parents describe themselves as beginners compared with only 7% of children, and only 16% of parents consider themselves advanced compared with 32% of children. Although most parents and children are confident in their searching skills, among parents, only one in three knows how to set up an email account and only a fifth or fewer are able to set up a filter, remove a virus, download music, or fix a problem. Yet children also struggle with the internet. Although they enthusiastically use the internet, proudly labeling themselves the *internet generation,* children too vary in confidence and competence when faced with the challenge of getting the best from the internet while avoiding its problems (Livingstone & Bober, 2003).

Some of these difficulties concern finding what they want. As Heather (17, from Essex) says, "Every time I try to look for something, I can never find it. It keeps coming up with things that are completely irrelevant to the actual thing that you search for. And a load of old rubbish really." Other difficulties are more subtle—for example, judging the reliability of information online. Faruq (15, from London) tells us, "It's like you don't know who's doing what, whose website it is, who wants what, who wants you to learn what. So you don't know who's put what information there, but . . . it's reliable—but you don't know who's put it, who wants you to gain what from that information." Indeed the survey findings confirm these limitations in internet literacy. Despite the stress laid on ICT in education policy, nearly one third (30%) of pupils report having received no lessons at all on using the internet, although most have been taught something: 23% report having received *a lot* of lessons, 28% *some,* and 19% *just one or two.* Many children, it seems, lack key skills in evaluating online content: 4 in 10 pupils ages 9 to 19 say they trust most of the information on the internet, half trust some of it, and only 1 in 10 are skeptical about much information online. Only 33% of 9- to 19-year-olds who go online at least once a week say they have been told how to judge the reliability of online information, and among parents of 9- to 17-year-olds, only 41% are confident that their child has learned how to judge the reliability of online information.

There is a danger, then, that this combination of factors—that children seek to evade parental invasions of their privacy, as they see it, and that children may be or may appear to be more expert than their parents in using the internet—will result in a failure of domestic regulation and, therefore, a failure to address children's (and parents') concerns. For, despite their considerable enthusiasm for the internet, children, like their parents, also worry about the internet. Ellen (10, from Hertfordshire) draws on the *thinkUknow* campaign (www.thinkuknow.com) when she observes that the internet can be dangerous "because adults can like turn their voices into younger children, and like they can ask for pictures and stuff and ask to meet you. If you give away your name and address, they could." Indeed the survey found that three quarters of 9- to 19-year-olds (74%) are aware of some internet safety campaign or have heard or read a news story that made them think the internet can be dangerous: 48% of daily and weekly users worry about "being contacted by dangerous people," 44% worry about "getting a virus," and 38% worry about "others finding out things about you."

MIND THE GAP?

As national regulation of the complex communication environment is ever more difficult to sustain, there is increasing interest in building parental regulation into national and international policy. This chapter has examined how parents and children are responding to this growing responsibility, as well as some of the difficulties they face. For parents, the emerging story of children's internet use is neither as positive as they hoped when first investing in the internet nor as worrying as the media panics would have us believe. For regulators, the emerging story is equally ambivalent—parents are making considerable efforts to manage this regulatory responsibility, but it is proving worrying and demanding. More important, the outcomes are, at best, mixed.

Empirically, we have identified a significant gap between parents' and children's experiences of the internet—one that impedes the effective regulation of children's internet use within the home. Parents, it appears, underestimate the risks their children are experiencing online. Children, it appears, underestimate the regulatory practices their parents are attempting to implement. Parental anxieties tend toward being both ill-informed and, in some ways, ineffective in supporting regulation. Children's enthusiasm for the new medium is resulting in some risky behaviors. Of course experiences vary considerably, and as the locations and forms of use multiply, some children are becoming adept at finding ways to do what they want to do online. Meanwhile, others are getting lost.

Although, of course, some discrepancies between parents' and children's accounts are to be expected of ordinary family relations, in this case, they also point up a problematic conception of family relations within academic and policy discourses. First, the dominant tradition of research tends to assume that domestic regulation consists of authoritative and responsible parents setting rules that reflect their level of concern about the media and innocent children dutifully complying. This view is easily undermined by the simple method of including both parents and children in the research design. It is no accident, nor simply an annoying impediment to the smooth implementation of a regulatory policy, that parents and children prefer flexible, contextualized strategies of domestic regulation, rather than a high level of consistent control. By contrast, ethnographic approaches—to the appropriation of new media within the household, rather than to the issue of regulation in particular—reveal families' everyday lives as occasioning a host of justifications for exceptions to any rule and, more important, reveal the home as a site of contestation between parents and children for the good reason that they have differing interests at stake (Hoover et al., 2004; Seiter, 1999).

Taking this a step further, it can be argued that the dominant view is implicitly technologically determinist (Mackenzie & Wajcman, 1999) in the sense that, like many parents, it construes the media as an external force that impacts on ongoing family life, directly modifying children's behavior unless parents provide a buffer in the form of parental mediation or restriction. Recent work on historical shifts in the family (Stacey, 1998) and in childhood (James et al., 1998) points toward an alternative view—one that recognizes the stresses and conflicts faced by the family in late modernity and positions the media as one among several convenient resources for families to work through their struggles over public and private boundaries for the home, dependence and independence of family members, generational shifts in moral values, and so forth (Hoover et al., 2004; Livingstone, 2002).

In late modernity, as Giddens (1991), Beck (1992), and others have argued, power relations within the family have shifted from a model of authority and generational hierarchy to the more egalitarian, democratized pure relationship. Parental authority exercised through control over rules and rewards is giving way, although not without a struggle, to a parent–child relationship that prioritizes trust and negotiation as mediated by the discourse of rights, including children's rights. Parental regulation of media provides, on this view, an occasion for relationship work, rather than a response to an external threat. Consequently, popular discussion of the benefits and risks of the media for children is imbued with a strongly moral undertone. Because it is the new media that mark the key transition for parents from the norms of their own childhood to those of their children's childhood, these discussions center on new media and have a strongly nostalgic flavor (Buckingham, 2000).

CONCLUSION

Where does this leave the policy of devolving regulatory responsibility to parents? We have suggested that a policy seeking to regulate children's access to the internet by, in effect, regulating parents is problematic. These problems arise, in part, from the apparent reluctance of policymakers to look inside the family, preferring to stop their regulatory scrutiny at the front door, as becomes immediately apparent when one adopts a child-centered approach. In practical terms, the policy neglects the ways in which children respond to being regulated and, therefore, the game of strategy and tactics being played out between parents and children in many homes. In theoretical terms, the policy positions regulation as a buffer against the impact of external media harms rather than a process embedded in the historically and culturally specific dynamics of parent–child relations. The game of strategy and tactics that results, albeit as an unintended consequence, from the traditional approach to parental regulation precisely undermines the trust-based negotiations within the family that are central to attempts to democratize the family. This matters not only because this is a goal for many parents, but also because it is central to other areas of policy—notably those concerned with family welfare and children's rights (Hill & Tisdall, 1997). There is an irony here that, in seeking to reduce top–down state regulation of the market, so as to further regulatory goals of freedom of markets and of individuals, pressure is placed on parents to reassert traditional hierarchical relations of authority with their children.

This chapter has not, for reasons of space, examined the reasons that devolving internet regulation to parents is increasingly promoted by the policy community in the UK and elsewhere. There are, we must acknowledge, considerable merits in such an approach—both practically (for the global internet is highly intractable for national regulation) and theoretically (for the empowerment of individuals can only be a worthy goal). Rather, our purpose is to add to the public discussion a sense of the difficulties that such a policy generates, both for parents and children and for the implementation and evaluation of the policy. Regulation—whether of organizations or individuals—institutionalizes a formal relationship of regulator to regulated, and it requires a consistency and standardization in its implementation, both of which fit poorly with the contemporary family. This message of standardization, as Oswell (1999) described it, is present, for example, in the well-meaning information and awareness campaigns directed at parents designed to achieve the domestic norms and practices necessary for consistently regulating children's internet access and use (and thereby achieving societal goals such as segregating pornographic content from children, preventing commercial invasions of their privacy, and, generally, policing the boundary between the activities of adults and minors). Again, we do not mean here to undermine these goals, but rather to identify the costs of seeking to achieve them in this way. After all, as Rose (1999) cautioned, from a critical, Foucauldian perspective, the more there is talk of children's rights and participation, the more society is moved to regulate the conditions of this participation. As our empirical work has shown, the more parents represent the tools for such regulation, the more uncertainty, confusion, and resistance, rather than standardization, seem to result.

In conclusion, this chapter has argued that relying on parents to implement consistent, effective regulation within the home is problematic—not necessarily because parents are unwilling or incompetent, but rather because for both practical and theoretical reasons, this is a difficult and, in some ways, inappropriate burden to rest on parents' shoulders. The realities of everyday family life, and the particular practices and expertise building around the internet, mean that such a policy is unlikely to be consistently successful. Further, to the extent that it does work (e.g., if parents are sufficiently frightened into exerting tight controls over their children's online activities), it is likely to undermine not only children's freedom and privacy to explore and express themselves online, but also to undermine the democratic negotiation of mutual rights, trust, and responsibilities between parents and children more generally.

ACKNOWLEDGMENTS

This chapter draws on a research project conducted by the authors entitled *UK Children Go Online* (UKCGO). The project has investigated 9- to 19-year-olds' access to and use of the Internet, combining 36 focus groups, interviews, and observations of children and young people from diverse backgrounds (see Livingstone & Bober, 2003) with a major national face-to-face survey conducted in homes with 1,511 children and 906 parents in spring 2004 (Livingstone & Bober, 2004). See Livingstone and Bober (2005) for the final project report and www.children-go-online.net for further project details and publications.

We acknowledge funding by Economic and Social Research Council grant (RES-335-25-0008) as part of the "e-Society" Programme, with co-funding from AOL, BSC, Childnet-International, Citizens Online, ITC, and Ofcom. This chapter also draws on research funded by an ESRC "Risk in Social Contexts" network grant (RES-336-25-0001). Thanks to the UKCGO project's Advisory Panel and Online Children's Panel for guidance during the project design and interpretation of findings. Thanks also to BMRB for administering the survey, Ellen Helsper for help in analyzing the data, and Nico Carpentier, Richard Collins, and Peter Lunt for comments on an earlier version of this chapter.

REFERENCES

Abelman, R. (1985). Styles of parental disciplinary practices as a mediator of children's learning from prosocial television portrayals. *Child Study Journal, 15*(2), 131–146.

Austin, E. W. (1993). Exploring the effects of active parental mediation of television content. *Journal of Broadcasting and Electronic Media, 37*(2), 147–158.

Beck, U. (1992). *Risk society: Towards a new modernity.* London: Sage.

Buckingham, D. (2000). *After the death of childhood: Growing up in the age of electronic media.* Cambridge: Polity.

Buckingham, D. (2002). The electronic generation? Children and new media. In L. Lievrouw & S. Livingstone (Eds.), *The handbook of new media: Social shaping and consequences of ICTs* (pp. 77–89). London: Sage.

Bybee, C., Robinson, D., & Turow, J. (1982). Determinants of parental guidance of children's television viewing for a special subgroup: Mass media scholars. *Journal of Broadcasting, 26,* 697–710.

Corsaro, W. A. (1997). *The sociology of childhood.* Thousand Oaks, CA: Pine Forge.

Currie, D. (2005). *Speech to the ISPA Parliamentary Advisory Forum.* Retrieved June 3, 2005, from http://www.ofcom.org.uk/media/speeches/2005/01/ispa#content

de Certeau, M. (1984). *The practices of everyday life.* Los Angeles: University of California Press.

Dorr, A., Kovaric, P., & Doubleday, C. (1989). Parent–child coviewing of television. *Journal of Broadcasting and Electronic Media, 33*(1), 35–51.

Drotner, K. (2000). Difference and diversity: Trends in young Danes' media use. *Media, Culture & Society, 22*(2), 149–166.

Eurobarometer. (2004, March). *Illegal and harmful content on the Internet.* Brussels: European Commission. Retrieved June 3, 2005, from http://europa.eu.int/information_society/programmes/iap/docs/pdf/reports/eurobarometer_survey.pdf

European Commission. (1997). *Green Paper on the Convergence of the Telecommunications, Media and Information Technology Sectors, and the Implications for Regulation Towards an Information Society Approach* (Green Paper No. COM(97)623). Brussels: Author.

Facer, K., Furlong, J., Furlong, R., & Sutherland, R. (2003). *ScreenPlay: Children and computing in the home.* London: Routledge Falmer.

Flichy, P. (2002). New media history. In L. Lievrouw & S. Livingstone (Eds.), *The handbook of new media: Social shaping and consequences of ICTs* (pp. 136–150). London: Sage.

Giddens, A. (1991). *Modernity and self-identity: Self and society in the late modern age.* Cambridge: Polity.

Greig, A., & Taylor, J. (1999). *Doing research with children.* London: Sage.

Harden, J. (2000). There's no place like home: The public/private distinction in children's theorizing of risk and safety. *Childhood, 7*(1), 43–59.

Hill, M., & Tisdall, K. (1997). *Children and society.* London: Longman.

Hoover, S. M., Clark, L. S., & Alters, D. F. (2004). *Media, home, and family.* New York: Routledge.

James, A., Jenks, C., & Prout, A. (1998). *Theorizing childhood.* Cambridge: Cambridge University Press.

Jowell, T. (2003). Press release, Department of Media, Culture and Sport. Retrieved June 3, 2005, from http://www.culture.gov.uk/global/press_notices/archive_2003/dcms83_2003.htm

Lazarsfeld, P. F. (1941). Remarks on administrative and critical communications research. *Studies in Philosophy and Science, 9,* 3–16.

Lin, C. A., & Atkin, D. J. (1989). Parental mediation and rulemaking for adolescent use of television and VCRs. *Journal of Broadcasting and Electronic Media, 33*(1), 53–67.

Livingstone, S. (1998). Mediated childhoods: A comparative approach to young people's changing media environment in Europe. *European Journal of Communication, 13*(4), 435–456.

Livingstone, S. (2001). *Online freedom & safety for children* (Research Report No. 3). London: IPPR/Citizens Online.

Livingstone, S. (2002). *Young people and new media.* London: Sage.

Livingstone, S. (2003). Children's use of the Internet: Reflections on the emerging research agenda. *New Media & Society, 5*(2), 147–166.

Livingstone, S. (in press). Children's privacy online. In R. Kraut, M. Brynin, & S. Kiesler (Eds.), *Domesticating information technologies.* Oxford: Oxford University Press.

Livingstone, S., & Bober, M. (2003). *UK children go online: Listening to young people's experiences.* London: London School of Economics and Political Science. Retrieved June 3, 2005, from http://www.children-go-online.net

Livingstone, S., & Bober, M. (2004). *UK children go online: Surveying the experiences of young people and their parents.* London: London School of Economics and Political Science. Retrieved June 3, 2005, from http://www.children-go-online.net

Livingstone, S., & Bober, M. (2005, April). *UK children go online: Final report of key project findings.* London: LSE Report. http://www.children-go-online.net

Livingstone, S., & Bovill, M. (2001). *Families and the Internet: An observational study of children and young people's internet use.* Retrieved June 3, 2005, from http://www.lse.ac.uk/collections/media@lse/pdf/btreport_familiesinternet.pdf

Livingstone, S., & Lemish, D. (2001). Doing comparative research with children and young people. In S. Livingstone & M. Bovill (Eds.), *Children and their changing media environment: A European comparative study* (pp. 31–50). Mahwah, NJ: Lawrence Erlbaum Associates.

Mackenzie, D., & Wajcman, J. (Eds.). (1999). *The social shaping of technology* (2nd ed.). Buckingham: Open University Press.

Montgomery, K., & Pasnik, S. (1996). *Web of deception: Threats to children from online marketing.* Washington, DC: Center for Media Education.

Ofcom. (2004). *Ofcom's strategy and priorities for the promotion of media literacy: A statement.* Retrieved June 3, 2005, from http://www.ofcom.org.uk

Office for National Statistics. (2004, April). *Internet access: 12.1 million households now online.* London: Author. Retrieved June 3, 2005, from http://www.statistics.gov.uk

Oswell, D. (1999). The dark side of cyberspace: Internet content regulation and child protection. *Convergence: The Journal of Research into New Media Technologies, 5*(4), 42–62.

Oswell, D. (2002). *Television, childhood and the home: A history of the making of the child television audience in Britain.* Oxford: Oxford University Press.

Rose, N. (1999). *Powers of freedom: Reframing political thought.* Cambridge: Cambridge University Press.

Seiter, E. (1999). *Television and new media audiences.* New York: Oxford University Press.

Stacey, J. (1998). *Brave new families: Stories of domestic upheaval in late twentieth century America.* Berkeley, CA: University of California Press.

Turow, J., & Nir, L. (2000). The Internet and the family: The view of U.S. parents. In C. C. Feilitzen (Ed.), *Children in the new media landscape: Games, pornography, perceptions* (pp. 331–348). Göteborg, Sweden: Nordicom.

Van Der Bulck, J., & Van Den Bergh, B. (2000). Parental guidance of children's media use and conflict in the family. In B. Van Den Bergh & J. Van Der Bulck (Eds.), *Children and media: Interdisciplinary approaches* (pp. 131–150). Leuven-Apeldoorn: Garant.

Chapter 7

Active and Calculated Media Use Among Young Citizens: Empirical Examples From a Swedish Study

Tobias Olsson
Lund and Växjö University

The development of digital media has brought renewed interest in well-rehearsed debates about audiences and their media uses. What is a media audience in the digital era? How do audiences engage with digital media and their content? How can researchers gain access to audience activities? The subtitle of a recently published analysis by media researcher Livingstone (2004) captures quite well the state of the art: "[W]hat is the audience researcher to do in the age of the internet?"

Turning to the established literature on digital media in general, and the internet in particular, three features in digital media have contributed to make prescriptive ideas on the media audience problematic. First, their *interactive form*, which means that the new media—as opposed to traditional media (i.e., books, newspapers, radio, TV)—are characterized by a user pull rather than a producer push (Jensen, 1998). Among other things, theoretically this means that users can develop a whole new approach to their media environments and become increasingly selective in terms of both what channels and what content to use. This feature creates questions about the established view of the relationship between media producers and their audience—the broadcasting model. When the former senders no longer naturally have the upper hand in their communication with what used to be peripheral receivers (McQuail, 1997; Siapera, 2004), the consultative mode of communication (McQuail, 1997) gains in importance. Furthermore, the new ICTs—especially the internet—have a multimedial (Dahlgren, 2002) character, which means that they bring together what used to be separate media into one infrastructure of communication, as well as bringing various kinds of communication together, ranging from interpersonal to mass communication.

In this context of vast media changes, one of the issues within audience research that has resurfaced is the question of audience activity (Bird, 2003; Livingstone, 2004; McQuail, 2000; Rice, 1999). Prior to the development of digital media, the debate within audience research had come to a standstill, or it had at least slipped from the top of the research agenda. After two decades of debates between different camps within research—between, on the one hand, researchers drawing on versions of Marxism, who understood the media audience as rather easy targets for seductive media messages (e.g., Gripsrud, 1995; McGuigan, 1992), and, on the other hand, researchers within the cultural studies (Fiske, 1989) and the uses and gratifications schools (Blumler & Katz, 1974), who proclaimed a view of the audience as active and resistant to the ideological biases of the media—a kind of compromise seemed to have been established. In the terms of this compromise, media researchers agreed that the audience consists of active interpreters of media content, but also that audience members have little— if any—influence over what content the media industry presents them with. As such, audience members' activity is severely constrained by powerful media institutions. Put somewhat differently, and paraphrasing Marx, one could say there was an agreement that audience members do write their own histories, but not under conditions of their own making (cf. Buckingham, 1998; Dahlgren, 1998; Thompson, 1995, for a more thorough discussion).

The intention of this chapter is neither to tear the compromise apart nor to repeat a discussion on whether media texts have an influence on people. The intention is rather to take on a more searching, exploratory approach in discussing what audience activity means and what it looks like in the era of digital media. However, this is not solely a digital question. Indeed it involves paying attention to traditional as well as digital media.

The empirical and analytical parts of this chapter follow after a short discussion of the theoretical background. The analysis explores and suggests four types of audience activity. The data I discuss are individual interviews with 19 politically active adolescents (16 to 19 years old) from four different Swedish political parties. Each semistructured interview lasted approximately 2 hours and covered areas such as the use and perception of traditional as well as digital media, political engagement, and everyday life.

The analysis starts by exploring two dimensions of audience activity that are specifically connected to the respondents' critical awareness of the media: (a) their critical awareness of media structures, in this case the institutional prerequisites that condition traditional media organizations' work (e.g., broadcasting networks), as well as the specific character of the

Internet's technological form; and (b) the young respondents' media re-flexivity. Thereafter, I move on to discuss and present examples of calculated media use among the respondents—in this case, their use of the media with the deliberate intention to develop their political skills. This is a special case of audience activity, and I show how they use TV to develop their rhetorical skills and, for the same reason, how they participate in public spheres on the Internet.

The chapter concludes by returning to the theoretical debate on the active audience, suggesting that closer attention should be paid to the dimensions of audience activity presented in this chapter. However, the conclusion also brings a note of caution against overemphasizing the notion of activity because, it is argued, the degree of activity vis-à-vis the media depends on different users' access to various kinds of resources.

THE ACTIVE AUDIENCE

It can be argued that the previously mentioned debate on the active audience has been rather one dimensional in terms of where it searches for and locates audience activity. So far the debate on the active audience has been quite exclusively interested in the relationship between media texts and members of the media audience: whether they are active (re)interpreters of media texts, or not. Concepts such as *oppositional decoding* and *discursive resistance*, which are frequently used in the characterization of the active audience, tell about the importance that has been ascribed to the encounter between the media texts and their audience (see Gripsrud, 2002, for an overview).

However, analyzing audience members' activity in their (re)interpretations—or decoding—of media texts is too narrow a focus. The development of digital media has certainly helped make it clear that attention needs to be paid to other dimensions of activity when it comes to people's use of the media. For instance, the great increase in media supply offered by the new media has made it clear that there is an important dimension of activity to be found in people's selection of media content to consume, not least when it comes to children and young people, who, to a greater extent than adults, tend to have naturalized the use of the so-called *new media* (Bergström, 2005).

In this chapter, I thus explore what I suggest are additional dimensions of audience members' activities. My interest is partly theoretical, in exploring further the idea of the active audience; but this idea also sheds light on the empirical results from our study of politically active Swedish youth. The empirical results suggest that the respondents' use of media is certainly active in the original sense of the concept (i.e., they are active [re]interpreters of media texts). But the respondents also present other kinds of practices and ways of thinking that can be interpreted as components of a more general notion of audience activity. Furthermore they even present what can be perceived as calculated use of the media; they invest time in both traditional media (especially TV) and digital media (i.e., the Internet) to enhance their rhetorical skills and develop their own political points of view.

CRITICAL AWARENESS OF MEDIA STRUCTURES

There still exists a malicious portrait of the media audience: as couch potatoes that are easy targets for ideological manipulation. The portrait claims, without further reflection, that the truth of news broadcasting, commercial advertising messages, and the subversive invitation to consumerism in popular culture easily persuade members of the audience. Of course the analysis presented in this chapter cannot be any general antidote toward such a view of the audience. However, it can bring a completely different view of the audience based on the interviews with the respondents, who are members in youth organizations affiliated with Swedish political parties.

To start with, these young, politically active respondents are well aware of the constructed character of news: They do not interpret news as a portrayal of the most important issues of the day. For instance, they are well aware that what makes up news is a construction on the part of journalists and the editorial staff. The fact that the selection of news items is based on the supply of newsworthy events is quite clear to the young respondents. Several of the respondents also call attention to the fact that their political interest makes them critical toward the media content offered to them. For instance, they claim to "look more critically at things now [after joining the political organization]" (Olsson, 2004, p. 98) and to interpret news "according to my ideological points of departure" (Olsson, 2004, p. 91).

A salient component in the politically active, young citizens' activity vis-à-vis media in general, but TV in particular, is thus their critical awareness of the part played by media organizations' institutional prerequisites. For instance, when Stefan, 18 years old, talks about what he perceives to be the most important political issues today, he mentions world trade, feminism, and media issues. The interviewer then asks him to develop his ideas about the media:

Stefan: Well, I think that the society needs free as well as democratic media, and then we [the people] must be able to influence the democratic media as much as possible. They [the democratic media] must also pay attention to what's really important, not just to what seems to attract a large

> audience. [. . .] There's so much . . . famine and repression
> of women in the world, that . . . and that they [the media]
> pay attention to global issues instead of . . . Well . . . Then
> I'm also critical when it comes to the U.S., they only have
> free media, no democratic media. Thus, there's no chance
> for minorities to get representation, they haven't got any
> chance against large groups of consumers.

Interviewer: When you say democratic media, what do you mean by
              that?

Stefan: I'm thinking of media that don't first and foremost try to
              attract large audiences. Instead, I think of media that looks
              for some kind of democratic representation, something
              that everyone can be part of.

Stefan obviously has done some thinking about the media in general:
When he is asked to talk about his political interest in media issues, he immediately starts to discuss the media's institutional conditions. He also uses
concepts such as *free media* and *democratic media* as if they were parts of his everyday vocabulary, no more unfamiliar to him than any of the subjects he
takes in school, although media studies is not part of his curriculum. He is
able to present quite informed arguments about the commercial role of the
media and the impact of this on their representation of minority groups.
The interview extract thus makes it obvious that we are dealing with a young
man who certainly knows his way around (economic) media structures and
is able to present sophisticated comments on them. One might even argue
that he is presenting more informed arguments around media structures
than many adults would be able to do.

Within the interviews, a great deal of attention was paid to the respondents' uses and perceptions of new media in general and the internet in
particular. Tina—a 16-year-old young woman, strongly affiliated with the
political left—insists that all traditional media (i.e., TV, newspapers, and radio) are racist and only aim at making people consumers. At first she seems
to be much less critical toward the internet than toward traditional media.
Although she is also furious that a few owners control all Swedish newspapers and argues that TV contributes to cementing conservative stereotypes
of men and women, she does not at first include the internet in this rather
massive (and spontaneous) media critique. But when the interviewer mentions that she seems to hold a more positive attitude toward the internet,
she explains her thoughts about the new digital media more carefully:

Interviewer: You seem to be much less critical when it comes to the in-
              ternet . . .

Tina: It feels more like the internet is a sphere for everybody, for the worst possible shit, but also for the things that I like. But it's also a matter of. . . . The internet is good, but it's also a lot of shit. I think there's a lot of unserious shit. It feels as if people don't need to feel as responsible for what you say on the internet as everywhere else, you can say whatever you want. It's like a whole ocean of shit, but also good things.

Despite its rather rough tone, the extract and overall content in this passage of the interview reveals Tina's critical awareness of the internet's technological structure or form (i.e., its openness and its ability to host all kinds of information). Tina is, for instance, well aware of the need to stay critical of one's sources while surfing on the internet. She understands the internet to be a place where anyone can present any kind of information—that truths are mixed with lies and serious points of view are mixed with jokes and strong exaggerations. Further, she also connects this situation with the fact that people do not feel as responsible for what they say on the internet as they do anywhere else—that they look on the internet as a place for saying and doing things that they normally would not do.

In general, Tina holds a positive attitude toward the possibilities brought about by the internet. At the same time, she is critically aware of the circumstances for publishing on the internet—that the internet has an open form and allows for pretty much anyone to publish any kind of information. Thus, it is not an exaggerated interpretation to claim that Tina also brings her critical awareness of the traditional media (TV, newspapers) with her into the digital world, although she generally holds a more positive attitude toward the internet.

MEDIA REFLEXIVITY

Another dimension of activity vis-à-vis the media among the young respondents is their media reflexivity. In Reimer's (1994) investigation of media use among different social and cultural groups of users, he used the concepts *high brow* and *low brow*. *High brow* refers to segments within the media output that are considered to be legitimate (Bourdieu, 1984) to consume. For example, among Swedish media users reading the morning paper and watching the TV news on the public service channels are two examples of high brow media use. *Low brow* refers to the opposite—to illegitimate media channels and content (e.g., American daytime TV serials).

The distinction between high brow and low brow is useful for describing the respondents' way of orienting themselves through their media environment. This is not so much because they mainly consume high brow content—which they do—but because they seem to have internalized these norms and are well aware of how various types of media content are popularly assessed.

Sandra is 18 years old and just about to finish upper secondary school. Just like the other respondents, she is a member of a political party and also holds a leading position within a project working for stronger democracy in Swedish schools. During the interview, she suddenly started giggling while telling the interviewer about her everyday media use:

> Interviewer: You said that you sometimes watch TV at home in the afternoon. What do you watch?
>
> Sandra: [Sigh] [Giggle] I guess I watch *Dr. Phil* and . . . whatever they put on in the afternoon . . . American sit-coms. . . . But there aren't any shows that I follow regularly.

The most interesting part in the extract is Sandra's way of talking about her habits. She sighs and starts giggling when she mentions *Dr. Phil*, and thus presents an ironic distance from her own media practice. It is quite obvious that she knows how others would assess the show—that it would not be considered good TV. It seems to be quite obvious to Sandra how a young woman with political ambitions should interpret a TV program such as *Dr. Phil*.

Another respondent, Sofie, comes from a small city in southern Sweden. At the age of 18, she is already representing her political party within municipal politics. Like Sandra, Sofie has internalized the norms for distinguishing good media from bad media:

> Interviewer: If we get back to TV. What genres do you prefer?
>
> Sofie: Genres . . . I really can't say . . . Well, I like *Friends* [laughs] but I don't like soap operas in general.
>
> Interviewer: So it is just that specific show?
>
> Sofie: Yes, I guess it's [laughs] *Friends, Sex and the City, Simpsons.* [With a serious voice] And then it's the news and current affairs program.

It is, of course, hard to get a sense of this through a written extract, but the shifts in Sofie's tone of voice reveal a competence to assess media content according to dominant discourses about what is good and bad. She laughs when she tells the interviewer about her habit of watching the American sit-com *Friends*. She keeps smiling while mentioning herself watching series such as *Sex and the City* and *The Simpsons*. But suddenly her tone of voice changes when she tells the interviewer that she also watches the news and current affairs, moving from an ironic and distanced tone to a serious one. The two extracts are just two out of many examples in the interviews illustrating the young respondents' media reflexivity. Arguably, this awareness of general assessments of various media and different kinds of media content can be looked on as a dimension of audience activity. Interestingly, digital media, or more specifically the internet, does not fit into these established distinctions between good and bad. In the case of TV, as earlier, the respondents make careful judgments between different kinds of content. Some genres are considered legitimate, whereas others are not. Overall, they do not reject TV as such. Instead, they reject various parts of the content presented on TV.

When it comes to the internet, the respondents do not seem to make the same kinds of careful distinctions in terms of content or activities conducted on the internet. For instance, they do not consider reading emails to be a good thing and surfing for entertainment as something bad. Instead they seem to assess the internet as a whole; and these politically active young respondents tend to fit the internet into the high brow parts of the media landscape. For example, Marcus—an 18-year-old boy living close to a big Swedish town—looks on the internet as a "whole different thing" when he is asked about his view on digital media in comparison to traditional media. He takes a very critical stance when he is asked about traditional media and also makes careful distinctions between different genres. But when it comes to the internet, it is judged as a whole and fits into his category of good media.

This might be an outcome of the fact that in the Swedish context the internet has been a widely celebrated medium. In popular as well as political discourses, the internet has been described as a tool for effective learning and a tool for bringing stronger democracy. But in these discourses, it is never clear what parts of the internet—email, the web, games—will bring about all these good things. Hence, neither of these official Swedish discourses offers a more fine-grained vocabulary for evaluating the internet, and it might be too much to ask young respondents in this study for a more complex conceptualization. Nevertheless, they remain very reflexive in terms of how the medium is popularly assessed.

CALCULATED MEDIA USE: TV AND INTERNET

The empirical illustrations presented so far are of course indications of an active attitude among the respondents toward traditional as well as digital media. But the young respondents' activity becomes even more salient when they talk about their reasons for watching political debates on TV:

They deliberately watch political debates to learn to get better at conducting debates, indicating a calculated use of media.

This extract from the interview with Marcus, whom we met in the previous section, is an evident example:

Interviewer: Does TV mean anything to your political engagement today, now that you are already involved in a political organization?

Marcus: Ehhh . . . Well . . . To get information about the other political parties, about their policies, I think . . . TV's no good. I rather . . . Basically, the reason why I watch television nowadays, when it comes to my political engagement, is to learn from the debates. I learn about rhetoric and look at rhetorical differences between different party leaders [. . .]

Interviewer: If you think about it, one could say that you use TV in order to . . . use it yourself one day?

Marcus: Yes, also . . . I guess it's kind of a general thing . . . You look at what rhetoric to use when you talk to different groups of people and in different contexts. Of course, TV's an important part of all that.

Rather than using the TV and TV debates to get information, Marcus chooses to take on a more cynical approach to the medium—he uses the TV as a tool for learning how to conduct debates. In this practice, he tells the interviewer later that he is also politically unfaithful; he does not care about whether he likes the arguments. Instead he focuses solely on ways of presenting arguments. By doing this, he develops his own rhetorical skills and his ability to get his political messages through more effectively.

Marcus is by no means the only respondent to talk about this type of calculated TV activity. Sofie is not as explicit as Marcus about her practice of ignoring the content of the debates to learn more about their form. Still this dimension appears in her interview as well:

Interviewer: In your opinion, what's the point in watching a TV program like *Debate* [a program on one of the Swedish public service channels in which current issues are debated]?

Sofie: Well you can. . . . For instance, if I've an opinion on a specific matter, then I can see what other people say about it: "Well, that's a good point. . . ." You can also pick up arguments that you might be able to use yourself, or at least see what other people—politicians and journalists—think about a specific issue.

This extract is preceded by a passage in the interview in which Sofie describes what she usually watches when she watches TV. She tells the interviewer that she often likes to watch the news and programs like the previously mentioned *Debate*. Thereafter, the interviewer asks Sofie why she is interested in that kind of program. Sofie indicates her calculated attitude toward TV—she watches *Debate* to learn about arguments that she can use and arguments that she might have to counter one day.

In Sofie's as well as Marcus' case, it is quite obvious that there is a calculated strategy in their watching of debates on TV. Both of them tend to focus more on the form of the TV debates than on their actual content. They also look on the TV debating as opportunities to learn about debates—they watch them to get better at presenting their own arguments.

These young, politically active respondents are also experienced users of the internet, not least within the frames of their political engagement. For instance, they routinely search for political information on the internet, they use the internet for organizational coordination, and they keep updated about the news through the web (Olsson, 2004). But in this context, when considering their calculated use of media, another aspect of the young respondents' internet use appears most interesting—their use of the internet for learning rhetorical skills. The practicing of rhetorical skills takes place in different contexts on the internet. Here we see two of them: the internal debate within the respondents' own political organizations, and in opposing parties' debates.

The empirical material suggests that it is useful to divide the group of 19 respondents into three when it comes to participation in their political organizations' internal debates. First, we have a group of about 10 respondents for whom the debate within their political organizations on the internet seems especially relevant. These respondents participate frequently in the internal debate. Second, we have a group of five respondents who participate in the internal debate on the internet from time to time. Third, we have a group of four respondents who, for various reasons, never participate in the internal debate (Olsson, 2004). Of course all of these groups are interesting, for various reasons, but the aim of this chapter suggests focusing on the first one.

Matilda and Sara belong to this group of users. Matilda is 17 years old. To Matilda, the Internet has become an important resource for her political activities, especially for participation in her political party's debates on the internet. In the following extract, she has just told the interviewer about her youth organization's web pages and the internal discussions they keep there:

Interviewer: Do you go there regularly [to the youth organization's web page]?

Matilda:	Oh, yes, I go there at least once a day.
Interviewer:	You go there during school?
Matilda:	Sometimes, but it can be at home as well. It depends on whether or not I've got time to do it in school.
Interviewer:	What do you usually do on the net?
Matilda:	I read the debate, and if there is something for me to react to, then I do it.

Matilda follows her political organization's debate on the internet every day—she even uses the concept *addicted* at a later stage in the interview to describe the extent to which she does this. She follows the debate mostly to keep track of what is happening, but also to actively participate by posting messages and responding to other participants' points of view. The debates that she participates in are local as well as regional and national, she notes at a later stage in the interview.

Sara, 18 years old, also pays attention to the internal debate on the internet. On the internet, she says, she reads current debates and—from time to time—also makes her own contributions to them:

Sara:	I used to hang around there a lot [on the internet debates]. I've done some writing on the mailing lists, but now it was quite a while ago. It's not too crowded there [ironic tone], not too many people are reading. [. . .] But you can write something for the discussions and then you get an answer.
Interviewer:	What have you been writing about on the lists?
Sara:	Pornography once . . . I've been writing about other things as well, but I can't remember what it was. I guess I've been writing about racism and then I've given answers to other messages.

The extract indicates that Sara feels at home in the debates on the internet, although she does not participate in them as much as Matilda does. Because she feels they are not too crowded, that not enough people participate in them, she seems to have lost some of her interest in participating herself lately. Nevertheless, she still visits the discussions to read the updates and occasionally comment on some messages.

This participation in the internal debates is interesting for various reasons. The debates are interesting as debates per se, as discussions in which opinions are shaped; but in this context, when looking specifically at calculated media use among the respondents, other dimensions appear even more interesting, especially that participation in these debates can be interpreted as part of an education for future political engagement. Through participation in these debates on the internet, the respondents learn about debating: They learn how to argue and how different readers receive different arguments. This knowledge is useful in future debates on the internet, but its relevance does not end at that. Knowledge of how to conduct debates also becomes useful in other contexts in their future engagement.

The practicing of rhetorical skills does not exclusively take place in internal public spheres on the internet. At least some of the politically active, young respondents also regularly use the internet to participate in debates in public spheres connected to other, opposing political parties. This participation accentuates the points made with reference to the respondents' participation in the internal debates: Here we have an even more advanced practice for learning how to debate.

Stefan (18), whom we met earlier, illustrates this point when commenting on media structures:

Interviewer: The last time you participated in a debate [on the internet], what was it about?

Stefan: Yes, well . . . it was the European monetary union. I discussed it with people on the [oppositional party] web site.

Interviewer: What do you think of that? When I visited your meeting . . . your idea of this campaign . . . it aims at reaching a lot of people, but the debates on the internet—on the other side—hardly include any people?

Stefan: No, it is mostly for myself, to test arguments and to see what kind of response I get. To try to ask a good question and see how they react to it.

Interviewer: How do they react then?

Stefan: It can be anything from not bothering to answer to a long answer stating how terribly wrong I am [laughter].

Stefan's use of the internet is extensive. He frequently uses it in school, and he is also a member of several internet communities. Besides using the internet as a tool for his political engagement, in the prior extract he describes how he uses the internet to get better at debating—he uses opposition political parties' public spheres on the internet. Through the resistance he encounters, he learns how to argue and what arguments to use in various contexts. It is also interesting to note how Stefan deliberately looks for opposition in these discussions. He is hoping—even calculating—for counterarguments because they help him enhance his arguments and develop rhetorical skills.

Annika, who is 16 years old and lives in a large city in Sweden, also realizes the usefulness of the internet when it comes to developing her arguments. She also presents a calculated use of the opposition political parties' public spheres on the internet. At this stage of the interview, she is talking about her everyday internet use:

Interviewer: Do you visit your political antagonists' web pages as well?
Annika: It happens. I've been to the antagonists' web pages a couple of times and that was quite fun, I was kicking up some fuss. It's especially good for testing one's arguments. . . . If you have an idea and you're not sure whether it will work out or not, then it's quite good. But sometimes people just do it in order to destroy the debate, that's no fun. [. . .] But I do think it's good that the debates don't get too internal and it's good for trying out arguments. [. . .] What do they answer if I say like this? You really get to learn quite a lot.

However, Annika indicates that it is somewhat problematic when people from other parties attend her party's internal debate. However, she basically holds a positive attitude toward a more inclusive discussion on the internet. She also adds that she—from time to time—uses the opposition parties' debates to get feedback on and develop her own ideas. Like Stefan, Annika is not there to make people change their minds; she is there to enhance her debating skills.

Stefan and Annika are not the only respondents to spend time with this kind of calculated activity. For instance, Marcus (18) does it as well. Marcus mentions how he has tested his arguments about equal rights for gays and lesbians within a debate among right-wing extremists on the internet. Once again he participated not so much because he wanted to make a difference, but because he wanted to practice his debating skills. Although it is only a minority of the respondents who engage in this kind of practice, it is worthwhile noting, not least as an example of how the internet is being shaped as a tool for the development of skills necessary for political debate.

NEW DIMENSIONS OF AUDIENCE ACTIVITY

The previous sections of this chapter have presented different aspects of an active and sometimes even calculated media use among members in youth organizations affiliated with the Swedish political parties. If we consider all of these practices and habits together, and also add that the empirical material on which this chapter is based brings additional examples of practices that could be subsumed under the notion of *audience activity*, it is quite obvious that we are dealing with audience members who certainly qualify as active and who actually might even be better understood as hyperactive (Dahlgren, 1998).

The respondents' hyperactivity is particularly interesting if looked on in the light of the long-lasting debate on audience activity in two separate but interrelated ways. First, as already stated, the politically active, young respondents' use of both the traditional media and digital media (the internet) suggests that there are additional dimensions of activity to pay attention to. The traditional debate on audience activity has tended to focus quite narrowly on the relationship between media texts and their interpreting audience members. Here we see additional dimensions of activity—dimensions to which the debate on the active audience has not attended so far.

Arguably, it is imperative that we attend to new evidence of audience activity because the kinds of activities presented here might be important components of a more general understanding of the changing media–audience relationship. It is crucial to our understanding of the ideological effects of the media to know whether the media audience is aware of the institutional prerequisites determining media output. For instance, knowing about these institutional circumstances may make it less likely that people interpret news as the truth about reality. Furthermore, it is also relevant to pay attention to people's reflexivity with respect to media output. The fact that audience members are aware of how various segments of the media are valued is also important to their interpretation of media content. For example, watching a soap opera while being aware of discourses that condemn the soap opera as a waste of time containing outdated and oppressive representations of women is something completely different from watching the same soap opera and not knowing these discourses. From the examples in this chapter, we can add the development of a calculated attitude toward the media as a dimension of audience activity. Media are rarely described as learning resources for audience members, but here they certainly take on such a role. Both TV and the internet are deliberately used by the young, politically active respondents to develop their rhetorical skills and make them better at presenting their arguments. These would be interesting dimensions of a more expanded notion of audience activity.

Second, although this chapter reports a high degree of media activity among the young, politically active respondents, we should be careful about making general conclusions about audience activity. The young respondents included in this study are by no means average members of the audience. Instead they have certain dispositions that make them well suited for being active and even calculated with respect to the media. For instance, they have good access to various kinds of resources that help them engage with the media. Considered as a group, the respondents in this study have access to material (Murdock et al., 1992) as well as social (Warschauer, 2003) and discursive resources (Bourdieu, 1984) that of course help them develop an active and at times even calculated attitude toward the media. In addition, their political engagement gives them particular political resources to draw on in their encounter with both traditional and digital media.

Therefore, this chapter should not be interpreted as yet another effort—as in the 1980s—to state that the audience is active rather than passive. The argument would rather be that the audience members can be active, but that the degree of activity nevertheless is dependent on what resources users bring to their encounter with the media. The empirical evidence does suggest that we cannot exclusively look for the audience members' activities in their interaction with and interpretation of media texts. The activity can also be identified in various attitudes to and practices around the media, of which we have seen several examples in the research reported here.

ACKNOWLEDGMENTS

This chapter is based on empirical material from the research project "Young Citizens, ICTs and Learning." The project is funded by the Swedish Knowledge Foundation's research program "Learn-IT."

REFERENCES

Bergström, A. (2005). *Nyhetsvanor.nu: Nyhetsanvändning på internet 1998–2003* [Newshabits.nu: The use of news on the internet 1998–2003]. Unpublished doctoral dissertation. Gothenburg: JMG, Gothenburg University.

Bird, W. (2003). *The audience in everyday life: Living in a media world.* London & New York: Routledge.

Blumler, J. G., & Katz, E. (Eds.). (1974). *The uses of mass communication.* Beverly Hills: Sage.

Bourdieu, P. (1984). *Distinction. A social critique of the judgement of taste.* London: Routledge & Kegan Paul.

Buckingham, D. (1998). Children and television: A critical overview of the research. In R. Dickinson, R. Harindranath, & O. Linné (Eds.), *Approaches to audiences: A reader* (pp. 131–145). London: Arnold.

Dahlgren, P. (1998). Critique: Elusive audiences. In R. Dickinson, R. Harindranath, & O. Linné (Eds.), *Approaches to audiences: A reader* (pp. 298–319). London: Arnold.

Dahlgren, P. (2002). Internetåldern [The age of the internet]. In P. Dahlgren (Ed.), *Internet, medier och kommunikation* [Internet, media and communication] (pp. 13–38). Lund: Studentlitteratur.

Fiske, J. (1989). *Reading the popular.* Boston: Unwin Hyman.

Gripsrud, J. (1995). *The Dynasty years: Hollywood television and critical media studies.* London: Routledge.

Gripsrud, J. (2002). *Understanding media culture.* London: Arnold.

Jensen, J. F. (1998). Communication research after the mediasaurus? Digital convergence, digital divergence. *Nordicom Review, 19*(1), 39–52.

Livingstone, S. (2004). The challenge of changing audiences: Or, what is the audience researcher to do in the age of the internet. *European Journal of Communication, 19*(1), 75–86.

McGuigan, J. (1992). *Cultural populism.* London: Routledge.

McQuail, D. (1997). *Audience analysis.* London: Sage.

McQuail, D. (2000). *McQuail's mass communication theory* (4th ed.). London: Sage.

Murdock, G., Hartmann, P., & Grey, P. (1992). Contextualizing home computing: Resources and practices. In R. Silverstone & E. Hirsch (Eds.), *Consuming technologies: Media and information in domestic spaces* (pp. 146–160). London: Routledge.

Olsson, T. (2004). *Oundgängliga resurser: Om medier, IKT och lärande bland partipolitiskt aktiva ungdomar* [Indispensable resources: On media, ICTs and learning among young, politically active people]. Lund: Media and Communication Studies Research Reports.

Reimer, B. (1994). *The most common of practises.* Unpublished doctoral dissertation. Stockholm: Almqvist & Wiksell International.

Rice, R. E. (1999). What's new about new media? *New Media & Society, 1*(1), 24–32.

Siapera, E. (2004). From couch potatoes to cybernauts? The expanding notion of the audience on TV channels' websites. *New Media & Society, 6*(2), 155–172.

Thompson, J. B. (1995). *The media and modernity: A social theory of the media.* Cambridge: Polity.

Warschauer, M. (2003). *Technology and social inclusion: Rethinking the digital divide.* Cambridge, MA: MIT Press.

Chapter 8

Youth as e-Citizens:
The Internet's Contribution
to Civic Engagement

Kathryn Montgomery
Barbara Gottlieb-Robles
American University

The growth of the internet has dramatically altered the ways in which individuals use media, and youth are at the forefront of these changes. Generation Y, the nearly 60 million individuals born after 1979, represents the largest generation of young people in U.S. history and the first to grow up in a world saturated with networks of information, digital devices, and the promise of perpetual connectivity (Neuborne & Kerwin, 1999). Although teens overall spend less time online than do adults (for a variety of reasons, including busy school and after-school schedules and the need to share internet access with others), they are much more involved in the interactive and communications aspects of the Internet (Jupiter Communications, 2000; Packel & Rainie, 2001). According to a 2001 study by the Pew Internet and American Life Project, for example, among internet users, teens far exceed adults in their use of instant messaging (IM) (74% of online teens as opposed to 44% of online adults), visits to chatrooms (55% to 26%), and playing or downloading games (66% to 34%) (Lenhart, Lewis, & Rainie, 2001). In another study of internet use by young people, one third of college students regarded themselves as *internet dependent,* and another one fourth described themselves as *cybergeeks* (Cyberatlas, 2001). As one industry trade publication put it, "Teens and college-age young adults . . . have not just adopted online technology . . . [they] have internalized it" (Youth Markets ALERT, 1999, p. 3). In perhaps the clearest indication of a fundamental shift in media consumption patterns, a July 2003 survey of teenagers and young adults revealed that for the first time this age group spent more time on the internet each week than watching TV (Reuters, 2003). All of these trends have made young people key defining users of new media.

Youth are more than just consumers of digital content; they are also active participants and creators of this new media culture, developing content, designing personal web sites, and launching their own online enterprises (Bunn, 2000; Sharp, 2000). The proliferation of youth-created web pages and message-board postings, and the popularity of IM among young people all contribute to the booming use of the digital media for communication among youth.

Much of the public debate over the internet and youth has been dominated by a concern about the darker side of online behavior. Throughout the 1990s, fears about pornography, predation, and other internet dangers prompted Congress to pass several laws to regulate cyberspace, most of which were successfully challenged in the courts by civil liberties groups (Voedisch, 2000). This public obsession over internet harms has spawned a spectrum of protective software and technologies, including filtering and blocking services, as well as labeling and rating systems, all aimed at shielding children and youth from harmful online content (COPA Commission, 2000).

Against this backdrop of public obsession over internet harms, a quite distinct development has quietly been unfolding. Scarcely audible amid the hubbub over pornography, a low-profile civic upsurge has been taking root on the net. Hundreds of web sites—created for and sometimes by young people—encourage and facilitate youth civic engagement by promoting thinking and dialogue about and participation in civic life, including partisan political participation, community involvement, volunteering, philanthropy, and social activism. Taken as a whole, they may be said to constitute a new, emerging genre on the internet that could loosely be called *youth civic culture*.

Our study, "Youth as E-Citizens: Engaging the Digital Generation," was designed to provide a broad, descriptive map of this online youth civic landscape, focusing not only on web site content, but also on the organizations and institutions creating that content (Gottlieb-Robles, Larson, & Montgomery, 2004). Our primary purpose was to document the existence of youth civic content and activity on the web, describing and categorizing what we found, to highlight and showcase aspects of the new digital media culture that have received little research or public attention. Another goal was to examine the various ways the civic sector is taking advantage of the special features of the Internet and digital communication. We were also interested in exploring whether these little-understood civic and political internet-based activities by youth could help reverse declines in civic and political engagement, a trend that has sparked alarm among experts in the United States (CIRCLE & Carnegie Corporation of New York, 2003; Delli

Carpini, 2000a, 2000b; Putnam, 2000). Finally, we wanted to help reframe the public debate about media and youth. Rather than focusing on simply protecting youth from the harms of new media, we hoped to build on the view that our media system should *serve* young people, providing them with resources—including opportunities to participate in the production of civic content—that can help them develop into competent and responsible citizens (Buckingham, 2000). We see the present research as laying the groundwork, then, for a formulation of practice and policy in pursuit of that larger goal.

DEFINING AND SEEKING "YOUTH CIVIC" WEB SITES

Our investigation of online civic content for teens and young adults—conducted between 2002 and 2004—identified more than 400 "youth civic web sites" and analyzed 300 of them systematically. In addition to undertaking a broad overview of youth civic activity on the internet, we also performed more detailed analyses of selected issues and projects, including several case studies of individual web sites, for which we conducted in-depth interviews with the sites' developers. We included sites in this study in accordance with their adherence to two criteria. First, sites needed to address civic topics, broadly defined; second, they needed to speak directly to youth.

We realized at the outset that this type of research would not be easy. The internet is so vast that it is impossible to grasp its full scope or plumb its depths. Unlike traditional print or broadcast media, with their discrete editions and programs, the internet is in a constant state of flux. Web sites can change very rapidly; their content can be altered, they can morph into other kinds of sites, or they can disappear altogether. Furthermore, many civic sites are difficult to detect through casual perusal of the web. For a variety of reasons, these web sites tend to be marginalized in dominant media culture. The nature of discourse and quality of conversation tends to be more serious-minded in content and more respectful in tone. The sites reflect a diversity of voices and experiences beyond those usually expressed in a commercial medium. Perhaps most important, most do not have budgets that permit them to advertise. Thus, we did not find them easily, but had to seek them doggedly.

We utilized a variety of methods for finding youth civic web sites. We drew initially on earlier research we conducted on web content designed for teens (Center for Media Education, 2001). Although that study concentrated on commercial content, it also identified a number of sites dedicated to promoting civic engagement. As is typical on the web, many of those sites offered links to other sites with similar missions, which in turn linked us to others. In the same manner, our interviews with site creators also brought up the names of relevant sites. Online research, however, was the primary means of locating online youth civic content, especially the use of search engines. We uncovered additional civic material, much of it relevant to our study, through the use of youth-specific portals such as Yahooligan! and through directories. Some civic content was located in unexpected places. For instance, we found portals for nonprofit job and volunteer listings, such as www.Idealist.org, to be gold mines of links to youth civic sites.

Most of our analysis was qualitative and descriptive in nature, with the primary goal of rendering as accurate and vivid a portrait as possible. We returned to some of the sites months after our initial observations in an effort to keep our data up to date, although we were not able to do so in most cases. We selected a few dozen web sites for closer, more in-depth examination, focusing on those we considered emblematic of certain trends or features of online civic culture. We supplemented our descriptive work with a questionnaire-based, quantitative analysis of various kinds of web site content. Because of the complexities of applying social science methods to the study of web content, we designed this part of the study not to provide a precise measure of what we found, but rather to give a sense of the range and distribution of certain features within the body of web sites we examined.

We believe that we have captured a reasonably accurate picture of the overall trends in this quickly changing environment. Although there were obviously parts of the new online youth civic culture that we were not able to look at closely, we believe we have provided a sufficiently wide-angle view of what is taking place on the internet to stimulate more detailed studies. Although we tried to provide the most up-to-date descriptions of the content of the web sites examined in our study, in some instances revisiting them numerous times to assess their evolution, this process can never be complete. Such is the ephemeral and dynamic nature of the web.

MAPPING THE CIVIC LANDSCAPE

The initial objective of our research was to document and map online efforts to engage young people in civil society. We believe we succeeded in creating the first rough map of "online youth civic culture" in its early phase. Besides identifying over 400 such web sites and analyzing 300 of them, we classified them into categories (described next) based on the type of civic activity they encourage. Although these categories are not mutually exclusive, with some web sites subject to placement in more than one grouping, we found this to be a useful way of organizing the mass of material we uncovered, and we have utilized it to showcase online some of the more outstanding youth civic web sites (see our http://www.centerforsocialmedia.org/ecitizens/-index.htm).

The vast number of web sites in the internet universe made it impractical to examine all the content we unearthed, and the fact that the universe is both uncharted and ever changing (web sites spring up and die with frustrating speed) made the selection of a representative sampling unrealizable. For this reason alone, our findings must be recognized as *indicative* of the field we studied, but not necessarily *representative* of it in formally quantified terms. Thus, when we refer to our data, we often use general terms—*the majority, over half, roughly a third*—so as to emphasize the imprecise nature of the quantified findings.

Over half of the youth civic web sites we unearthed were created by nonprofit organizations, both small and large and primarily U.S.-based, that work with young people. Widely recognized institutions comprise only a small segment of the online civic landscape for youth. Most online civic content is produced by little-known organizations that serve cities, counties, or local neighborhoods. In addition, a sprinkling of civic web sites (under 10% in each case) was created by educational institutions, governmental offices, or commercial endeavors. (Some commercial interests that address youth, such as MTV, have developed highly visible campaigns designed to serve civic purposes.) A tiny proportion of the sites were launched by individuals, sometimes young people themselves, and were clearly a labor of love.

To create a map of the youth civic web, we organized these web sites into the following 10 categories. What follows is a brief profile of each category, illustrating the differing approaches the sites take to promoting civic engagement.

1. Voting. In recent decades, the United States has experienced a severe decline in voter turnout, nowhere more marked than among young people. The 2004 presidential election witnessed an upsurge in the youth vote, and some of the web-based initiatives identified in our study may have played a significant role. However, it remains unclear whether this recent rise will constitute a reversal of trends in the long run (CIRCLE & The Carnegie Corporation of New York, 2003). Roughly 15% of the youth civic web sites we studied encourage youth participation in the electoral process by urging young people to vote, facilitating registration using an online registration form, and promoting interest in elections and campaigns. Those web sites include efforts both small and large. The best known is Rock the Vote (http://www.rockthevote.org/), established 15 years ago by music industry leaders. The group organizes voter registration drives, get-out-the-vote events, and voter education efforts for young adults and offers a voter registration form online ("Engaging the Next Generation," 2000). In addition, this boldly colored, Flash-enhanced web site also spurs young people to take political and social action. For example, in an online "Action Center," visitors are urged to "protect the issues you believe in" by personalizing and signing prewritten electronic letters addressed to politicians, which Rock the Vote submits electronically. The site also allows young people to sign up online for offline action, such as street teams that set up voter registrations stands at concerts and community events. Rock the Vote follows the lead of commercial marketers of clothing and music by combining traditional advertising with grassroots visibility and viral marketing.

2. *Volunteering.* Nearly half of American young people believe that volunteering for community activities is important. In 2002, in fact, 40% of American youth and young adults donated time to a group (National Public Radio, 2002). In light of these statistics, it is not surprising that web-based appeals for volunteers are common. One third of the web sites we surveyed provide opportunities for or links to volunteer activity. Some simply invite young people to volunteer with the organization that posted the site. Others are portals through which young people can access volunteer opportunities in hundreds of nonprofit organizations—local, national, or even international. One of the premier volunteering portal sites is SERVEnet (http://www.servenet .org), created by Youth Service America (http://www.ysa.org). Site visitors enter their zip code or city and state and then specify their skills, interests, target population, and availability. Within seconds, an array of relevant local organizations seeking volunteers appears on the screen. A single mouse click takes the user to the selected organization's web site, where details are provided on the organization and its volunteer needs.

3. *Youth Philanthropy.* Studies have found that 89% of all American households make charitable donations (World Vision, 2002). Yet there is growing concern that philanthropic behavior is a lesson that younger Americans have failed to master. When donations were studied by age group, 18- to 35-year-olds were by far the least giving, both in the percentage that gave and the median amount they contributed (Independent Sector, 2002; World Vision, 2002).

Fully a third of the sites we surveyed offered some kind of opportunity to learn about philanthropy, become involved in philanthropy, or make a donation. Some sites sport a "Donate Now" button to facilitate donations by credit card. For teenagers, many of whom do not have credit cards, YouthNOISE (http://www.YouthNOISE.org) offers a variant. For each visitor who clicks a designated "Just One Click" button, a host sponsor donates a small amount of money, such as five cents, to a specified cause. Youth for Life (http://members.tripod.com/~joseromia/), a prolife web site for young people, is one of many sites that encourage philanthropy by teaching about fundraising. Youth for Life offers its local affiliates a whole chapter of fundraising information, including 18 suggestions for fundraising activities and a range of sources for donations.

4. Local Community Involvement. Community-based web sites are too numerous to count and often fly under the radar of researchers. Our study highlights some that make innovative use of the web's interactive features. Among the most imaginative is the Community Information Corps (http://www.westsidecic.org/) of St. Paul, Minnesota. This is an expansive site concerned with exploring, documenting, and sharing the riches and resources that a neighborhood has to offer. The site demonstrates varying applications of mapping—taking an inventory of local resources and plotting them in a colorful, engaging, and informative online geographic display. In one, young people conducted 98 interviews to identify learning opportunities in their neighborhood. In another, CIC hired teenagers to develop an online tour of street murals in St. Paul's West Side. The result is a map of public art on display in West Side's streets and parks. Accompanying the map is a page of clickable photos of the individual murals, many of which reflect the neighborhood's immigrant roots, from its large Mexican-American community to its more recent Hmong arrivals. Most are accompanied by fascinating accounts of the area's history, drawn from interviews the youth conducted with mural artists or long-time neighborhood residents.

5. Global Issues and International Understanding. An emerging aspect of youth civic engagement is the understanding that the civic role can extend beyond the borders of nation-states. This awareness is evident in web sites for young people that promote international awareness and collaboration. Approximately 5% of the sites in this study are efforts to explore global affairs or foster international understanding among youth. Some sites have also found innovative ways to help young people interact with their peers in other countries and cultures. iEARN, the International Education and Resource Network (http://www.iearn.org), is a nonprofit online global network enabling young people to engage in collaborative educational projects. The site advertises itself as an inclusive, culturally diverse community linking 15,000 schools in 100 countries through a safe and structured online environment. There youth communicate through online school linkages to share materials for one another's classroom projects. iEARN's aim is to both "enhance learning and make a difference in the world."

6. Online Journalism and Media Production. If, in relation to youth, the primary difference between the old and new media could be reduced to a single word, that word would be *participation.* As opposed to the one-way print and broadcast media of the past, the new online media afford youth an opportunity to respond. They are doing so in astonishing variety. One means is through youth journalism. Nearly half of all the youth civic web sites we surveyed invite youth to participate online in some fashion, and almost a third provide opportunities for visitors to submit essays, articles, reviews, op-eds, or artwork to their sites (see also Olsson, chap. 7, this volume).

One such site is WireTap (http://www.wiretapmag.org), an online magazine that refers to itself as "Youth in pursuit of the dirty truth." Created by Alternet, a progressive online magazine and news service, WireTap serves up youth-written reporting, analysis, and cultural reviews on a wide range of contemporary issues—from the job market for young people, to politicians' attitudes toward youth, to the importance of hip-hop music in youth culture. WireTap serves as a training ground for young writers, and the quality of the writing is uneven; yet at the same time, individual voices are clear and perspectives can be refreshing and unexpected.

The internet also offers an inexpensive tool for multimedia production and distribution. Many young artists, authors, and activists, with assistance from supportive institutions, have found creative ways to publish civic-minded text, images, video, audio, and animation. One example is the Appalachian Media Institute, a Kentucky-based organization where young participants acquire web, video, and audio skills. Its web site (http://www.appalshop.org/ami/) offers an online catalog of youth-produced documentaries that give voice to their mountain communities, struggling to be heard in the modern world.

7. *Access and Equity.* To focus on the potential civic impact of the internet on disadvantaged youth, we must traverse what is called the *Digital Divide*—where the haves enjoy access to computers (and, by extension, to the internet, its information, and its openings for civic engagement), whereas the have-nots are cut off (Cha, 2002; Warschauer, 2002). Beneath the surface issue of technology acquisition lie the more complicated issues of social use, community integration, and civic engagement. The issue now is not simply whether the wiring is complete in any given community or neighborhood, but also whether the circuits are open and the pertinent civic, informational, and expressive content is flowing—in *both* directions.

HarlemLive (http://www.harlemlive.org/) is a web site dedicated to creating just that kind of community-based conversation. Launched in 1996 by a former New York City public school teacher, HarlemLive is an online magazine written, edited, and produced by Big Apple teens. It is notable for the community spirit that infuses its writing and for enabling participants to come to terms with many of the social, political, racial, and cultural issues that affect their lives. Because young people choose the topics and write the articles, HarlemLive addresses issues that young people have passion for or that affect them directly. Adult advisors appear to guide with a light hand.

8. *Diversity and Tolerance.* From online auctions of Nazi memorabilia to the World White Web of the Aryan Nation Brotherhood, the internet has given new voice to those who would gladly stifle the voices of others. Much less heralded are those individuals and organizations that have seized on the web as a platform to promote tolerance, understanding, and respect

among diverse groups and cultures. Yet these web sites do exist—many of them created for youth. Tolerance.org (http://www.tolerance.org) is a web project of the Southern Poverty Law Center that offers its audience information and skills to promote tolerance and fight hatred. Unlike sites offering one-size-fits-all programming, Tolerance.org arranges its content according to age level, with separate sections for parents, teachers, teenagers, and children. "Mix It Up," the teen section, promotes an activist approach to fighting self-segregation and social boundaries in schools, whether based on race, religion, or school-based clique. Other site features include online tests based on rapidly shifting images—a particularly apt use of the internet's capabilities as an electronic medium—to help the user discover his or her own less-than-conscious associations and value judgments about minority populations.

9. Positive Youth Development. Positive youth development programs—those that focus on youths' strengths and assets, as opposed to deficit-based approaches that focus solely on youth problems—have long been a part of U.S. civic fabric in the form of scouting and similar efforts. Web sites for the traditional youth organizations often serve mainly as online brochures or newsletters for the offline programs. However, a number of groups utilize the web's interactivity to offer additional resources and opportunities for involvement. For example, the YWCA site (http://www.ywca.org) contains links to a digital archives project with information about important women in U.S. history and women's events; to the YWCA's international site, World YWCA; and to a special web site for teenage girls, the Young Women's Web.

10. Youth Activism. The 2004 U.S. presidential election spotlighted the power of the internet as a tool for political organizing. Grassroots activists have likewise embraced the net, which lends itself to the kinds of informational, analytical, and organizational strategies on which activism depends. Digital media have become a fundamental component of many social action projects (McCaughey & Ayers, 2003). Free the Planet! (http://www .freetheplanet.org) illustrates how young people utilize the web to expand the student environmental movement, provide resources for activists, and help students win campaigns for environmental protection. Its campaigns have taken aim at such corporate giants as Ford Motors and Kraft Foods, among others. In each case, the web site offers a Problem, Solution, and What You Can Do—from sending an email to a corporate or political decision maker, to urging colleges to opt for Integrated Pest Management instead of heavy pesticide use. The web site points up the interaction between online and offline efforts, offering fact sheets and campaign guides in PDF form for downloading and offline use, announcements of offline training programs for student activists on its homepage, and an online listing of environmental jobs and internships.

NEW TECHNOLOGIES, NEW VOICES

In the quest to engage young people more fully with their communities, their government, and the process of solving societal problems, the web provides a wealth of material and plentiful opportunities for participation. In addition to mapping the civic resources available to youth on the Internet, we identified a number of key issues and trends. These include facets of civic engagement, as well as the ways in which the new networking technologies lend themselves to fostering such engagement.

Youth Voice

First, digital technology holds the potential to position young people as creators as well as consumers, as participants as well as spectators, enabling them to articulate and disseminate a youth voice in civic affairs. This capability is particularly important for adolescents, who are not only in the process of defining their personalities and constructing their understanding of their role in the world, but who also now have ready access to the technologies that can enhance these tasks. Civic web sites offer a range of opportunities for youth expression and communication. Online polls and questionnaires invite them to register their opinions, and web sites use them as one way to increase youth involvement and youth-generated content. Almost a third of the web sites we surveyed provide opportunities for visitors to submit essays, articles, reviews, op-eds, poetry, or art work to the site. Some web sites take youth involvement even further, allowing youth to determine what topics will be addressed online, choose the topics for message boards, design polls, and even serve on editorial boards. Recent technological innovations, such as blogging software and online political tools, have further enhanced the Internet's capability for youth expression and participation.

Civic Identity

By encouraging young people to articulate their views and positions, by creating the expectation of talking back and debate, and by welcoming youth initiative in responding to problems, the web may also assist in the formation of civic identity—developing the appropriate values, perspectives, and behaviors for a lifetime of civic involvement (Flanagan & Faison, 2001). The internet facilitates exposure to civic and political ideas and perspectives much more varied than anything a young person is likely to discover within the family, among friends, in school, or on TV. Although the quantity of content on the Internet is overwhelming and potentially confusing, it is not without organizing tissue: Hyperlinks from one web site to another provide a sense of the relations, clusters, and webs of interrelated connections among the issues and groups to be found online. Thus, the internet may lead a young person along a journey of discovery: of issues, concerns, values, and ideas.

At the same time that the Internet may lead a young person to experiment with new and unfamiliar identities, it can also lead him or her to a greater understanding and acceptance of his or her own identity. The web allows specific populations to strengthen their identities, building knowledge, pride, and a sense of belonging through a network of contacts and resources. It serves to link young people of a given racial or ethnic group. For example, the Ahimsa Youth Organization (http://www.ayo.org) introduces itself in its web site as a "charitable and educational organization dedicated to educating and promoting the culture of South Asia to the general public, specifically non-South Asians, and assisting the less fortunate through community service." This group helps a minority youth population represent itself to the larger surrounding culture. Similarly, Out Proud (http://www .outproud.org/), the web site of the National Coalition for Gay, Lesbian, Bisexual & Transgender Youth, exists to provide "outreach and support to queer teens just coming to terms with their sexual orientation and to those contemplating coming out."

Civic Skills

Civic skills are many and varied, including communications skills such as active listening, taking turns, and public speaking; intellectual skills such as critical and reflective strategies for processing information, formulation and expression of opinions, perspective taking, and principled reasoning; leadership and organizational skills such as organizing meetings, understanding and tolerance for diverse points of view, bargaining and compromise in group decisions, public problem solving, and coalition-building; and civic-specific skills such as contacting public officials (Flanagan & Faison, 2001).

Almost half of the web sites we surveyed cited the promotion of team building or leadership skills as a goal of the site or of the organization behind it, whereas two thirds cited promotion of the skills necessary for youth to promote and engender change. Many of the skills underlying these goals are by definition practiced in a group, and as such are not readily transferable to web sites built for individual participation. This might suggest a limitation in the capacity of the internet to teach certain civic skills, although web sites may be useful in directing young people to offline programs where the desired skills may be acquired in person.

In any case, web sites can certainly model such skills as listening to and engaging with different ideas and perspectives. This function is frequently played by online bulletin boards—sometimes well, sometimes poorly. We found in our study that message boards offer hands-on practice of such relevant skills as formulating and expressing opinions, debating opposing views, and taking turns. Whether users actually do reflect on the views expressed by others, respond with sound and principled reasoning, and whether they are open to changing their own viewpoints in response to what they learn was often difficult to determine. Youth message board participation is frequently sporadic as opposed to sustained, and our study did not permit direct observation or interviews with site users. However, Olsson's study (chap. 7, this volume) provides evidence that some youth use message boards for political activism in a sustained and calculated way.

Organizational skills are more directly taught. Advice about how to raise money is often featured on the youth civic web sites of national organizations; the information is intended as a resource for local chapters, but is available to any site visitor. Such online fundraising training can be found, for example, at the web sites of Youth Crime Watch of America (http://www.ycwa.org/start/index.html), United Students Against Sweatshops (http://www.usasnet.org/), and Youth for Life (http://www.members.tripod.com/~joseromia/).

In general however, it appears that the web is currently an underused venue for teaching civic skills. Some civic skills are modeled in practice on some web sites, but rarely do web site producers point out or highlight the specific skills involved. Nor do they explicitly draw attention to civic skills as valuable tools that young people should seek to acquire. In very few cases do web sites set out deliberately to teach civic skills. These shortcomings strike us less as an inherent weakness of the web and more as a lost opportunity. Most civic sites are focused on their immediate goals—civic, to be sure—and seem not to have given much thought to using the web as a training ground for the young people who will presumably be an organization's members and supporters in a few short years. Future efforts to promote civic engagement might choose to address nonprofit organizations, focusing their attention on the ways they could utilize the Internet to inform, motivate, and train young people as emerging active citizens.

Civic Literacy

The web's most important contribution to youth civic engagement may be its role in building civic literacy. In years past, primarily high school government and civics classes played that role. For today's adolescents, many of whom have virtually no classroom instruction in these topics, levels of civic and political knowledge are positively associated with parental levels of education as well as any civic content they do learn in school, classroom discussions of current events, and participation in student government and community service (Flanagan & Faison, 2001). We would add to that list the civic-related content that young people encounter on the web.

Three quarters of the web sites surveyed stated that "promoting knowledge about a particular issue or set of issues" is a goal of the site producer (commonly on the organization's mission statement). Online civic information abounds, including background information on particular issues and problems, discussions of proposed solutions, identification of key decision makers, strategies for contacting those decision makers, and opportunities to make one's voice heard.

Unfortunately, much of the information available online is noninteractive in form. Many civic web sites present valuable information, but in ways that fail to exploit the internet's potential to promote active engagement and dialogue. Frequently, information is presented as static text that could as well be found in a printed newsletter or book, underutilizing the internet's powerful technological interactivity, and, in so doing, missing out on an array of options for engaging young people more directly with civic content. Yet even where a web site utilizes only the most static types of technology to post civic information, its contribution to civic literacy is noteworthy. Most obviously, the electronic nature of the web makes reams of civic information accessible across the limitations of space and time.

Even information presented in static form helps to carry young people across the first threshold for youth civic involvement: that of awareness. Without an initial awareness of the societal issues and challenges that exist, the ways they are being addressed, and the means of youth participation, young people have no idea how to become involved. Thus, any medium that provides windows into the civic realm plays an integral role in making youth civic engagement possible. Civic literacy has also been found to correlate positively (in adults, at least) with attitudes or values that are necessary for a democratic society to function, such as tolerance, and with the actual behavior of engagement in community affairs (Flanagan & Faison, 2001). For all these reasons, even the simplest and most static function of the civic web is potentially of great significance.

THE IMPACT OF ONLINE YOUTH ENGAGEMENT

Our study did not—and could not—measure the *impact* of the web in promoting youth civic engagement, an important task that lies ahead. Rather, our study was based primarily in an analysis of online civic content designed for young people. To a lesser extent, through interviews and secondary source materials, we also looked at the organizations behind the web sites, in an effort to understand their intended goals, the strategies they employed, and the obstacles they encountered. What we were able to analyze, then, were *efforts* at promoting civic engagement. What fell beyond the scope of this study was an assessment of *results*.

Nonetheless, several initial observations can be made about the impact of civic web sites. First, it is clear that the web is already integrated into most young people's window on the world, and that it offers them a broader perspective than any before. In many ways, the web constitutes an enormous informational resource on a wide variety of topics (including civic affairs), offering young people a handy library, Yellow Pages, referral service, and more. Informational use of civic web sites is most apparent in individual quests for information. Given the key role that the classroom can play in promoting civic engagement, further study should be devoted to the extent to which schools draw on this rich resource and the ways in which they do so. Beyond informational use, youth civic web sites open doors to access and participation in civic projects. Which young people utilize these web sites, how, and with what effects over time are all topics that call for more systematic research.

Second, research into youth development suggests that, as a source for learning civic skills, values, and behaviors, web sites will be most effective if used over an arc of time (Larson, 2000; McLeod, 2000). Our study did not allow us to perceive how often any individual user visited a given web site or how sustained this use was over time. Where some glimpses of this are possible—for example, on message boards—it appears that many users come and go. This intermittent use is not likely to reinforce behavior-based skills, which require repeated use and practice. This suggests that web sites may offer their greatest impact in teaching civic skills when used within a well-defined community that can commit to sustained use—whether a youth group, a school, or a civic organization with a program designed for ongoing as opposed to one-time involvement.

Third, given the hundreds of civic web sites that exist, and their tremendous variation, generalizing about their impact is not fruitful. Impact inevitably depends on which web sites are used, how they are used, by whom, with what kind of guidance, and for what purposes. If civic web sites are to be utilized in the classroom—and we believe they should be for the richness of their content and the introduction they offer to real-life issues and situations—they will have to be used selectively. To maximize their impact and appropriateness, educators and researchers need to develop rigorous criteria in developing online content and selecting web sites that meet young people's needs, as well as pedagogic and curricular standards.

PROSPECTS FOR THE FUTURE, AND RECOMMENDATIONS

The body of material that we have studied is little known compared with the mass of flashy, heavily advertised commercial content for youth. Yet it embodies a vibrant civic and political online culture. As we try to assess its significance, both current and potential, it is clear that additional research is needed to systematically assess the impact of these web sites on the young people who use them. What influence can web sites have on the civic values, thinking, and behavior of American youth? What types of impact are most readily achieved? How should web sites be designed? What kinds of online interaction should be offered to attract young people? Are the same approaches appropriate to teach them or to engage them in action? Will online techniques work for all youth or only for some? Can online engagement have a long-term effect on young people's lifelong civic values and behavior? Only when further inquiry answers these and a host of related questions will we be able to make clear statements about the lasting value of these intriguing efforts.

More immediately, can online youth civic culture grow and flourish? Can it compete against or at least exist side by side with the commercial digital media juggernaut? That, to date, is an unanswered question. The abundance of civic content, its variety, vitality, and (in some places, not all) its quality, indicate that digital media are poised to serve civic and political engagement. Furthermore, the field is vibrant and fast changing: Our study unearthed many promising practices and innovations. If we add to that the importance of the youth demographic, plus the widespread concern for youth civic involvement, online civic culture seems likely to grow in size and scope in the coming years.

To survive, this mass of civic material needs to become more prominent in the online landscape. Many appealing and informative civic web sites are marginalized by near invisibility, submerged as they are in the vast sea of content that is the World Wide Web. If civic online content is to have any impact on the digital generation, it must be made easier for young people to find. To date, there has been little effort to organize a critical mass of this material into a coherent, clearly marked online civic sector. Raising the profile of civic web sites would not only increase the likelihood that they were more widely used; it would also facilitate the task of articulating the nature of this online civic world and the reasons it is worthy of support.

An equally important concern is the financial sustainability of an online civic sector. This question is inextricably linked to both the health of the nonprofit sector, whence much of the civic content is derived, and the future shape of the digital communications system. Here again, at least in the United States, issues of telecommunications public policy—the nature of the transition to broadband, the question of open access—will largely dictate who shapes the internet (Center for Digital Democracy, 2005). The youth who use the internet for political and civic efforts have not yet been educated about these issues or involved in them. Yet as stakeholders, they should play an active role in the debate over the future of the media system. The challenge of involving them, and of incorporating their tastes and needs into the design of our future communication system, faces media activists, educators, and foundations alike.

Despite the many questions that surround the future of a civic internet, we are optimistic that it will continue to expand and evolve, generating new means for youth to learn about and participate in local, national, and global society. We hope that our study stimulates future initiatives to help grow this youth civic culture and place it in the foreground of the digital media culture for young people.

REFERENCES

Buckingham, D. (2000). *The making of citizens.* London: Routledge.

Bunn, A. (2000, July/August). The rise of the teen guru. *Brill's Content,* pp. 64–69, 123–129.

Center for Digital Democracy. (2005). Retrieved May 19, 2005, from http://www .democraticmedia.org/issues/openaccess/index.html

Center for Media Education. (2001). *TeenSites.com: A field guide to the new digital landscape.* Washington, DC: Author.

Cha, A. E. (2002). *"Digital divide" less clear.* Retrieved July 18, 2002, from http:// www.washingtonpost.com/ac2/wp-dyn/A63831-2002Jun28

CIRCLE & The Carnegie Corporation of New York. (2003). *The civic mission of schools.* New York: Carnegie Corporation. Retrieved December 4, 2003, from http://www.civicmission ofschools.org/

COPA Commission. (2000, October 20). *Final report of the COPA commission.* Retrieved December 3, 2003, from http://www.copacommission.org/report/

Cyberatlas. (2001, August 8). *U.S. college students use net for shopping.* Retrieved September 3, 2001, from http://www.cyberatlas.internet.com/big_picture/demographics/article/0, 5901_432631,00.html#table

Delli Carpini, M. (2000a). *Gen.com: Youth, civic engagement, and the new information environment.* Working paper. Retrieved December 4, 2003, from http://jsisartsci.washington.edu/ programms/cwesuw/carpini.htm

Delli Carpini, M. (2000b). *The youth engagement initiative strategy paper, Pew Charitable Trusts.* Retrieved August 10, 2000, from http://www.pewtrusts.com/misc_html/pp_youth_strategy_ paper.cfm

Engaging the next generation: How non-profits can reach youth adults. (2000). *Research Center.* MTV & The Ad Council. Retrieved May 14, 2005, from http://www.adcouncil.org/ research/engaging_next_gen/

Flanagan, C., & Faison, N. (2001). Youth civic development: Implications of research for social policy and programs. *Social Policy Report, 15*(1), 3–16. Retrieved from http://www.srcd.org/ sprv15nl.pdf

Gottlieb-Robles, B., Larson, G., & Montgomery, K. (2004, March). *Youth as e-citizens: Engaging the digital generation.* Washington, DC: American University, School of Communication, Center for Social Media website. Retrieved from http://centerforsocialmedia.org/ ecitizens/youthreport.pdf

Independent Sector. (2002). *Giving and volunteering in the United States 2001.* Retrieved November 18, 2003, from http://www.independentsector.org/programs/research/GV01main. html

Jupiter Communications. (2000, September 12). *Teens spend less than half as much time online as adults.* Retrieved May 10, 2001, from http://www.jup.com/company/pressrelease.jsp ?doc+pr0009127

Larson, R. (2000). Toward a psychology of positive youth development. *American Psychologist*, 55(1).

Lenhart, A., Lewis, O., & Rainie, L. (2001). *Teenage life online: The rise of the instant-message generation and the Internet's impact on friendship and family relationships.* Washington, DC: Pew Internet & American Life Project.

McCaughey, M., & Ayers, M. (2003). *Cyberactivism: Online activism in theory and practice.* London: Routledge.

McLeod, J. M. (2000). Media and civic socialization of youth. *Journal of Adolescent Health, 27*(2).

National Public Radio. (2002). *Civic lessons beyond the classroom: Volunteering may not teach students about the problems roots.* Retrieved June 25, 2005, from http://discover.npr.org/features/feature.jhtml?wfld#905341

Neuborne, E., & Kerwin, K. (1999, February 15). Generation Y. *Business Week,* pp. 81–84.

Packel, D., & Rainie, L. (2001, February). *More online, doing more.* Washington, DC: Pew Internet & American Life Project.

Putnam, R. (2000). *Bowling alone: The collapse and revival of American community.* New York: Simon & Schuster.

Reuters. (2003, July 24). *Youth spend more time on web than TV-study.* Retrieved December 4, 2003, from http://www.forbes.com/technology/newswire/2003/07/24/rtr1037488.html

Sharp, R. (2000, May 29). Teen moguls: Internet-savvy kids are turning their fun and games into million-dollar businesses. *Business Week,* pp. 108–118.

Voedisch, L. (2000, January 17). *You must be 18 to enter.* Retrieved December 4, 2003, from http://www.cnn.com/2000/TECH/computing/01/17/are.you.18.idg/index.html

Warschauer, M. (2002). *Reconceptualizing the digital divide: First Monday.* Retrieved July 15, 2002, from http://www.firstmonday.dk/issues/issue7_7/warschauer/

World Vision. (2002). *Survey finds Americans more generous last year.* Retrieved April 23, 2002, from http://www.worldvision.org/worldvision/pr.nsf/stable/20020423_barna

Youth Markets ALERT. (1999, September). Generation Y is internalizing Internet-driven values. *EPM Communication, 3.*

Chapter 9

Cyber-Censorship or Cyber-Literacy? Envisioning Cyber-Learning Through Media Education

Julie Frechette
Worcester State College

With the growth and popularity of the internet, particularly in schools and educational institutions, there has been a growing concern about the safety of using computer-mediated communication technology. Globally, parents and schools have approached cyber-travel with concerns about racist web sites, pornography, pedophiles, and the like. From schools to governments to computer industries, there has been a concerted effort to cyber-patrol the internet. In December 2000, the U.S. Congress passed the Children's Internet Protection Act (CIPA), requiring schools and libraries that receive federal money for internet connections to adopt internet safety policies, including the use of audit-tracking devices, safe sites, and software filtration devices such as *Safesurf* and *NetNanny*. Yet such proposed solutions and policies ignore the more relevant question of how private computer companies, internet service providers, corporations, and governments stand to gain financially and politically by deciding what kind of information will be censored and what kind will be promoted.

In fact it could be argued that the cyber-safety crisis dominating public policy and mainstream media coverage has produced a cultural climate ripe for the commercial exploitation of vulnerable parents and educators. In this chapter, I argue that the discourse of cyber-safety and cyber-censorship manufactures consent through a hegemonic force that overlooks the invasion of online advertising or marketing strategies targeted at children. By examining the rhetorical and financial investments of the telecommunications business sector, I contend that the mainstream articulation of cyber-paranoia attempts to reach the consent of parents and educators by asking them to see *some* internet content as value-laden (i.e., nudity, sexuality, trigger words, or adult content) while disguising the interests and authority of profitable commercial and computer industries (in the form of advertising, marketing, tracking, and filters).

Equally interesting is the fact that articulations of cyber-safety and cyber-censorship have emerged at a time when the internet continues to surpass traditional communications media as an alternative source of information, offering diverse perspectives otherwise absent from the mainstream media. Although transnational corporate conglomerates such as Time Warner and Microsoft continue to gain a stronghold on controlling the means to cyber-access at home and at school, educators and parents need to realize the potential of the internet as a powerful and important learning medium for the 21st century. By outlining how to develop cyber-literacy skills in media content, grammar, and medium theory, this chapter ventures toward the articulation of transformative possibilities within cyber-space through media education.

EASY SOLUTIONS FOR COMPLEX PROBLEMS

According to figures provided by the U.S. Census Bureau (2001), more than half of school-age children (6 to 17 years) had access to computers both in school and at home in the year 2000 (57%). With some 17 million children using the internet in some capacity, including email, the web, chatrooms, and instant messaging (Silver & Garland, 2004), the Census Bureau estimates that 21% percent use the Internet to perform school-related tasks, such as research for assignments or taking courses online.

Although these statistics underscore the growth and popularity of the internet, particularly in schools and educational institutions, ensuing concerns have grown about the safety of using computer-mediated communication technology. Since the internet became a mass medium in 1995, parents and schools have approached online content with reservations. As such, politicians, educators, child-advocacy groups, and, most important, the computer industry have been vocal advocates for patrolling the internet and censoring certain kinds of illicit or objectionable content.

Likewise, educators have expressed concerns about online information overload. According to one school administrator, accessing the internet in schools is less predictable: "If you used to bring your class to the school library, you pretty much had a sense of what was available for the children to research; now you have no idea . . . they are going to hit sites that are appropriate and sites that are inappropriate" (personal interview; cited in Shyles, 2003, p. 176).

Despite a commitment to online security in schools, libraries, and homes from so many constituents, few recommendations have materialized into solid strategies or funding initiatives. Almost all of the proposed solutions and policies ignore the more relevant question of how private computer companies, internet service providers, corporations, and governments stand to gain financially and politically by deciding what kind of information will be censored and what kind will be promoted. What's more, the democratic potential of the internet as a means to access alternative information and perspectives otherwise absent from the mainstream media continues to be threatened by the consolidation of increasingly powerful global media giants, such as Time Warner and Microsoft, which have much to gain from controlling the content internet users access at home or school. Consequently, an examination of the political and economic forces on the internet is necessary for librarians and educators interested in understanding the benefits and limits of the internet as a means of alternative communication.

EXPLORING THE MEANS TO FILTERING ONLINE CONTENT

Parental Guidance

As a result of the concerns I have outlined, a number of solutions have been advanced to ward off illicit online content appearing on the computer screens of young internet users, beginning with parental guidance. CyberTipLine grew out of the 1997 Internet/Online Summit and is currently in operation today. Run by the U.S. government and the National Center for Missing and Exploited Children, parents can notify authorities of incidents of online child pornography and child predation. Another derivative of the summit's "America Links Up" project is the industry-sponsored "GetNetWise" web site, which was launched in 1999. The user empowerment service, which involves a coalition of numerous internet industry partners and advocacy organizations,[1] offers parental advice, including information about filters to block sexually explicit material, as well as a variety of tools to help parents and caregivers monitor a child's online activities and find browsers for kid-friendly sites. As one sponsor, AT&T, notes in its promotional material, "Our involvement with GetNetWise reflects our commitment to help users have the best possible online experience" (GetNetWise, 2004).

---

[1]For example, AT&T, Dell Inc., Microsoft, Verizon, America Online, Inc., American Library Association, Amazon.com, Center for Democracy & Technology, Comcast, Earthlink, Inc., Recording Industry Association of America, Visa USA, Wells Fargo, Yahoo!

A more well-known parental guidance initiative passed in April 2000 was the Children's Online Privacy Protection Act (COPPA). In accordance with COPPA, the Federal Bureau of Investigation offers "A Parent's Guide to Internet Safety," which advises parents to "utilize parental controls provided by your service provider and/or blocking software" and "Monitor your child's access to all types of live electronic communications [chat rooms, instant messages, Internet Relay Chat, etc.], and monitor your child's e-mail" (FBI, 2004, n.p.).

Other parental guidance measures have been created to address online advertising and marketing as well as issues of privacy. Parent advocacy groups, such as Commercial Alert, Consumer Action, The Center for Media Education, and Computer Professionals for Social Responsibility, have taken up the cause of parents concerned about online marketing measures targeted at children. For example, Commercial Alert has made requests to the Federal Communications Commission (FCC) and the Federal Trade Commission (FTC) to require disclosure of embedded advertising in a variety of media and has created a Parent's Bill of Rights seeking to empower parents in the face of an aggressive commercial culture (Ruskin, 2003).

Proof-of-Age/Shielding Systems

In addition to parental guidance, many online providers and web masters have adopted proof-of-age/shielding systems that use credit card access as another means of content filtering. Although COPPA sought to protect children ages 13 and under, those located in the 14- to 18-year range were not covered by legislation. Providing proof of age before being allowed to access the content of a desired online site emerged as a means to address this gap. This system works in the same way that fraud-screening technology works: Merchants collect user information at their web sites for instant age or identity verification. Once online users submit their name, zip code, date of birth, and age, they are checked through an international electronic database of government-issued identifications. This allows site providers or merchants to determine the consumer's identity within seconds. Sometimes additional measures, such as online name signature, are required so that user signatures are bound to a public record.

Proprietary Environments

Another reaction to the discourse of online safety has been the advocacy of proprietary environments, where content is screened by editors into specific categories. For example, the leading internet service provider, America Online (AOL), provides a blocking service that allows users (ostensibly parents) to limit a child's selected screen name to either a Kids Only area, which is recommended for children under 12, or to a preteen/teen environment, with restricted use of chatrooms or newsgroups. According to the site, Kids Only is a collection of educational resources and entertainment areas as well as a preselected collection of child-oriented internet sites, with AOL staff monitoring of message boards and chatrooms. AOL also promotes the company's Parental Phone Line for instructions and advice on choosing and maintaining the settings of this product (the premise here is that the settings are likely to be tampered with by savvy teens and preteens).

In addition to Kids Only, AOL has aggressively marketed its *AOL@School* service, which has been adopted by more than 14,000 schools by 2004 (Williams, 2003). AOL@School offers six online learning portals for Grades K–5, middle school, and high school so that students can access web sites that have been preselected by educators as content and age appropriate. The software needed to access the portals comes with AOL's parental controls designed to "help ensure a safe, secure, age-appropriate experience" that includes school-controlled email, chat, and instant messaging (AOL, 2004). The popularity of child-safe proprietary environments has not waned as web browsers and popular search engines have created their own directories in an attempt to create safe havens for (and develop customer loyalty from) younger online users. Yahooligans' Web Guide for Kids is a collection of predominantly commercial links to online games, music, TV, science, news, jokes, cool pages, arts and entertainment, and sports. Like most commercial proprietary environments, Yahooligans is riddled with advertisements and synergistic ties to commercial media products.

Internet Ratings Systems

For those seeking additional regulatory measures, internet rating systems offer another approach. Unlike the rating system for TV content that is uniformly and centrally organized by the TV industry, internet ratings are not assigned consistently by a centralized group of online content providers. However, the goal is the same: industry self-regulation over government regulation. According to ratings system advocates, many of whom work in the software and computer industry, internet ratings are designed to make it safe for schools and parents to let their children access nonpornographic material without government directives. According to Resnick (1997), chairman of the World Wide Web Consortium group at the MIT Laboratory for Computer Science, which includes AT&T Laboratories and Microsoft, the Platform for Internet Content Selection (PICS) was originally created to allow parents, teachers, and librarians to review questionable materials that they would not want their children to come across on the Net.

Resnick (1997) explained, "prior to PICS there was no standard format for labels, so companies that wished to provide access control had to both

develop the software and provide the labels. PICS provides a common format for labels, so that any PICS-compliant selection software can process
any PICS-compliant label" (p. 106). Yet unlike uniform rating labels,

> a single site or document may have many labels, provided by different organi-
> zations. Consumers choose their selection software and their label sources
> (called *rating services*) independently. This separation allows both markets to
> flourish: companies that prefer to remain value-neutral can offer selection
> software without providing any labels; values-oriented organizations, without
> writing software, can create rating services that provide labels. (Resnick, 1997,
> p. 107)

One of the leading internet rating systems that uses PICS is SafeSurf, a
group that offers ratings along with other tools to help parents and net citizens filter online information. One means to achieving its goal is to encourage online content providers to fill out a questionnaire using content
descriptors to rate their web sites. Unlike government or industry-wide regulatory labeling efforts that may brand content, SafeSurf is interested in
maintaining First Amendment rights by offering content providers greater
latitude to self-rate their web material. For example, rather than branding
content that includes nudity as pornographic, users can distinguish their
inclusion of nudity as scientific, sociocultural, artistic, titillating, graphic, or
illegal.

Once content providers rate their web sites or directories, they can
download the SafeSurf-rated logo of their choice. A SafeSurf staff member
verifies the rating and sets up the chosen ratings label. Parents and educators can then use PICS-compliant software/browsers to read the settings
and use the ratings to filter content that is not desired. As the SafeSurf
group explains, "PICS allows content providers to rate their pages and parents to set passwords and levels for their children. Then, PICS compliant
software/browsers will read the settings and use the ratings to filter content
that is not desired" (SafeSurf, 2004a).

The Internet Content Rating Association (ICRA) is another international, independent, nonprofit organization that seeks to "empower the
public, especially parents, to make informed decisions about electronic media by means of the open and objective labeling of content" (ICRA, 2004).
ICRA's dual aims are to "protect children from potentially harmful material
and to protect free speech on the internet." Like SafeSurf, web authors
complete an online questionnaire describing the content of their site, on
which ICRA generates a content label using PICS computer coding, which
the author adds to his or her site. Parents and internet users can then set
their internet browser to accept or decline access to web sites based on the
labels and user preferences. PICS is now a standard feature included in internet software and browsers such as Microsoft Explorer.

Third-Party Rating Systems

Although ratings systems are designed to allow content providers to voluntarily label the content they create and distribute, third-party rating systems "enable multiple, independent labeling services to associate additional labels with content created and distributed by others. Services may devise their own labeling systems, and the same content may receive different labels from different services" (ICRA, 2004). In other words, online watchdog groups interested in protecting children from online predators or illicit material can offer their own set of restrictive control tools for material they deem objectionable. One such group is WiredSafety, formerly known as CyberAngels, led by Parry Aftab, an experienced international attorney and author of *The Parents Guide to Protecting Your Children In Cyberspace* and *A Parent's Guide to the Internet.* Lauded as "one of the internet safety's most influential players," Aftab has emerged as a nonprofit leader who has created coalitions with many governmental and nongovernmental agencies, including the FBI's Innocent Images antichild pornography and exploitation task force (Hill, 2000). She was appointed the founding American director of UNESCO's global Child Safeline project and currently heads WiredSafety, "the largest online safety, education and help group in the world." With more than 9,000 volunteers worldwide, the group is a coalition of various internet safety groups, such as WiredKids.org, WiredTeens, Teenangels, CyberMoms and CyberDads, and their affiliate, WiredCops.org, all of whom patrol the internet for child pornography, child molesters, and cyberstalkers. Additionally, WiredSafety offers a variety of educational and help services for online users. Some of its volunteers access and review family-friendly web sites, filter software products and internet services, and post their findings on the web. The group even has a Cyber911 help line that offers net users access to help when they need it online. Surfwatch is another online ratings system designed for parental supervision. It too prevents access to web, gopher, and ftp sites that Surf Watch's team of net surfers have found objectionable. They maintain an updated list of not-for-children web sites that can be subscribed to electronically.

Commercial Filtering Software and Databases

A more intensive effort to censor inappropriate online content has come from commercial filtering software companies (often working in conjunction with powerful internet content providers and third-party ratings systems). Also known as censorware, these filtering products, which include NetNanny, CyberPatrol, Cyber Sitter, and N2H2, range from $25.99 to $80 and are heavily marketed to parents, educational administrators, and libraries. Designed to be installed on home or school computers or to work with network routers, firewall, cache, or proxy devices, these products claim to offer safety measures for youth using computers for online research and recreation. Essentially, most of these programs work by using a combination of filtering and blocking strategies, such as the blocking of web sites denoted through keywords and databases, and the blocking of individual web sites by specific URLs.

One of the first filtering programs—and most commercially lucrative—is NetNanny. According to its promotional web site, NetNanny® 5 is "the world's leading parental control software, [and] provides customers with the broadest set of internet safety tools available today. Our award-winning software gives customers control over what comes into and goes out of their home through their internet connection, while respecting their personal values and beliefs" (netnanny.com). Launched in 1998, NetNanny is a tool allowing parents, teachers, administrators, and librarians to screen incoming and outgoing internet information, particularly pornographic material. By identifying and blocking various sites and subjects considered inappropriate, the program blocks the web addresses of known pornographic and illicit sites. Parents can add to the collection of forbidden code words used to detect and flag sites. The program works with all major online providers and in email. It can also prevent children from accessing specific files on a PC's hard drive, floppy, or CD-ROM. Like audit-tracking software programs, NetNanny keeps a record of a child or student's internet perusal, meaning that parents and teachers can check up on the sites that a child has perused.

Another commercial service, CyberPatrol, works in the same way as NetNanny by filtering harmful web sites, newsgroups, and web-based email. Also commercially successful, CyberPatrol licenses its CyberLIST database of site ratings to several additional vendors. Among its ratings categories are: violence/profanity, partial nudity, full nudity, sexual acts, gross depictions, intolerance, satanic or cult, drugs and drug culture, militant/extremist, sex education, questionable/illegal and gambling, and alcohol and tobacco.

Likewise, Cybersitter blocks sites and subjects deemed unacceptable by internet users. It offers site lists for automatic blocking and allows parents to have added input in restricting programs, files, and games. According to *PC Magazine*, Cybersitter offers the strongest filtering and monitoring features, blocking content related to violence, hate, sex, and drugs (Munro, 2004). It also allows parents to choose from 32 content categories, such as free email sites, file sharing, wrestling, cults, and gambling, for those interested in added blocking categories. As with other similar products, it lets parents filter and monitor their children's activities without their knowledge and can record both sides of instant messaging (IM) sessions.

Joining in the mix of filtering software providers is N2H2 (acquired by Secure Computing in 2003), a company endorsed by eTesting Labs and the

Kaiser Foundation as "the most effective and accurate" filtering program and offering an extensive database of objectionable internet sites (N2H2, 2004). It offers two product lines: Sentian, which is geared toward helping businesses manage their employee internet access; and Bess, a popular program and database adopted by many schools and endorsed by the American Library Association to help schools and libraries meet CIPA rules for young internet users.

With so many companies vying to be the best provider of filtering software, it is not surprising that Microsoft would venture into this area by offering its own industry standard internet filter aimed at regulating youth-directed online content. As part of its monopoly on the internet browser software Internet Explorer (which accompanies its Windows platform), Microsoft has also implemented a filtering system that can be configured to block or log all data transfers including World Wide Web pages, newsgroups, types of messages within any newsgroup, Internet Relay Chat, or internet hosts known to have objectionable material to children.

TESTING CONTENT CONTROLS
FOR CYBER-CAPITALISM

The hegemonic impulse of online safety profiteers becomes clear when we take a look at some ratings organizations, online proprietary environments, ISPs, and databases recommended by parents, the government, educational institutions, and the industry. First is SafeSurf, a rating organization that claims to be "dedicated to making the internet safe for your children without censorship." Through an information database of objectionable sites, a proprietary environment for children, and safety tools for parents, Safesurf believes they "will enable software and hardware to be developed that will enable more effective use of the Internet for *everyone*" (italics added).

My skepticism about claims that everyone benefits through SafeSurf's methods developed when visiting the SafeSurf homepage, where I reviewed their policies, claims, and method to create an environment that is child-tested and parent-approved. What first drew my attention to their web site were the various advertisements centered on the page. One ad displayed a large colorful rectangular for *Card Service Online*, "the leader in online real-time credit card processing" featuring *Mastercard, Visa, Discover*, and *American Express*. Directly under it was an ad for *Child Magazine*, on sale at the reduced price of $7.95; its pitch: "One year for the price of a bottle." Beneath this was a bold advertisement link to "Update Microsoft's Internet Explorer to support SafeSurf Ratings." Combined, these ads validated my forewarning about the interconnections between powerful computer firms, such as Microsoft, and blocking software products.

My findings led me to presume that more advertising would emerge on the *SafeSurf Wave* link, which offers *Kid's Wave*, a list of top sites purportedly "devoted to educating and entertaining children." On the *Kid's Wave* front page, I was informed, "There are great places to take your children online." Below was a grid of partial listings of SafeSurf-approved sites by category. The first category was the "favorite site of the month," which was *Squigly's Playhouse.* By clicking on the cartoon graphic, my hypothesis was reaffirmed: The unfolding visual displayed a large color advertisement for *Disneyland* with moving graphics and a photo of the Magic Kingdom. The flashing text read, "[Frame 1: photo and text depicted Disneyland Resort] To really enjoy yourself here [Frame 2: photo of Mickey Mouse described as 'the Disneyland Trip Wizard'] . . . Pick up your custom schedule here."

In case the ad was overlooked, each separate clickable *Kid's Wave* link for an activity or game was infused with the Disney Resort campaign. For instance, the Squigly's Games page had another large, flashing, color ad for Disney at the top that read, "[Frame 1—photo of Mickey Mouse] Are you the Ultimate Disney fan? [Frame 2—photo of Goofy] Click here—enter to win"; on the bottom, a three-frame flashing ad targeted at parents read, "[Frame 1] You know what you put on your card, [Frame 2] but do you know what *he* put on your card? [picture of a crowd with a man circled in red], [Frame 3] Find out with your free credit report online." Other pages, like Squigly's Writing Corner or Brainteasers, featured separate Disney ads as well as credit card ads (presumably targeted at parents, but also a new generation of consumers).

Disney, it seems, is a frequent advertiser on filtering software products. In addition to selling nonsoftware products, such as $40 embroidered golf shirts, NetNanny's internet web site had an advertisement for *Disneyland* featured on its front page. Most troubling, however, is that advertising clients are also the sponsors of NetNanny content. Among its safe sites for kids were fun links to Disney, Crayola, and Kids Channel. Under the category Education was a *Colgate* Kidsworld link with prominent product advertisements for *Colgate* toothpaste. Describing its mission in philanthropic terms, *Colgate Palmolive Co.* purportedly maintains the internet site "as a service to the internet community." A closer look at the page proves otherwise. First, I had to type in my first name and specified password of the day, *toothpaste*, to enter the No Cavities Clubhouse. There I was greeted by Dr. Rabbit, who appeared in his clubhouse holding a toothbrush and *Colgate* toothpaste. Although this web site offered "interesting oral care facts, games, and stories aimed at raising children's awareness of oral health," I couldn't get away from Dr. Rabbit and his *Colgate* endorsement no matter what activity I clicked on. Moreover, despite its intention to adhere to the Children's Advertising Review Unit (CARU) Guidelines for advertising on the internet and online services, my name and e-mail were still requested so that the

Tooth Fairy could send me an email message—no doubt carrying her Colgate toothpaste and brush in cyber-flight.

Although not nearly as plastered in advertising as SurfWatch or Net-Nanny, CyberPatrol's web unquestionably catered to and partnered with commercial web sites, including Disney's internet empire of kid-targeted web addresses. A recommended safe site was *Toy Story* Games, a game developed by Disney based on its *Toy Story* movie. Not surprisingly, Disney's homepage was saturated with child- and adult-directed advertising. Although the advertising contained here was 2nd level, meaning that I had to click on the recommended sites before being inundated with ads, the sites contained on the page remained uncontested as child appropriate.

As evidenced within these kid-designated web sites, the far-reaching clutches of advertisers are rendered invisible in the discourse or underlying rationale of internet protectionism. Although children are deemed to be impressionable when it comes to sex, pornography, adult content, and nefarious language, concerns about manipulative advertising campaigns go largely undetected within kid-safe internet domains.

QUESTIONING THE VIABILITY OF ONLINE SAFETY INITIATIVES

What form might media literacy take in relation to the internet? Although some of these internet resources and restrictions make sense for certain schools depending on the age group and grade level of internet users, there are some problematic areas within each method that should be cause for concern. The main underlying difficulty raised by these quasi-solutions is that they narrowly define what is inappropriate, relegating most objections to issues of nudity, sexuality, trigger words, or adult content. This focus neglects to confront the invasion of advertising or marketing strategies directed at children. In many respects, internet commercialism seems to be a more serious concern, but one would never guess considering the ad-strewn and content-compromised solutions to appropriate internet content.

Although child-directed advertising might not be as blatantly offensive, it certainly fosters values that, at present, are not considered objectionable to most governmental, parental, and commercial watchdog groups. Although the first tenet of media literacy explains that *all media are constructions,* the problem with advertising and marketing strategies is that they are so much a part of our social landscape and our everyday life that they appear to be natural. Subsequently, the conceptualization of what is inappropriate for children or students only helps to sustain the interests of a commercial system through the omission of advertising: Advertising is omitted and thereby deemed appropriate. Parents, educators, and anticommercial groups such as Commercial Alert have protested against the commercial imperatives of satellite-delivered school programs such as Channel One, a company that offers schools free satellite equipment in exchange for a captive audience of students forced to watch its daily advertisement-driven programming and the computer equivalent, ZapMe!, which tried to turn "the schools and the compulsory schooling laws into a means of gaining access to a captive audience of children in order to extract market research from them and to advertise to them" (Commercial Alert, 2000). Likewise, we need to be equally circumspect about the amount of advertising and marketing proliferating on Kids Only sites and via kid-safe filtering software (Schiffman, 2000).

Moreover, sustaining an internet-based market economy whereby consumer software programs and proprietary environments become the antidote to inappropriate material is directly at odds with democratic means of dealing with these issues through public discourse, political action, and critical media literacy skills. Most of the products previously analyzed are produced and distributed by profit making and publicly traded enterprises, such as the media conglomerates Time Warner, Microsoft, and Yahoo! Obviously, it is good business to create and sell blocking software products or to offer third-party rating systems that decide—for parents, educators, and librarians—what is in their (both children/students and the company's) best interests. In a self-fulfilling business transaction, reports of inappropriate content as well as media and political hype about the internet as an unsafe environment lend credence to, or create a functionalist need for, such products. As stated earlier, advertising is overlooked as inappropriate content because it is part of everyday consumer culture, unlike pornographic and hate sites, which exist beyond the boundaries of what is deemed good for children and teenagers. As Marxist philosopher Gramsci (1971) noted, hegemony works within the terrain of everyday life and requires the consent of audiences—or, in this case, parents, educators, and librarians. Hence, the commonly employed rhetorical elements that create paranoia about internet content within the mainstream attempt to reach the consent of parents and educators by inviting them to see some internet content as value-laden or problematic while camouflaging the interests and authority of a profitable computer software and hardware industry.

Although serious discussion about government regulation goes beyond the purviews of this study, several concerns must be raised regarding commercial software programs. First, the decision to block some sites over others is a subjective decision. The problem with this kind of regulation is that some groups and individuals might attempt to censor material (under the guise of concerns for safety) that threatens their own political and/or religious agenda. Dependence on commercial internet service providers and related filtering products limits the democratic principle of the free flow of

information and puts commercial enterprise at the helm of online navigation, a troubling fact given that corporate culture can often be extremely
conservative and self-serving when it comes to making censorship decisions.
In one instance, America Online was charged with using filters to block out
several web sites associated with liberal political organizations. One of the
top stories featured in *Censored 2001* was AOL's liberal blacklist, whereby
sites for the Democratic National Committee, Ralph Nader's Green Party,
Ross Perot's Reform Party, the *Coalition to Stop Gun Violence*, and *Safer Guns
Now* were labeled as "not appropriate for children" (Phillips & Project Censored, 2001, p. 111). Ironically, the youth filters did not prevent access to
nudity or conservative groups, including the National Rifle Association
(NRA). Designed for America Online by The Learning Company, an educational software company owned by Mattel, such filtering programs confirm suspicions about the process of labeling and omitting web sites according to political and economic interests.

This kind of censorship raises flags about the capabilities of large media
conglomerates to limit access to material deemed politically at odds with
commercial interests. In the same way that Disney was in a position to
revoke the distribution of *Fahrenheit 9/11*, Michael Moore's political documentary produced through Disney's Miramax film division, large multimedia conglomerates are poised to censor content that is politically or economically damaging to their enterprise.

Second, some of the trigger words used to block internet sites might be
legitimate subjects for research. For example, the often-sited example of an
internet user not being able to access research on breast cancer or sex education (if these words were denoted as trigger words) is indeed troubling.
As PC Magazine reviewers of Cybersitter 9.0 explain, "Cybersitter errs on
the conservative side, by default it may block sites you would deem okay"
(Munro, 2004, n.p.). A telling example of this problem is offered in an article featured in *Electronic School Online*. Author Kongshem (1998) wrote

> Cybersitter yanks offending words from web pages without providing a clue to
> the reader that the text has been altered. The mangled text that results from
> this intervention might change the meaning and intent of a sentence dramat-
> ically. For example, because "homosexual" is in the list of Cybersitter's forbid-
> den words, the sentence, "The Catholic church is opposed to all homosexual
> marriages" appears to the user as, "The Catholic church is opposed to all mar-
> riages." (n.p.)

Likewise, Karen Schneider, a librarian for the Environmental Protection
Agency (EPA), has led a filtering software assessment project involving
more than 30 librarians around the world. She found that filters "are not reliable and they're hard to maintain" (cited in Gebeloff, 1999). In one example, recipes using chicken breast are blocked due to sensitive word triggers.

Third, students and computer hackers have already found flaws with such programs and have managed to acquire information from sites that have been blocked. When product evaluators at *Consumer Reports* tested over nine different web content filters, including AOL's parental controls, they discovered that, although AOL offered the best protection, as much as 20% of easily located web sites containing sexually explicit content, violently graphic images, or promotion of drugs, tobacco, crime, or bigotry slipped through the filters. In fact, "NetNanny displayed parts of more than a dozen sites, often with forbidden words expunged but graphic images intact" (ConsumerReports.org, 2001, n.p.).

Fourth, there is an inherent conflict of interest when the main advocates challenging the government's attempts to protect children from online predation and pornography are the very same groups that seek to profit directly from a free marketplace of online smut. In its June 2004 press release, SafeSurf applauded the U.S. Supreme Court for its ruling in the internet pornography case *Ashcroft v. ACLU* "because the High Court concluded that internet filtering solutions, such as those originally proposed by SafeSurf over nine years ago, are a better way to proceed than the government restrictions imposed under the Child Online Protection Act" (Jules, 2004, n.p.). As the chairman of SafeSurf Ray Soular exclaimed, "This decision has revealed that the High Court has seen the *wisdom* in protecting the internet from governmental censorship and in enabling parental discretion through an intelligent filtering and labeling system. Maybe now, Congress will focus more attention on what has become known as the 'Safe Surfing' method of protecting children online" (Jules, 2004, n.p.; italics added). Yet the court's *wisdom* is more the result of intense lobbying than constitutional insight. SafeSurf has been lobbying Congress about the constitutionality of the Child Online Protection Act (COPA) since its implementation, arguing its case before the Congressional Commission on Child Online Protection in July 2000, just a few months after COPA's passage.

With laws mandating the use of various forms of censorware to meet government regulations like the Children's Internet Protection Act (CIPA) and liability issues at school, the library, or work, it is no surprise that the marketplace of ideas has increasingly channeled its financial resources into for-profit filtering products. Companies easily win over school and library administrators by guaranteeing adherence to government legislation as well as liability protection and parental approval. For $14.95, SafeSurf markets *Safe Eyes* as an effective tool that "uses the N2H2 web site database which has been proven time after time to be the most accurate database available. . . . In recent tests, both the U.S. Department of Justice and the Kaiser Family Foundation found N2H2 to be the best" (SafeSurf, 2004b). Official endorsements from prominent governmental, industry, and educational groups are an added selling point, such as N2H2's official stamp of approval from the American Library Association for meeting CIPA rules.

As for the pervasiveness of filtering products, a poll conducted as early as 1998 at the Technology and Learning conference revealed that 51% of surveyed teachers, technology directors, school board members, and other educators had adopted some form of censorware for all or some students in their district (cited in Kongshem, 1998). Another poll conducted in 2000 by MSNBC.com found that:

> many users rely on an Internet service provider, or ISP, to do the filtering for them. The big names in the market are America Online, The Microsoft Network, Mayberry USA, Rating-G Online and Getnetwise.com. Filters that are popular with Christians and conservatives include Family.Net, Integrity Online and Hedgebuilders.com. (Nodell, 2000, n.p.)

With no centralized board or groups to review the practices of these filtering companies or ISPs for their effectiveness or appropriateness, it is easy to see how those seeking to meet the needs of their schools, libraries, work, or homes turn to various programs without clear indication of their validity and reliability, especially institutions pressured to have some safety plan to meet CIPA legislation or issues of liability.

Accordingly, it is no surprise that filtering producers and marketers stand to gain financially by lobbying for nongovernmental solutions to censorship, as well as a deregulatory media environment allowing telecommunications firms to continue to merge and expand their online assets and streamline web content. MSNBC's interest in polling internet user preferences for filtering is not purely for newsworthiness given its partnership with Microsoft. The same is true for AOL Time Warner. What is more, in addition to cornering the market for libraries, schools, and homes, many of these companies have ventured into the work environment. As MSNBC .com reporter Bobbi Nodell (2000) explained, "many filter companies are moving into the corporate market, which is booming because employers are concerned about workers 'wasting time' on the job and want to keep them from shopping, checking investments and playing games . . . the corporate market is expected to grow from $60 million in 1999 to $500 million in 2004" (n.p.).

Subsequently, if the internet content accessed by K–12 youth is patrolled by capitalist institutions, rather than by the government, educational institutions, public libraries, or communitarian groups, it will inevitably become more difficult "to turn the one-way system of commercial media into a two-way process of discussion, reflection, and action" (Thoman, 1998). As Resnick (1997) explained, no matter how well conceived or executed, any labeling or blocking system will tend to stifle noncommercial communication since the time and energy needed to label will inevitably lead to many unlabeled sites: "Because of safety concerns, some people will block access to materials that are unlabeled or whose labels are untrusted. For such people, the internet will function more like broadcasting, providing access only to sites with sufficient mass-market appeal to merit the cost of labeling" (p. 106). This form of censorship is a serious problem as the possibilities for a decentralized and openly available information network will once again be delimited by a capitalist hierarchy where noncommercial or alternative sources of information will remain peripheral.

Finally, information filtering does not prepare students to learn how to analyze and evaluate information once they are no longer using the internet within an educational setting. This point has gained momentum as media literacy educators, librarians, and scholars have been grappling with the need for solid media literacy curricula that include a critical and analytical approach to learning with and about online communications technology (Fabos, 2004; Frechette, 2002; Paxson, 2004; Tyner, 1998).

DEVELOPING A CURRICULUM FRAMEWORK

In documenting the obstacles to the development of media education in the United States, Kubey (1998) contended that there is a lack of support from parents, as well as teachers and administrators, who want their children to be computer literate rather than media literate. Traditionally, *computer literacy* has referred to one's technological proficiencies using particular software or hardware components or computer applications. Computer literacy prioritizes skills-based learning that emphasizes the technological medium over the process and objective of learning. Obtaining computer skills has often been associated with upward mobility within the realm of commerce and business. As Kubey (1998) explained, "parents believe that computer expertise can equal a leg up in the job market" (p. 60). Although workplace concerns have long dominated American education, the merging of computer, information, and media literacy skills is long overdue. With the proliferation of computer-mediated information technologies in schools, students are faced with the challenge of learning not only how to acquire useful information through new technologies, but, more important, how to critically analyze and evaluate information once it has been retrieved and deciphered. This critical learning process is only becoming more arduous with the proliferation of information forms and sources.

A curriculum framework for media literacy with technology can be built using the three multiple literacies offered by Meyrowitz (1998)—media *content* literacy, media *grammar* literacy, and *medium* literacy. Teachers can "help students become critical consumers of information through an experiential learning process that teaches both 'about' and 'through' media" (Quesada & Summers, 1998, p. 30). This requires teaching methods that encourage group dialogue through the use of questioning strategies aimed at encouraging the higher levels of cognitive learning outlined in Bloom's taxonomy. For critical autonomy or independent critical thinking to be attained, students must be motivated to learn for the sake of personal empowerment, rather than acquisition of marketable skills, through analysis, reflection, synthesis, and evaluation of media. Although Bloom developed these cognitive measures well before the widespread use of computer and the internet in education, their relevancy remains. As Gilster (1997) explained, digital literacy requires "the ability to read with meaning and to understand" (p. 33) as it applies to the internet. Just as Bloom established measures for learning competencies that enable learners to make informed judgments after a series of cognitive development processes, Gilster believed that cyber-cognition demands similar measures. He explained that making informed decisions about what is found online requires knowledge acquisition through developing and applying online search skills; that analysis and synthesis come from assembling knowledge from diverse sources using internet tools, and that critical thinking must be developed "using the model of the electronic word—hypertext and hypermedia" (pp. 2–3).

Media Content Literacy

One of the most important elements of internet access involves not only how much information we can acquire, but the quality of the information we receive. When using the internet, three essential questions need asking to evaluate what we stand to gain with this new technology: (a) how well can we make discerning judgments about what we receive? (b) what ideas and issues are available on the internet? and (c) what absences and silences exist—in other words, what is *not* to be found? Unfortunately, although there is accurate and important information accessible through the internet, there is also much that is inappropriate for learning purposes. This is especially troubling for teachers. Crossman (1997) explained:

> [many] teachers whose students use the Web are concerned about the question of authenticity and reliability of information on the internet in general and the Web in particular. Even the most casual evening of Web surfing reveals incredible amounts of trivia, misinformation, bad manners, hostility, stupidity, and other vagaries of humankind. (p. 31)

Using Meyrowitz's (1998) *media-as-conduits* metaphor, Internet *content* litereracy carefully considers the value and reliability of information acquired online. Although few education models apply content literacy to the internet, library media specialists have been in the forefront of devising content literacy skills enabling students to question the veracity of the information they receive online. Drawing from Grassian's (2000) UCLA College Library online resource, there are many analytical questions to be asked when thinking critically about discipline-based internet resources. The majority of these questions center on content and evaluation.

The Information Source. One of the first evaluative questions for web resources investigates the information provider or source. By asking who the originator, creator, or author of a web site (or email) is, students can determine whether a web site represents a group, organization, institution, corporation, or governmental body. At the root of this question are concerns regarding the reliability and representativeness of the information acquired. Teachers would want their students to look at the URL address provided on the home or front page of the site to get clues as to whether the information comes from a trustworthy institution, such as a school or university, or whether it is from an anonymous individual whose credibility would need verification. It would be advisable for students to verify the qualifications of content authors, sponsors, or supporters. Students would want to find out whether the web site is officially or unofficially endorsed or sponsored by particular groups, organizations, institutions, and the like, as this again impacts on the credibility of the information acquired.

Influences on Content. The next set of evaluative questions aims to discover whether the web site or email describes or provides the results of research or scholarly effort. In terms of basic research skills, it makes sense for teachers to instill in their students a curiosity regarding whether there are sufficient references provided to other works to document hypotheses, claims, or assertions. By asking whether there is enough information to properly cite the document, students can decide whether the information they have found is appropriate for a research report. Students would want to know whether the web site/email combines educational, research, and scholarly information with commercial or noncommercial product or service marketing because this affects the underlying goals or objectives of the site.

By inquiring into the economic or political influences of internet content, students should question whether the ratio of useful information to superfluous information is adequate. They would want to pay attention to the amount of advertising, as well as unrelated graphics or links, because these factors necessarily impact the content. For instance, if information on oral hygiene is provided by the manufacturer of a toothpaste seeking to influence brand-name loyalty, students should be more skeptical of the claims being made within the site. Other profit motives include fees for the use of access to any of the information provided at a site. Naturally, students would want to determine whether such fees are warranted or whether similar information could be found for free on other sites or through other research tools. In terms of politics, students would want to discover the motives, values, and ideas influencing the content so they can better sort through and evaluate the claims and assertions projected on a web site.

Ideally, the purpose of a web site should be clearly indicated. Because this is not always the case, further investigation through the use of evaluative questions helps students better determine the motivations of the content providers.

Timeliness. Finally, the timeliness of online information would need to be fathomed so that students could discern whether the study or research on the web site/email is up to date. If the date of the information is not easily located within the content, students could look for the last update to the page or site at the bottom of the front or homepage. This enables students to judge the accuracy of the information presented based on their knowledge of recent scholarship, discoveries, or perspectives that would affect previous findings.

As Meyrowitz (1998) explained, content literacy skills are not exclusive to any media per se, but are easily applicable from one medium to another. Students can employ these same evaluative questions in studying books, newspapers, magazines, TV programs, and other texts. Certainly, internet content presents some unconventional circumstances that set it apart from other research tools. Vast amounts of information are available on any given topic, allowing students more flexibility in conducting research than a school library might offer. Nevertheless, students must first figure out how to find the type of information they are looking for, which requires skills in conducting effective online excursions using various search engines. Whereas students can always go to a librarian or teacher for search tips or strategies, it is not always easy to figure out what internet sites are worthy of perusal and which ones should be avoided. Librarians and teachers still need to offer students online resource sites that help students find educational sites that are reliable and useful.

Media Grammar Literacy

Although there is nothing novel in applying critical evaluative questions to the internet, the critical study and utilization of the internet is distinctive in terms of its media grammar and form. For this reason, media literacy in cyberspace must go beyond online *content* literacy by addressing the peculiarities of the internet as a communication technology. Media *grammar* literacy for the internet requires an understanding of the production elements used to alter people's understanding of messages communicated electronically. As such, teachers would want their students to learn graphic design principles so they could better understand how web pages are created or infused with carefully crafted signifiers. Vibrant colors, large or unusual fonts, flashing text, striking visuals, and music used to draw or divert attention need to be decoded so that students ascertain the function, intention, or goal served by the graphics, icons, and design elements.

Consequently, the basic elements of graphic design, usually reserved for art or vocational curricula, need to be integrated across the curriculum so that students can better comprehend how various production elements work to signify or connote particular meanings in cyberspace. Because the internet is necessarily nonlinear in form, there are many design elements used to feature certain areas, visuals, or links. Whether these elements are used for business, educational, or civic means, students would want to evaluate the creativity and effectiveness involved in the structural design of the message by examining: (a) what media elements are being used for communication (i.e., words, pictures, sounds, videos, animations, etc.), and (b) how content is organized (i.e., through user-controlled hypertext or hypermedia links).

As a component of media *grammar* literacy, visual literacy theory has been used to encourage students to produce and interpret *visual* messages. In *Visual Messages: Integrating Imagery Into Instruction,* Considine and Haley (1992) explained that like traditional literacy, visual literacy embraces what might be termed a reading and writing component. Students can be taught to recognize, read, recall, and comprehend visual messages. Accordingly, students who understand the design and composition of visual messages can better communicate through visual means. With the rapid increase in student-designed web pages, design elements converged around internet technology are becoming more necessary. By using the components of visual literacy that have been applied to audio, moving images, and still graphics, students can better think *about* and *through* the images and multisensory components of the internet.

Medium Literacy

Media grammar literacy, or visual literacy, includes an understanding of the *medium* and the message, the form, as well as the content. In terms of the internet, *medium literacy* would require students to examine the variables previously described in Meyrowitz's (1998) multiple literacies model and those extrapolated from Meyrowitz's sample medium variables. In particular, Internet technology impacts: (a) the multisensory types of information conveyed, as it conveys messages through visual, aural, and textual means; (b) the uni/bi/multidirectionality of the communication, which is affected by internet postings, e-mail correspondence between individuals, and chatroom discussions between two or more people; and (c) the speed and degree of immediacy in encoding, dissemination, and decoding, which are altered by the internet's instantaneous message transmission and its ability to bring otherwise disjointed individuals or groups together in nonface-to-face encounters. One of the most important applications of medium theory would lead students to examine how message variables, both content and visual, are uniquely acquired and represented in cyberspace. Students must learn to question whether the information they find is unique to the internet or is available through print and other noninternet resources. This inquiry leads students to understand the potential of the internet as a decentralized form of technology because it greatly increases the amount of information and perspectives (both dominant and nondominant) available on any given topic. This presents creative opportunities for students to find ideas and messages that infrequently unfold in mainstream media. Moreover, through user-controlled hypertext or hypermedia links, students can interactively determine what informational course they want to navigate. Educational prospects such as these can only unfold in the critical thinking classroom, whereby students are encouraged to discover, compare and contrast, and critique the messages communicated through computer information technology.

CONCLUSION

Media literacy scholar Masterman's (1985) explanation of critical autonomy, to "develop in pupils enough self-confidence and critical maturity to be able to apply critical judgments to media texts *which they will encounter in their future*" (p. 24), does not fit within the logic of commercial filters and the self-regulated corporations attempting to control and streamline internet content. As Thoman (2002) clarified, "the media have become so ingrained in our cultural milieu that we should no longer view the task of media education as providing 'protection' against unwanted messages" (n.p.). Hence, a learning model of awareness, analysis, reflection, action, and experience leads to better comprehension, critical thinking, and informed judgments.

Contrary to filtering mechanisms designed to censor or reduce student exposure to inappropriate web sites and online information, a much better approach toward new information technologies is to go beyond teaching students about how to use computers, email, web browsers, and so on. First and foremost, the goals of media literacy must go hand in hand with computer training and online access through the instruction of critical skills by which students learn to discriminate all types of information. Although there are hazards to overregulation and underregulation of the internet, educators and librarians have an important role to play in developing on-line media literacy initiatives so that students can become discerners of the types of information they need. The goals for taking media literacy to the internet must go beyond the critical evaluation and use of information to include an analysis and understanding of the impact of political and economic forces that drive and control much of the internet. Within a media literacy in cyberspace model, the issues of ownership, profit, control, and related questions are essential to helping students formulate constructive ideas for action that will impact on their own internet choices and surfing habits (Frechette, 2002). As PICS chairman Resnick (1997) admitted, "no labeling system is a full substitute for a thorough and thoughtful evaluation" (p. 108). In the end, if the power of internet content labeling, ratings, and restrictions are left to a third party or profit-making companies, then educators, librarians, and parents need to ensure that they serve the *public* interest, rather than private commercial interests.

REFERENCES

AOL. (2004). *Welcome to AOL@School.* Retrieved September 28, 2004, from http://www.aolatschool.com

Commercial Alert. (2000, January 19). *Coalition asks states to protect children from ZapMe!* News release. Retrieved on September 28, 2004, from http://www.commercialalert.org/index.php/category_id/2/subcategory_id/40/article_id/63

Considine, D., & Haley, G. (1992). *Visual messages: Integrating imagery into instruction.* Englewood, CO: Teacher Ideas Press.

ConsumerReports.org. (2001, March). *Digital chaperones for kids: Which Internet filters protect the best? Which get in the way?* Retrieved on July 12, 2004, from www.consumerreports.org/main/content/display_report.jsp

Crossman, D. (1997). The evolution of the World Wide Web as an emerging instructional technology tool. In B. H. Khan (Ed.), *Web-based instruction* (pp. 27–42). Englewood Cliffs, NJ: Educational Technology Publications.

Fabos, B. (2004). *Wrong turn on the information superhighway: Education and the commercialization of the Internet.* New York: Teachers College Press.

FBI. (2004). *A parent's guide to Internet safety.* Retrieved on September 29, 2004, from http://www.fbi.gov/publications/pguide/pguidee.htm

Frechette, J. (2002). *Developing media literacy in cyberspace: Pedagogy and critical learning for the twenty-first century classroom.* Westport, CT: Praeger.

Gebeloff, R. (1999). *Screening zone: The trouble with net filters and ratings.* Retrieved on September 28, 2004, from http://www.talks.com

GetNetWise. (2004). *AT&T.* Retrieved on September 28, 2004, from http://www.getnetwise.org/about/supporters/att

Gilster, P. (1997). *Digital literacy.* New York: Wiley.

Gramsci, A. (1971). *Selections from the prison notebooks.* New York: International Publishers.

Grassian, E. (2000). *Thinking critically about World Wide Web resources.* UCLA College Library Online Resources. Available at http://www.library.ucla.edu/libraries/college/help/critical/index.htm

Hill, L. (2000, March 29). *Second coming of cyberangels.* Retrieved on September 28, 2004, from http://www.wired.com/news/culture/0,1284,35279,00.html?tw=wn_story_related

ICRA. (2004). *About ICRA.* Retrieved on September 28, 2004, from http://www.icra.org/about/

Jules, V. (2004, June 29). *Supreme Court finds SafeSurf's solution is better than COPA.* Press release. Retrieved on September 28, 2004, from http://www.safesurf.com/press/press28.htm

Kongshem, L. (1998, January). *Censorware: How well does Internet filtering software protect students?* Retrieved on July 14, 2004, from http://www.electronic-school.com/0198fl.html

Kubey, R. (1998). Obstacles to the development of media education in the United States. *Journal of Communications, 48*(1), 58–69.

Masterman, L. (1985). *Teaching the media.* London: Comedia.

Meyrowitz, J. (1998). Multiple media literacies. *Journal of Communication, 48*(1), 96–108.

Munro, J. (2004, August 3). *Cybersitter 9.0.* Retrieved on July 14, 2004, from http://www.pcmag.com/article2/0,1759,1618830,000.asp

N2H2. (2004). *Homepage.* Retrieved July 12, 2004, from http://www.n2h2.com/products/index

Nodell, B. (2000, August 9). *Filtering porn? Maybe, maybe not: Shielding kids from the Web's dark side isn't a science yet.* Retrieved on September 28, 2004, from http://www.msnbc.com/news/438174.asp?cp1=1

Paxson, P. (2004). *Media literacy: Thinking critically about the Internet.* Lincoln, NE: GPN Educational Media.

Phillips, P., & Project Censored. (2001). *Censored 2001.* New York: Seven Stories Press.

Quesada, A., & Summers, S. L. (1998). Literacy in the cyberage: Teaching kids to be media savvy. *Technology & Learning, 18*(5), 30.

Resnick, P. (1997, March). Filtering information on the internet. *Scientific American,* pp. 106–108.

Ruskin, G. (2003, September 30). *Commercial alert asks FCC, FTC to require disclosure of product placement on TV.* Retrieved on September 28, 2004, from http://www.commercialalert.org/index.php/category_id/I/subcategory.html

SafeSurf. (2004a). *SafeSurf: The original rating system.* Retrieved on September 28, 2004, from http://www.safesurf.com

SafeSurf. (2004b). *SafeEyes.* Retrieved on September 28, 2004, from http://www.safesurf.com/filter/safeeyes.htm

Schiffman, B. (2000, November 28). *ZapMe kills computers in the classroom.* Retrieved on September 30, 2004, from http://www.forbes.com/2000/11/28/1127zapme.html

Shyles, L. (2003). *Deciphering cyberspace: Making the most of digital communication technology.* Thousand Oaks, CA: Sage.

Silver, D., & Garland, P. (2004). "Shop online!" Advertising female teen cyberculture. In P. Howard & S. Jones (Eds.), *Society online: The Internet in context* (pp. 157–171). Thousand Oaks, CA: Sage.

Thoman, E. (2002). *Media literacy for the '90s—U.S. style.* Retrieved June 15, 2005, from http://www.medialit.org/reading_room/article128.html

Tyner, K. (1998). *Literacy in a digital world: Teaching and learning in the age of information.* Mahwah, NJ: Lawrence Erlbaum Associates.

U.S. Census Bureau. (2001). *Home computers and internet use in the United States.* Washington, DC: U.S. Government Printing Office.

Williams, T. (2003, October 23). *AOL@SCHOOL expands its free online learning service with new alliances and expanded relationships with industry leaders.* Retrieved September 28, 2004, from http://www.lexisnexis.com/universe

IDENTITIES AND ONLINE COMMUNITIES

Following on from the internet research presented in Part II, the chapters in Part III address different aspects of online communities, focusing specifically on the experience of girls, on gay and lesbian youth, on blogging, and on informal learning in online communities. Together the chapters provide fascinating insights into how identities are being practiced, defined, supported, and experimented with in different online cultures.

In chapter 10, "It's a gURL Thing: Community Versus Commodity in Girl-Focused Netspace," Michele Polak contrasts corporate web sites aimed at tween and teen girls with web sites designed by the girls themselves. The chapter outlines how company-owned and -created web sites have found an audience in the rising trend of *gurls*, the computer-savvy girl who surfs the net with avid familiarity. These web sites offer gurls advice, information, and a netspace to claim as their own. What is also prevalent, however, is commodification: Most of the web sites created for gurls by corporations exist to promote company-produced products. Such web sites are rhetorically designed in ways to cater to this generation of girls—ones with spending power. The visual design with such web sites is traditionally girl-designated while enforcing the rhetoric of the site's commodity-driven purpose. This girl-focused netspace is not limited to commodity rhetoric, however, as gurl-created web sites replace the presence of commodity with community. Here, gurls have designed their own web sites, shifting site content to include community in a text that is written in the familiar language gurls utilize in online forums such as chatrooms and message boards. This shift from commodity to community may prove that girls of this digital generation are more rhetorically aware than many media creators assume.

Chapter 11 follows on from Polak's chapter by examining blogging, a particularly popular activity with teenage girls. In this chapter, Lois Ann Scheidt analyses what she terms the *unseen audiences* of blogs. Unlike the paper-based adolescent diaries of previous generations, which primarily served as personal archives, in monologue, for thoughts and daily activities, blogs are publicly accessible spaces where adolescents can target their words to a variety of different external audiences in spaces that allow writers to develop active dialogues with their readers. In these spaces, the familiar assumptions that the diary is kept only for the diarist and that it is an intensively secretive and private enterprise need to be rethought. Clues to their idealized or known audiences can be found in the narratives that diarists or bloggers create. The research for this chapter classifies adolescent blogs into five categories, referring to the types of audiences for narrative performances. The implicit and explicit readers are categorized in the following terms: as witnesses to the experiences reported on in the story; as therapists and emotional supporters of the storyteller; as cultural critics commenting on the events that produced the story; as narrative analysts of the systems of discourse embedded in the narrative; or as passive observers.

Julia Davies (chap. 12, this volume) also looks at young people's online communication by focusing on two very specific online groups; wiccan and a community of young people with myalgic encephalopathy (ME). Davies describes how teenagers' use of digital technologies allows them a nomadic existence, offering opportunities to experiment with voice and identity. Digital technologies facilitate young people's chances to keep in perpetual contact and demonstrate that they inhabit the same life rhythms as each other. This anchors *screenagers* to a sense of community that has been referred to as a *virtual ideology*, which is collectivist in orientation. This chapter provides evidence from two teenage online communities and uses the notion of *communities of practice* to help understand the evolution and development of the groups' respective cultural practices. The analysis is based on evidence from web sites and message boards, as well as from online correspondence with members of the communities. The chapter explores how the lives of participants are enriched by their internet activities and looks at how they negotiate relationships and skills that benefit them in both their offline and online worlds. It suggests that although these communities can be highly beneficial to individuals and the groups to which they belong, there is also an important role for more formal systematic teaching, albeit using an approach that takes account of how digital technology works socially and culturally and its embeddedness in users' lives.

The role of online communities in providing support for young people is analyzed further in Susan Driver's "Virtually Queer Youth Communities of Girls and Birls: Dialogical Spaces of Identity Work and Desiring Exchanges" (chap. 13, this volume). This chapter explores the creative expansion of youth-oriented and -produced web sites, analyzing some specific developments of grassroots projects such as e-zines, online communities, and news groups created by, for, and about youth who have been historically marginalized within mainstream commercial mass media. It focuses on self-defined *grrrls*, challenging sexist media, and queer youth working to affirm their differences and challenge heteronormativity. The transformative approaches adapted by youth internet projects effectively destabilize binary forms of meaning-making through which youth make sense of their identities beyond reified social norms and ideals, as dynamically in flux. This chapter analyzes a few web sites in depth for the unique ways they design and utilize multimedia images/words as a process of self-representation and communication. This involves a detailed interpretation of the visual and narrative styles that make up counterhegemonic youth cultures on the internet. Languages are studied for how they generate participatory dialogues among youth on specific social issues affecting their lives locally. At the same time, the analysis examines common elements that link diverse internet sites together in terms of content and form, thereby suggesting some global dimensions of new media.

The chapters in this section provide insights into the communicational activities of young people online, particularly how communication supports the important role of online communities. In contrast to public discussions that are often characterized by portrayals of young people helplessly being subjected to various online risks, together the chapters give evidence that the internet is providing valuable audiences for many different purposes, as well as development of communities for encouragement, entertainment, advice, and support.

Chapter 10

It's a gURL Thing:
Community Versus Commodity
in Girl-Focused Netspace

Michele Polak
Miami University

"You asked what was wrong and I said nothing. Then I turned around and whispered everything" (Jennifer, 2004). I found this quotation on the home page of an AOL-hosted web site entitled *Jennifer's Hell*. As a scholar doing research on online discourse, I find it difficult to avoid the large part of the internet that has been appropriated by gURLs, a virtual space that is surfed, occupied, created, criticized, and well managed by tech-savvy girls. That girls would occupy such a space, one both private and public at the same time, is curious because given the option to speak aloud—or occupy space and claim recognition—is not a position of familiarity or comfort for most adolescent girls and many girls often opt for silence and nonrecognition of their identity. The move to silence in girls at the onset of adolescence has been well documented by girl culture researchers. Pipher (1994) wrote, "Something dramatic happens to girls in early adolescence" (p. 19); Stern (2002b) noted, "Girls use their silence as a strategy for navigating safely through life" (p. 226); and Gilligan (1982), the psychologist who first noted the shifting of voice as girls reach adolescence, indicated that, "Girls struggle against losing voice and against creating an inner division or split" (p. xxiii). That Jennifer would choose to place such a quotation on her home page, however, is fitting: The internet has allowed her to be comfortable in the familiarity of her silence, yet has also allowed her a space to explore the voice she is learning to use. Jennifer uses her voice in this space well, by creating a home page full of graphics and animations and a banner that reads: "Can't sleep. Clowns will eat me."

As Driver argues in this volume (chap. 13), "Youth make use of the internet as a realm to try out, play with, and perform their identities and desires through provisional combinations of images, words, and narratives." As such a platform for exploration, cyberspace allows girls to enter in search of identity, in search of a voice. A venue that allows the preteen or teen girl to try out her changing identity and maturing voice against—or with—both textual and graphical imagery can offer a step toward empowerment, leading to that sense of self that often eludes the adolescent girl. As such a space, a girl-focused netspace that is permeated by all interests marked *girl* is occupied by web sites designed *for* girls and *by* girls, all adding their pages to a girl-defined virtual space.

Yet the internet, however vast and malleable it may be, needs to be evaluated in terms of purpose and audience interaction if it is going to contribute to the development of adolescent girls. When I began analyzing girl-focused netspace, a clear division became evident: There are web sites created for girls by corporate sponsors—commercial web sites—that are clearly marked for promoting consumer culture (Hawisher & Sullivan, 1999, p. 274), offering girls a space that allows for play and sometimes interaction. Yet the concept of product is always in the forefront, framing these web sites in a commodity structure; web sites created for girls by nonprofit or educational sponsors—institutional web sites (Hawisher & Sullivan, 1999, p. 277)—teetering between aiding the growth of girls' development and benefiting the sponsor who hosts the site; and personal web sites created by the girls, with no commercial input unless hosted on a freeserver, which limits commercial ads to top or side banners. The audience is clear in these personal web sites: girls and all things girl defined both by textual input and imagery. The rhetorical aim for the personal web site is overwhelmingly to build community. Here girls have created a space for playing with identities and for their voices not only to be heard (or seen), but also to be shared with other girls—a space in which girls can enter and speak in their own language and with content that best addresses their interests. A space to enter is exactly what the developing adolescent girl most needs.

The metaphor of navigation through unfamiliar space is prevalent in the many texts that discuss girls and their relation to the cultural environment. As early as 1982, Gilligan noted that there is often "an active process of dissociation, of knowing and then not knowing" (p. xxii), a moment of uncertainty when a girl's identity is not yet established. Pipher (1994) argued that the surrounding cultural environment makes claiming an identity difficult because girls "are coming of age in a more dangerous, sexualized and media-saturated culture" (p. 12). This loss of self and loss of voice hinders not only emotional stability through adolescence, but also creates a fragmented self as girls enter into adulthood: "The edge of adolescence," argued Brown and Gilligan (1992), "has been identified as a time of heightened psychological risk for girls" (p. 2). Eating disorders, sexual promiscuity, and body modification such as cutting and branding are patterns that develop in adolescence and can carry into adulthood. Girls often take to "writing on the body" in this manner in their struggle to find their voice, a space in which to be recognized. Girls' struggle to be seen and heard is not just manifested in such physical acts, but also in "the makings of an inner division as girls come to a place where they feel they cannot say or feel or know what they have experienced" (Brown & Gilligan, 1992, p. 4). Silent girls grow up to be silent women as "[w]ith loss of voice also comes loss of self" (Iglesias & Cormier, 2002, p. 259). This notion of navigation becomes one of difficulty given the cultural environment that girls must learn to manage in the search for their sense of self. The sexualization of Western culture, in which a well-defined body image plays a role in popularity, can often be a negative force in an adolescent girl's development. Add to it the trappings of commercial advertising and girls barely stand a chance.

COMMERCIAL WEB SITES

"Think GIRL POWER to the Max! Fashion, accessories, toys and so much more. . . . In other words—it's all about YOU!"

—EverythingGirl.com

As American girls alone are "spend[ing] $60 billion [dollars] annually" (Dunn, 1999, p. 108), it is important to recognize the impact that consumer culture has on adolescent development. Quart (2003) noted that "kids are forced to embrace the instrumental logic of consumerism at an earlier-than-ever age" (p. xii), and this notion of buying products is what helps fuel the social spaces that girls occupy. The commodification of youth culture does not offer a position girls are able to navigate when a lack of ability in reason or maturity might hinder choices made. Reaching the buyer is the main purpose for advertisers, and what better way to create a cultural product than to make the product part of the cultural language of the consumer? Although access for use and command of Internet activities is still unarguably class- and culturally defined, online discourse is better utilized by this generation of youth than the previous ones. For advertisers aiming to market to the current youth generation, cyberspace is a logical medium as "the Internet is [. . .] a force for peer-to-peer marketing" (Quart, 2003, p. 39), with the communal sharing of information among its users. Girls have become major players in cyberspace. Do the proper cyber-search for girls web site (omitting the words *sex* and *sexy*) and your results will total in the thousands. Stern (2002a) noted, "by offering self-selected descriptors, girls more easily create the selves they want others to perceive" (p. 271), and with the personal versus private platform that the internet allows, identity is up for grabs. As Addison and Comstock (1998) noted in their work on youth and cyberspace, "Electronic networks make it especially difficult and inadvisable to draw fixed borders between on-line and off-line cultures and subcultures" (p. 370). Creating a consumer culture online to parallel that of real-time culture was destined to become successful because there is no separation here: Girls visit commercial web sites as they shop the mall, "wield[ing] tangible power in dictating popular culture [. . .] confident consumers, secure in their opinions" (Dunn, 1999, p. 111). The rhetorical aims of such web sites, however, need to be addressed.

My analysis revealed that seldom is a commercial site designed with a girl and her still-forming identity in mind. Although outwardly the site may consist of images that match contemporary girl interests and the visual layout may be pleasing to a young conventionally feminine eye with girl-defined colors and images, the purpose is pure product promotion. Commercial web sites design pages created in template and column format, which run ads in banners, usually on two or more sides, completely framing the page in product. Procter and Gamble's *beinggirl.com*—"There's lots to explore about being a girl" (beinggirl.com, 2004)—is a web site created for both the younger teen and the older teen, with topics varying from "Self-Discovery" to "Private Issues." Although the site does offer an option for girls to post questions and opinions, it is completely framed in graphics of the company's feminine sanitary product line. The site content maintains its focus on puberty and the physical aspects of the growing adolescent girl, but much of this is meshed in with different advertising on each page through its banners and sidebars of the same products. Unlike the banners on freeservers, which host many girls' personal pages, commercial web sites' banners often include animation. Thus, not only is the page framed in product, but the product promotion rotates the entire time the page is onscreen. In addition, pop-up boxes occur every time the user moves to a new screen, thus offering more product promotion. In magazine web sites such as *ELLEgirl.com* (http://ellegirl.com/eg/) or *CosmoGIRL.com* (http://cosmogirl.com/), ads appear not only for subscriptions to the magazines, but also for the products sold within its pages. Essentially, commercial web sites may allow for a girl-focused netspace, but it is one that must be shared with marketing.

A girl-focused netspace is seldom guaranteed on commercial web sites. For example, *kylieklub.com* (http://www.kylieklub.com/), a web site hosted by the British department store, Mackays, emphasizes a club environment, with club activities and discount benefits for members. On the site, however, members have no real interaction: Girls cannot actually submit any writing, nor are there forums for posting. *Barbie.com* is another web site that limits interaction with other girls. Although the parent's page emphasizes,

"*Barbie.com*'s mission is to engage, enchant, and empower girls" (Site Mission, 2004), there is no forum within the site for girls to use their own voice. As much as these web sites may create a space for girls to play, offering quizzes, polls, and games, the only real interaction for girls in many of these commercial web sites is to submit names and email addresses, making girls part of the company database, securing their position as a demographic. Mattel's *EverythingGirl.com*, a site that showcases a variety of Barbie-related dolls, opens the top left corner of their site with "NEW? Join now!" (EverythingGirl.com, 2004) and provides login spaces for members who have already joined the site. Joining requires not only an email address from the user, but also a parent's email address.

For many of these web sites, demographics will show that there is a girl market, and the site design plays to such a market. Many commercial web sites exhibit conventional and stereotypical girl imagery in their design using stock photography and pastel colors. A Procter & Gamble competitor in the feminine sanitary product industry, Kimberly-Clark, offers *girlspace.com* (http://www.girlspace.com/), a site much like beinggirl.com with quizzes, polls, and games focusing on adolescent health care. The site background can be chosen by the user with options of "flower-riffic" pink, "groovy green," "blue dazzle," and "jump 'n roll" yellow, with changes in artwork such as flowers and butterflies. *zip4tweens.com* (http://www.cool-2b-real.com/), a site created by America's Beef Producers aimed at promoting more red meat consumption among America's adolescent girls, exhibits pink, lavender, and yellow pastel backgrounds with ornate fonts for text. Balloons and smiley faces are used to anchor headings in each column or as link buttons to open new pages. What these conventionally feminine design formats do is inscribe a specific idea of what constitutes *girl* and seldom allow the girl who is searching for that sense of self to explore beyond what consumer culture provides her. In reality, "the idea of a girl market locating a specific demographic of girls is confounded by the difficulty of defining girls," according to Driscoll (2002, p. 268)—girls "who dramatically exceed, even for marketing discourses, any singular age range or other criteria." By confining girls to the narrative of the conventional feminine, even in visual representation, girls' voices are silenced.

INSTITUTIONAL WEB SITES

"Who says girls aren't good at math and science?"

—*girlsinc.com*

Silencing is a theme that must be addressed in relation to girl-focused netspace, where institutional web sites are concerned as these web sites often vacillate between promoting empowerment and creating a false sense of girl space. Web sites such as *girlsinc.org* (http://www.girlsinc.org/gc/) have social organizations behind them that might ensure users that they create a space for girls in which healthy and positive messages are available. Institutional web sites can offer marginalized girls a space for exploration and learning about their own cultural community free from the trappings of commodification. *sistagirls.org* (http://www.sistagirls.org/) is one such site. Not only is the content posted by the host organizations of institutional web sites geared toward the healthy development of the adolescent girl, such web sites accept submissions from girls, allowing them to explore their developing identities and voice. *SmartGirl.org* (http://www.smartgirl.org/), an institutional site sponsored by the National Science Foundation and the University of Michigan, offers three main pages for their users: "Speak Out," with forums for offering opinions on posted questions; "Express Yourself," a creative writing forum; and "Spread the Word," with options for girls to write reviews, articles, and commentaries on a variety of topics. Many institutional web sites offer several outlets for discussion, such as electronic bulletin boards, and (like commercial web sites) quizzes, polls, and games. These are the web sites often recommended by educators and in after-school programs, which is why many of them receive heavy traffic: Users can be assured to interact with a variety of girls of different ages and from diverse backgrounds.

I hold institutional web sites up to the same rhetorical analysis as commercial web sites, however. As Hawisher and Sullivan (1999) noted in their research on women and cyberspace, "institutional sites emphasize dispensing information, though not from an innocent or neutral position" (p. 277), and this is evident in many of these web sites. Feminist author Audrey Brashich hosts a site for girls entitled *Culture of Modeling*, for example, complete with a message board for asynchronous discussion. Although such a space for girls can be lauded for promoting critical discussion with forum titles such as "What Profession Should Earn the Most Money?", it should be noted that the first forum on this message board is "Help Audrey With Magazine Articles She's Writing!" (Brashich, 2004). Like commercial web sites, girl-focused netspace in some institutional web sites is shared with the host site's main purpose—one that may not necessarily be completely oriented toward girls.

A shared space is what must be accounted for when considering silence or space for voice. What type of censoring occurs if a girl's input does not coincide with a web site's theme or audience? Moderators are often an issue. Jake, who is credited as the site tech coordinator, moderates *purple pyjamas*, an all-girl community-created site. Jake is also referred to as the "PurplePJ's knight in shining armor" (Spotlight, 2004), an indication that girls might not actually be capable of running the site. In addition, keeping a site active and current is never an issue with commercial web sites because they must promote the most recent and available product. With institutional web sites, however, an active site is not always available. Because many of these web sites are created and posted by summer workshops or after-school programs, they are not always kept current once the program ends. *gURLwURLd.com* (http://www.gURLwURLd.com/), for example, a web site created during an after-school program in Austin, Texas, was last updated in September 2000. An outdated web site such as this limits the opportunity for girls to interact on a web site because links often become inactive and both content and graphics can become outdated.

Interaction is important for girl-focused netspace because interaction leads to community building. In writing about voice and identity development in girls and women, Iglesias and Cormier (2002) realized that "what adolescent girls desperately want is real communication" (p. 267). Because "when they are not in school, [girls] most spend their waking hours with one form or another of electronic equipment, sometimes simultaneously" (Dunn, 1999, p. 108), electronic media is a familiar tool for girls' communication. Many contemporary girls know how to use the tools of digital technology, and their input to the many web sites created for them is clear evidence to this argument. Dunn (1999) pointed out that "this is the first generation [. . .] to grow up with true images of female empowerment" and perhaps because of this, "leagues of articulate, thoughtful, and strong girls are actively creating and maintaining progirl home pages" (Takayoshi, 1999, p. 95).

PERSONAL WEB SITES

> "Wendy. Female. Chinese-Canadian. From Hong Kong. 16 years. High school. Grade ten. Hetero. Lives in Ontario, Canada. Aries. Not as boy-crazy. Romantic. Opinionated."
>
> —Wendy, *Overprotected*

I have found that personal web sites fall into the position of combining both the pop culture and contemporary content interests of commercial web sites and the empowerment messages created by institutional web sites. Here is where gURLs—and they self-identify as gURLs—are finding a girl-focused netspace free from product promotion and censors with a guaranteed space for their voice and space for creating identity, both textually and visually. In her writing about girls and cyberspace, Takayoshi (1999) emphasized, "by recognizing that girls have created spaces in what can be a hostile environment, we reveal that girls are not powerless (as the negative representations of the web would suggest), but they may have overcome significant challenges in creating Web space for themselves" (p. 96). Likewise, Quart (2003) argued, "teen authors have become the architects of their own trademarked identities, strong-willed and mercenary in equal measure" (p. 177). gURLs can find a sense of self here, creating not only a girl space for their own voices, but a space for other girls to interact, argue, discuss, brag, and vent about anything with no limitation on topics tied to any traditional feminine narrative. gURLs voice opinions on topics ranging from the latest beauty product to world politics. With the anonymity the internet provides, a diversity of themes are up for discussion.

gURLs' personal web sites are not hard to find, and many are listed in the several hundred home page directories that inhabit cyberspace. A directory may list a variety of different home pages by creators both male and female; well-maintained directories offer a description of not only the site theme, but a small biography of the site owner. When entering the gURL community, it is easily recognized that home pages are grouped by interest and similarities: Fan web sites and fan listings, for example, reflect the site owner's interest, usually in an issue related to popular culture. Such web sites often share graphics pulled from several sources and seldom are officially approved by the interest they promote. Electronic bulletin boards and forums for discussion are also grouped together by interest, with specifications on the level of moderator activity. Graphics and blends are web sites created strictly for showcasing knowledge of digital graphic and painter programs. Such web sites offer not only server space for members, but also competitions, tutorials, and design feedback. Portals are web sites in which gURLs use web cams to communicate. Collectives, cliques, webrings, and listings are all grouped by interest or common theme.

gURLs' home pages—and *pages*, plural, is appropriate because some web sites contain links to many screens depending on the amount of information in the site—vary visually, some elaborately constructed with digital art created by the gURLs, some with clip art pulled from around the web. Depending on the age of the gURL and her level of technological expertise, gURLs may design their pages using a template provided by a software program or use computer coding to work outside a restrictive design framework. Content, however, is usually consistent among the pages: There is always a biography that reveals either age, location, sometimes either a screen name or a real name, or a mixture of all these elements. Many biographies also include photographs of the site owner/creator. All web sites also include some way of reaching the gURL by way of email. Some gURL web sites include the owners' writing, from poetry to essays they may have written for a class assignment or digital artwork created either by hand and scanned or with the aid of graphics programs. There may be links to quizzes, polls, and games, and there is often a listing of pop culture interests such as favorite films or TV shows. What seems to be currently popular in many web sites is the central location of blogs, or weblogs, the daily journal of the site's creator. In addition to blogs, a user may find tagboards, which allow for responses from readers. Many web sites include a site map, and here is where users can navigate pages of links to things that may not be prominent on the home page.

Tori's Stories (http://www.taskoski.com/tori/index.html), the home page of 11-year-old American Tori, is an entry-level example of gURLs' home pages. Basic in its design, Tori's picture is the largest image on the page, with wrapped text stating who she is and link information running down the left side of the page. The home page background is a clip art graphic of a chalkboard with ruled lines that represent school homework paper. Her links include "Read A Story," which are posted essays about class trips and short stories, and "Soccer," which includes pictures of Tori in her soccer uniform beginning at age 6. Compare Tori's home page to that of 15-year-old Canadian Sarika whose *Without Love* (http://sarika.avania.co .uk/) home page changes design on a rotating basis. Sarika's page seldom exhibits a basic design format as images sometimes frame the page, some-times balancing text on either side. She often plays with colors for her page and routinely changes the images to match her popular culture interests. Central to Sarika's page is her blog, which often discusses not only personal issues in her life, but the process and ideas on how her home page is de-signed. Links on Sarika's page include "Where To?", a navigation sidebar for the many pages in her site, and "Right Now?", a listing of Sarika's cur-rent interests and emotional state of being. There is certainly an indication that for many gURLs, a home page "crafts a self out of [their] textual and graphical choices" (Hawisher & Sullivan, 1999, p. 281). In every gURL site, without fail, are links to other gURL web sites as either a collective, an affili-ation, a webring, or a signature in a guest book (which is often signed by adding a URL).

It is here that gURLs' personal web sites differ from commercial or insti-tutional web sites. The rhetorical purpose here is community. I have yet to find a gURL site that does not list links to other gURL and gURL-related web sites. Many of these web sites structurally support each other by sharing artwork or frames for design. It is common to see the same gURLs posting in various web sites within a webring. Despite many of these gURLs knowing each other only virtually (geographical distance most likely prohibiting real-life meetings), they know each other well, and many of the discussions and arguments that arise in the text reveal this. As Davies (chap. 12, this vol-ume) argues in her research on teens online, "they develop a sense of self as part of such groups," and in gURL web sites, it is clear that community is central to the exploration of self. Although gURL web sites can be just as moderated and censored as both commercial and institutional web sites— they are at the whim of their owner after all—community is the purpose, an exploratory space for sharing, and so keeping users interacting with the site is purpose alone for allowing voice. Stern (2002b) noted that gURLs "use their home pages as a forum of self-disclosure, especially as a place to engage in self-expression" (p. 224). As girls venture outside that space of silence and make attempts at using their voice, creating identity, they search for like-minded individuals to garner support. Finding an entire community only enforces that support system.

What I find most exciting about surfing personal web sites is the vast variety of experience that gURLs bring to this space and how cleverly they use it. Some web sites are basic in content and the design clearly follows a template provided by a freeserver host space. *JessicaOnline* (http://www .geocities.com/jessicataurins/), owned by 11-year-old Australian Jessica, is hosted at Geocities and is created using the host site's software program. The design is gridded, divided into six sections, each containing links to different pages. Likewise, *Laura's World* (http://www.angelfire.com/la2/ lbeanz/), hosted at Angelfire, a freeserver site created for building web sites, exhibits 13-year-old Canadian Laura's page. Like the simple elements found in Tori's page, Laura uses the central design space to introduce herself, with the left side of the page reserved for links. In addition, she plays with animations of bouncing flowers and deflating smiley faces. When a gURL moves from freeserver space to owning her own site domain (usually paying a monthly or yearly fee), her design experience becomes part of the visual space that is viewed. *Sweet Catastrophe* (http://nikki.twenty-five.org/), owned by 17-year-old Nikki from Australia, includes not only the lyrics of a song superimposed over a blend of images, but also a blog central to the design space with links to her other graphic work. *Blueberry Wings* (http:// www.blueberry-wings.org/home.html), a blend/fan listing site owned by 16-year-old Tina from Germany, uses her central design space to encase a scroll bar template, which exhibits her blog and links to other pages within her site. For Tina's site, the scroll bar portion becomes part of the design layout and part of the artwork, the same color as the images that frame the site.

As Hawisher and Sullivan (1999) have pointed out, girls online "manage to use visual discourse to construct multiply rich selves" (p. 288). Their use of color and imagery often differs from what commercial and institutional web sites exhibit, and this in itself is a visual rhetoric. gURLs are often aware of the feminine stereotypes to which they have been confined, and many make the effort to break out of that structure when designing their web sites. One gURL writes on her home page, "The color scheme for this page is magenta, not pink. THIS is pink, thank you" (Bad Girls, 2003), and she provides a color bar of pastel pink against a bright magenta background. On a home page entitled *FizzY poP* (http://www.angelfire.com/bc/ fizzzypop/), the site creator chose to code the title and the heading above a

list of links, "YO CHEK these OUT," the same color as the page background. Readers of this site on opening see no text unless they use their
cursor to highlight the page, thus making any invisible text the color of the
highlight preference set in their computer software. gURLs often play with
both imagery and text in this manner, and knowing how to read the design
elements in many of these web sites is part of recognizing the emerging
voice gURLs are finding in such a netspace. Photos in the biography area
may be jumbled in screen static until a cursor pass reveals a clear image, allowing the site owner to both hide and reveal herself at the same time.
Fonts may be distorted or pasted into the page in reverse, mirror direction,
a play on how the text should read both by content and image. Colors such
as deep purples, browns, blacks, and monochromatic hues of one color palette replace the conventionally feminine of pastels. gURLs are clear on who
they want to be online, and very few home pages parallel the description of
who the commercial web sites think girls might be.

The styles in which gURLs write also create part of this visual rhetoric.
Younger gURLs have adapted *netspeak* using letters and numbers in linguistically different combinations. On one freeserver site created by a 12-year-
old American girl, a poem to her friends reads: THoSe MaNY DaYs We
sPeNT ToGeTHa../THeY WiLL aLwAyZ STaY iN mY <3 4eVa (HeY GuYz -
n- GiRLiEs!! I <3 YoU aLL, 2004)—a playful use of both capital and lowercase letters, with the "<3" representing a sideways heart. Older gURLs also
frequently play with linguistic styles, creating elements of a new language
within the community. There is an appropriation of the word *girl*, for example, and many gURLs wear that title with pride, using it to create links to
their biographies, such as with "the girl most likely" or simply, "The Girl."
Home page titles for owned domains reveal a side of a gURL that commercial web sites may not realize: *anti-reality* (http://anti-reality.net/), *Punk
Pixie* (http://www.punk-pixie.net/blends/main.htm), *not so graceful moments* (http://graceful.yellow-bubbles.net/index2.html), *Frisky Butterfly*
(http://frisky.cuddle-bug.net/indexx.html), and *Life On Display* (http://
lod.lost-memories.net/) are examples of titles that may be an indication of
an identity the site owner is attempting to create. However, much as commercial web sites may try to be current and contemporary, language styles
here are very fluid, and this is also what separates the commercial sites from
gURLs' personal home pages.

But it is the growing need for community in personal web sites that sets
them apart. Eleven-year-old Ashli from the United Kingdom titles her
home page "If Your [*sic*] a Girl You've Come to the Right Place Because
This Place is Just For Girls!" Her site links to "cool web sites that are just for
girls" (Ashli, 2002). American 14-year-old, Kelly, owns *A World Full of Drama*,
a personal web site that features a blog, pictures of Kelly and her friends,
and a links page that is introduced with, "Here are some links of friends. . . .

If you want to be put on here then just email me or tag me one hehe . . ."
(Kelly, 2003). Like Ashli, links to girl-specific web sites are provided; link titles include "Rachel's Journal" and "Brittany's Poetry." Although links to
both commercial and institutional web sites created for girls are posted in
many personal pages, Stern (2002a) found that "the most common type of
links girls presented was to other girls' homepages" (p. 281). *Toxic-Bliss*
(http://toxic-bliss.org//), a personal site created by 18-year-old Akasha
from Canada, lists not only links to a collective—a listing of all the web sites
by an individual owner categorized with similar web sites (such as fan listings)—but also affiliates, which may be web sites of personal interest to the
site owner or web sites of similar style. For Akasha's page, she adds links to
family listings, which are other web sites that are hosted by the same server
as the one that hosts her site. In addition, Akasha links to a random hostee,
other web servers that host yet more personal pages. From this one site
alone, links to personal pages are endless, and this is very common in the
community building among gURLs. Essentially, a gURL can find the link to
one personal page through a web directory and from there navigate her
way inside a completely girl-focused netspace.

Much of this community building creates a bonding over shared interests, ideas, and platforms for interaction. Many pages list personal interests
as either a central feature in the design or as a linked page. In addition to
personal writing and artwork, many gURLs will share music selections, with
either a song overplaying as the page opens or a playlist with links to MP3
files and lyrics to favorite songs. Graphic web sites that are created for featuring artwork, such as blend web sites, are hosted at domains with larger
server space so that users can save their artwork to the site. Challenges are
often posted at such blend web sites, and collective work is created with one
person starting an image and saving it on the server, with other community
members adding to it until the completed image is then posted and archived. Blog postings on personal pages reveal intimate issues, and allowing
for responses to the tagboard opens up discussion among users. This sharing of interests and intimacies is part of the process of building a strong
sense of self. By adding a link to their site in a Webring or by joining an online collective, these gURLs are finding like-minded individuals who not
only allow for a voice, but also help create a space that contributes to the
formation of identity.

In writing about voice and identity development in girls and women,
Iglesias and Cormier (2002) wrote, "girls from diverse groups need to be
given ways to tell their stories" (p. 269), and personal web sites have allowed
for such stories, told not only by the gURLs who have created these web
sites, but also by the gURLs who read and post to them. I find postings on
personal web sites, both in text and graphics, very revealing. The personal
and private space often meshes together for gURLs as they make attempts

at being heard—in many cases, to find support or others like them. As Hawisher and Sullivan (1999) discovered, women online "begin to forge new social arrangements by creating a visual discourse that startles and disturbs" (p. 287). The same is true of gURLs, and this is perhaps even more powerful given their still-forming identity. *Tragic-Beauty*, a site owned by 17-year-old Amber from the United States, uses a blog as its central design. A posting on July 17, 2004, revealed Amber's struggle with body modification as she spent the day with her grandmother: "She was screeching at me, to wear a shorter shirt so i pulled my sleeve up and was like **I Can't**. She automatically went into 'sad grandma' mode and started lecturing me about how I should've called her instead of cutting." This same entry also reveals Amber's struggle with her emerging sexuality: "My cousin ronda already suspects I'm a dyke cause I have nothing but girls on my [computer] desktop" (Amber, 2004). It is in this hybrid of personal and private space that gURLs are able to play with their identities, using such space to maintain their anonymity while garnering support from a community that interacts.

It is important not to avoid the issue of social inequalities here, as internet access can only happen in specifically marked socioeconomic settings. Aside from the hardware required, a gURL must also have a working knowledge of the software needed to design web sites; the vast variety of home pages available reveals a range of existing experience. The benefit of institutional web sites is the opportunity for *all* girls to have that virtual space to play in; while personal web sites are communal, *how* much interaction is still at the discretion of the site owner. Over the last few years, there has been a change in the diversity of gURLs online. Although once American, Canadian, and British gURLs dominated girl-focused netspace, this space has since opened to include Western and Eastern European, South American, and Middle Eastern gURLs. There seems to be a large subculture in itself based on the J-Pop phenomena (Japanese popular culture), which has opened up girl-focused netspace to many Asian gURLs.

With the internet having few limits, I also need to address where boys lie in relation to cyberspace. Whereas directories for gURLs' personal web sites are numerous in search engines, both Stern (2002b) and Takayoshi (1999) agreed that "there is no corresponding collection of boys' sites on the Web." I have found that of the personal web sites created by boys, the majority were created by boys in their late teens and older, with younger boys' web sites focusing on the gaming community. This is not to say that boys do not interact on gURL web sites; on older gURLs' web sites, they often do. gURLs, however, manage a loud and commanding voice online. If a boy (or an adult) has entered a space that has been marked as personal or private for a specific community, or he has not been invited into discussion, members will react by *trolling* him out, calling him on his presence, and rejecting his posts by either ignoring him or having his IP (Internet Protocol address) banned by the site owner. Posts by someone other than a gURL can be identified in a variety of ways: through language use, style, and the context of posts, given the community and the environment in which it appears. gURLs recognize when someone other than a gURL is present among the community, and they are very protective of their space. I do want to emphasize, however, that although the owner's gender and age are often reflected both explicitly and implicitly in the site framework (Stern 2002b), there is no real guarantee that members are who they say they are—and this, of course, is why this space for shifting identities can be both safe *and* dangerous for gURLs.

CONCLUSION

Many commentators have attested to the silencing of adolescent girls without a venue to explore their voice and create an identity. Gilligan (1982) noted, "as girls become the carriers of unvoiced desires and unrealized possibilities, they are placed at considerable risk and even in danger" (p. xxii). As gURLs find their space online, "traditional narratives are re-created with new technologies" (Hawisher & Sullivan, 1999, p. 288), and this opens up a whole new space of empowerment for the adolescent girl. Disappearing is the idea that girls cannot manage technology. According to Takayoshi (1999), "these girls' experiences assert that the relationship of women to technology is neither fixed, predetermined, nor stable across the categories of women's lives" (p. 91). Online space offers girls an opportunity to play with voice and try on new identities—a space that is worked and reworked according to girls' wants and needs. In the few months since my research for this chapter moved from conference presentation to book chapter, many of the original personal home pages I initially referenced have been redesigned with new text and images. Some have even become defunct. This is testimony to the ever-changing needs of gURLs and their continual search for voice and identity. Although a girl-focused netspace is not without its instabilities—commercial web sites do not seem to be diminishing and internet safety is still an issue—the fact that there is a space for the adolescent girl to go to audition her voice and create her identity is at least a step toward a healthier, more emotionally stable, and more independent girlhood.

REFERENCES

Addison, J., & Comstock, M. (1998). Virtually out: The emergence of a lesbian, bisexual and gay youth cyberculture. In J. Austin & M. N. Willard (Eds.), *Generations of youth: Youth cultures and history in twentieth-century America* (pp. 367–378). New York: New York University Press.

Amber. (2004, July 17). *Tragic-Beauty.* Retrieved July 20, 2004, from http://www.tragic-beauty.net/

Ashli. (2002). *Homepage.* Retrieved July 16, 2004, from http://hometown.aol.com/ashlibear/index.html

Bad Girls. (2003). *Homepage.* Retrieved July 18, 2004, from http://www.angelfire.com/film/moofrog/slayers/

beinggirl.com. (2004). *Homepage.* Retrieved July 20, 2004, from http://beinggirl.com/en_US/teen/younger/pages/y_home.jhtml

Brashich, A. (2004). *Message board forum.* Retrieved July 18, 2004, from http://modelingculture.proboards4.com/index.cgi

Brown, L. M., & Gilligan, C. (1992). *Meeting at the crossroads: Women's psychology and girls' development.* New York: Ballantine.

Driscoll, C. (2002). *Girls: Feminine adolescence in popular culture and cultural theory.* New York: Columbia University Press.

Dunn, J. (1999, November). The secret life of teenage girls. *Rolling Stone,* pp. 107–121.

EverythingGirl.com. (2004). *Homepage.* Retrieved July 18, 2004, from http://www.everythinggirl.com/home/home.aspx

Gilligan, C. (1982). *In a different voice: Psychological theory and women's development.* Cambridge, MA: Harvard University Press.

girlsinc.com. (2005). *Homepage.* Retrieved April 18, 2005, from http://www.girlsinc.com/gc/

Hawisher, G., & Sullivan, P. (1999). Fleeting images: Women visually writing the Web. In G. Hawisher & C. Selfe (Eds.), *Passions, pedagogies, and 21st century technologies* (pp. 268–291). Logan: Utah State University Press.

HeY GuYz -n- GiRLiEs!! I <3 YoU aLL. (2004). *Homepage.* Retrieved July 16, 2004, from http://hometown.aol.com/__121b_0P2Gp75EWULE52VkSt7aXzitJNSDIDc5u8clz32sP06ZQVqLwK26KDepbBVlflwJ

Iglesias, E., & Cormier, S. (2002). The transformation of girls to women: Finding voice and developing strategies for liberation. *Journal of Multicultural Counseling and Development, 30,* 259–271.

Jennifer. (2004). *Homepage.* Retrieved July 16, 2004, from http://hometown.aol.com/RajunCajun1389/

Kelly. (2003). *Links page.* Retrieved April 18, 2005, from http://personalweb.about.com/gi/dynamic/offsite.htm?site=http%3A%2F%2Fdarkserenity.2ya.com%2F

Pipher, M. (1994). *Reviving Ophelia: Saving the selves of adolescent girls.* New York: Ballantine.

Quart, A. (2003). *Branded: The buying and selling of teenagers.* Cambridge: Perseus.

Site Mission. (2004). *Parents page.* Retrieved July 20, 2004, from http://barbie.everythinggirl.com/parents/

Spotlight. (2004). *Homepage.* Retrieved July 18, 2004, from http://www.purplepjs.com/

Stern, S. (2002a). Sexual selves on the World Wide Web: Adolescent girls' home pages as sites for sexual self-expression. In J. D. Brown, J. R. Steele, & K. Walsh-Childers (Eds.), *Sexual teens, sexual media: Investigating media's influence on adolescent sexuality* (pp. 265–285). Mahwah, NJ: Lawrence Erlbaum Associates.

Stern, S. (2002b). Virtually speaking: Girls' self-disclosure on the WWW. *Women's Studies in Communication, 25*(2), 223–253.

Takayoshi, P. (1999). No boys allowed: The World Wide Web as a clubhouse for girls. *Computers and Composition, 16,* 89–106.

Chapter 11

Adolescent Diary Weblogs and the Unseen Audience

Lois Ann Scheidt
Indiana University

Previously the preserve of a few enthusiasts, blogging (weblogging) is increasingly becoming a mainstream activity of the digital age. In refining their model of blog populations, Perseus Development Corporation estimates that as many as 31.6 million weblogs "have been created on services such as BlogSpot, LiveJournal, Xanga and MSN Spaces, with 10 million created in the first quarter of 2005 alone" (Henning, 2005, n.p.). The corporation's previous study found that up to 66% of the blogs have been either temporarily or permanently abandoned (Henning, 2003). Therefore, their 31.6 million is both an underestimate of the population of blogs available online, because there is no reliable count of blogs available outside of the hosted sites, and an overestimate, because there is no accounting for inactive blogs and as many as 20.8 million of the blogs included in their study may be abandoned, potentially leaving 10.7 million active sites on the listed hosts.

The growing presence of weblogs in online communication has led to increased academic scrutiny. Previous research has considered the genres of weblogs (Herring, Scheidt, Bonus, & Wright, 2004b), political weblogs (Cherry, 2003), weblogs as journalism (Gallo, 2004), and weblogs as community (Blanchard, 2004; Wei, 2004). In our work on genre, the Blog Research on Genre Project (Herring et al., 2004b) found that diary weblogs, particularly those produced by adolescent webloggers (Herring, Kouper, Schedit, & Wright, 2004a; Herring et al., 2004b), were among the most numerous type found online. A special issue of *Biography: An Interdisciplinary*

Quarterly entitled "Online Lives" (vol. 26, no. 1, Winter 2003) presented academic studies outlining the transition of diary and autobiography to online spaces such as weblogs (McNeill, 2003), little academic interest has been drawn to adolescent use of these spaces (Herring et al., 2004a; Huffaker, 2004).

In principle, blogs may be targeted at many different audiences. But in all of these genres, the formal audience, rather than being defined by the communication media, needs to be seen as a construct of the discursive practices utilized and something that is embedded into the narrative through the author's choices during production (Anderson, 1996). Likewise, Bloom (1996) suggested that diary authors may have many implied audiences in mind as they construct their written work—children, spouses— as well as a larger generalized audience of strangers.

This chapter situates adolescent diary weblogs and their implied audiences and then applies a typology of audience for personal narrative performance to a sample of diary weblog posts to ascertain whether the typology fits the implied audiences present in the post text.

WHAT ARE WEBLOGS?

Weblogs, aka blogs, have been defined as "frequently modified web pages in which dated entries are listed in reverse chronological sequence" (Herring et al., 2004b, n.p.). Although this definition is accurate, it articulates less specificity than that given by Stuffer (2002) in his book, *Blog On: The Essential Guide to Building Dynamic Weblogs*:

> A weblog or blog is a website that's designed to be updated with items in a linear, time-based fashion, similar to a personal journal or diary, except that the contents are meant specifically for public consumption. Often implemented using special software, weblogs contain articles or entries that are grouped primarily by the date and time they are posted. (p. 4)

It should be noted that although some weblogs are meant for public consumption and are therefore available to any viewer, many other web sites that could legitimately be classified as weblogs are available only to those who have been granted access through such techniques as passwording on diary weblogs or intranet-only access for k-logs (see later discussion). Therefore, modification of Stauffer's definition is appropriate, and the following is used in this chapter: A weblog is a frequently modified web site that allows updating with items that are grouped primarily by the time and/ or date of posting. Entries usually appear in reverse chronological order. Contents of the weblog may be available publicly or through restricted access. Weblogs may also utilize special software designed for this implementation.

In our article "Bridging the Gap: A Genre Analysis of Weblogs" (Herring et al., 2004b), we identified five genres of weblogs:

- Filters. These are potentially the oldest form of weblog, and their roots can be traced to Berners-Lee (1992), who posted a list of links to all the new websites as they came online (Winer, 2002). A filter weblog has content that is external to the weblogger, such as national and international events (Blood, 2002).
- Diary or personal journal weblogs. These weblogs typically focus on the blogger's personal thoughts and feelings (Blood, 2002).
- K-logs. Knowledge-logs are weblogs that have been created as repositories for knowledge sharing (Festa, 2003). An example of this category would be *a klog apart: Phil Wolff's subversions* . . . (http://dijest.com/aka/).
- Mixed purpose. These combine the functions of two or more genres—diary/personal journal weblogs, k-logs, or filter weblogs (Herring et al., 2004b).
- Other. These blogs served miscellaneous functions not accounted for in the preceding four categories (Herring et al., 2004b), such as acting as a repository for song popular lyrics.

In our study of a random sample of publicly available English-language weblogs, we found that 70.4% of the sample met the definition of diary blogs (Herring et al., 2004b). As the largest genre of weblogs, diary weblogs are a locus for life-writing (McNeill, 2003). Diary weblogs bear a resemblance to their paper-based antecedents in that they are usually written by a single author (Fothergill, 1974) in first person (McNeill, 2003). They tell an episodic story (Walker, 2003) that may be fragmentary (Hogan, 1991) and is always in process (Culley, 1985a). The continuation is open ended and terminates when the writer ceases to make entries (Bunkers, 2001).

However, two time-worn assumptions about paper diaries fall away when looking at diary weblogs. First, the view that diaries are kept only for the personal consumption of the author (McNeill, 2003) is unsuitable when the diary is posted online. Second, the view that diary keeping is a private and secret effort (Bunkers, 2001; Lejeune, 2001) is out of place when the diary is available for public access. Online forums provide what Kitmann (2004) called *connected privacy*, a place where connections between persons and communities exist, albeit with permeable boundaries allowing access and interaction to persons outside the basic connection set. Even so, within these insecure boundaries, privacy is possible.

The uniqueness of weblogs comes from their ability to blend personal narrative with performance characteristics, like stage settings, through the use of color and image and interaction with the audience by way of reciprocal discussion in comments, posts, and via communication lines outside the weblog space, using channels such as email and instant messaging (IM). These channels are controlled by the author and limited only by the technology and the author's capability to use the technology. While these characteristics can be found in webpages as well, the frequent updating that defines weblogs provides for a higher level of performance and interactivity.

ADOLESCENTS AS BLOGGERS

As mentioned earlier, the rapid growth of weblogs has been marked by increased academic interest (e.g., Gurak, Antonijevic, Johnson, Ratliff, & Reyman, 2004; http://www.blogtalk.net/). However, published research has focused primarily on adult users while marginalizing the activities of adolescent webloggers (Herring et al., 2004a). This limited research underrepresents adolescents' presence online, with an estimated 73% of American teenagers ages 12 through 17 using the internet (Lenhart, Rainie, & Lewis, 2001). Likewise, the "UK Children Go Online" study found that 92% of the 9- to 19-year-olds interviewed had access to the internet at school, while 75% had access from home (Livingstone & Bober, 2004).

Many adolescents and young adults have adopted weblogs as a communication form. Henning's (2003) finding that 92.4% of weblogs are produced by authors under 30 years of age positions weblogs as the province of adolescents and young adults. We have found that between 34.3% (Herring et al., 2004b) and 38% (Herring et al., 2004a) of weblogs were written by adolescents, with diary weblogs the predominant genre produced (Herring et al., 2004b). Orlowski (2003) went further, asserting that a majority of bloggers are teenage girls.

Like homepages before them, weblogs are prominent venues for adolescents to present themselves in textual and multimedia fashion. Weblogs give adolescents the opportunity to "exercise their voices in personal, informal ways, and indirectly promote digital fluency" (Huffaker, 2004). Authors of weblogs, like authors of webpages, use the space to communicate and reach an audience (Stern, 2004).

In American culture, adolescence has been seen as a liminal period (Turner, 1982): The adolescent is not exactly a child and not exactly an adult. This period is seen to end abruptly on the 18th birthday, when a teen is accepted as a legal adult. As can be observed from the academic works cited in this chapter, the definitions of *adolescent*, *teen*, and *youth* have been applied quite flexibly to identify individuals ranging in age from 9 to 21. The new category of *emerging adulthood*, ages 18 to 25 (Arnett, 2000), is also gaining currency as it encompasses and extends the transitional years. For this chapter, I have adopted Steinberg's (2002) definition of adolescence as the second decade of life—ages 10 to 19. This definition creates an easily understandable age range that can be viewed similarly across a range of research.

Once a term such as *adolescence* is defined in a research project, the next question is: What data do we collect to measure the variable? There is an active concern among parents and their children who use online spaces that adults pretending to be children and adolescents are present in internet venues (Livingstone & Bober, 2003). There has not been much academic scrutiny of the issue, although there has been previous discussion of the phenomenon of participants in online forums masquerading as another gender (Danet, 1998; LaPin, 1998; Reid, 1991, 1994). In looking at these two points, it is clear that the same issue is present in both discussions—the ease in creating alternative identities online, which bear little resemblance to a participant's offline life (Donath, 1999).

Within an online space, accurate determination of participants' identity characteristics is difficult, but not impossible. For this research, determination of the weblog author's proper classification as an adolescent is made through triangulation. First, a thorough examination of any direct references to the participant's age is conducted (e.g., in the post text or in the profile). Then a careful reading of the weblog posts is done, with special emphasis on topics such as school, after-school jobs, sports, and dating. Consideration is also made of language structure and use: for example, is it consistent with the stated or apparent age of the author? Finally, where there are no strong reasons to doubt the author's veracity, age is accepted at face value.

Adolescents may be particularly drawn to diary weblogs because of their growing self-consciousness and self-awareness (Steinberg, 2002). During adolescence, individuals may have the egocentric feeling that they are always being watched by an imaginary audience (Elkind, 1967). As Steinberg (2002) put it, "The imaginary audience involves having such a heightened sense of self-consciousness that the teenager imagines that his or her behavior is the focus of everyone else's concern" (p. 63). Likewise, the adolescent may develop personal fables around the belief that their experiences are unique (Steinberg, 2002). Both of these developmental characteristics may push adolescents to perform their personal fables in diary weblogs for the audience they believe is already interested in watching them.

AUDIENCE

Historically, the concept of *audience* refers to a collocation where individuals come together to "create the motive and the site for public presentation" (Anderson, 1996, p. 75). The implied connectivity of the audience through collocation has been broken as technological advancements have allowed communication portability. Ong (1982) pointed out that the term *audience* has been extended to include groups of readers as a collective. Likewise the expansion of this definition has been made to include dispersed audiences for television (Bird, 2003; Brooker & Jermyn, 2003; Hay, Grossberg, & Wartella, 1996) and the internet (Hine, 2001; McLaughlin, Goldberg, Ellison, & Lucas, 1999).

Online communication goes beyond the limitations of these primarily textual narrative environments. In her study of email and memoranda, Cho (in press) found that electronic communication exhibits characteristics of both written and informal oral communication. In much the same way, Langellier and Peterson (2004) pointed to weblogs as "sort of like" conversation with an approximation of audience feedback. Both of these articles suggest that there is a continuum ranging from historically familiar forms of communication (such as memoranda or performances) to those that are characteristic of new communication media.

Langellier (1998) presented five types of audience for personal narrative performance. In this typology, the audience acts as (a) a witness testifying to the experience; (b) a therapist unconditionally supporting emotions; (c) a cultural theorist assessing the contestation of meanings, values, and identities in the performance; (d) a narrative analyst examining genre, truth, or strategy; or (e) a critic appraising the display of performance knowledge and skill.

Following are examples of each of Langellier's audience types drawn from our research on adolescent weblogs. Because Langellier did not include narrative definitions of each audience type, I have used her titling as a jumping off point in developing the codebook for this project. Each example includes a screenshot of the weblog that will be used in illustration. With the illustration is the text entry, in part or in whole, of a weblog post that exemplifies the category of audience. Weblog text examples begin with <snip> and end with </snip>. Text examples are presented verbatim, including misspellings, emoticons, irregular capitalizations, bold, and italics. I have, however, excluded in-text embedded links and the associated underlining because they are outside the purview of this chapter.

As a Witness Testifying to the Experience

This audience category is the most general of the five and is the type of audience most people expect to be part of when observing a performance. In these personal experience narratives, the author presents a story of an experience from the past (Denzin, 2001), asking the audience to observe the experience framed for them by the author. The narrative for this type of entry is usually presented in a linear fashion, including transitions such as "after that we/I" and "then we/I" (see Fig. 11.1).

kissy crayon at 8:26 PM

)-Yellow T-Shirt, navy blue jersey shorts, yellow scrunchie
nytail
g- U2, Achtung Babyl, "One". {track #3}
Mango water ice from Rita's.
¦- Kitchen Confidential
g- My E-mail box get fuller and fuller

:s. WHAT?! I AM UPDATING?! NO WAY!

nt to Dorney Park yesterday. Happy, happy, joy, joy. It wasn't all that bad, actually. I woke up an hour late because I set my ala
m. instead of seven a.m., but nevertheless my Dad woke me up at eight. So I hoped in the shower and ran around in order to pi
d get to the art studio. I put on my new Good Charlotte shirt, so when I got to the studio there was **NO WAY** I was going to pa
im, however. I just decided I would draw a sketch of Adam Clayton from U2. The picture that I wanted was stuck on my compu
rever. So, I will take that picture of Adam next week. Instead I started to Johnny Rotten, from the Sex Pistols. His eyes are c
the picture, but he is still really cute! I am one of the only people who finds him attractive in the least. Johnny isn't Larry Mullen I
r for U2) hot, but cute. Anyway, after I was finished at the studio my family and I were off to Dorney Park. Rachel, my brother's
, went with my mom and dad and I in my dad's car. Colin, and his friend Ryan (aka Carry) went in my brothers blazer. Of course \
the park we had to park a zillion miles away in the "1" section of the parking lot. I said the I stood for "I Will Follow", a U2 song.
iy overpacked family walking with two huge bags across the sweltering lot with bathing suits under our clothes. After what seer
ut three hours following behind Carrey in between rows of cars, I saw the entrance. Thank Bono! So, basically for the first thirty
it was all about walking around in the heat, trying to find our lockers and such. Alas, when we got over to the water park, Colin,
ey of course left me with my parents. Because I ride, NOTHING, my Mom sat on a bench and my Dad and I went into the "Water
at little kids and fat men with water guns. Haha. (Please, do not send me complaints. I will say what I want to.) I was just wantir
ien I saw Rachel! Woo! She got really sick and blacked out in line for some crazy water slide ;-(. So, everybody decided we woul
back to the "dry" part of the park. First, Rachel, me, and my mom had to face the adventure of trying to shower in the Dorney Pa
j room. Yeah, us and about five hundred other women. I am not even going to go there. In the end everyone was clean and grov
an and Rachel got on the Talon. It looked crazy! My stomach can't take that whole upside-down thing! After that they ran to "Ha
iu sit down and flip around and around. My Mom was hiding behind my Dad and saying,
r! My baby is there! Oh my gosh, oh my gosh!"
a, "MOM! I AM THE BABY! HE IS OLDER THAN ME!"

FIG. 11.1.   16 crayons! Available at http://16crayons.blogspot.com/

<snip> So, I went to <u>Dorney Park</u> yesterday. Happy, happy, joy, joy. It wasn't all that bad, actually. I woke up an hour late because I set my alarm for seven p.m. instead of seven a.m., but nevertheless my Dad woke me up at eight. So I hoped in the shower and ran around in order to pick up Vickie and get to the art studio. I put on my new <u>Good Charlotte</u> shirt, so when I got to the studio there was **NO WAY** I was going to paint. . . . Anyway, after I was finished at the studio my family and I were off to Dorney Park. </snip>

In this entry, the author takes the audience step by step through her day, from arising in the morning through her time spent with her family at the water park. She tells the audience the story, asking them to become part of the experiences through her description of her activities. The text of her post uses long sentences with simple words and containing extensive detail. The narrator relays the story in first-person major character by placing themselves in the center of the story through the extensive use of I.

As a Therapist Unconditionally Supporting Emotions

In this category, the authors consciously or unconsciously ask the audience to validate and unconditionally support their emotional positions. Tone is a primary indicator of this type of post (see Fig. 11.2):

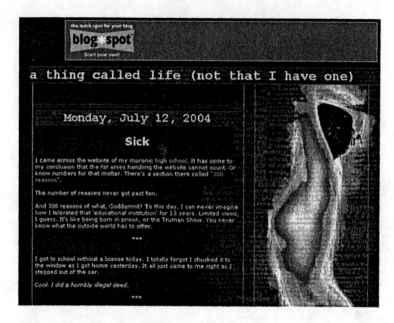

FIG. 11.2. A thing called life (not that I have one). Available at http://anonymuse.blogspot.com/

<snip>The inevitable has taken place. I have once again stepped within the walls of an institution frequented by asylum-deprived eccentrics and egocentrics. But I love it.

No longer a freshie . . . This cannot be happening. No more excuses to be ignorant. No more innocent eyes. No more fun classes . . . *sniff*

But enough of that. The new freshies are here. Gotta show them who's boss. They're easy to spot. They usually go in herds, eagerly sticking to everyone so as not to get lost.

Reminds me during freshie, first sem reg, EVERYone spoke to each other in english, hoping not to give themselves away as tagalog-speaking regular students. But of course that only lasted a few days. A week max. Then everyone discovered the joys and comfort of speaking their own tongue (blogging is a different story, dear).

Anywhoo, you should've seen the freshies today. So scared to stay away from each other with the fear of becoming the block outcast. tsk tsk. It's been a year, God damn it. A frekkin year. Pathetic. A college sophomore yet already filled with nostalgia. Wait till I turn 35. </snip>

In this post, the author asks the audience to validate her experience as a new freshman and support her assertion that she has gone beyond what she now views as immaturity and inexperience. Now she is a sophomore, nostalgic and accepting that she can fit in the college environment. In this post, the narrator fluctuates between first-person major character and second-person point of view (Yordon, 1999), the transition being marked by the change in focus from I to you, thereby directly addressing the audience and inviting them into the story. She tells us this using short sentences with complex words and textual actions, such as *sniff*.

As a Cultural Theorist Assessing the Contestation of Meanings, Values, and Identities in the Performance

In this category, the audience is asked to apply their understanding of the blogger's and their own cultures in evaluating values, beliefs, meanings, and identities, including race, social class, and gender issues described in the post (see Fig. 11.3):

<snip>things that piss me off: no. 1 . . . anti-bush protestors
 i live in the uk, and upon george bush's recent state visit here, hundreds o' thousands of people went out into the streets protesting at his visit, calling him 'the most evil man on the planet' and so on . . .
 where the hell were these protesters during all the years of oppression that the iraqi people faced? probably eating mcdonalds and driving ford cars to work
 why do these people not protest against E.U farming subsidies, which undeniably contribute to poverty amongst african/asian farmers? possibly because they are too busy watching the latest episode of nieghbours (oh my god!

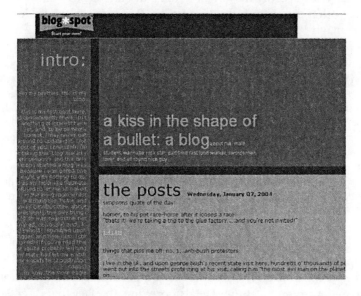

FIG. 11.3. A kiss in the shape of a bullet. Available at http://coquet .blogspot.com/

steph has cancer! she had better pull through . . . max and the kids deserve
better!) </snip>

In this post, the author asks the audience to share his cultural and personal values in assessing issues of belief and social class. He presents a comparison between political protestors in Britain turning out in large numbers to protest the U.S. President George W. Bush's visit and the smaller
number of protesters who appear in the street to picket against European
Union (E.U.) farm subsidies, an issue the author sees as more important.
The text of his post is presented without the standard capitalization found
in formal English sentences. The narrator tells us the story from the first-
person major character perspective, but also invites us into the performance by the use of questions to call forth the author's point of view. Unlike
the standard first-person major narrator, however, he utilizes limited omni-
science in telling us what other values the protestors hold more highly—
"eating at mcdonalds" and "watching the latest episode of nieghbours"—
than concern for groups of disenfranchised persons—"iraqi people" and
farmers.

As a Narrative Analyst Examining Genre, Truth, or Strategy

In this category, the author asks the audience to examine the production of
narrative. This category may include meta-discussions of weblog narrative,
as well as other online or offline narratives. Posts may include references to
real or imagined audience reactions to the narrative (Fig. 11.4):

> <snip>i have to start thinking about applying to college. not that i havent
> been doing that for the last two years, but now i have to start acutally writing
> my essays and applying. i should definitely talk about being muslim and jewish
> and how unique and amazing and diverse and all that other fuckingshit my
> experience is. for some reason the thought of talking about that just makes
> me cringe. maybe because i havent figured all that out myself and i'm not re-
> ally sure *what* i am.
>
> for georgetown, one of the essays is 'describe an experience that describes
> you' or some bullshit to that effect. i really dont feel like doing that. you see,
> i've been really busy lately. first of all, now theyre doing that 70s show reruns
> ALL THE TIME. how could i miss those, right?</snip>

In this post, the author is discussing the construction of essays that must
accompany his college applications. He introduces the idea that his personal essays will address his experiences as an adolescent of mixed religious
ancestry—Jewish and Muslim. He also presents the fact that discussing his

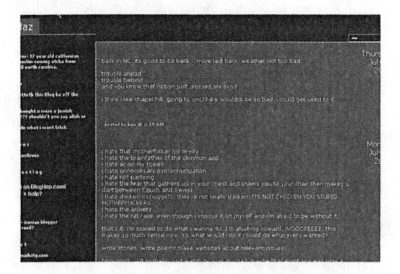

FIG. 11.4. benlaz. Available at http://home.nc.rr.com/benlaz/

ancestry is difficult, as he himself has yet to integrate the meaning and impact of both facets on his life. This entry utilizes a first-person major character narrator with transition into second-person through the use of "you see" in the last paragraph. The author uses lowercase letters in many places one would expect to see uppercase in formal English sentence structure. Likewise, he has chosen to replace commas in complex sentences with periods, or with no punctuation. This creates a somewhat mixed message when reading the section.

A Critic Appraising the Display of Performance Knowledge and Skill

This type of weblog post asks the audience to assess the merit of the author's performance. The appraisal request may refer to performances within or outside the weblog space. Possible examples include artwork, poetry, dance or singing, song writing, and lyrics (see Fig. 11.5):

<snip>I just threw this image together, and I think it turned out nicely . . . </snip>

In this entry the author is displaying a new graphic design to the audience and asking for feedback on his design prowess. In this post the words are overshadowed by the much larger graphic of which the author speaks.

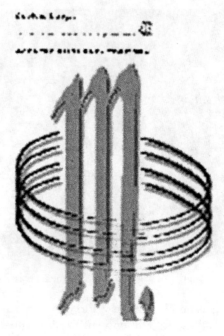

FIG. 11.5.   arador's abode. Available at http://www.arador.org/

BLOGGERS AND THEIR AUDIENCES

Who are bloggers, and which types of audiences do they address? To explore this question, I undertook a content analysis of an opportunity sample ($N = 12$) of adolescent diary weblogs. The sample was drawn from the EatonWeb Portal (http://portal.eatonweb.com) under their Teen category (http://portal.eatonweb.com/cat/Teen). EatonWeb was originally a hand-coded list of all the weblogs available online (Rhodes, 2002). As the number of available weblogs increased, the site was reconfigured to allow for self-submission of weblogs and keywording by the authors/submitters through a JavaScript file (Rhodes, 2002). Each entry in the teen category was reviewed on April 3, 2004, to ascertain that (a) the listed web site was available and met the definition of a weblog, (b) English was the weblog's primary language, and (c) the weblogger met the age criteria of the study at the time of the review. The first page of all weblogs that met the criteria were then archived for coding. All entries on the first page of the weblog were coded for audience category and demographic data. In every weblog reviewed, I was able to assign the authors to a sex category based on their statements in the text or in the profile. The 12 weblogs were evenly divided between female and male authors.

The sample included 102 entries, 89 of which could be fully coded. Thirteen entries from the sample did not meet the requirement of posts with text that appeared to have been written by the weblogger—including blank posts, picture only, and popular song lyrics. The average entries per main page were 8.5, with a range of 4 to 21. The female authors averaged fewer entries per page than the males. Females averaged 6.8 entries, ranging from 5 to 14 entries on the main page and produced 41.6% of the entries. Males averaged 10.2 entries, with a range of 4 to 21 entries and produced 58.4% of the entries in the corpus. When the outlier, 21 entries, was removed, the males averaged eight entries per page, with a range of 4 to 14 similar to the female average. Over 85% of entries reviewed were written in first person.

The average age of the authors was 16.9 years, with a range from 13 to 19 years old. Males were slightly more likely than females to have listed an age in either the text or the profile, with five males providing the information compared to four females who did so. Females were slightly older than males, with an average age of 17.8 years for females (range 15–19) and 16.5 for males (range 13–17; see Fig. 11.6).

The weblogger's country of origin was explicit or implicit in every weblog reviewed. Seven of the authors were from the United States, two each were from the Philippines and Singapore, and one was from the United Kingdom.

When applying Langellier's audience typology, I found the predominant category was "audience as witness to the experience," accounting for 50.6% of the entries. The category with the second highest occurrence, with 25.8% of the entries, was "cultural theorist assessing the contestation of meanings, values, and identities in the performance." The "therapist unconditionally supporting emotions" category accounted for 12.4% of the 89

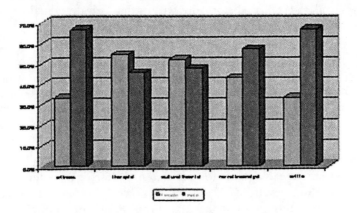

FIG. 11.6.   Posts by category.

posts coded. The "narrative analyst examining genre, truth, or strategy" category accounted for 7.9% of the posts. Finally, the remaining 3.4% of the posts asked their audiences to function as "critic appraising the display of performance knowledge and skill."

The type of audience address was then broken down by the sex of the author. Males created more "witness to the experience" type posts than did females, with 66.7% produced by males compared with 33.3% by females. More entries seeking "therapist" audiences were created by females than males—54.5% versus 45.5%. Likewise, females authored more "cultural theorist" posts than did their male counterparts—52.2% to 47.8%. Conversely, males (57.1%) authored more "narrative analyst" type posts than did females (42.9%). Finally, males also produced more "critic" type posts than did females—66.7% to 33.3%.

These gender differences may reflect broader differences in the construction of masculine and feminine gender identities. Thus, it has been suggested that the diary is a feminine form of self-presentation because it often concentrates on the everyday activities and experiences of the writer (Hogan, 1991). A diary weblog, like any other locus of action and interaction, is "socially and culturally constructed and reflects ideas about how we interact within a culture and how that culture influences us" (Huff, 1996, p. 123).

Research on diaries underscores Friedman's (1988) point that "women often explore their sense of shared identity with other women, aspects of identity that exists in tension with a sense of their own uniqueness" (p. 44). The young women whose weblogs have been analyzed herein illustrate this tension through a tendency toward seeking support for their individual struggles with appeals to the envisioned audience. It is clear that the individual webloggers envision a female audience, clearly their quest for nurturance resonates with the private domain that has been associated with women (Culley, 1985b). Historically, within that private domain, women's diaries, as a form of autobiography,

> . . . rarely mirror the establishment history of their times. They emphasize to a much lesser extent the public aspects of their lives, the affairs of the world, or even their careers, and concentrate instead on their personal lives—domestic details, family difficulties, close friends, and especially people who influenced them. (Jelinek, 1980, pp. 7–8)

Nevertheless, the female webloggers who have undertaken "cultural theorist" posts in their weblogs are, to some extent, differing from Jelinek's view. These young women are exercising their power to observe their cultures and record their thoughts in a way that allows them both public and private moments of reflection.

Likewise, men show a somewhat similar bifurcated audience focus, from internal evaluation in posts, sharing their world by asking us to witness the events and requesting comment on their personal performance, to an external evaluation through narrative analysis. Both of these views are consistent with Jelinek's (1980) comments on the autobiographies of men:

> . . . consensus among critics is that a good autobiography not only focuses on its author but also reveals his connectedness to the rest of society: it is representative of his times, a mirror of his era. This criterion is adequately supported by the many male autobiographies which concentrate on chronicling the progress of their authors' professional or intellectual lives, usually in the affairs of the world, and their life studies are for the most part success stories. (p. 7)

In particular, the production of "narrative analyst" and "critic appraising the display of performance knowledge and skill" type posts allow men to illustrate their intellectual lives and prowess through their ability to conduct meta-dialogues and to produce and critique the narratives around them.

The male webloggers in this study invite the reader into their "glorification of a man, a career, a political cause, or a skillful strategy . . . limited almost entirely to the public sector of existence" (Gusdorf, 1980, p. 36). Their first-person narratives in which the audience witnesses their experiences may not be wholly limited to the public sector, the writers elevate the private into the public sphere by their choice to present the tale on a weblog. Likewise, these formerly private narratives do not embody the same level of personal emotion found in the women's appeals for support—a form that is more truly private than the process narratives of "witness to the experience" type posts.

CONCLUSION

It is clear from this research that Langellier's typology can be successfully applied to adolescent weblogs—and that it also highlights some significant differences between masculine and feminine orientations toward this emerging medium. Such attempts at cross-disciplinary theory application are necessary during the early days of research into a new communication medium. However, the researchers must be conscious of the effect that medium may impart on communication, so they do not fall into what Hawkens (2004) referred to as "medium blindness" (p. 392).

Online communication mediums, weblogs in particular, are sites of author audience interaction that differ from face-to-face performance and traditional reader relationships. Laurel (2001) argued that when "the audience joins the actors on the stage," they "become actors," rather than continuing to be an audience in their new location (p. 110). It is clear that weblogs create new loci of audience and author interaction through interactive communication as well as such added enhancements as comments. We are just beginning to untangle the threads that lead to a level of co-authorship/co-audience creation through feedback and calibration, we may someday be forced to develop new theories that transcend our old notions of implied and explicit audience.

REFERENCES

Anderson, J. A. (1996). The pragmatics of audience in research and theory. In J. Hay, L. Grossberg, & E. Wartella (Eds.), *The audience and its landscape* (pp. 75–93). Boulder, CO: Westview.

Arnett, J. J. (2000, May). Emerging adulthood: A theory of development from the late teens through the twenties. *American Psychologist, 55*(5), 469–480.

Berners-Lee, T. (1992). *What's new in '92.* Retrieved August 30, 2004, from http://www.w3.org/History/19921103-hypertext/hypertext/WWW/News/9201.html

Bird, S. E. (2003). *The audience in everyday life: Living in a media world.* New York: Routledge.

Blanchard, A. L. (2004). Blogs as virtual communities: Identifying a sense of community in the Julie/Julia Project. In L. J. Gurak, S. Antonijevic, L. Johnson, C. Ratliff, & J. Reyman (Eds.), *Into the blogosphere: Rhetoric, community, and culture of weblogs.* Minneapolis: University of Minnesota. Retrieved July 2, 2004, from http://blog.lib.umn.edu/blogosphere/blogs_as_virtual.html

Blood, R. (2002). *The weblog handbook: Practical advice on creating and maintaining your blog.* Cambridge, MA: Perseus.

Bloom, L. Z. (1996). I write for myself and strangers: Private diaries as public documents. In S. L. Bunkers & C. A. Huff (Eds.), *Inscribing the daily: Critical essays on women's diaries* (pp. 23–37). Amherst: University of Massachusetts Press.

Brooker, W., & Jermyn, D. (2003). *The audience studies reader.* London: Routledge.

Bunkers, S. L. (2001). *Diaries of girls and women: A midwestern American sampler.* Madison, WI: University of Wisconsin Press.

Cherry, S. M. (2003). The blog of war. *IEEE Spectrum, 40*(6), 48.

Cho, N. (in press). Linguistic features of electronic mail. In S. C. Herring (Ed.), *Computer-mediated conversation.* Cresskill, NJ: Hampton.

Culley, M. (1985a). *A day at a time: The diary literature of American women from 1764 to present.* New York: The Feminist Press at the City University of New York.

Culley, M. (1985b). Introduction. In M. Culley (Ed.), *A day at a time: The diary literature of American women from 1764 to present* (pp. 1–26). New York: The Feminist Press at the City University of New York.

Danet, B. (1998). Text as mask: Gender, play, and performance on the net. In S. G. Jones (Ed.), *Cyberspace 2.0: Revisiting computer-mediated communication and community* (pp. 129–158). Thousand Oaks, CA: Sage. Available from http://atar.mscc.huji.ac.il/~msdanet/mask.html

Denzin, N. K. (2001). *Interpretive interactionism* (2nd ed.). Thousand Oaks, CA: Sage.

Donath, J. (1999). Identity and deception in the virtual community. In M. A. Smith & P. Kollock (Eds.), *Communities in cyberspace* (pp. 29–59). London: Routledge.

Elkind, D. (1967). Egocentrism in adolescence. *Child Development, 38*, 1025–1034.

Festa, P. (2003, February 25). *Blogging comes to Harvard.* Retrieved February 25, 2003, from http://news.com.com/2008-1082-985714.html?tag=fd_nc_1

Fothergill, R. (1974). *Private chronicles: A study of English diaries.* London: Oxford University Press.

Friedman, S. S. (1988). Women's autobiographical selves: Theory and practice. In S. Benstock (Ed.), *The private self: Theory and practice of women's autobiographical writings* (pp. 34–62). Chapel Hill: University of North Carolina Press.

Gallo, J. (2004). Weblog journalism: Between infiltration and integration. In L. J. Gurak, S. Antonijevic, L. Johnson, C. Ratliff, & J. Reyman (Eds.), *Into the blogosphere: Rhetoric, community, and culture of weblogs.* Minneapolis: University of Minnesota. Retrieved July 2, 2004, from http://blog.lib.umn.edu/blogosphere/weblog_journalism.html

Gurak, L. J., Antonijevic, S., Johnson, L., Ratliff, C., & Reyman, J. (2004). *Into the blogosphere: Rhetoric, community, and culture of weblogs.* Minneapolis: University of Minnesota. Retrieved August 25, 2004, from http://blog.lib.umn.edu/blogosphere/

Gusdorf, G. (1980). Conditions and limits of autobiography. In J. Olney (Ed.), *Autobiography: Essays theoretical and critical* (pp. 28–48). Princeton, NJ: Princeton University Press.

Hawkens, L. (2004). Code: Textual theory and blind spots in media studies. In M.-L. Ryan (Ed.), *Narrative across media: The languages of storytelling* (pp. 391–404). Lincoln, NE: University of Nebraska Press.

Hay, J., Grossberg, L., & Wartella, E. (1996). *The audience and its landscape.* Boulder, CO: Westview.

Henning, J. (2003). *The blogging iceberg—Of 4.12 million hosted weblogs, most little seen, quickly abandoned* (Perseus Development Corporation White Papers). Retrieved October 4, 2003, from http://www.perseus.com/blogsurvey/

Henning, J. (2005, April 12). *The blogging geyser* (Perseus Development Corporation White Papers). Retrieved April 13, 2005, from http://www.perseus.com/blogsurvey/geyser.html

Herring, S. C., Kouper, I., Scheidt, L. A., & Wright, E. (2004a). Women and children last: The discourse construction of weblogs. In L. J. Gurak, S. Antonijevic, L. Johnson, C. Ratliff, & J. Reyman (Eds.), *Into the blogosphere: Rhetoric, community, and culture of weblogs.* Minneapolis: University of Minnesota. Retrieved July 2, 2004a, from http://blog.lib.umn.edu/blogosphere/women_and_children.html

Herring, S. C., Scheidt, L. A., Bonus, S., & Wright, E. (2004b). Bridging the gap: A genre analysis of weblogs. In *Proceedings of the 37th Hawaii International Conference on System Sciences* (HICSS-37). Los Alamitos: IEEE Press. Retrieved January 6, 2004b, from http://www.blognija.com/DDGDD04.doc

Hine, C. (2001, June). Web pages, authors and audiences: The meaning of a mouse click. *Information, Communication & Society, 4*(2), 182–198.

Hogan, R. S. (1991). Endangered autobiographies: Diaries as a feminine form. *Prose Studies, 14*(2), 95–107.

Huff, C. A. (1996). Textual boundaries: Space in nineteenth-century women's manuscript dairies. In S. L. Bunkers & C. A. Huff (Eds.), *Inscribing the daily: Critical essays on women's diaries* (pp. 123–138). Amherst: University of Massachusetts Press.

Huffaker, D. (2004, January). Spinning yarns around the digital fire: Storytelling and dialogue among youth on the internet. *First Monday, 9*(1). Available from http://www.firstmonday.dk/issues/issue9_1/huffaker/

Jelinek, E. C. (1980). Introduction: Women's autobiography and the male tradition. In E. C. Jelinek (Ed.), *Women's autobiography: Essays in criticism* (pp. 1–20). Bloomington, IN: Indiana University Press.

Kitmann, A. (2004). *Saved from oblivion: Documenting the daily from diaries to web cams.* New York: Peter Lang.

Langellier, K. M. (1998). Voiceless bodies, bodiless voices: The future of personal narrative performance. In S. J. Dailey (Ed.), *The future of performance studies: Visions and revisions* (pp. 207–213). Annandale, VA: National Communication Association.

Langellier, K. M., & Peterson, E. E. (2004). *Storytelling in daily life: Performing narrative.* Philadelphia: Temple University Press.

LaPin, G. (1998). *"Pick a gender and get back to us": How cyberspace affects who we are.* Retrieved August 30, 2004, from http://www.fragment.nl/mirror/various/LaPin_G.1998.Pick_a_gender_and_get_back_to_us.htm

Laurel, B. (2001). Computers as theatre. In D. Trend (Ed.), *Reading digital culture* (pp. 109–114). Malden, MA: Blackwell.

Lejeune, P. (2001, Winter). How do diaries end? *Biography: An Interdisciplinary Quarterly, 24*(1), 99–112.

Lenhart, A., Rainie, L., & Lewis, O. (2001, June 20). *Teenage life online: The rise of the instant-message generation and the Internet's impact on friendship and family relationships* (PEW Internet & American Life Project). Retrieved November 27, 2002, from http://www.pewinternet.org/reports/pdfs/PIP_Teens_Report.pdf

Livingstone, S., & Bober, M. (2003, October). *UK children go online: Listening to young people's experiences.* London: Economic & Social Research Council.

Livingstone, S., & Bober, M. (2004, July). *UK children go online: Surveying the experiences of young people and their parents.* London: Economic & Social Research Council.

McLaughlin, M. L., Goldberg, S. B., Ellison, N. B., & Lucas, J. (1999). Measuring internet audiences: Patrons of an on-line art museum. In S. G. Jones (Ed.), *Doing internet research* (pp. 163–178). Thousand Oaks, CA: Sage.

McNeill, L. (2003, Winter). Teaching an old genre new tricks: The diary on the internet. *Biography: An Interdisciplinary Quarterly, 26*(1), 24–48.

Ong, W. (1982). *Orality and literacy: The technologizing of the word.* London: Routledge.

Orlowski, A. (2003, May 30). *Most bloggers "are teenage girls"—survey.* Retrieved May 30, 2003, from http://www.theregister.co.uk/content/6/30954.html

Reid, E. M. (1991). *Electropolis: Communication and community on internet relay chat.* Unpublished honor's thesis, Department of History, University of Melbourne. Available from http://www.nicoladoering.de/Hogrefe/reid91.htm

Reid, E. M. (1994, January). *Cultural formation in text-based virtual realities.* Unpublished master's thesis, Cultural Studies Program, Department of English, University of Melbourne. Available from http://www.aluluei.com/

Rhodes, J. S. (2002). In the trenches with a weblog pioneer: An interview with the force behind Eatonweb, Brigitte F. Eaton. In J. Rodzvilla (Ed.), *We've got blog: How weblogs are changing our culture* (pp. 99–103). Cambridge, MA: Perseus.

Stuffer, T. (2002). *Blog on: The essential guide to building dynamic weblogs.* New York: McGraw-Hill/Osborne.

Steinberg, L. D. (2002). *Adolescence* (6th ed.). New York: McGraw-Hill.

Stern, S. R. (2004). Expression of identity online: Prominent features and gender differences in adolescents' WWW home pages. *Journal of Broadcasting & Electronic Media, 48*(2).

Turner, V. (1982). *From ritual to theatre: The human seriousness of play.* New York: PAJ.

Walker, J. (2003, June 28). *Final version of weblog definition.* Retrieved August 30, 2004, from http://huminf.uib.no/~jill/archives/blog_theorising/final_version_of_weblog_definition.html

Wei, C. (2004). Formation of norms in a blog community. In L. J. Gurak, S. Antonijevic, L. Johnson, C. Ratliff, & J. Reyman (Eds.), *Into the blogosphere: Rhetoric, community, and culture of weblogs.* Minneapolis: University of Minnesota. Retrieved July 2, 2004, from http://blog.lib.umn.edu/blogosphere/formation_of_norms.html

Winer, D. (2002). *The history of weblogs.* Retrieved August 30, 2004, from http://newhome.weblogs.com/historyOfWeblogs

Yordon, J. E. (1999). *Roles in interpretation* (4th ed.). New York: McGraw-Hill College.

Chapter 12

"Hello newbie! ☺**big welcome hugs** hope u like it here as much as i do! ☺": An Exploration of Teenagers' Informal Online Learning

Julia Davies
University of Sheffield

As I write, my teenage daughter is thoroughly absorbed in using the family PC (I am relegated to using a laptop), and she is dextrously moving from window to window, using instant messaging (IM) to talk to online friends and, at their suggestions, clicking about to visit a range of web sites. She has her online diary (weblog) open, carefully shielding it from my view. She deals in texts with multiple layers, with icons, music, hyperlinks, and images; her mobile phone is by her side. She often laughs as she types, seeing witticisms, reading visual jokes, seeming to feel closer to her online friends than she is to me, just a meter or so away. She is involved in a range of complex literacy activities that take her focus beyond her immediate environment. I am drawn to the idea that this is very important, and I seek to understand more about what skills she and her peers are developing. I want to understand these new literacy practices, and I believe that such understandings might help us implement a more meaningful pedagogy for digital education. I have written elsewhere (Davies, 2004, 2005), as have others (Ito & Okabe, 2004; Schofield Clark, 2005), about the importance of perpetual contact to many of the digital generation, and it is through this endeavor that many teenagers are learning through social practices online. Polak (chap. 10, this volume) is clear about the motives of gURLS on the sites she has investigated: to build community. Her gURLS, like the teens I have been observing, are looking to share values, interests, and a space to be with like-minded others.

In this chapter, I provide evidence from two teenage online communities and use Lave and Wenger's (1991) concept of *Communities of Practice* to help understand the evolution and development of the groups' respective cultural practices. Through examples of data taken from teen sites, I show how *screenagers* (Rushkoff, 1996) present themselves through particular identity formations, learn from each other, and create communities through online practices. I begin, then, with an introduction to the notion of Communities of Practice prior to illustrating its applicability to the communities I have observed.

COMMUNITIES OF PRACTICE

In their delineation of Communities of Practice, Lave and Wenger (1991) described a process of enculturation where learners are not formally instructed, but learn through being part of a group. Newcomers are apprenticed into ways of relating to other community members and, through their interaction with others, develop shared understandings of concepts, terms, and values. Wenger (1998) emphasized that although Communities of Practice may not have their focus on learning, being engaged in particular Communities of Practice is a learning process. He argued that learning occurs continually through "mutual engagement, negotiation of an enterprise and development of a shared repertoire" (Wenger, 1998, p. 95). The notion of Communities of Practice is therefore built on a notion of learning as a social practice.

The features listed next are characteristics I have observed in online Communities of Practice and are those that Lave and Wenger also described. Communities of Practice:

- Enculturate newcomers
- Apprentice learners with experienced practitioners
- Facilitate communal activities
- Develop a shared history
- Develop shared meanings
- Build identities in association with a specific community
- Benefit from the empowerment of group values

As can be seen from this model, apprenticeship involves the learning of cultural and social values alongside skills and knowledge, and the boundaries between them are blurred.

Moreover, in my observations of teenage web communities, participants seem to develop a sense of self through group membership and exhibit, through their blogs, web sites, and message board interactions, determinations to consistently exhibit behaviors that repeatedly demonstrate their claims and rights to membership. In turn, this allows the community to retain a sense of itself *as* a community and gives it coherence. As such, individuals construct online identities that help them retain membership in the way Wenger (1998) described:

> Building an identity consists of negotiating the meanings of our experience of membership in social communities. The concept of identity serves as a pivot between the social and the individual, so that each can be talked about in terms of the other. (p. 145)

Bearing in mind Wenger's idea that identity formation within a Community of Practice is a dual process of identification and negotiation, I move now to a discussion of the web communities I have observed.

COMMUNITY ONE: THE MAGIC WEB

This community is populated by teenagers who identify themselves as witches and/or express the values of the Wiccan religion. The sites I examine declare no affinities with TV series such as *Buffy the Vampire Slayer, Sabrina the Teenage Witch, Charmed,* and so on. In fact, these sites vehemently disassociate themselves from such superficial groups and declare associations with serious religious books, pagan beliefs, and historical events. It is significant that the community is keen to articulate who are insiders and who are outsiders according not just to their affiliations to serious Wiccan matters, but that additional interests (e.g., *Sabrina*) disqualify them from the main group. It is partly through declaring what they are not that helps delineate and define the community. As Wenger (1998) described, "A learning community is therefore fundamentally involved in social re-configurations, its own internally as well as its position within broader configurations" (p. 220). Moreover, the Wiccan communities show an awareness of an inherited social history, of ties to an ancient community that articulated a prescribed code of conduct, such as "The Wiccan Rule of Three," which begins "Bide the Wiccan law ye must" and continues with a series of exhortations to follow a particular code, set of beliefs, and way of behaving (Achilles Sun, 2000).

Induction to the community means that newcomers, or *newbies*, are warned about being superficial, about the need to follow the Wiccan code, and about the need to learn about the culture, beliefs, and so on. For example, one site declares on its home page,

This is a web site for serious teen witches. If you are just into witchcraft as a teen rebellion thing, this ain't your kind of web site. Not trying to discriminate against anyone, just trying to be clear about intentions. . . . No spell begging. (Teenwitch, 2005)

This site clearly signals that there are insiders and outsiders, as well as interlopers. It warns about features that identify outsiders and shows a value for seriousness. One site lists characteristics of fakers:

10. "I learned how to make a stoplight change!"
 9. "Can you teach me how to make a rain cloud come around?"
 8. "Well, I saw this really cool Ricky Lake show . . ."
 7. "I'm a natural witch!" . . .
(Skyfire, 2005)

Although this feature appears on a light-hearted section of this site, it nevertheless signals underlying values expressed earnestly elsewhere, such as, "Witchcraft follows the rules of nature," "Magic is the art of teaching your mind to make changes subconsciously," or "Magic is not like what you see on TV" (Amber Skyfire, 2000a, 2000b).

Again, with its explicit declaration, the Wiccan rede is given a pride of place on many sites, detailing rules for living:

Bide the Wiccan laws ye must
In perfect love and perfect trust
Live and let live. . . .
(Paganus, 2005)

In such ways, cultural beliefs and codes of conduct are articulated, often especially for newbies, and many sites give lengthy lists of books to read, information about different paths to take, and so on (Terra, 2005; Witchcrafted.com, 2004). Cultural values are also expressed implicitly, for example, via linguistic means.

Technical terms for mundane objects, such as *besom* for broomstick or *yule* for the Christmas period, are uniformly used, while *A Book of Shadows* is the insider word for a spell book, and *magick* is spelled in a particular way, marking it as Wiccan rather than associated with trickery or conjuring for mere entertainment. Ritual language provides the community with identity and territory markers; to use the language betrays insider knowledge. The frequently used greeting "Merry Meet" and the parting salutation "Blessed Be" denote membership and frame exchanges so that any content is imbued with Wiccan connotations—for example, "Merry Meet. Welcome to the Purple Raven site" (Arianwitch, 2004).

Newbies often announce themselves and request support for their own induction, but usually it is clear they have carefully researched the community and noted the important linguistic and textual markers. Take this example from an English-speaking Latvian girl who has left a message on a board:

> I'm new, any1 want a penpal? Sveiki all Latvian Witches!

> Merrymeet witches, I just started Wicca last Sept., but I discovered I had technicly been "Wiccan" b4 I even knew it! By the way, Tekaru or however ur name is spelled, how do u make it rain? Isn't it like against the Wiccan code 2 mess w/nature? I'm just looking for a coven in my area, I'm 13 and my mom still thinks this is like something Im going 2 grow out of, help! Also, if n-e-1 wants 2 B penpals w/me, my e-mail is witchkitty1313@yahoo, e-mail me pleez!

> BB!!
> ~Pixie
> (Pixie, 2004)

A range of identity markers are expressed here—of age, nationality, and Wiccan identity—as well as the struggle to separate from her mother. This girl is taking an "opportunity to play with . . . identity and to try out new ones" (Turkle, 1996, p. 356) as she uses language in an experimental way. The post uses "Merrymeet" as an opening greeting and ends with the salutation "BB," an abbreviation of "Blessed Be," words to signal departure. Where possible she uses numerical figures, although there are some elements that betray her naiveté despite her efforts to blend in. The way in which Merrymeet is used as one word is nonconventional; she seems uneasy with the exotic name, "Tekaru," and her desire to join a coven immediately would be frowned on by many veteran Wiccans (Wildspirit, 2004a, 2004b). She chooses a name, Pixie, that reflects other kinds of fantasy play, and this does not collocate with other names likely to be found on these sites, such as Black Amber, Socharis, raven, and so on. She asks a series of questions, explicitly seeking information to help her transition into the community; she declares natural membership however ("been Wiccan b4 I even knew it!"), and her desire to make firm bonds is shown in her request for individual friends to e-mail her. This awkwardness is also shown in her inconsistency of language, where abbreviated texting conventions are nevertheless used among expansive sentences and explanation. Here we see the process of enculturation in its infancy. Nevertheless, others accept her contribution as sincere and respond with support, giving her advice and explaining more about Wicca.

In the earlier extract, we have seen the early moments in the construction of an online identity and one that seeks guidance from others. As we see later, and also as documented by Thomas (2005), this guidance sometimes occurs in face-saving backstage spaces, such as through IM, e-mail, or private message systems. Turkle (1995) explained this process of gradual enculturation, "as they participate they become authors not only of text but of themselves, constructing new selves through social interaction" (p. 12)—a process that is further exemplified later.

Some pages show participants demonstrating membership through the use of artifacts and lifestyle arrangements:

Witching up your Room

Yeah, so you're a Witch. You've got your altar set up in your room, and everything is all wonderful and happy, right? Of course! But when you look from the altar to the rest of your room (where said altar probably is), you realize how bloody mundane and boring the place looks! Whatever can you do? You don't have anywhere else to use for your altar and, let's face it, you sort of don't *want* it anywhere else, right?
(Darksomenight, 2005)

The slick, colloquial style from this web page emulates a teen magazine and confidently gives explicit advice. The tone assumes audience solidarity ("Yeah, so you're a Witch") and that readers are seeking ways to express group membership through artifacts. In so doing, the writer sets herself up as expert and as one who rejects other lifestyle choices—the notion that non-Wiccan artifacts are boring is implicit. The tactical series of questions assumes agreement and in this way assumes a like-minded readership. This piece emphasizes the message that true Witches saturate their lives with Wiccan emblems. This blend of the personal with a strong sense of performance echoes Scheidt's (chap. 11, this volume) observations of blog writers and reflects the uniqueness of the opportunities to self-publish on the web. The piece is witty, powerful, and, like Thomas' (2005) creative writing community, empowered through her online practices.

Many Wiccan home pages show a blend of Wiccan and everyday worlds in a bricolage of multimodal emblems such as music and images of witchy paraphernalia alongside images of their own faces or homes. Personal home pages offer possibilities for presenting identities to others, exploiting the public/private affordances of online spaces. Stern (1999) compared girls' home pages to their bedroom walls, where self-expression and public presentation come together as textual constructions of self. Yet these are complex textual constructions that reflect tensions across multiple selves, showing what "in some way the selves girls think they are, the selves they wish to become, and most likely, the selves they wish others to see," as Stern (1999, p. 24) explained.

Like home pages, weblogs are prominent venues for adolescents to present themselves in multimodal ways. The strong sense of audience as described in Scheidt's work (chap. 11, this volume) is very clear in the communities I have looked at and is particularly poignant where teenagers address the audience directly or present themselves through blogs. Moreover, these blogs allow the Wiccan teens to illustrate the embeddedness of Wiccan culture in their lives. The blogs reflect a perpetual consciousness of all things Wiccan/occult. Blogs pose as windows into teenagers' worlds; typically representing lives that are entirely consistent with professed beliefs, all experiences seem to be seen through a Wiccan lens. Discourses are saturated with references to Wiccan beliefs as here in Laura's blog:

> I have finished "In the circle—Elen Hawke" it is a really good book, and took me no time to read! I'm going shopping soon so i'll pick up another book :)
> ... I'm re-reading "Witches night of fear—Silver Ravenwolf" its a follow up to "Witches night out" there are three books in the series. . . . I'm waiting for my "witchfest 2002" tickets to come through, its only been a week but i'm so excited. I think i'm going to meet Celia (Wildspirit) at witchfest to which will be great because we have been "internet" friends for about three years.
> (Laura, 2002)

This is a very typical entry; reading lists abound, and there is a strong sense that Laura is a secure member of a clearly defined group. The books are culturally potent for the group, and the blog foregrounds the notion that Laura carries the values of the community beyond her online world. Wiccan cultural activities are in profusion; the mention of the annual Witchfest, which is advertised both on and off line, is suffused with insider kudos. To attend is to be part of an inner group, which does more than just talk online, and it seems that online participants often meet there for the first time, outside the Web. The second intertextual reference is to Wildspirit, another teenage Wiccan with whom Laura once hosted a very popular site, The Silver Circle, and Laura's casual, familiar use of her name implies a certain access to social capital. Yet it is only through repeated mention of her name in the community that has allowed such meanings to accrue, and they are only likely to have currency here.

The coherence and cohesiveness of the community is shown through the repeated citation of the same names across many guestbooks; the way they vote for associated sites in various online polls; their listing of links to each other's sites on their home pages; as well as their referencing of each other's contributions to discussion boards. This coherence allows participants to move swiftly through the community, tracing paths and conversations through sites in a seamless manner, making the various discussions seem as one. In this way, values and discourses become promoted, shared, and assumed. Take, for example, this reference to The Silver Circle site where anxious community members have been unable to connect to it for a few weeks: "Oh no!!!! I hope it comes back soon. I love the site and find it quite inspirational" (Ravenwing, 2004). This value for specific people and sites is built up gradually, as Wenger (1998) explained, and meanings are negotiated over time.

Conversely, intense discussions about outsiders' sites also take place. For example, one thread in The Silver Circle discusses a site that many discussants believe is naive and dangerous. Here Wildspirit comments on Rowan's reservations about teenagers being in covens:

> Rowan, yeh I agree . . . although I know Silverfire is in a coven? *looks at Silverfire*
> Also the fact that a 15 year old is teaching 11 year olds and holding rituals and study circles . . . bizarre.
> Okay, so here's a question then: should teenagers really be creating covens and claiming titles like "high priestess"?
> (Wildspirit, 2004a)

Within this piece, the contributor refers to two others by name (both of whom have their own sites) and shows a confident familiarity with them. She assumes shared values and asks a question of them. She implicitly expresses the values of the group—that a 15-year-old "teaching 11-year-olds and holding rituals . . ." is wrong. There are clear social and cultural values being expressed and a sense of the community policing itself, "claiming titles like 'high priestess' " being under clear disapproval. The closeness is demonstrated through the words "*looks at Silverfire*," which identifies a kind of metaphorical presence and unspoken, assumed tacit understandings. As Wenger (1998) noted, the disruption of the smooth running of groups can help members identify who belongs and who does not. A fresh articulation of community definitions, rather than a less visible negotiation and enactment of belonging, might sometimes be seen as a requirement at crisis points. The members of the group on this board are renowned and well-established members of the teen online Wiccan community, and Wenger's (1998) words here are most apt:

> Sustained engagement . . . gives rise to boundaries. These boundaries are a sign that communities of practice are deepening, that their shared histories give rise to significant differences between inside and outside . . . boundaries are inevitable and useful. They define a texture for engaged identities, not vague identities . . . boundaries define them as much as their core . . . boundaries are a sign of depth. (p. 254)

Within this online community, a number of sites produced by key individuals seemed to take the lead, such as those who first set up The Silver Circle. Indeed the girls reported to have met successfully at the Witchfest, as well as when they were filmed by the British Broadcasting Corporation (BBC). Their site started a petition (Silvercircle, 2003) protesting about a Channel 4 documentary (*Teenage Kicks*) on the lives of teenage witches. This influential challenge to hegemonic representations of Wicca was brought to the attention of the BBC, which later filmed a response program with Wildspirit as the star. Wildspirit is a catalyst to many online events: Much like one of Rheingold's (2003) *Smartmobs*, she seems to innovate and lead. She is at the heart of influential happenings, and her diaries offer a strong sense of theater, of display, of life being represented with some aspects magnified. My recent e-mail correspondence with Wildspirit, to gain permission to use evidence from her site, describes in detail how online activities have been empowering:

> I think one of the things about online communities, is that sometimes they become real-life communities. It's a wonderful way of communicating and opening the world up. I met a really valuable friend through my message-board and my online diaries, and we now talk on the phone regularly, and he travels down from Birmingham often for group ceremonies and rituals. In fact, almost everyone, in one of my ritual groups, I know through my website. It's been an amazing benefit in that way.
> Even the BBC stuff was a great (although somewhat bizarre) experience, that generated from the internet. Just today I got a call from Mizz magazine who wanted to do an article on a young pagan, the BBC passed my number on. I think it's exciting how those threads seem to weave together, and one things leads to another thing. Again, ultimately, it's all stemmed out of the internet and the communities I've been a part of in the past.
> (Wildspirit, 2004b)

The internet can be a space to evade the parental gaze, and many sites show young people talking about upset friendships or disputes with teachers and parents. The strange way in which so many of these interactants see the internet as both an intimate area for exchange, as well as a place for public display, challenges our perceptions of these boundaries. Yet it is all these qualities that are exploited here, so that interactants can demonstrate their shared values while also hiding aspects of their identity if they wish. Online diaries, like message board interactions, allow the narration of a common, although asynchronic, experience. As Driver (chap. 13, this volume) explains, online spaces allow the performance of emerging identities that have varying degrees "of distance and closeness, fiction and reality, self-reflection and social dialogue." There is a suggestion of real time, and teenagers can enjoy playing with aspects of their identity—not only presenting themselves to others in a particular way, but also to view themselves in specific ways, speaking a common language that binds them together and weaving a narrative across boards to create a community with clear cultural markers.

COMMUNITY TWO: THE AYME MESSAGE BOARD

In the next part of this chapter, I look at data from the online message board (AYME, 2004) set up by The Association of Young People with ME (AYME). Access was negotiated through the charity's Board of Trustees, and members were alerted to my presence as a researcher. Some interactants corresponded with me via e-mail.

The board is largely used by teenagers, but some AYMERs are in their early 20s. The data for this chapter are drawn from a larger set in a project considering how message board participants use the web to improve the quality of their lives, gain a sense of community, and interrogate the outside world's notion of their illness. For many AYMERs, the internet is their main means of maintaining a sense of self and making new friends. These young people use the internet to create a peer network that replaces previous social interaction; their digital literacy practices thus become their main means of communication for self-presenting to peers. Membership of the group is therefore powerful in a more nuanced way than for those who can easily leave their homes. These youngsters see the board as the gateway to reengagement with the outside real world.

> When my condition was worse I relied on the MB a lot to have contact with other people (as I had lost all my healthy friends) and more importantly other people who could understand how I was feeling and not judge my condition. I found that my main activity would be logging on to the board, it was something I could do whenever I wanted to when I felt up to it. Often it would make my day seem more enjoyable and was a good way or meeting new people or just being entertained! (I often used a laptop in bed at this stage.)
> (Lois, 2004)

For many AYMERs, their previous sense of identity as children, where they were expecting to grow in independence, is challenged by the restrictions that their illness has placed on their lives. Many of them no longer attend school, and they can lose a sense of themselves as friends, pupils, and members of a peer group. They become in many senses like a much younger child—more dependent and based mainly in the home, relying on others to bring life to them, rather than finding fun in parks, street corners, youth clubs, or in school. Many use the internet to discuss their losses, discover and redefine themselves as members of a new group, and re-create social aspects of their former lives. They use the group to explore and gain a new sense of power. Despite the special and unfortunate circumstances that have brought the group together, they share much in common with other web communities in their development of a specific Community of Practice. Take, for example, Fig. 12.1. Notice the way this newbie makes her entry to the board.

The messages shown below appear onscreen, in a tabulated form, with many icons available for members' use. These link to: a profile of the member, containing as many personal details as she or he wishes to reveal; a quick link to e-mail; a link to that person's web site if she or he has one; a link to their IM forum; a link to AYME's private message database; and finally a copying facility that allows a member to quote from another's contribution. Confident use of these icons shows a strong and secure member of the group, and acquisition of the skills is clearly driven by the desire to communicate. The more often a member visits the board, the more skilled she or he will become, with digital literacy experiences increasing simultaneously with social interaction and a more intensive relationship with the

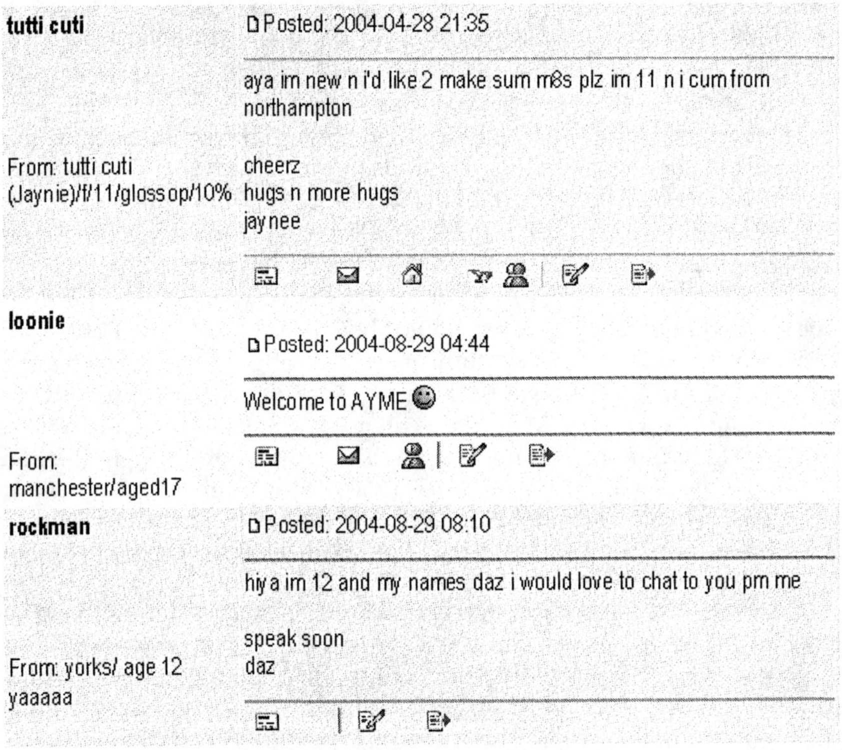

tutti cuti	☐ Posted: 2004-04-28 21:35
	aya im new n i'd like 2 make sum m8s plz im 11 n i cum from northampton
From: tutti cuti (Jaynie)/f/11/glossop/10%	cheerz hugs n more hugs jaynee
	▣ ✉ ⌂ 📷 👤 📝 ➡
loonie	☐ Posted: 2004-08-29 04:44
	Welcome to AYME ☺
From: manchester/aged17	▣ ✉ 👤 📝 ➡
rockman	☐ Posted: 2004-08-29 08:10
	hiya im 12 and my names daz i would love to chat to you pm me
From: yorks/ age 12 yaaaaa	speak soon daz
	▣ 📝 ➡

FIG. 12.1. Welcome hugs—apprenticeships.

community. In this way, the Community of Practice facilitates social and digital learning.

It is noticeable how, even as a newbie, tutti cuti's text is littered with abbreviated text message conventions, as with the earlier Wiccan newbie. The strong presence of these showing membership to the digital generation is signaled more strongly than in, for example, Wildspirit's interactions earlier. It is as if, in seeking acceptance, certain rituals are more important than others at the start. Although she is online, she reveals where she lives, and this information is given quite often in this board (pseudonyms and different locations are given here). Although these boarders have screen names, they have all also chosen to reveal their real names too. This is an interesting play with multiple identities that actually provides discussion material in other postings where boarders ask the meanings of each other's names. Thus, screen names are not used to mask identity, but to suggest an aspect of that person's character to other AYMERs. In this way, there is a sense in which multiple selves are brought to the board; membership is biologically determined, but stronger other identities are brought to the fore to build up a sense of community beyond the illness. Unlike the Wiccan teens, the members of this group, who are anchored to one specific site, do not always want to focus on the characteristic that links them in the first place. The community builds up other kinds of relationship; ironically what brought them together is the thing they wish to be liberated from.

As mentioned earlier, it seems that sometimes relationships are negotiated openly, purely on the board for all to witness, while others are conducted backstage. Thus, daz (rockman) asks Jaynie (tutti cuti) to pm (private message) him so they can leave private messages. In order to pm someone, a boarder clicks on one of the icons in that person's message cell and he or she is then taken to a separate area of the site where he or she can type a message to that person without it being read by others. This system means that a member can accumulate a host of personal messages and pieces of information to look back on at a later time, thus representing a personal history for each AYMER and allowing him or her to experience a relationship within the community, but this time without being in the public eye. This backstage talk, as Thomas (2005) showed, means that newbies can often be helped by more experienced others to learn the conventions of the groups and then participate without disturbing the sense of community already established.

The IM facility meanwhile, also available by clicking on another icon, allows synchronic discussion that is not stored on the board's database. This discussion would be hosted by one of the many international providers such as YAHOO, AOL, or Microsoft. Such discussions represent a break away from the main community, indicating that new friendship groups are forming as satellites to the host group.

All this insider knowledge is quite complex and requires management of technical knowledge about how the board works, as well as the social skills to discriminate about the type of discourse individuals want to have with others. Rockman's invitation to tutti cuti, therefore, is a means of apprenticing her to the various modes and dimensions of the board community. Thus, the warm welcome goes beyond even the surface structure of the words; it is an invitation to use a different dimension or affordance of the web site. Here again we see learning as a social process, underpinning the community's activities, with the desire to communicate as primary.

I discussed earlier the importance to communities of gaining a sense of themselves as a group by way of their relation to others. In Fig. 12.2, we see AYMERs cheerfully establishing themselves as a group that clearly identifies outsiders to that group. Within Fig. 12.2, "non M.E. believers" are othered, and a sense of security across the friends is shown. Rachel, alias "Scotty McMad," refers to Lois several times, almost as if she were in the same place, but in fact other parts of this thread reveal that they are not together, but also involved in an IM chat that allows them to talk backstage together.

The AYMERs are involved in a charade in Fig. 12.2, apparently throwing people into a hole—a scenario that another AYMER quickly accepts and builds on, and this thread develops into a long piece with nine contributors imagining the black hole and throwing in contenders. Here also in this section, we see the convention of asterisks around present-tense verbs to de-

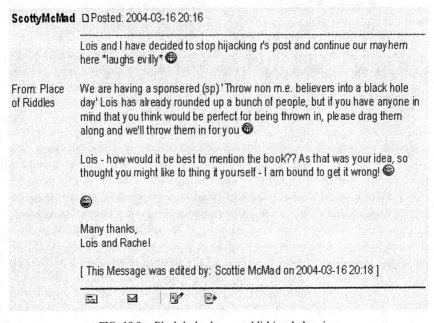

FIG. 12.2. Black hole day—establishing belonging.

scribe paralinguistic features. This is something common across internet discussion boards, but is used by AYMERs very often, bringing in much needed drama to their lives. They learn this through observation it seems, occasionally giving help where needed if asked, again a characteristic common across sites I have observed elsewhere (Davies, 2005). The charade allows an opportunity to share aspects of their lives in an upbeat way and forms part of a series of vignettes developed over a period of weeks, which together build up a cultural history for regular boarders. The sense of performance is strong, with AYMERs able to become fully accepted as the group just by joining in the linguistic ritual. The blend of personal narrative, where one by one AYMERs say who they would like to throw in and why, is balanced with a sense of fun and a strong feeling of audience. The humor is slapstick, although the undercurrents are clear—many people do not believe in ME as a credible illness. Through this role-play, to paraphrase Wenger (1998), these AYMERs are involved in the social configuration of their group and establishing it in relation to broader configurations.

The discussions on the AYME site are usually upbeat, linguistic jokes are common, and screen names tend to be elaborate and witty. The fun is often by way of complex and absurd role-play discussions, and the board chat frequently involves collaboratively composed narratives as a way of sustaining the interaction. The interactants tend to bring all they can to the screen because a great number rarely leave their houses and have a heightened sense of linguistic agility. Figure 12.3 reflects a fast-paced (note the numerical notation of timings) absurd piece of drama. It is clear that the interactants are jointly envisaging a scene of farce.

These AYMERs are clearly typing very fast, and sometimes one AYMER's contribution will overlap with another's response. Asterisks mark off actions, and capitals are used for emphasis in a way that adds to the dramatic feel. The present tense is used, and there is a sense of real-time hesitation implied: "But I don't want a . . . wait I'll have that." Here DiscardedLozenge asks the others to imagine she is reacting to something she can see. The narrative takes on a deeper dimension and draws the group in close. The joke continues over time and later these AYMERs repeatedly refer back to this charade, again building it as part of their social history. The bonding thus operates on a number of levels: graphically (e.g., through asterisks and emoticons), grammatical (e.g., present-tense stage directions), lexical (e.g., vocabulary from the kitchen combined with colloquial expressions), and syntactical (e.g., the layout as if a script in a play, with one piece of dialogue answering another). There is a sense of the writing imitating speech, but in fact the AYMERs are careful to use markers to indicate what is spoken and what is not and to use emoticons to indicate mood. The shared application of all these features in this online game marks the community off as one with specialist meanings for everyday words and phrases, where cutlery be-

Ringyding

☐ Posted: 2004-03-04 16:29

hiiii jet - here, have a new spoon

DicsrdedLozenge ☐ Posted: 2004-03-04 16:29

can I have a spoon?

Author
Ringyding ☐ Posted: 2004-03-04 16:30

no. they are reserved for jet and jet a lone. here, you can have a nice plastic fork instead.

DiscardedLozenge ☐ Posted: 2004-03-04 16:31

but I dont want a...wait! I will have that, it'll make a very good wepon! ☺

Tricksie ☐ Posted: 2004-03-04 16:33

Hi, Roberta. *offers tissue and disposable fork*
EVERY NEW MAMBER GETSA PIECE OF CUTLERY- NEXT PERSON TO JOIN GETS AN EGG CUP (ok that doesnt count as cutlery but near enough - kitchen type supllies then!)

FIG. 12.3.   Spoons—creating social history.

comes an ironic symbol of friendship. The humor is sophisticated and closes the community tighter.

   Discussions sometimes refer to the way in which time passes slowly for AYMERs (see Fig. 12.4). As before, the board has a strong sense of place for the AYMERs—a playground feel that is frequently emphasized through metaphors (e.g., "it's been really quiet lately . . ."), as well as in the charades described in earlier examples. The interactants on this site seem to explore a range of topics with each other, and discussions often show timings that go right through the night because ME frequently causes reverse sleep patterns. Another aspect of typical message board discussion features refer-

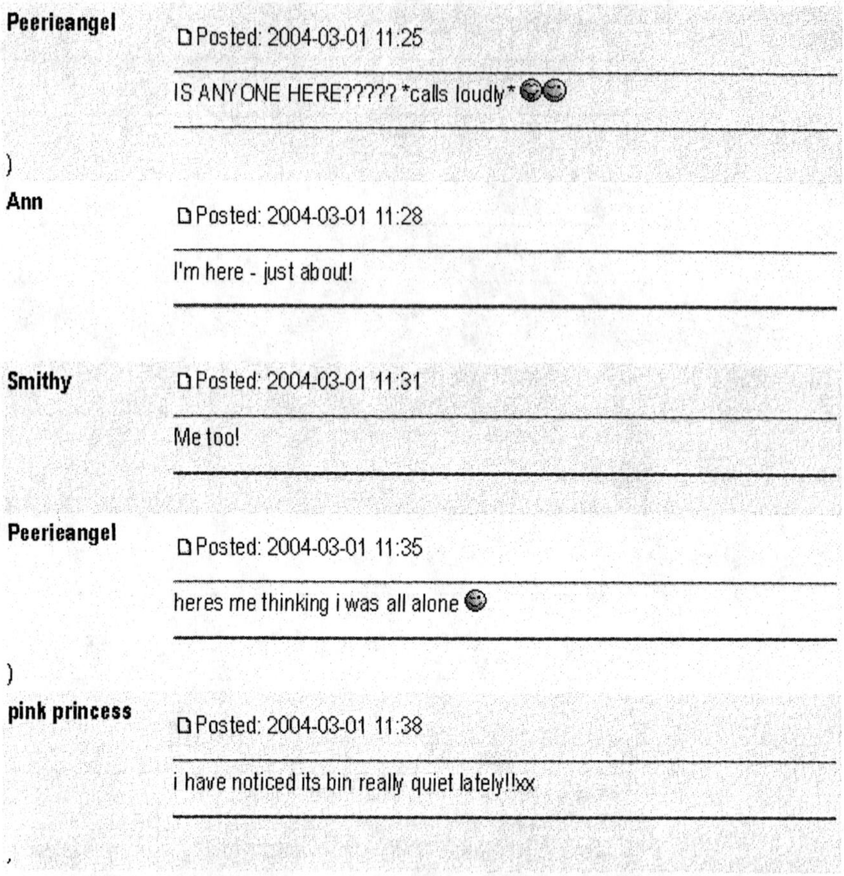

Peerieangel

☐ Posted: 2004-03-01 11:25

IS ANYONE HERE????? *calls loudly* 😊😊

)

Ann

☐ Posted: 2004-03-01 11:28

I'm here - just about!

Smithy

☐ Posted: 2004-03-01 11:31

Me too!

Peerieangel

☐ Posted: 2004-03-01 11:35

heres me thinking i was all alone 😊

)

pink princess

☐ Posted: 2004-03-01 11:38

i have noticed its bin really quiet lately!!xx

,

FIG. 12.4.   A sense of space—is anyone here?

ences to other Web sites and addresses are given. There is a sense in which
AYMERs "leave the house together" or watch TV with each other and gain a
sense of sharing and community as they express opinions on other sites.
Thus, the internet provides for such people the company they crave, but
that they cannot get from their living companions. It is clear that these
youngsters are able to develop points of view and remain creative and stim-
ulated in ways not possible without digital technologies.

FINAL COMMENTS

The landscapes of many children's lives are woven through with digital
technologies, sometimes replacing, at other times enriching, offline meat-
space lives. Wenger (1998) argued that there is "a profound connection be-

tween identity and practice" and went on to explain how "the formation of a community of practice is also the negotiation of identities" (p. 149). Wenger justified this through an argument concerning the interrelatedness of identity and worldview, with language, cultural artifacts, shared understandings, as well as participation in a range of communities. The fact that many of the young people meet first on web sites and then off line is one indicator of the influence of the internet; but the potency of many of the exchanges and the depth of debate and expressed feelings in some of the groups betray a different kind of profundity in online experiences.

In this chapter, I have shown two well-defined communities that have a strong sense of who they are and who they are not. In many ways, it is through this self-conscious definition of parameters and the negotiation of identity in relation to those parameters that seems to sustain the communities.

Turkle (1995) explained that, "In the real-time communities of cyberspace, we are dwellers on the threshold between the real and virtual, unsure of our footing, inventing ourselves as we go along" (p. 10). The development of self within communities, as I have shown earlier, involves a sense of empowerment. As a sense of writing the self develops, a sense of possibility as an active agent in one's own life emerges. This can become a real lived experience for those involved, whether talking as Wiccan online teens or imagining themselves playing even when not healthy enough to leave their beds.

REFERENCES

Achilles Sun. (2000). *The Wiccan rede.* Retrieved June 2, 2005, from Teen Wiccan Page: http://www.geocities.com/RainForest/2111/index.html

Amber Skyfire. (2000a). *I want to do spells.* Retrieved June 2, 2005, from http://www.witchcrafted.com/articles.htm#So%20Then,%20What%20is%20Witchcraft,%20Really

Amber Skyfire. (2000b). *Books for teen witches.* Retrieved June 2, 2005, from http://www.witchcrafted.com/books.htm

Arianwitch. (2004). *Welcome to the purple raven.* Retrieved June 2, 2005, from http://arianwitch.tripod.com/thepurpleraven/

AYME. (2004). *Messageboard.* Retrieved March 1–March 31, 2004, from The Association of Young People with ME: www.AYME.org.uk

Darksomenight. (2005). *Witching up your room.* Retrieved June 2, 2005, from http://www.witchcraft.org/Guest/guestbook.php?lang=en&layout=CoA%20Guest&start=920

Davies, J. (2004). Negotiating feminities online. *Gender and Education, 16*(1), 35–49.

Davies, J. (2005). Nomads and tribes: Online meaning-making and the development of new literacies. In J. Marsh & E. Millard (Eds.), *Popular literacies, childhood and schooling* (pp. 161–176). London: Routledge/Falmer.

Ito, M., & Okabe, D. (2004). *Intimate connections: Contextualising Japanese youth and mobile messaging.* Retrieved May 5, 2005, from http://www.itofisher.com/mito/archives/itookabe.texting.pdf

Laura. (2002). *Laura's diary.* Retrieved October 5, 2003, from http://www.dreamwater.net/bluemoon/october

Lave, J., & Wenger, E. (1991). *Situated learning.* Cambridge: Cambridge University Press.

Lois. (2004). Private e-mail correspondence with author, April 2004.

Paganus. (2005). *Resource centre.* Retrieved June 2, 2005, from http://www.geocities.com/paganus83/wicca/wr.html

Pixie. (2004). *The Children of Artemis guestbook (page 1).* Retrieved June 2, 2005, from http://www.witchcraft.org/Guest/guestbook.php?lang=en&layout=CoA%20Guest&start=920

Ravenwing. (2004). *Messageboard.* Retrieved September 20, 2004, from http://www.dreamwater.netsilvercircle/messageboard

Rheingold, H. (2003). *Smartmobs: The next social revolution.* Cambridge, MA: Perseus.

Rushkoff, D. (1996). *Playing the future: How kids' culture can teach us how to thrive in an age of chaos.* New York: HarperCollins.

Schofield Clark, L. (2005). The constant contact generation: Exploring teen friendship networks online. In S. R. Mazzarella (Ed.), *Girl wide web: Girls, the internet, and the negotiation of identity* (pp. 203–221). New York: Peter Lang.

Silvercircle. (2003). *TeenageKicks.* Retrieved September 1, 2003, from http://www.witchcraft.org/Guest/guestbook.php?lang=en&layout=CoA%20Guest&start=920

Skyfire, A. (2005). *Just for fun.* Retrieved June 2, 2005, from http://www.witch-crafted.com/humor.htm#14

Stern, S. R. (1999). Adolescent girls' expressions on web home pages: Spirited, sombre and self-conscious sites. *Convergence: The Journal of Research Into New Media Technologies, 5*(4), 22–41.

Teenwitch. (2005). *Homepage.* Retrieved June 2, 2005, from http://www.teenwitch.com

Terra. (2005). *Main menu.* Retrieved June 2, 2005, from http://www.angelfire.com/wi/spiralpath/intro.html

Thomas, A. (2005). Children online: Learning in a virtual community of practice. Retrieved May 5, 2005, from *E-learning, 2*(1), 27–38: http://www.wwwords.co.uk/elea/

Turkle, S. (1995). *Life on the screen: Identity in the age of the internet.* New York: Simon & Schuster.

Turkle, S. (1996). Constructions and reconstructions of the self in virtual reality. In T. Druckey (Ed.), *Electronic culture: Technology and representation* (pp. 354–365). New York: Aperture.

Valentine, G., & Holloway, S. (2001). Technophobia parents' and children's fears about information and communication technologies and the transformation of culture and society. In I. Hutchby & J. Moran-Ellis (Eds.), *Children, technology and culture: The impacts of technologies in children's lives* (pp. 58–77). London: Routledge Falmer.

Wenger, E. (1998). *Communities of practice.* Cambridge: Cambridge University Press.

Wildspirit. (2004a). *Forum.* Retrieved September 20, 2004, from http://www.witchcraft.org/Guest/guestbook.php?lang=en&layout=CoA%20Guest&start=920

Wildspirit. (2004b). Private e-mail correspondence with author, September 2004.

Witch-crafted.com. (2004). Retrieved October 24, 2005, from http://www.witch-crafted.com/map.htm

Virtually Queer Youth Communities of Girls and Birls: Dialogical Spaces of Identity Work and Desiring Exchanges

Susan Driver
Wilfrid Laurier University

> *The birl community is very important to me. We, as birls, and other groups that break the gender barriers of the world, hold a very special place in my heart and in my mind. They are a constant reminder that age-old gender stereotypes are, to be frank, a load of crap and nobody has to act or look a certain way merely because of their gender. That not everything is as it seems, and that not everything follows the same pattern and routine. Diversity is something that is many times attempted to be stifled, and communities such as that of birls keep diversity alive.*
> —Birls Live Journal (2004)

Cyber-communities are expanding the very terrain of social interaction and identification for gay, lesbian, bisexual, transgender, queer, and questioning (GLBTQQ) young people coming out and growing up within geographically scattered and culturally distinct contexts. There has emerged such an expansive range of communities for/by/about queer youth that it would be impossible to cover even a fraction in a single chapter. They range from national groups like *Alterheros* in Canada, *Queer Youth Alliance* and *Gingerbeer* in the UK, and *Youth Resource* in the United States, to more specific groups like the *Transproud* online community and the *Transyouth webring*. There are several youth positive lesbian dating forums such as *Superdyke, Lesbotronic, Gaydar,* and *Pink Sofa,* as well as digitally savvy sites such as *Technodyke* and creative forums for lesbians of color such as *Pheline.* Not only is there a proliferation of community forums, but within them the modes of communication include message boards, ezines, chatrooms, live discussions, community blogs, webrings, and listserves. The time has come when there is virtually a group to suit the needs of most young queers in cyberspace.

Online communities help to provide multilayered spaces of self-representation, support, and belonging for youth who are marginalized on the basis of their gender and sexual differences. Designing, moderating, and joining groups in which to talk with others, queer youth are at the forefront of do-it-yourself digital media. Such developments spur many questions: What is the form and content of these community spaces? How do youth construct, access, and participate in online communities? In what ways is community queered? How are community boundaries drawn? Who is included/excluded? Do these virtual communities have a connection to the real worlds of queer youth? What do youth say about them? How do we study youth online communities as adults without being unwanted lurkers?

Community is not a given for queer youth: It is lost, taken away, refused, and re-created at a very vulnerable time of life when articulating a sense of self and belonging becomes intensely urgent and uncertain. Connecting up with other queer youth through new media becomes vital way for youth to access and sustain links with queer mentors, friends, and acquaintances. Owens (1998) wrote in his book, *Queer Kids*, that "within a support network, especially one consisting of other teens, individual internal conflicts can subside and a youth can begin to heal. Self-esteem can be rebuilt" (pp. 149–150). In this way, communities for, by, and about queer youth may help to strengthen social trust and hope. Although queer youth may be isolated and individualized within their everyday lifeworlds, they are also cunning community builders learning to use new media to create innovative social networks. According to Addison and Comstock (1998): "As a result of their isolation and increasing access to the internet and the WWW, it seems that more and more les-bi-gay youth have begun to employ technology in order to understand and express their experiences and demand that they be considered culturally significant members of society" (p. 368).

Facing an especially hard time getting social recognition within their local families, neighborhoods, or schools, many youth are compelled to actively pursue new community forms and practices. I would argue that queer youth develop critical consciousness about the difficulties, conflicts, and compromises of partaking in communities as part of their coming-of-age and survival. There is a strong degree of intentionality in the making and sustaining of queer youth groups because they are forged from a crisis of not fitting into the norms of traditional community frameworks. This converges with the requirements of internet communities that demand a high level of intentionality, which is very different from the concrete bonds of physically situated communities. Online communities are such that "symbolic boundaries and resources are all fodder for the imagination of what a given community consists of and can be, as well as the kinds of interaction that this new type of engagement reflects" (Shumar & Renninger, 2002, p. 6). Queer youth are socially and culturally positioned to take advantage of these transformative dimensions of online communities, staking out new terms and territories of identification and belonging. Shumar and Renniger wrote that, "the internet has altered our sense of boundaries, participation and identity. It allows for the recasting of both self and community, meaning that through the Internet a person or group can revise his or her sense of possibilities" (p. 14). Allowing for flexible spatial and temporal boundaries of community participation, online community offers chances for dispersed and marginalized youth to align themselves through multiple and shifting interests, ideas, sentiments, and values.

Within these informal, grassroots communities, there is a great deal of room for experimentation and improvisation with visual and verbal styles. Although some youth speak directly about themselves, others use popular culture or fiction to introduce themselves or represent an idea. Using personalized handles and icons, it is possible to join discussions without ever disclosing a self, mingling with others through a concealed or possibly an invented identity. At various stages of coming out publicly, youth make use of this self-representational flexibility to show themselves at their own time and in their own specific and often quirky ways. A 19-year-old comments that "I've come out to people online, in large groups in chat rooms, which is much easier than in person or one-on-one" (Huegel, 2003, p. 82). Entering a community through a poem or song lyrics, a fragment of a Webcam shot, images of pets, or a drag self-portrait, youth are able to manipulate the signs through which they are read within the group. There is a striking diversity of modes of representation that not only leaves room for youth to explore how they will present themselves, but also enables diversely queer selves to join in. As such, community is not based on the transparency or stability of the identity of all members, but on the personal and collective work of signifying the details and transitional signs of experiences. Although deception is possible, misrepresenting a self in a completely false guise is rarely a problem in these groups because the point is not to tell the truth, but rather to respond to others with understanding, care, and reciprocity. GLBTQQ youth instigate performative dialogues online, encouraging creative practices of self-representation in relation to participation in community.

I use the term *queer* throughout this chapter to focus on the performative enactment of gender and sexual identifications through visual and textual languages. In this way, queer is not a descriptor so much as it is a process of signifying desire and selfhood within online modes of communication. Queer youth become meaningful as a category of analysis honed at the level of the creative practices through which youth resist binary heteronormative ways of thinking. Within cyberspace, queer youth actively challenge fixed notions of girl/boy, male/female, and heterosexual/homosexual that proscribe diverse desire and identifications. Young people in my research alternatively refer to themselves as lesbian or bisexual to name their desire for girls, transgendered to signify that their chosen gender identity as masculine and/or male differs from their ascribed sex as female. They call themselves genderqueer in an attempt to refuse either/or labels, and at other times the youth avoid such categorizations altogether to question and explore possibilities. Across a broad range of youth cyber-communities, self-presentation, and definition is often an unstable and changing cultural process. This affirmation of a queer self in flux lines up with Turkle's (2001) idea that "the culture of simulation may help us achieve a vision of a multiple but integrated identity whose flexibility, resilience, and capacity for joy comes from having access to our many selves" (p. 249). The contingent and mobile relations of internet media link up with the transitional queer self-formations of youth in ways that are mutually reinforcing. Through interactive social environments, youth are complicating the very terms through which they name their sexual and gender embodiments and experiences.

STUDYING VIRTUALLY QUEER YOUTH COMMUNITIES

After surfing online for a couple of months, I decided to focus on a close content analysis of daily dialogues within two communities that are part of the larger blogging site called livejournal.com. I selected the ikissgirls and birls communities because they are extremely active and popular open forums with a continuous and diverse flow of talk by youth about gender and sexuality. They are also useful because they are linked to the blogs of individual members, giving other members, and me as a researcher, access to personal and contact information. In this way, there were multiple possibilities for interaction between individuals, one on one and collectively, expanding the means through which youth communicate and connect with each other. The two forums are also fully archived and contain a very flexible range of topics as well as a mix of textual and visual forms of communication.

I was also interested in the groups' distinct yet overlapping modes of address to "girls who kiss girls" and "girls who identify as boys." The two groups are sometimes connected through dual memberships of individuals, yet they are also distinct in terms of the sexual and gender boundaries they construct. While ikissgirls focuses on desire between girls and birls converges around masculine identifications, in practice these communities also share some of the same members, topics, and conversational styles.

Both birls and ikissgirls are driven by a causal pleasure in idle talk, a collective sense of conviviality, and playfulness balanced with support, advice, and caring relations. Their members range loosely from 14 to 24 years of age, and they include hundreds of members with varying degrees of participation.

I closely followed the textual contents and forms shaping these communities for several weeks, and I also undertook a close and detailed interpretive analysis of a single week's worth of archived discussions. Drawing heavily on the words and dialogues developed by youth, I decided to use as many direct quotes as possible to convey living dynamic voices within these communities. The trick becomes learning how to convey a sense of individual spontaneity and differences with collective patterns of identification and meaning. As I became intensely focused in my observations and analysis, I began to feel uncomfortable and unsure about my status as a middle-age queer woman; I was an obvious outsider to these communities. Although I could enter cautiously, reflexively, and empathically as an ally, I could not pretend or force my belonging. I wondered if my presence would be considered invasive? Prying? or Prurient? Was I an unproductive lurker taking information without giving anything back in return?

I decided to ask randomly some of the youth if they minded me studying their community dialogues. Although ikissgirls and birls are open public sites and I decided to maintain the anonymity of the youth, I approached each person I quoted for permission to use their words. I was amazed by their unanimously affirmative responses. Queer youth want to be heard, quoted, understood, and respected. They want their words to have broader social significance—to be part of a bigger picture in which their experiences and perspectives are taken seriously. In many informal conversations I had with these youth through email, I discovered that although youth enjoy spontaneous self-directed exchanges with other youth online, they are more than willing to have their words used to support an expansion of knowledge about their lives. In the face of social invisibility and silence, after years of being dismissed as strange, immature, deviant, and confused, many youth are pleased to have their words recognized as valuable and publicly meaningful. They want their words carefully contextualized, left open for contradictions and changes, treated as intelligent and creative, and protected from negative moral judgments. This is the burden of responsibility and the gift of recognition that needs to be fostered within research about queer youth online. It is not an exact science, but a caring engagement that acknowledges failure, partiality, and emotional investment. Hopefully, my readings that follow offer a glimpse of the rich dialogues shaping queer youth communities, sharing intimate words for the sake of expanding public awareness of complex identities, desires, and social relations enacted by, for, and about youth online.

IKISSGIRLS: BY, FOR, AND ABOUT QUEER GIRLS

Bonnie, the Ikissgirls.com originator, wrote:

> I started up this site after many unsuccessful attempts to find a friendly online community for young females who are attracted to other females, simple as that. All the sites I found were aimed at all genders and/or sexual orientations, seemed threatening in some way, or were specifically for older women. I was looking for something personal, something I could easily relate to, something non-commercial and created by someone like me. As for the age thing, I myself realized at the age of ten that I was attracted to girls. Discovering one's sexuality should never be restricted to adults. (About IKG, 2004)

As one of the most active youth forums in livejournal.com, ikissgirls (*I Kiss Girls Live Journal*, 2004) community is an extension of a youth-owned and -operated web site named *I KISS GIRLS* that includes a gallery of pictures, a webring, a message board, storytelling pages, and an advice column. This elaborate internet site emerged out of a simple idea of creating "a friendly community for girls who kiss girls" (*I Kiss Girls Homepage*, 2004). Hailed as a "resource for young lesbian, bisexual, and bi-curious women," this community draws its boundaries according to specific age, gender, and sexual identities, and it is designed to encourage the showings and tellings of girl-on-girl erotic desires and relations (*I Kiss Girls Hompage*, 2004). The forum, ikissgirls, is an offshoot of the *I KISS GIRLS* web site and extends its interactive possibilities through ongoing threads of discussion and hypertextual links to the individual blogs of each member. Started in 2003, it already lists over 1,000 members and produces up to 35 threads of conversation a day. It is here that the interests, meanings, and purposes of this community rebound across a wide range of subjects from girl crushes to homophobia in schools to coming out and sexual adventures. Dealing with much more than personal lifestyle issues, this community has developed to provide members with a place to talk about vulnerable experiences that take on broader social significance as youth speak to each other with insight, care, and humor.

Ikissgirls provides a relaxing virtual community to casually talk with, listen to, and look at images of young queer girls. There are very few rules governing membership, nor are there many restrictions as to the content or form of discussions. Relaying minute details of a date, seeking out hair or fashion advice, exhibiting revealing pictures of oneself, telling of heartbreak, showing off a new tattoo, sharing a poem or song, passing along a comic, introducing a pet, debating about gay marriage, asking questions about sex toys—these are all engaging topics carried forth by members of ikissgirls. This community is not bound by a single interest. Rather it co-heres in providing a space to talk openly. Being able to participate in a relaxed spirit of openness provides a liberating space where sexual preference, although an important part of their sense of belonging, does not define all aspects of these girls' lives. As such, this virtual community's purpose and meaning is as fluid as a group of young people hanging out, gossiping, and laughing together in real life. Yet such simple activities are often harder for queer youth to access and thus are especially valued online as a supplement to offline life. A 16-year-old self-identified lesbian writes that:

> I do have a fairly large amount of GLBT friends, and I love them. But ikissgirls is different. It gives people a place to open up and share things. You can talk about personal subjects and issues that you wouldn't be able to address with close friends. People in the ikg community are of all ages and from all over. You can get an honest outside opinion on something, which is what I really enjoy. You can also get all kinds of support and advice. GLBT teen communities have helped many people I know become familiar with their sexuality and come out. It is a wonderful thing.

The idea of being able to talk more freely about personal subjects within the community is especially relevant when it comes to the topic of desire and romance. It is here that the physical distance and anonymity of a virtual community becomes useful for eliciting emotionally risky talk about love. At times the agony of teen love comes across through the added loneliness of silence. When a girl talks about falling in love with her best friend or confessing that a girlfriend has cheated on her by sleeping with a boy, it is often expressed for the first time online, out of reach of those who might scorn her. Many secrets about love are told precisely because they are addressed to other lesbian or bisexual girls who can relate and share feelings. These youth go to great lengths, providing details and analysis, as they try to communicate their romantic predicaments and receive detailed accounts in return.

After comforting someone who was dumped by a girlfriend, a member thoughtfully reflects on a similar event and reaches out: "If you want to talk, I'm usually always signed onto AIM . . . I know I'm a complete stranger, but sometimes talking to a stranger, who doesn't have any bias, is better than talking to a friend who knows you. =) *hugs*" The offering of unbiased support gets reiterated often within this community, especially when it comes to intimate struggles of love and loss. Yet an even more creative interplay of confession and assistance emerges as girls take on the imaginary role of lover. Here is an example of a bisexual girl who responds by saying, "im sorry she's cheating on you . . . your such a great person and if you were here . . . i would never cheat on you . . . well i would have a boyfriend too . . . but no cheating on you with another girl:) i love you." Wounded from real-life romance, girls are met with the promise of a better kind of romance fictionalized online. Community emerges as a place for healing and hope: Through brief moments of symbolic romance online, these girls help each other feel better and move on.

Although some youth articulate a secure sense of sexual identity and desire for girls, others use ikissgirls to talk about their doubts and fears. Some as young as 14 seek out advice from older members, asking: "What is gaydar?" "how to know if a girl is straight or queer?", and "what is the best way to make the first move?" At the beginning stages of their sexual explorations, many of these girls use the forum to get information and learn through their shared experiences. As a form of self-help dialogue, they teach each other conventions of lesbian culture. A 20-year-old writes that this community "is a good place for the younger generations that are going through tough times because of their alternate lifestyles, to converge and gain support and guidance from the older generations that have already mustered their way through." It is interesting that a 20-year-old is considered part of the older generation. Although this is a sign of the age lines implicitly drawn by members, it does not mean that age determines sexual confidence or experience. Seeking out sexual help and admitting vulnerability is a common element of many posts—almost a requisite of belonging to ikissgirls insofar as it creates a common sense of needing to hear back from others with similar frustrations and curiosities.

A remarkable feature of this community is its fluid sexual boundaries. Although the focus is on girls who kiss or want to kiss girls, many participants are openly and proudly bisexual. The very status of sexuality gets articulated as bisexual girls speak up about their need to be understood and respected, telling stories of not being taken seriously in either straight or lesbian communities. Several girls refuse to identify in clear-cut terms, leaving their sexuality open to multiple interpretations. A 17-year-old comments that she is "a lesbian with heterosexual tendencies," remaining coyly ambiguous and eliciting positive feedback. There is a remarkable openness toward bisexual and questioning youth in this community that gives them permission to ask questions without being shot down or ignored. A 16-year-old girl writes that "I find it weird that being more straight than bi, that I enjoy lesbian porn more than straight porn . . . why is that? *shrugs*." This question offers a rare chance to hear about youth enjoyment of porn and calls for responses from girls to exchange ideas about its pleasures. The visual identity icons selected by members are frequently highly eroticized images of girly porn stars or celebrities. I was struck by the prevalence of bold sexual visuals. Of course these icons are their personal tags that circulate among many communities, but they have special queer significance in this site, providing conversation pieces about how hot they are as figures of girl desire. Explicit sexual dialogues take place about buying sex toys, wearing dildos, and making do-it-yourself harnesses. Mixed in with practical comments about where to purchase and how to use toys, these youth talk about their fantasies and inhibitions. Ikissgirls incorporates sex as part of this community of queer girls in ways that overcome the regulative, taboo, illicit, and shameful tenor of discourses within the dominant culture, where girls are framed as either sexual prey or innocent and unknowing kids.

Although the ikissgirls community is largely devoted to personal talk about self-image, leisure, romance, and sex, and is not ostensibly a political forum, even its most intimate exchanges touch on issues of invisibility, power, and exclusion. I came to this community expecting light, friendly chats, but I was very moved by expressions of loneliness, fear, and isolation interwoven into the dialogues. Sharing experiences of coming out is very common among the members of this community. They have a chance to talk about the process of coming out with other young girls without judgment or adult scrutiny. Over the course of a week's entries, I counted more than a dozen times in which the issue of coming out was talked about. It was in the context of family relations and fear of rejection that the girls expressed the most worry, driving them to seek out advice. One girl writes: "Speaking of coming out to my mom . . . ANYONE HAVE ANY ADVICE???? She's really anti-gay and very Christian, so she's going to kill me." She is offered sympathetic, diverse pieces of advice. From short quips that advise her to keep quiet and get away from her mom as soon as possible, to longer analyses of right-wing Christian attacks on gays and lesbians, a responsive context is developed to place individual experiences in social perspective. While some recount their own struggles with intolerant parents, focusing on the dangers of coming out without a safe degree of independence and outside support, other girls tell of strengthened bonds with their mothers and fathers and possibilities of shared learning across generations. Many come forward with their struggles to understand and name their own desires, suggesting how coming out to oneself may be a drawn-out, difficult process. Girls also speak out about the empowerment of refusing to live in secrecy and shame by making their lesbian or bisexual identities public. Wildly diverse stories of coming out intermingle uneasily in this community, encouraging the youth to figure out their choices in relation with others. This community frames coming out as an ongoing social process, helping queer girls to see themselves as less isolated and alone in claiming their sexual identities.

Talking about coming out includes talk of the risks of losing social recognition and love, broaching larger issues of oppression. Although issues of homophobia and heterosexism are not explicit topics of discussion, they enter fragments of narratives as these youth admit to losing friends, being excluded at school, or having their rights denied. The more abstract aspects of gay rights are brought home when a girl desperately appeals for feedback on her decision to join the military. Raising doubts about the "don't ask, don't tell" policy, she worries that her career aspirations may force her to sacrifice her desire for girls, and asks "would any of you go out with a lesbian serving in the military?" Although she is greeted with support and confirmation that there are girls who would still want to date her, this thread marks an important glimpse of the fear provoked by institutional barriers facing queer youth today.

Acknowledging that problems of injustice reach into the religious heart of American culture, this community grapples with the power of anti-queer forces. After watching a story about a gay bishop on the TV news magazine *60 Minutes*, a girl questions the ignorance that surrounds her, both inside and outside her immediate family. In response, a 15-year-old girl asserts the need for political action and a movement when she comments that "it would be so cool if there was a gay type of Martin Luther King who can stand up for us." This seemingly apolitical youth community does not skirt more substantive issues of injustice that are raised out of the urgency of power inequalities and conflicts in the material world of the here and now.

In this way, the personal desires and identities of these girls emerge as inextricably political as they are grounded in the daily realities of the heterosexist social worlds they have grown up in and continue to survive as young queer people. As I turn to the birls community, complex enactments of self and community throw into question the gender parameters through which I have been referring to queer girls. What about girls who identify as masculine? What about genderqueers who desire boys? Where do boyish girls go to hang out, chat together, and enjoy conviviality? For those youth born female whose identity does not fit into girl terms or ideals, virtual communities are emerging to provide alternative spaces of social bonding.

BOYISH GIRLS UNITE IN THE BIRLS COMMUNITY

> see i'm just a little girl boy,
> trying to make my way in a man's world ("Best Cock on the Block," Bitch and Animal, quoted in *Birls Live Journal*, 2004)

In my search to understand the range and specific community practices of queer girls online, I realized that the very concept of being a girl is being transformed by those who define themselves and seek out others who identify outside the clear-cut lines of being girl/boy, straight/queer, and female/male. Many youth-organized virtual communities are creatively resisting normative identities. Whereas ikissgirls takes for granted the gendered status of being and desiring girls, other groups purposely defy them. Some communities adopt a more generalizing approach that embraces all who refuse gender binary categories: "This community is for those of us who don't feel we fit the binary gender system in use by most of society. Ungendered, many gendered, a gender other than the one society thinks you should be?" (*Genderqueer Live Journal*, 2004). In an attempt to overcome rigid identity-based community forums, this community defines itself through open-ended gender ambiguity and inclusivity. What is shared in common is a desire by many young people for movement across the gender spectrum without the compulsion to fit into or self-identify with a predetermined single spot. Genderqueer communities are actively structured through disinvestment and disidentification with normalizing categories of difference, linking individuals through shared interests in flexible gender systems.

Such virtual genderqueer spaces of dialogue and belonging mark new frontiers of community in ways that disrupt a more specific focus on queer girl online connections. Transgender youth groups often elicit and produce a provocative flux of identity: "new . . . girl . . . boi . . . ME! . . . . I'm 16 . . . I dont identify with a gender . . . or a sexual orientation/preference. I'm just me" (transyouth livejournal community). Transgender communities can also work to challenge heteronormative gender ideals while embracing specific sex/gender identities as a new basis for community. In this way, transgender ftm (female-to-male) youth groups embrace male and masculine aspects of their transitioning or transitioned selfhood. For youth who join these communities, talk is of becoming boy—of progressing toward the achievement and status of becoming a man. The passage is conceived as unidirectional, away from being a girl or having been seen as a girl. A 17-year-old on an ftm open community writes:

> And ever since I was little I've always felt I belonged in the so-called "male world." All my best friends growing up were guys, and I've always acted far more "boyish" than my (few) female friends. I've only just recently begun to look into things; mostly because I'm finally beginning to get disgusted with the body and social role I seem to be trapped in. I'm looking into someday (when I have money and am away from my mother) making the trip across the spectrum.

I came across a few sites that combine transgender and girl identities, simultaneously using and transforming their meanings as a basis for community formation. The birls forum describes itself as "a community dedicated to boyish/androgynous girls" with open borders such that "all people who don't define themselves as birls are welcome as well, including femmes, bio-boys, androgynes, and transguys . . . or you could just make up your own label for who you are" (*Birls Live Journal*, 2004). Birls draws together many boyish girls who gather to talk in detail about their self-images, romance, family, hobbies, and social struggles to be accepted. As an open and flexible community, members and friends come and go without restrictive codes or conventions. Listing over 800 active and inactive members and up to 30 new and distinct threads of discussion every day, this community stands out as attracting and maintaining the interest of a large group of youth. Naming oneself a birl is a celebrated act that encourages others to join in and get involved in the inventive development of self-presentation and interaction between birls. It is precisely the made-up quality of this identity that provides virtual community with a unique space for connecting girls who look, act, and feel like boys without delimiting who this includes.

Community among birls in this forum begins with a mutual appreciation of the value of being a birl in the face of widespread social misunderstanding, as one birl describes: "Some folks can't grasp that just because some girls are butch/boyish/androgynous/birly doesn't mean that they aren't female under their clothes . . . there's something insanely sexy about being able to look at someone and not be totally sure what sex they are, just that they're insanely hot." Affirmation of the desirability of birls is a key element throughout this online site even when complex issues of gender and sexual positioning are being worked through. There are many threads of discussion engaged in a process of defining birls and, more specifically, of trying to answer the question: "Why am I a birl?" In this sense, the community provides a collective place to dialogue publicly about identity, to share alternative ways of inhabiting in between genders. A youth introduces him or herself in the following ways: "I am a boyish girl (and a girlish boy) because I fluctuate between feminine and masculine. My gender identification is different all the time. I love to wear skirts, but I also love to bind, pack and wear ties. I am comfortable being called she most of the time, but other times I prefer he." Expressing a creative ability to live in the world as both boy and girl, this birl invites responses. In return, the community offers warm praise ("You are a doll") and encouragement ("I'd love to see you post more!"). Gender ambiguity becomes a source of pleasure and bonding among these youth, taken as a sign of being interesting and worth knowing.

At times the very concept of gender is up for grabs, boldly theorized by youth beyond heterogendered frameworks. A 19-year-old writes:

> I was born a girl and I can be pretty femme, but I no longer claim gender. I only id as queer . . . I reallly HATE gender labels, and all the million new labels seem to cram people into even smaller boxes. The thing that bothers me so much about labels are the stereotypes that go with them. Girls are supposed to be fragile and nurturing, and boys are supposed to be feelingless and tough. Majority of the time my general persona is equivalent to that of the stereotypical gay man. It seems as though the only way to defy gender is to be a butch girl or a flamboyant man.

Visual presentations of self are a vital way through which birls represent themselves. Images are an integral part not only of the introduction of a new birl to the community, but to the maintenance of contact and connection. Showing off a new haircut or eyeglasses, asking for fashion advice, posing seductively for a web-cam photo, and revealing friends and pets make up the content of frequent posts. Photos provide a visual immediacy that helps birls come to know each other in more intimate ways. But even more important, these photos are the basis for demonstrating and talking about birl embodiment. Here visual evidence of clothes, gestures, tattoos, accessories, and movements work to characterize the individual enactment of birliness. Personalized snap shots become a dynamic locus of birl talk, much of which is centered around praising and complimenting a person's looks (e.g., "mmmm very cute!"). Valuing physical appearances works to reverse and displace the negative perceptions of the dominant culture and invisibility of masculine girls in mass media, creating an empowering social realm in which to reenvision oneself as beautiful, attractive, and sexy precisely for being a boyish girl. Everyone who reveals themselves is received with embracing compliments, a remarkably effective way to encourage even the shyest to make themselves visible. A pervasive tendency of members is to flaunt their physical image, to assert themselves as camera whores, and to pose for the community over and over again.

Talk surrounding the physical details of looking boyish goes beyond a playful narcissism. It is also a site for sharing stories about degradation and social restriction. Barriers to birl self-expressions such as parental disapproval are shared for feedback and support: "Does anyone else have the problem of your mom telling you to be more feminine? If so, what do you say?" This person calls out to other birls to offer insight and strategies for dealing with pressure within families to conform to feminine ideals. The responses are generous and revealing of diverse perspectives and practical advice. Although some dismiss the parents as ignorant and not worth the effort, others raise questions and begin an analysis of the dilemmas they face: "I mean I can understand their desire to have their daughter look more like their daughter than their son, but seeing as I was that daughter who wanted to look like a son I understand that side too." Several older members recount the history of their struggle with moms and dads, holding onto their masculinity and sometimes finding acceptance. Narratives of resistance against parental judgments provide a powerful collective cultural system through which youth can draw encouragement and knowledge to deal with potentially devastating family rejection.

Although much talk revolves around the physical presentation of birls and the social reactions based on surface looks, many members stress that appearances are not everything, claiming that no prescribed look constitutes a birl since, as one birl commented, it has "everything to do with personality." The very question of *looking* masculine or feminine versus *being* masculine or feminine is at stake, as members seek to include girls who look girly into the birls community. Defending her place in this forum, a young girl writes that, "for those of you who don't think I'm a birl, you're under no obligation to click this link. So don't . . . a dress only makes me feel girly for a few moments, anyway." Simple assumptions of gender identity are rejected as more subtle elements of embodied consciousness enter discussions. There is an outpouring of support to include girly birls as members speak passionately about this girl's right to belong:

> Being a birl has as much to do with your inside as it does with your outside, and I think one of the biggest points of this community is to be who you are. You're an artist, a girlie girl and a birl . . . and I for one love the fact that you share that with all of us. You're awesome and beautiful, so don't let it get to you.

Talking about who belongs to the birl community provides an opportunity for questioning commonsense notions of boyish girls, exploring the emotional, mental, physical, and social variability of this subject position. Rather than simply define birls through a static set of attributes, this community creates coherence through an ability to dialogue, interpret, and personalize meanings.

Although gender identity, not sexual preference, is the focus of this community, many of the discussion threads address birls lusting after girls, desiring other birls, loving queer femmes, or exploring their bisexuality. Desire pervades birl talk. Being lesbian, gay, or bisexual is not a prerequisite of this community, yet much of the friendly banter takes on an erotic charge of queer attractions. Commenting on the sexual allure of birls becomes a daily ritual of birl members, reinforcing self-confidence and collective bonding. It is remarkable that virtually everyone posting pictures is told that they are cute, hot, sexy, or adorable. Such affirmation unites this community as a place to find sexual acceptance. Their mutual belonging rests on a mutual appreciation of their appeal as birls. Much of the exchange is light and flirty, filled with playful dialogues that teasingly suggest possibilities of encounters:

A: I've got some ties you can have . . . for a small fee
B: And what fee would that be, pray tel? ;)
A: Yeah umm . . . stop by my house. lol
B: I'll be right over . . .

This online community is scattered with imaginary promises of off-line connections, many of which are sexually driven. These moments are often brief and ephemeral within the public realm of the community, but they are important to sustaining interest and openness between birls and the girls who love them. It seems that erotic recognition is an ongoing dynamic of community involvement, acting in performative ways to create a shared sense of their desirability as birls.

Beyond the enactment of sexual flirtations and seductions online, this community asks questions, shares frustrations and pleasures, and tells stories about sexual relations occurring in their off-line experiences. A recurring theme is the problem of lusting after and dating straight girls:

> I am hopelessly in love with a straight girl
> completely head over heels
> I love everything about her
> except when she talks about boys
> and how they hurt her

Birls express how risky it is to pursue straight girls, who use them to try something new and experiment with their sexual identities. It is in relation to straight girls that members talk about wanting to be boys: "I wish I was born a guy, everything would be simpler." Positioning straight girls as deeply desirable, they are also represented as elusive and deceptive—they provoke vulnerability, fear, and anger among this community. This ambivalence creates a division between birls and straight girls. In the process, these youth reinforce boundaries marking those inside/outside the birl community. Sympathizing and relating to the dilemmas of desiring straight girls becomes a common means of bonding as birls. Although not all birls are interested in straight girls, this experience signifies more general difficulties of being a boyish girl in a society that favors bio boys or feminine girls. In a disturbing way, straight girls mark the other to this community, sometimes longed for and sometimes loathed as reminders of gender-restrictive powers and pleasures.

This online community of birls is complex and shifting in the ways it marks its boundaries, identities, and interests. It builds its collective momentum through the affirmation of the physical, social, and personal qualities of boyish girls, left open to continual performances, representations, and interpretations. As a symbolic space of community interaction and belonging, these youth express joy and a sense of belonging in their masculine qualities. What is at stake is a sharing of experiential stories and visual images that becomes the basis of virtual interconnectivity. In this way, the content of most community discussions are grounded in the material worlds of these youth. Individual fragments of this material get taken up, reworked, questioned, exchanged, and mediated within an online sphere to become the basis of a collective discourse.

Crossing between off-line and virtual experiences is the crux of the birl forum, leading some to fantasize about their coming together: "I want a big abandoned house right off the beach, filled with birls," "well you know what kid, birls stick together dammit!!;)" Some birls dream of actualizing this community in time and space. Although this may be impossible, this imaginary projection of community is empowering in the ways it compels these youth to envision alternative gender relations. Such imaginative work is potentially transformative, according to Shumar and Renninger (2002), who write that "the fluidity of boundaries and flexibility of how community is defined make it possible for participants to enact forms of community in the virtual world and extend the definition of community as a function of social imagination" (p. 9). These youth are continually learning how to construct a community based on acceptance of differences. In the process, they come up against the challenges of sustaining an inclusive environment, as is cautiously commented on by a birl who gets right to the tenuous heart of the matter: "I think once we start excluding people, that will be our downfall."

CONCLUSION

The ikissgirls and birls communities are informal realms of social engagement that challenge us to think beyond the binaries of private subjective spaces and public political spheres. They do not draw lines separating sexuality from issues of family, work, or school because these issues are interwoven in their embodied and symbolic experiences. The banal details of fashion are not outside deep questions of belonging; sex is not only about bodies and pleasures, but also the limits of social acceptance and political rights; talk of tattoos is not a purely subjective issue of adornment, but also a mode of communication; and coming out is not merely a psychic process, but a painful confrontation with heterosexist culture. The performative work of young queer self-definition and social analysis is enacted in many combinations, spurring new ways of understanding youth and community.

Reaching beyond static sex/gender systems, the youth quoted throughout this chapter are at the forefront of elaborating forms and practices of virtual community that transform the public voices of youth today, calling for more nuanced ways of naming and leaving identities open for reinvention. Queer youth cyber-communities challenge simplistic divisions between the virtual and the real, the imaginary and the physical, the textual and the embodied, the experiential and the fictional. They provide insights into the in-between spaces where youth work out the unique contours of their sexualities and genders, as they communicate their identifications and desires in words and images shared with others across diverse contexts. It is online that young people find ways to safely and creatively explore their queer differences as lesbian and bisexual girls, transyouth, genderqueers, and birls. Putting their bodies, fantasies, and experiences on the line, queer youth refuse to tame or censor themselves through fear of adult predators or moral regulators. Desire becomes a language negotiated and owned by these youth, turned toward the detailed dilemmas they face day by day. In this way, the erotic lives of youth are explored by, for, about, and toward those who are also willing to talk about their lives as young people resisting heteronormativity. It is intimate acts of care, exchanged back and forth within informal public spheres, that invite a relaxed flow of chat, gossip, stories, jokes, and flirtations. Integrating intersubjective bonds of empathy, pleasurable conversations, and politicized talk of oppression and exclusion, youth are in the process of devising interactive and intertextual collective spaces shaped according to the whims and needs of queer youth.

REFERENCES

About IKG. (2004). *About I Kiss Girls.* Retrieved August 4, 2004, from http://www.ikissgirls .org/!.php?about

Addison, J., & Comstock, M. (1998). Virtually out. In J. Ausin & M. Willard (Eds.), *Generations of youth* (pp. 367–378). New York: New York University Press.

Birls Live Journal. (2004). Userinfo. Retrieved July 20, 2004, from http://www.livejournal.com/ userinfo.bml?user=birls

Genderqueer Live Journal. (2004). Userinfo. Retrieved August 1, 2004, from http://www .livejournal.com/userinfo.bml?user=genderqueer

Huegel, K. (2003). *GLBTQ: The survival guide for queer and questioning teens.* Minneapolis: Free Spirit Publishing.

I Kiss Girls Home Page. (2004). Homepage. Retrieved August 3, 2004, from http:// www.ikissgirls.org/

I Kiss Girls Live Journal. (2004). Userinfo. Retrieved August 3, 2004, from http:// www.livejournal.com/userinfo.bml?user=ikissgirls

Owens, R. (1998). *Queer kids: The challenges and promise of gay, lesbian and bisexual youth.* New York: Haworth.

Shumar, W., & Renninger, K. A. (2002). Introduction: On conceptualizing community. In S. Wesley & K. A. Renninger (Eds.), *Building virtual communities* (pp. 1–27). Cambridge, England: Cambridge University Press.

Turkle, S. (2001). Who am we. In D. Trend (Ed.), *Reading digital culture* (pp. 236–250) Oxford: Blackwell.

Part IV

LEARNING AND EDUCATION

This final part of the book focuses on a theme that has cut across several of the preceding contributions: education and learning. The difference here is that all these chapters focus on initiatives that involve more or less explicit *teaching* via the use of digital media. Even so, the contexts addressed here are extremely diverse, crossing the digital divide from rural South Africa to the United Kingdom and the United States, and including formal settings such as schools alongside more informal youth and community-based projects. Although all of these chapters offer relatively optimistic accounts of the potential of digital learning, they all point to the importance of the social context and pedagogic relationship between teachers and students (or adults and young people). They all suggest that the technology will not teach in and of itself: It needs to be embedded within productive social and educational settings, and it needs to be actively and creatively used, rather than simply applied in an instrumental manner.

Bill Holderness (chap. 14, this volume) addresses an issue that has only been marginally considered in the chapters thus far: the so-called *digital divide.* Focusing on South Africa, but drawing lessons for the continent as a whole, he argues that the digital divide is merely a reflection of much broader historical, socioeconomic, and generational factors, as well as the degree of urbanization and access to resources (such as electricity). He considers the considerable challenge of equipping educators and learners in remote, rural, nonelectrified schools and homes with basic technological knowledge and competencies. Holderness argues that past initiatives utilizing new media to bring about educational reform have only succeeded when they have gained the active participation of teachers. He suggests that such attempts to bridge the digital divide must take account of the mediating role of teachers and community leaders, and the nature of traditional rural cultures. This chapter concludes by looking forward to potential partnerships and more ecological solutions to closing educational and technological gaps in sub-Saharan Africa.

Andrew Burn and James Durran (chap. 15, this volume) report on work currently being undertaken in the very different context of a specialist media arts school in Cambridge, England. In many respects, the teaching they describe is at the cutting edge of media education. Significantly, the focus here is not simply on the use of digital technology in student production, but also on how this technology can be used to help students analyze and deconstruct existing media texts. Using digital editing programs, their students are able to unpick media texts, transform, and rework them, thereby giving them direct hands-on experience of the ways in which images and sounds can be selected, manipulated, and combined to create new meanings. Rather than seeing analysis and production as two separate activities, Burn and Durran propose that analysis can be creative, productive, and affective. More broadly, they suggest that technologies such as digital video editing software can enable schools to intervene in—and even to begin to equalize—the power relationships between media producers and their audiences.

Liesbeth de Block and Ingegerd Rydin (chap. 16, this volume) present experiences from an innovative pan-European research project, where video production was used to promote intercultural communication. This project established after-school media clubs for refugee and migrant children between ages 10 and 14 years in six European countries. The children made and edited short videos and then exchanged them on the internet. This chapter focuses specifically on a small set of productions using the genre of rap music: It discusses two video exchanges between Sweden and the United Kingdom, drawing on observations of the production and exchange processes, the videos as texts, and on broader observations and interviews over the course of the fieldwork. The authors caution against celebratory accounts of rap, showing how the genre became the basis of some complex social negotiations among the children: Although technology offered the possibility of global dialogue, this was not by any means unproblematic. However, they also show how such global cultural forms are refracted through local variations, and that digital media can permit the production of hybridized texts that reflect the multiple and diverse cultural identifications of such global young people.

The final chapter focuses on a similarly informal setting—in this case, a community-based youth project in a deprived urban neighborhood in the United States. Carol Thompson and her colleagues from the Hopeworks project (chap. 17, this volume) address the aspiration, explicitly or implicitly contained in various youth programs, that technology will provide the means for healthy identity construction for disenfranchised youth. They argue that digital technologies are insufficient tools for this purpose. Rather, they are a means toward apprenticeship in which younger youth learn from more experienced peers how to develop their skills and self-respect. This chapter traces the identity development in one youth trainee over a period of 1 year, as well as analyzing the broader organizational culture of the project. It shows how young people act initially as apprentices and then as leaders, grappling with new kinds of knowledge, the needs of customers, the social networks in which they find themselves, and the global vectors of which they are a part. While the GIS technology used in the project is intellectually stimulating and provides the means for this trainee to alter his understanding of his city, his identity shifts are equally a result of his relations with peers, mentors, the team he now leads, and various civic groups to whom he makes presentations.

In different ways, these chapters seem to conclude by arguing that we need to look beyond technology and focus on the sociocultural contexts in which it is used. Despite the rhetoric of the digital generation, it is clear that technology cannot teach—let alone overcome social inequalities or transcend cultural differences—in and of itself. Technology can undoubtedly make a significant difference to learning, and hence to young people's identities and life chances; but whether and how it does so will depend crucially on the motivations of those who use it.

Chapter 14

Toward Bridging Digital Divides in Rural (South) Africa

Bill Holderness
Nelson Mandela Metropolitan University

A chapter that considers remote rural schools and communities in Africa may seem out of place in a book that focuses on cutting-edge technological and educational developments among children and young people in First World countries. But there is a general and serious tendency to overlook the needs of *digitally disadvantaged* generations of children and young learners living in lesser developed contexts. The contrasts between First and Third World countries with regard to technological access and utilization are stark. African societies currently experience major digital divides, which reflect historical, socioeconomic, and generational factors, as well as differing degrees of urbanization and access to resources (e.g., electricity). Such divides are growing exponentially as rapid technological advances are made in highly industrialized countries, and this in turn has significant negative implications for the economic potential of the developing continent. This chapter considers some of the challenges, difficulties, and potential advantages of equipping communities, and especially educators and learners in remote, rural, nonelectrified schools and homes, with basic technological knowledge and competencies.

In considering possible approaches to bridging the digital divides, this chapter draws on past initiatives and current efforts that have made use of relatively new media to reach rural schools and educators with limited access to key information and educational opportunities. These initiatives have made use of interactive learning materials, as well as TV, video lectures, and even computers—in venues that have access to electricity. The intentions of the interventions have ranged from supporting and improving the performances of rural educators and school leaders, to enhancing the quality of education experienced by children, to benefiting remote schools and the communities they serve. Through various media, educators and learners have been exposed to key knowledge and varieties of formal and informal pedagogies. The chapter concludes by looking forward to potential partnerships that can harness technological advances such as alternative energy sources and mobile internet to address educational gaps and bridge the digital divides in lesser developed contexts.

PART I: DIGITAL DIVIDES

The Global Divide

The global problem of a major digital divide between developed and developing countries is long standing and growing. Six years ago, an investigation by the United Nations Development Program (UNDP, 1999) found that only 2.5% of the world's population was connected to the internet—and approximately one quarter of the digitally connected in the world resided in one country—the United States. Ninety percent of internet host computers were based in the highest income nations, but these same nations were home to only 16% of the world's population.

More recently, sobering global statistical reports have been published on the Caslon Analytics web site (2005). These include the 2002 findings of the International Telecommunications Union (ITU) that of 141 million Internet hosts across the globe, some 106.2 million are in the United States and a mere 0.274 million in Africa (0.238 million in South Africa). The estimated number of personal computers in the United States is 178 million, in Australia 10 million, and in all of Africa 7.55 million.

Watkins (2000) pointed out that children in developing countries spend far less time in education than those in developed countries. On average, a child entering primary school in a developed country can expect 15 to 17 years of education. However, in sub-Saharan Africa, the average school-life expectancy is only 5 to 6 years, and it is less than 3 years in Burkina Faso, Mali, Niger, and Mozambique. With reference to levels of deprivation measured in terms of the Education Performance Index, Watkins (2000) pointed out that South Asia is 32% lower than the average for all developing countries. However, Africa is 40% higher than the average for all developing countries.

African Digital Divides

Although the main concern of this chapter is with the plight and potential of the marginalized rural areas of the African continent as a whole, most of the specific details relate specifically to South Africa—to which the writer owes most of his rural field experiences and insights. Many features of living in a South African rural context—in particular, the lack of access to Information Technology—are considered sufficiently common to the continent as a whole to justify using the term *rural Africa* in this chapter. However, this should not lead us to ignore the considerable diversity of political and socioeconomic conditions that exist in Africa. Indeed, when considering Future Possibilities in Part IV, the need to recognize differences in African settings is emphasized.

Given the range of factors that determine the use of information technologies and the many lines along which the divide falls, it becomes more helpful to conceive of the problem in the plural—in terms of a number of digital divides, both within and between countries. For example, the UNDP study referred to earlier identified a number of factors that caused divisions both between and within countries—factors other than simply access to technology. In terms of *language*, English was used in almost 80% of web sites, yet less than 1 in 10 people in the world spoke the language. In terms of *income*, the average Internet user in South Africa had an income seven times above the national average. The average Bangladeshi would have to spend 8 years' income to buy a computer, compared with just 1 month's salary for the average American. In terms of **gender**, only 17% of Internet users in South Africa were women, and in terms of age, most users were under the age of 30.

Norris (2001) supported the idea that there are multiple divides to consider: a *global divide* between industrial and developing societies; a *social divide* between the information rich and information poor in each nation; and, within the online community, a *democratic divide* between those who do and do not utilize technology and information to engage in public life.

South African Inequalities

Divides in the South African context can be identified not only between hemispheres and countries, but also among provinces, regions, districts, and generations. For example, until 2003 the Eastern Cape was considered the poorest province in South Africa, and now it is second poorest to the Northern Cape, which has no major urban development or industry. Even within the Eastern Cape, there are major divides between those who live in the Nelson Mandela Metropole (around Port Elizabeth) and the deep rural hinterland (around Mtata). Within these same regions, further divisions are experienced between urban and rural dwellers and among the young people, teachers, and semiliterate parents.

The most recent South African Schools Register of Needs (Department of Education, 2001) depicts an educational context riddled with digital divisions. By far the majority of schools are rural (at least 60%). About half of South African schools (47%) have no electricity and therefore no access to electronic teaching aids such as TV, video recorders, overhead projectors, let alone computers. The situation is probably far worse in many other countries of Africa given that South Africa enjoys a relatively high Gross Domestic Product (GDP) and strong economy. South Africa is acknowledged as one of the most developed countries in Africa, yet 34% of schools have neither a telephone line nor access to running water.

Many schools are, of course, situated in urban areas. However, of South Africa's 27,000 schools, only 6,581 have one or more computers—and where there is one, it is generally used only for administration purposes and seldom, if ever, for teaching and learning (if it is working). Eighty percent of schools have no media centers, and those that do generally have few educational resources and cannot afford the luxury of a computer or the running costs required to maintain it or an Internet connection. Moreover, the lack of computer literacy among teaching staff puts a further brake on digital developments.

Significance of Divides

Why is it important to narrow the digital divides? Clearly there are political, social, and economic reasons. Civil rights activists in developed countries, such as Chapman and Rhodes (1997), argue that "access to the internet is as important a part of civil life as parks, public transport, libraries, and cultural centres." Certainly in rural Africa, failure to address imbalances in access to and the ability to use IT will certainly entrench imbalances between the rich and poor, the historically privileged and disadvantaged, and the information haves and have-nots. It will widen existing gaps in levels of education and seriously limit the opportunities for young rural Africans to compete in the mainstream economy, find employment, and participate in civil society.

In his address to the National Union of Educators, the Superintendent-General of the Department of Education (Edley, 2005) stressed that the "chasm between rich and poor schools must be narrowed—yet it has widened." He went on to warn that the huge disparities between haves and have-nots have historically caused social unrest, conflict, and even revolution. Kofi Annan (UN Secretary General) and James D. Wolfensohn (former president of the World Bank) agreed that exclusion from digital access poses a threat likened to lack of drinkable water, jobs, shelter, food and health care. Wolfensohn went on to state that "the digital divide is one of the greatest impediments to development and it is growing exponentially" (cited in Norris, 2001, p. 40).

Debates Around Divides

It is important to define what we mean by the term *digital divides*. The understanding that policymakers and others attach to the concept largely influences how they respond to and legislate about the matter. Servon (2002) pointed out that the popular conception of the digital divide tends to be simplistic, equating inclusion in the information society with access to computers and the internet. Policymakers and the media have tended to define the term narrowly and incompletely. Instead, she argued that we need a broader and more complex understanding of the problem than simply possession of, or permission to use, a computer and the internet. It needs to include both training and content issues:

> Access is a necessary precondition but that engenders a need for training in order to use the tools. Once people have facility with the tools, they demand content that serves their interests and meets their needs. The process of redefinition must also be informed by an analysis of how different groups use IT and for what purposes. (Servon, 2002, p. 8)

Are digital divides a diminishing problem? Will advances in technology and their increasing availability at reducing costs enable the person in the street to afford, access, and benefit from information technologies? It is true that, at least in developed countries, the gap between digital haves and have-nots has been closing rapidly as access to information technology has increased at a rapid rate. Some writers maintain that the problem of the digital divide will basically disappear with time as technology becomes more readily accessible to all sectors of society. Compaine (2001) went so far as to say that we should "declare the war against the digital divide won and move on to issues with higher stakes" (p. 301).

However, this chapter maintains that a larger problem still remains—particularly in Third World contexts, such as rural Africa. The high levels of illiteracy in rural areas (Norris, 2001) and the expectations that computer/internet users will be able operate at a fairly sophisticated level in English all act against the likelihood of a rapid narrowing of digital divides in Africa. Morisett (2001) stated that "no technology, in itself, will ever eliminate the differences that arise among people who effectively utilize a technology and those who do not . . . between those who can read well and those who cannot . . ." (p. x). Servon acknowledged that, even in the United States, deep divides continue between those who possess the resources, education, and skills to reap the benefits of the information society and those who do not. Persistent gaps remain between different racial and ethnic groups, people with and without disabilities, single- and dual-parent families, the old and the young, and people with different levels of income and education.

The next section provides a more social and humane perspective on the rural African context because an understanding of such factors is a necessary backdrop and precursor to any ambitious interventions aimed at bridging digital divides. We begin by examining some of the ways in which digital divides get played out in the lives of young and old in industrial and rural societies. This illustrates issues such as those raised by Cuban (2002) regarding the components of an effective intervention, such as the need for stakeholder participation, content training, and sustainability.

PART II: CONTEXTUAL CONSIDERATIONS

Contrasting Youthful Experiences and Opportunities

Most of the younger generation considered in other chapters of this book have access to personal computers—if not at home, then at least at the schools they attend. Livingstone and Bober (2004) reported in the *UK Children Go Online* (UKCGO) survey that 75% of 9- to 19-year-olds in Britain have accessed the Internet from a computer at home, and almost all children and young people (92%) have accessed the internet at school. An even higher percentage (98%) has used the internet at least once. Only 7% of adults had used the internet at one place or another in 1996, but 97% had already had access to and used the internet by the time of the survey in 2004.

The different degrees of sophistication in the use of computers and the internet by young people are examined elsewhere in this book and are the subject of many recent studies in the developed world. For example, in their UKCGO survey, Livingstone and Bober (2004) revealed "a plethora of ways in which children and young people are taking steps towards deepening and diversifying their internet use, many of them gaining in sophistication, motivation and skills as they do so" (p. 51).

By contrast, we turn our attention to those children and young people who reside on the other side of the digital divide. For them, an average of only 4 years of education can be expected, whereas their counterparts in Europe can expect 15 years (Watkins, 2005). To make the contrast a little more vivid, here are photographs of two classrooms I visited close to where I lived.

Classroom Contexts

The class depicted in Fig. 14.1 was being taught on a baking hot summer's day, with little protection given by the corrugated iron sheets. Without desks to work at or books to write on—and certainly no electrical point— the opportunities to learn about computers and modern technology in such a classroom are virtually nonexistent. Indeed, children in such contexts (by no means the worst in rural Africa) are largely dependent on the presence of an informed adult for any form of education, and she in turn is particularly reliant on the existence of a book in her hand.

When children have no books to read or desks to work at, it is not surprising that the teacher reads aloud and dictates to the whole class, and they in turn learn through chorused repetition and memorizing. Over 20 years ago, Hawes (1979), in his book, *Curriculum and Reality in African Primary Schools*, identified such responses as *survival teaching*—an apt term and

FIG. 14.1. Class in a corrugated iron structure.

one that still applies in large areas of the rural world today. He argued that
for hard-pressed, disillusioned teachers working for long hours in tough,
bleak conditions and with low recognition, formal teacher-centered approaches may well represent the only possible alternative for a struggling
teacher to adopt. But this is a far cry from the kind of independent, asynchronous, and outcomes-based learning opportunities that computer-
based education requires and promotes today. So it is no wonder the digital
divide is growing rapidly and exponentially.

Classes are often held *under trees* (see Fig. 14.2) or in hot, temporary dwell-
ings, simply because there is no permanent classroom available. Both figures
depict scenes that are not uncommon in rural Africa. Of course, some excel-
lent teaching can happen under trees, but, from a digital education perspective, if there is no alternative venue, such children are deprived in obvious
ways. Not least of these is that schooling cannot happen during heavy winds,
dust storms, and thunderstorms. Again, the divide widens where there are no
working surfaces, let alone telephone lines for modems and internet expo-

FIG. 14.2.   Class under the best shade in the village.

FIG. 14.3.   Class in a local church.

sure. Close by in the same school, another class has been allowed to use the local church (see Fig. 14.3). But again, writing through church pews does not give learners much practice in computer-based learning.

The Older Generation

In such developing world situations, the key role of the teacher for the advancement of young learners is evident. Thus, to facilitate the development of a digital generation in *rural* Africa, this older generation of mature (mostly Black female) teachers will need to be involved, particularly if they are expected to play the role of gatekeepers in future years—in line with current developments in industrialized countries (Livingstone, 2005). If the teachers are exposed to the possibilities of computers and other new media, there is more likelihood that they will be well disposed toward advocating and promoting them in the schools. If not, this older generation, which makes up the teaching force in rural areas, may continue to view such advancements negatively and as a potential threat to their teaching positions.

Furthermore, the traditional structure of the family in rural Africa plays a large role in the decision-making processes of patriarchal and hierarchical rural communities. Families belong to the clan, and so the traditional leader or chief of the clan is the most important person in his particular area. The leader, along with his advisors and the heads of households, are therefore vital to include in any venture, above and beyond informed educators and teachers. It is the traditional leader who grants people the right to teach in *his* school, to start a church or business, or to buy property. This is another important argument for the inclusion of the older generation in closing the digital divide. This inclusion may be achieved through such simple strategies as requiring learners to ask their parents, guardians, or older siblings what they need or want researched on the internet. However it could and should include more direct involvement too. Wisely managed, advances in technology could support existing family structures, rather than undermine them. In this way, a positive *reverse socialization* (Buckingham, 2006) could occur, whereby children in rural Africa could help their parents or elders adapt to technological developments.

AIDS Orphans

The HIV/AIDS pandemic is having catastrophic consequences in rural Africa; it has been leaving increasing numbers of children without parents and many schools without teachers. Where there are no willing or able grandparents, aunts, or uncles, then child-headed homes—even with little or no income—become the best option (better than the alternative of the street). At least child-headed homes contain some of the children who may have access to school environments, and therefore the potential for a digital education; but once children are on the street, there is little intervention and even less infrastructure available to find them and reintegrate them back into normal society.

What chances does Africa have to break through the vicious cycle of digital deprivation and disadvantage depicted earlier—when so many of her children arrive at school boiling hot or freezing cold, barefoot, and starving after a long 10-kilometer walk in the early morning? The last farm-school class I visited in winter was huddled around a wood fire made in the middle of the classroom—in an attempt to keep warm. What relevance do such social and contextual anecdotes and pictures have for a book dealing with digital generations? I argue that the realities they depict are fundamental to understanding the ways young people and new media can move forward. In the next section, we consider what insights might be gained from previous and current initiatives to bring about large-scale innovation and improvements, such as would be required to bridge Africa's rural divides.

PART III: RURAL AFRICAN REFORM INITIATIVES

The chapter now draws on the field experiences of a number of large-scale education projects in which I have been intimately involved. All of these initiatives have, in various ways, attempted to provide support and bring about improvements or alternative approaches in marginalized rural schools. As such, they can serve to inform and caution, guide and inspire future efforts to bridge the divides. The final part of the chapter considers future possibilities and partnerships in addressing the digital divide issue and bringing rural children, schools, and communities quickly and smoothly into the 21st century.

The following two school-improvement projects were two of the largest South Africa has known. They were both particularly ambitious and are therefore interesting to compare. Both the Primary Education Upgrading Programme (PEUP) and the Thousand Schools Project (TSP) were bold initiatives, each of which ultimately sought to bring about improvements and changes in almost 1,000 needy schools in the country.

The first project grew and endured in the northwestern region of South Africa over a 16-year period (1980–1995), by which time it was fully accepted by the local Department of Education and thus became an institutionalized innovation. (More details may be found in the publications listed later.) The TSP, by contrast, took a lot more time and money to get started (1993–1994) and yet, despite its much stronger funding base, for various reasons failed to endure beyond 18 months (1995–1996)—and made little if any impact. However, valuable lessons for future projects can be learned from these initiatives, which should inform any future planning to introduce alternative school structures.

Primary Education Upgrading Programme (PEUP)

In essence, the PEUP was a self-help, school-improvement program. It developed its own system of in-service teacher education courses and classroom visits and relied primarily on local communities for its support base. It began as a quiet and humble effort by a group of junior primary educators to improve the Grade 1 classrooms and teaching practices in their disadvantaged, Black primary schools. From almost unnoticed beginnings in seven semirural, village schools, the project grew rapidly into a major primary education improvement program, involving over 900 schools and in all class levels (from Grades 1–6).

As a result of its efforts, many of the kinds of schools described at the outset of this chapter (and shown in Figs. 14.1–14.3) were transformed into stimulating places of learning. In addition, their teaching methodologies were modernized and revolutionized over a period of time, and local village communities began to play more active roles in matters relating to schooling provision. But how was this achieved, and what lessons can be learned for future efforts to bridge the digital divides in Africa?

Various factors such as local community involvement, project ownership, and personnel empowerment have been identified by the author (Holderness & Altman, 1992) as having contributed to the success and sustainability of this project. Starting with the Grade 1 teachers and their principals, the upgrading process moved year by year up the school until the classes in all six grades were engaged in improving themselves. At the same time, these schools invited neighboring schools to visit them—to encourage them to be part of the upgrading process. Eventually almost all of the 900 primary schools in the 17 education circuits were at least nominally involved and were supporting each other in their efforts, through fortnightly meetings at each others' schools and through regular in-service courses planned and run by locally elected circuit team teachers for each grade level (Holderness, 1986).

With minimal if any external financial support, the PEUP relied heavily on local community support and fundraising efforts to bring about improved classrooms. Supported by regular in-service courses and writers' workshops, local teachers participated in the production of learner-centered materials and were involved in providing hands-on coaching to their counterparts at neighboring schools—on an ongoing, year-by-year basis and without receiving any extra remuneration. Where electricity was available, these short courses employed basic media such as video lectures and tutorials using a TV monitor.

The resourcefulness of rural African communities in improving educational provision for their children was demonstrated throughout the region in many marginalized schools, of which the one that follows is an example. In the background of Fig. 14.4, we see an outdoor storeroom used as a temporary classroom—without tables or chairs. However, the children—and their parents or caregivers—were motivated by their PEUP teachers to undertake self-help, community-based fundraising activities, such as holding concerts, collecting bones (for fertilizer), and collecting empty tins and cans (for recycling).

As a result of their efforts, during the following year, these same children were able to move from their inadequate classroom to an upgraded, mod-

FIG. 14.4. A heap of tins collected by learners for upgrading their classroom (behind).

ern-styled classroom—with desks and chairs, their pictures displayed on the walls, and shelves and lockers installed along the side walls on which new learning materials could be stored (see Fig. 14.5). Here teacher-made work cards (relatively new educational media at the time) could be stored in shoeboxes to enable group work and cooperative learning (then considered to be radically new teaching approaches).

For those who live in developed contexts such innovations may be judged as nothing new, but for the participants it was a radical and liberating move into a new age of independent and interactive learning, where children could begin to work at their own pace and to their maximum potential—a forerunner to computer-based, asynchronous learning.

Clearly an essential requirement for such transformations at schools is a change of attitude among the teachers. The PEUP experience was that teachers—particularly in isolated rural contexts—need to see and believe that something different is possible and desirable; they must want to make a change and know, with a degree of confidence, that they can make that change. This insight needs to be heeded when planning how to bring rural communities into the digital age.

Countless failed ambitious projects litter Africa primarily because they have failed to take this basic need into account. In the PEUP, a sense of mission and confidence among teachers was achieved primarily through school visits and by holding in-service courses at representative, pilot rural schools where teachers could see for themselves that such transformations were possible. They could stand around the sides of the classrooms, observing teachers (like themselves) working effectively with classes of 50 pupils, making use of new approaches and learning media. After these observations, they could go outside and practise using the new methods and materials with groups of

FIG. 14.5. Talking about "new" media in an upgraded classroom.

children. After watching others use these new interactive approaches and taking turns to receive guidance and hands-on coaching from fellow teachers, they generally felt confident and excited to return to their own schools and introduce the innovations there (Holderness, 2003).

A similar process should be followed when introducing new media and computer-based learning in African rural schools. The teachers (and even community leaders) need to be informed and convinced if they are going to actively support such innovations. Most teachers in rural areas in South Africa are over 40 years of age and have never before sat in front of a computer. This presents an additional—but not insurmountable—challenge. Rural teachers need to be equipped with what are *necessary* and *appropriate* knowledge, skills, and attitudes for the introduction of new digital media in their schools. Thereafter, they should receive ongoing support during the year as they implement new media and approaches. In terms of PEUP experience, such support can most effectively be provided through regular in-service get-togethers and classroom visits organized by fellow teachers, functioning in locally identified circuit teams.

Thousand Schools Project (TSP)

Following after the PEUP, but on a much grander and more costly scale from the outset, was another ambitious school improvement project. This project was an initiative of a South African government development facilitation agency (the Independent Development Trust) that had received a founding grant of R2 billion. The Trust involved more than 80 educational NGOs in its attempt to improve the quality of schooling in South Africa by focusing on the notion of *whole-school development.*

Unlike the PEUP's quiet beginnings in seven schools, the Thousand Schools Project deliberately publicized its ambitious intentions of beginning on a national scale with the identification and servicing of the 1,000 neediest schools in the country. For various reasons, the TSP failed to gain the lasting support of its teaching body—and was thus short-lived (1995–1996). Mouton concluded that "no proper, i.e. consistent and comprehensive implementation of the TSP took place!" (Babbie & Mouton, 2001, p. 363). While acknowledging that it was an "ambitious and worthwhile initiative," he believes that "the general socio-political and educational climate in most provinces was not conducive to the implementation of such a complex educational intervention" (Babbie & Mouton, 2001, p. 363).

What it did succeed in showing, however (Ashley, Holderness, & Padayachee, 1996), was that the introduction of a major innovation, such as alternative school structures or new teaching media, is indeed a complex matter. If an innovation is to be adopted and rolled out smoothly, all stakeholders should share a common goal and principles and observe certain practices, such as realism, participation, and good communication. The stakeholders should include not only principals, teachers, and the Department of Education, but also business, nongovernment organizations (NGOs), community leaders, politicians, and school-governing bodies.

Two achievements of the TSP are particularly noteworthy for future efforts in bridging digital divides. First, the community-based identification of the 1,000 neediest schools in the country occurred remarkably harmoniously. Second, an ingenious system was devised to enable funds to be controlled and moved by the Trust's computer in Cape Town directly to the respective NGO accounts—but only after the successful delivery of requested services had been confirmed by the individual schools. In the event of a large-scale initiative to bridge the digital divide in Africa, such a system brings many potential advantages, such as avoiding time delays and cash having to change hands while ensuring that the improvements are largely school-driven and there is no payment without delivery.

Writing to Read Project (WTR): Computers Into Rural Schools

As indicated earlier, a central concern of this chapter is to consider how to bring children of rural Africa into the digital age. A major international, well-intentioned, and generously funded project was attempted in this regard, and I served as regional evaluator of the project. WTR was in many ways ahead of its time: Its intention was to use a computer-assisted program to teach reading and writing to Grade 2 learners in African primary schools. With funding in the region of $20 million, it provided purpose-built, air-conditioned classrooms to serve as computer laboratories in 18 of South Africa's township and rural schools—6 each in the North West Province, Gauteng, and Kwa-Zulu Natal Provinces. Each classroom was generously equipped with computers and learning stations for the American-based (IBM) WTR program aimed at Grade 2 learners. The second phase was intended to grow this to include 42 schools before eventually moving from Cape Town to Cairo.

Sadly, many of our evaluators' warnings went unheeded: The young children (Setswana-, Xhosa-, and Zulu-speaking) struggled to comprehend the audiotapes spoken in American English, there were negative effects on the rest of the school curriculum and on excluded teachers, and the project coordinators had failed to consider adequately the financial upkeep of equipment by the schools and the need to proactively address rivalries of neighboring schools. For example, teachers sometimes felt marginalized and humiliated as young unemployed local matriculants, who had been sent to the United States for 2 weeks training as technicians, took over control of the class periods. Once again, however, the evaluation of such an initiative provides us with valuable lessons in planning our future ventures into marginalized communities (Bauer, Holderness, & Letsolo, 1986). For example, it is important to respect the traditional structure of African communities and to address problems proactively by gaining full support for the vision before, or as soon as possible after, the project has begun. Hence, the project proposed at the end of this chapter emphasizes the need to work closely with existing community structures and to observe village protocols. The WTR project, in its failed introduction of new media, could have paved the way for success by more effectively introducing and piloting the new intervention. If innovations are to succeed, relevant stakeholders need to be clear about, and generally in agreement with, the desired effects or outcomes of the interventions.

Insights Gained

In summary, it is imperative to recognize that a successful project, especially if it is an intervention project, has an obligation to put social development at its core. This implies that bridging the digital divide requires more than just handing out computers and providing computer literacy classes.

In light of the various field experiences and lessons indicated earlier, certain key questions need to be asked, and time-tested principles observed, when planning innovative ways to bridge digital divides in Africa. Project designers should ask themselves:

- Is there a shared vision and clear understanding about the innovation?
- Is there participation by the stakeholders in the development and decision making?
- Is there a sense of ownership of the innovation / project?
- Are the change agents credible to the participants? Are they accepted and convincing (e.g., Do they hold shared values? Have they experienced a similar environment?)?
- Are the new media appropriate for the given contexts (including financially, linguistically, and culturally)?

PART IV: LOOKING AHEAD

In looking to the future, what can be done to overcome the digital divides experienced by rural Africa and to bring teachers and children into the age of new media?

Aid—With Wisdom and Caution

On the one hand, there is justification for optimism that the marginalization of rural Africa will receive attention and that solutions can be found to bridge the digital divides. In addition to Africa's own program for development—the New Partnership for African Development—the continent has recently come to feature highly in the councils of the world, such as the G8 meeting in Scotland in July 2005, the British Prime Minister's Commission for Africa, and the campaign to cancel much of Africa's debt and to double aid from £25 billion to £50 billion a year over the next 5 years. Indeed, it has been said that the developed world can no longer sleep while Africa suffers.

However, there is a need to exercise caution and wisdom in the way this aid is dispensed and utilized in Africa. In a recent address to the International Institute for Strategic Studies in London, Oppenheimer (2005, p. 9) warned that aid is a poor substitute for real African solutions. He advised that aid should be targeted on a few critical goals: capacity building, assisting African governments in their battle against the AIDS pandemic and other endemic diseases, and promoting business and direct investment (i.e., trade rather than aid). With regard to the latter, he pointed out that countries such as Mozambique and Botswana owe their progress to hand-up business and investment, rather than to hand-out aid. If digital divides in Africa are going to be bridged, effective distance education programs will have to play a major role as a key contributor. These programs will need to enable and motivate local and international efforts to narrow the divides.

Differentiating Within Africa

In tackling development challenges in Africa (such as bridging the digital divides), Oppenheimer (2005) advised that:

> The West must predicate and nuance its policy on the realisation that there are at least three categories of African states: those that have successfully reformed and with which strategies for reinforcing success have to be developed; those that have stabilized and need to work in partnership or move into a higher growth trajectory; and those failed or failing states which remain to be stabilised and to which unique attention has to be given. In essence, Africa and its states should be differentiated—a reality too often ignored by continent-wide commissions and other bodies whose outlook is rooted more in the past and less in tomorrow. (p. 9)

Developed countries can help rural Africa build human capacity, combat diseases through promoting essential health messages and practices, and find a route out of poverty—by investing directly and wisely in strategies that bridge Africa's digital divides. Ultimately, the aim should be to enable a well-governed Africa to throw off the shackles of aid dependency and compete on equal terms in a globalized world. Some African countries are already doing so and others will certainly follow.

Future Possibilities

It is likely that rural Africa will take a rather different trajectory from industrialized societies in bridging technology gaps. For example, because most rural areas have little in the way of telephone lines, they may well skip that stage and move almost directly to widespread use of wireless and mobile technology (Servon, 2002). By so doing, rural areas may make considerable progress in narrowing the technological gap, at least in terms of access. It is encouraging to note that in only 7 years, the number of adults in the UK who had used the internet increased from 7% to 97% (Livingstone & Bober, 2004). However, mindful of points raised earlier regarding the nature of digital divides, it is important to take account of the other factors that inhibit progress toward accessing and utilizing information technologies in rural African settings. These factors include differentials in income, gender, age, and especially language, as well as the need for appropriate training and relevant content.

Village Community Technology Centers

Recently, a project specifically to help bridge digital divides in rural areas of Africa has been proposed by ProFound (Projects Education Foundation)—a nonprofit organization based at the Nelson Mandela Metropolitan University in the Eastern Cape Province of South Africa. The proposal is built on an idea drawn from a couple of web sites: www.fundisa.co.za and www.greenstar.com. It resembles in some respects community technology centers (CTCs) or telecenters that are being used in some First World countries to reduce digital divides. These are usually locally based, nonprofit organizations that link community residents to IT resources. When effectively managed, such centers can address digital divides comprehensively and advance larger social, political, and economic goals in the process (Servon, 2002).

In the United States, people who have initially gone to CTCs to gain access have continued to use the centers even after they own their own computers because of what they continue to learn there and because of the people they have met (Chow et al., 1998). Thus, CTCs have created communal spaces in which neighborhood residents have been able to learn about and use IT, as well as gather together, exchange ideas, and build relationships (Servon, 2002).

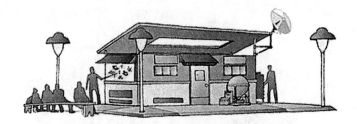

FIG. 14.6.   An artist's impression of a Greenstar Community Center.

How might such a resource be adapted and utilized in rural African contexts? With advances in technology, alternative energy sources could be used to power computer-and-technology, teaching-and-learning centers that are made available in villages, townships, and informal settlements. Of course, in the light of what has been discussed earlier, appropriate village protocol must be observed and, where appropriate, a local school could be involved in the hosting of this resource provided general accessibility is not impeded.

A center such as the one depicted in Fig. 14.6 could certainly benefit the community it serves. It can be transported to a site, where it would be relatively quick to install and inexpensive to maintain (with hardy, dust-free features and secure but replaceable hard drives). It can be fitted with value-added portions such as clinics, water purifiers, and outside lighting. Such centers can help communities generate income and provide workable means for alternative education at various levels, including adult and teacher education. They can be used to promote rural communities; publicize their traditional arts, crafts, and music; as well as market their agricultural and other produce at appropriate, competitive prices. For example, children in rural farming communities could feasibly help their parents research the price of corn in the city, and this would help them negotiate a better deal with the brokers and middle men.

Environmentally Powered Wireless Resources and the Internet

Yet another type of educational resource, made possible through wireless technology and alternative energy sources, is the Apple Mobile Curriculum Lab (Fig. 14.7). This is a step up from the mobile book and resource libraries pushed on trolleys from class to class that were used in the PEUP project. Conceivably, a next step would be for rural learners to gain access to mobile technology (e.g., laptop computers) as they are rolled into the classroom for the allocated period each day.

Although businesspeople and politicians might have a field day with the rhetoric and bottom-line profits surrounding such technology being intro-

FIG. 14.7. The Apple Mobile Curriculum Lab.

duced into nonelectrified schools, the possibility for success does exist, provided the educators and learners it is bringing across the digital divide are
motivated to cross the bridge. The programs and software available to users
will need to be varied and culturally appropriate. In this regard, lecturers
and researchers, such as the readers of this book, and those from the region's participating universities could be invited to participate in the designing of curricula, writing of materials, delivering of lectures, and even
providing of online supervision. At relatively minimal cost, existing courses
could be made available to rural-based learners for downloading or studying online. (It is the *preparation* of courses for uploading that is expensive,
but much of this cost will have already been borne by the more economically advantaged communities in Africa and the First World.)

The content of the programs would also include essential health and environmental messages for rural communities. In this regard, topics and approaches, such as those promoted by the London University's Child-to-
Child Project (Hawes, 1997) and the European Commission's introduction
to the internet (www.educaunet.com), could be most suitable and would
encourage the development of health-promoting schools, computer literacy, and economically productive internet usage in rural areas. Likewise,
sound ecological, environmental practices will also be promoted (such as
permaculture, food gardening, waste recycling, and water management).
Of course, there could also be opportunities for learning through games, interactive programs, and video lectures/tutorials, some of which are mentioned elsewhere in this book.

Conclusion

This chapter argued that recent advances in information technologies and alternative energy sources, coupled with wisdom gained from large-scale intervention initiatives in rural African settings, make it possible to address the deepening and detrimental digital divides experienced in rural Africa in informed and effective ways. In a spirit of cooperation, progress can be made on an ongoing and sustainable basis, requiring minimal outside funding and intervention. However, projects that are mainly externally driven and funded are likely to lack local initiative, have a reduced sense of ownership and commitment, and most likely have a shorter lifespan.

By contrast, as in the case of the PEUP, new teaching media and approaches in rural schools may be most effectively introduced by educators observing and participating in live classroom demonstrations, followed up by individual practical applications with small groups of learners. All stakeholders (including educators and community leaders) need to be appropriately informed and involved if new media and digital resources are to take root and bear fruit for their communities.

With increasing advances in technology—such as solar-powered and wireless internet—almost limitless opportunities exist for developing countries to take accelerated steps into the new media age. Against the backdrop of current initiatives by developed countries to cancel debts and increase financial aid to Africa, the time is right to harness the creative energies and academic capacities of the technologically advanced so that children and young people in lesser developed contexts can be brought across widening, computer-related chasms to participate fully in the new media age. With increasing wisdom and insights afforded by field-based experiences in rural contexts, such advances can be achieved with informed sensitivity to national and local contexts.

REFERENCES

Ashley, M., Holderness, W. L., & Padayachee, M. (1996). *The implementation of the Thousand Schools Project during 1995: An interim evaluation.* Cape Town: Independent Development Trust.

Babbie, E., & Mouton, J. (2001). *The practice of social research.* Cape Town: Oxford University Press.

Bauer, G., Holderness, W. L., & Letsolo, A. (1986). *Evaluation report on the IBM "Writing to Read" project: Bophuthatswana region.* Mafikeng: University of Bophuthatswana.

Buckingham, D. (2006). Is there a digital generation? In D. Buckingham & R. Willett (Eds.), *Digital generations: Children, young people, and the new media.* Hillsdale, NJ: Lawrence Erlbaum Associates.

Caslon Analytics. (2005). *Internet metrics and statistics guide: The digital divide's overview.* Retrieved on May 21, 2005, from http://www.caslon.com.au/metricsguide8.htm

Chapman, G., & Rhodes, L. (1997). *Nurturing neighbourhood nets: Technology review.* Retrieved on July 21, 1999, from http:www.techreview.com/articles/oct97/chapman.html, p. 3.

Chow, C., Ellis, J., Mark, J., & Wise, B. (1998). *Impact of CTCNet affiliates: Findings from a national survey of users of community technology centers.* Newton, MA: Community Technology Centers' Network (CTCNet), Education Development Center, Inc.

Compaine, B. M. (Ed.). (2001). Declare the war won. In B. M. Compaine (Ed.), *The digital divide: Facing a crisis or creating a myth?* (pp. 315–335). Cambridge, MA: MIT Press.

Cuban, L. (2002). *Underused and oversold: Computers in the classroom.* Boston: Harvard University Press.

Department of Education. (2001). *South African schools register of needs.* Pretoria: South African National Department of Education.

Hawes, H. (1979). *Curriculum and reality in African primary schools.* Harlow, UK: Longman Group Ltd.

Hawes, H. (Ed.). (1997). *Health promotion in our schools.* London: Child-to-Child Trust.

Holderness, W. L. (1986). *Upgrading primary education in the seventeen circuits: 1980–85* (Occasional Publication 2). Mafikeng: University of Bophuthatswana.

Holderness, W. L., & Altman, M. (1992). The PEUP: Factors contributing to sustainable innovation. *Journal of Educational Evaluation, 2*(1), 41–57.

Holderness, W. L. (2003). Transforming large-class teaching in South Africa. In M. Cherian & R. Mau (Eds.), *Teaching large classes: Usable practices from around the world.* Singapore: McGraw-Hill.

Livingstone, S., & Bober, M. (2004). *UK children go online.* London: Media@LSE.

Morisett, L. (2001). Foreword. In B. M. Compaine (Ed.), *The digital divide: Facing a crisis or creating a myth?* (pp. ix–x). Cambridge, MA: MIT Press.

Norris, P. (2001). *Digital divide: Civic engagement, information poverty, and the internet worldwide.* Cambridge, UK: Cambridge University Press.

Oppenheimer, N. (2005, June 19). Aid is a poor substitute for real African solutions. *Business Times,* p. 9. (Edited version of a speech to the International Institute for Strategic Studies, London.)

Servon, L. J. (2002). *Bridging the digital divide: Technology, community, and public policy.* Oxford: Blackwell.

Watkins, K. (2000). *The Oxfam education report.* Oxford: Oxfam.

Watkins, K. (2005, June 15). Interview on the TV program "Talking Point" on SABC2 South African Broadcasting Corporation Channel 2.

United Nations Development Program. (1999). *United Nations Human Development Report 1999.* New York: UNDP/Oxford University Press.

Chapter 15

Digital Anatomies: Analysis as Production in Media Education

Andrew Burn
University of London

James Durran
Parkside Community College

We want to talk, in this chapter, about some of our work that relates to the use of new technologies within media education and how it relates to the understanding, interpretation, and analysis of media texts. Our examples and interviews come from the first specialist Media Arts college in the UK, Parkside Community College in Cambridge, a small comprehensive school in which one of us worked formerly and one of us is still working. This school has been working with digital video since 1997, and we have published a number of accounts of work in this field (Burn, 2000; Burn & Durran, 1998; Burn & Reed, 1999; Burn et al., 2001).

For us, the phrase *digital generations* suggests that the difference of digital is an absolute distinction—it implies a rupture between the technologies and cultures of the digital and analogue ages, a generation gap between the groups of people caught up in these ages, a linear past and a nonlinear future, a former swamp of dinosaur technologies, and a future utopia of dazzling digital manipulations (and a present caught uncomfortably between the two).

Needless to say, we want to resist and question these rhetorics of rupture. Our main focus in this chapter is on digital video in school-based media education, and it challenges the generational rhetoric of rupture in a specific way. Digital Video editing software, although it has been bundled with i-macs for some time now and with Windows XP for three years, is not as much used by teenagers as the cyberkid rhetoric would suggest. Although there are clearly some digital technologies that young people make their own—Instant Messaging (IM) and chat, computer games, and SMS being obvious examples—there are others that they do not use so readily, so intuitively, or so automatically—Web-authoring software, graphics software, animation software like Macromedia's Flash, and Digital Video Editing software. To return to the generational theme, we might compare this with the domestic use of cameras over the 20th century. Although most households owned cameras, took holiday and family snapshots, and made photo albums, very few people made and used their own darkrooms, although the technology was not particularly hard to come by and use for an ambitious amateur. In the same way, the domestic ownership and use of camcorders is now widespread and in many ways is an obvious successor to the still camera. But just as the extra step into the darkroom, a space between the domestic and professional realms, was a step too far for most people, it may be that the same thing is happening with digital video editing. Access is not the problem—but the motivation to take point'n'press a step further toward production seems to be limited to an enthusiastic minority at one level, with their own culture of specialist magazines and web sites, and the world of semiprofessional independent film making a step further beyond that. We want to argue that the interstitial space between domestic camcorder use and professional video and film work is exactly the space education is best suited to occupy.

The problem here for education is how to respond to the use of media technologies in the domestic sphere. If children (or anyone else for that matter) can perfectly well learn to use such technologies informally, then education has nothing to add. If they can learn to use them functionally, but do not necessarily acquire a critical understanding of them, then education can offer to develop this. Alternatively, if only some people learn to use them informally, others only partially or not at all, then education has a clear role to level the playing field. Williams (1989) considered this problem in a prophetic essay about the future of communication technologies, arguing:

> The most basic social skills, of a kind acquired in quite primary development and relationship, gave access to the motion picture, the radio broadcast, the television program, at the level of reception, while very easily learned skills gave more general access, including some production, to the photograph and telephone. Thus the new technologies were inherently more general, and less apparently subject to systems of training. . . . It was not only that the institutions of the new technologies, in the very course of their development, and especially of autonomous production, became, in themselves, training systems. In immediate ways, types of speech, points of view, catch phrases, jingles, rhythms were in effect taught. . . . (pp. 189–190)

The question now, then, is whether Williams' notion of *training systems* provided by the technologies—in effect, that they teach the skills needed to use them—will render formal training and education systems redundant for this purpose. Our argument is that Williams missed the crucial interstitial space between the domestic and the professional. This is the space where the realm of the amateur minority, who have self-trained in more advanced skills, overlaps with the educational realm where similar skills are provided for the many who would not otherwise acquire them. To take Williams' example of photography, there was an obvious case for education to make photography for all an important mode of expressive work in schools through the 20th century, in step with the importance of this medium in global culture more generally. Equally obviously, the curriculum of the West, dominated by the imperatives of print literacy in particular, failed to respond to this challenge. It may be that we now face a similar opportunity—the chance to widen the expressive and communicative repertoires of our students to include the variety of moving image practices and cultures so important in their lives and ours; but also the danger that this kind of work will be relegated to a few specialist courses or an enthusiastic minority while the center of gravity of the curriculum performs a wholesale retreat into narrow models of print literacy more characteristic of the early and mid-20th century. Against this pull, advocates of media education argue that everyone should have the chance to enter the space between the domestic and professional spheres to taste a little of what it is like to make something in the audiovisual media. This experience gives them a more explicit understanding of media technologies, the grammars they use, and the contexts in which they are deployed. We hope this makes a difference to their understanding and perception of their world and how it is represented.

To narrow the focus a little, we want to concentrate on the relation between the new possibilities for production and the analytical and interpretive work of media education. Obviously, no one wants these to pull apart, but pull apart they do. At one level, there is the difficulty of the production sandwich: the bacon of practical video making encased by the stodgy bread of analysis; abstract decoding before the production work and abstract written work afterward. The more the two pull apart, the more they become stereotyped and caricatured; analysis becomes dry, arid, abstract, paper-bound, alienating, joyless, and inauthentic; production becomes creative, expressive, concrete, digital, pleasurable, and authentic.

This rather begs the question of what the analysis is for: Why might we want children to analyze the media? We do not have space to address this question in any detail, but we briefly say that, as is commonly the position in media education these days, we do not see children as dupes of the media, but as active readers, spectators, players, and makers who appropriate media images, themes, sounds, and words for their own purposes, the building and testing out of their identities, the imagining of their futures, and the construction of their cultures and tastes. However, we also believe that media education can extend both their critical understanding of the media and their technical and creative ability to make their own media texts, and that these two are intimately related, even inseparable, the recto and verso of the media education page. This is by no means a new argument. Indeed, it is a central thesis of the collection of essays by Buckingham, Grahame, and Sefton-Green (1995) in *Making Media*, and we acknowledge the pioneering essay by Sefton-Green in that collection, one of the earliest explorations of the use of digital video in the classroom.

We also follow Buckingham (2003) in considering the conceptual learning involved in media production from a viewpoint provided by Vygotsky's (1986) model of conceptual development through social interaction. As Buckingham pointed out, although Vygotsky's argument that *spontaneous concepts* emerge from social interactions is certainly opposite to a social account of media cultures, his notion of the *scientific concepts* developed by formal education is oddly asocial. We explore examples of the kinds of scientific concept promoted by media education and how they might be socially located.

What we hope to contribute here is a more detailed examination of how children learn about specific aspects of the language of the moving image through the use of digital production technologies for analysis; how this draws on their existing knowledge of film; and how it is, at the same time, a creative enterprise. But we also want to challenge the stereotypes we referred to a little earlier. On the one hand, we want to challenge the idea of analysis as sterile, arid, paper-bound, inauthentic, and uncreative. On the other hand, we want to challenge the idea that production is always undertaken for its own sake, justified as a creative enterprise only and purely expressive in function. We want to suggest, rather, that the technologies of production can be tools of *anatomy*, which children can use to undo the fabric of media texts, pulling them apart to see what structures hold them together. At the same time, we want to suggest that this process is not just an exercise, just a *deconstruction*, to misuse that word for a moment. We may have this purpose in mind, but for the children in our classes, this kind of anatomical work also involves re-assembly, re-presentation, and a kind of creativity that is about ideas as well as the pleasurable manipulation of the material medium.

We describe two units of work followed by students at Parkside. In part, each addresses an aspect of film language at the microlevel—the grammar of how shots are sequenced to make meanings. In effect, this is the language of the continuity system in film (see e.g., Bordwell & Thompson, 2001). There is a debate about how adequate this system is to describe the moving image as a signifying system, and elsewhere we have proposed an alternative system based on a view of the moving image as an assemblage of different communicative modes, which we have termed the *kineikonic* mode

(Burn & Parker, 2003). Such a system accounts for the meaning students are reaching for at certain moments more exactly than the traditional grammar of film.

EDITING *ROMEO AND JULIET*

At Parkside, Year 8 students (ages 12–13) work on Baz Luhrmann's *Romeo and Juliet*. Having watched the film and discussed in general terms Luhrmann's style and approach, students look closely at one short sequence:

Tybalt: Turn and draw!

Romeo: I do protest, I never injured thee
But love thee better than thou can'st devise.

These three lines occupy 13 seconds of film and 12 discrete camera shots. Students have seen the sequence in context when watching the film, but now have to try to visualize it just from the soundtrack, played several times. They are then given the camera shots as still images on small laminated cards and attempt to put them in sequence. This is, in a sense, already a production activity—the students are experimenting with making meanings with images, but it is production for the purpose of anatomizing the sequence.

The activity is familiar to children through text sequencing tasks in English lessons. It is social and active, and it requires complex speaking and listening as ideas are negotiated and revised. It is much harder than might be expected, and it is therefore productive to intervene after a few minutes, asking the class what methods and principles they are using to sequence the shots. In this discussion, students start to list these principles or conventions on the board.

This exploration and puzzle solving is followed by a more formal, instructional part of the lesson, in which the students decide as a class on a technical description of each shot and its function in the sequence. The conventions listed include: reverse angle shots; clues in the eye lines of characters; continuity of action; point-of-view shots, juxtaposed with shots that identify the character looking; the avoidance of jump cuts; and reaction shots. This is not arduous, however: the active reconstruction of the sequence and the associated discussion of its grammar make this analytic thinking straightforward (Fig. 15.1).

This sequence of activities involves movement between informal understandings and categorizations of aspects of the moving image and more formal ones. This movement exemplifies Vygotsky's (1986) distinction between spontaneous and scientific concepts. At the same time, the conceptual learning here depends heavily on the use of what Vygotsky (1978)

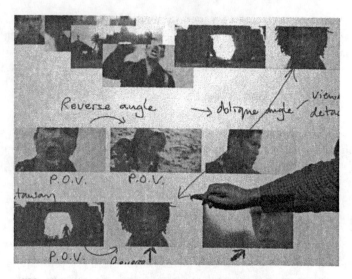

FIG. 15.1.   Modeling film language on an interactive whiteboard.

called semiotic *tools* and *artefacts*. Wells (1994) developed the distinction between these two categories: artefacts are the concepts offered to learners in the form of language, and tools are the semiotic processes through which the learners manipulate the concepts. In this course, there is a complex sequence in which concepts provided by the teacher as artefacts in both speech and writing are transformed by students using a range of tools, which include different kinds of writing, different kinds of talk, and the use of digital video editing software.

This is an iterative process in which the concepts are offered to the students for their *conscious* manipulation, which is one of Vygotsky's criteria for scientific concepts. The rehearsal of the concepts begins with speech, emerging from the work with laminated screen shots; it then moves to writing in the discussion and whiteboard activity. Finally, although language is most frequently seen as the prime tool for concept naming, in this case, the written label is co-present with the exemplifying image, and with the spoken word in the discussion between students, and between student and teacher. Although the word (e.g., *reverse shot*) indisputably possesses generality and systematicity (two more of Vygotsky's criteria for scientific concepts), the multimodal link with the visual image provides a concrete specificity that both remediates the abstractness of the word and makes a connection with the social meanings from which the concept derives, and with the practical anatomical process of ordering the screenshots.

In the next stage, students are then given a chance to rehearse these understandings further in an editing activity, using Adobe *Premiere* editing software. They are provided with the individual shots from a longer se-

quence in the film, of about 1 minute, when Romeo is being pursued across
Verona as he tries to reach the dead Juliet. These have been arrayed in the
bin and are ready to insert on the timeline. However, students are not asked
simply to reconstruct Luhrmann's original film: as well as the individual
camera shots from this sequence, they have at their disposal a number of
shots from other parts of the film, which they can use as flashbacks. In addition to the original soundtrack for the sequence, they have romantic music
from the lovers' first meeting and tragic music from the finale in the tomb.
They are therefore able to make a wide range of new versions of the sequence, creating different moods, and making references to other parts of
the narrative (Fig. 15.2).

As well as using their understanding of moving image grammar to establish continuity and to make the narrative coherent, they start to make new
meanings. In fact these might move beyond the strict conventions of the continuity system and use forms of juxtaposition between shots and between image and music more characteristic of the montage elaborated in particular by
Eisenstein (1968). This sort of juxtaposition can also be understood in terms
of multimodality theory (Kress & van Leeuwen, 2000): the kineikonic mode
combines a range of different signifying systems, the important ones here being music, visual dramatic sequences, and the affordances of editing—shot
structure, transitions, duration, pace, and rhythm.

FIG. 15.2. Adobe *Premiere* editing interface showing student re-edit of *Romeo
and Juliet.*

Interviewing students, it is clear that they appreciate the learning that comes from this activity—from the anatomizing of film that it allows. To Guthrie, the activity was like the "opening of a portal." It was about learning.

> . . . the use of being able to cut from shot to shot, instead of being, like, in a theatre and watching the whole thing on one screen constantly . . . how you can create emotions using particular techniques.

The comparison with theater here indicates a particular conceptual leap in moving image literacy that recognizes the disjunctive nature of film. Lottie identified the importance—as a learner—of being able to design, rather than just analyze, a sequence:

> When you did it yourself, you could see so many things that you could do with it, that you wouldn't have thought of doing . . . if you'd seen a picture of a clock, you wouldn't have put it maybe with, like, the police car, but when you can see it, and you can dissolve it into each other . . . and you can see it and how it changes it, how it makes it more interesting or do different things. . . .

This kind of design is not so much about continuity editing, which emphasizes narrative sequence; it is much more reminiscent of the montage principle of Eisenstein—it suggests the principle of the third meaning produced by montage from the juxtaposition of quite disparate shots, and by coincidence recalls Eisenstein's (1968) account of a montage of clocks in his film *October*.

To Richard, the concrete experience of manipulating film footage makes it stick mentally:

> . . . you remember more practical work, rather than just sitting there with a piece of paper, saying why they did this and why they did that.

Very apparent in these students' spoken comments is the pleasure of this sort of anatomizing of text. But the pleasure is also in being creative—of becoming a producer rather than just a reader of text; or perhaps a kind of textual infiltrator, which is suggested by Richard's metaphor of injection:

> I found it quite fun because it was like making your own movie . . . inject ourselves into the film.

Writing about the activity, Charlotte ended:

> What I like most though is that I'm the producer of my own film and I can have whichever clips I want!

Several students commented on how the editing activity affected their general perceptions and awareness of film.

Guthrie: ... [it's about] not taking for granted our media surroundings ... seeing their complexities and how they're structured ...

Ben: I now often walk down the street and find myself imagining my own film sequence ...

Lottie: I don't think I shall be able to go to the cinema, or watch another movie, without thinking about all the different shots and sounds in a small scene again ... I found the idea that you could make a shot with the camera much longer or shorter, or faster or slower ... fascinating and clever. I thought the shot was however long you filmed it with the camera for.

This is a good example of how students can learn key principles of the grammar of editing by doing—the revelation that editing reworks the filmed material, and that speed is also a variable of edited pieces.

This *Romeo and Juliet* course models a distinctive process of teaching and learning in media, illustrating the dialogic and dynamic learning described by Buckingham (2003) in *Media Education*. In the sequencing activity, students are working in small groups to discover meanings and structures in text, making sense out of their implicit understandings. Teacher intervention and instruction are folded into this process, introducing some formal grammatical concepts and scaffolding the articulation of new understandings (Bruner, 1983). As students use the editing software to redesign part of the film, they rehearse and consolidate the scientific concepts they have learned. Having acquired these initially as semiotic *artefacts*, they develop their use of them through the semiotic *tools* provided by the editing software, in which the abstract concept becomes process and the fixity of the written label becomes the fluidity of working practice.

The digital medium makes possible a specific kind of learning. Any moment in the process is always provisional, as the display of the edit in the interface, like all digital compositions, is governed by what Manovich (2001) called the principle of *variability*—media objects in a database held in a temporary configuration by algorithmic instructions. This principle produces iterative design, in which ideas are tried out, rejected, revised, continually varied, and reshaped. There are, then, two parallel processes. In one, the digital medium is revised in an iterative process; in the other, the concepts in play are further rehearsed and consolidated. In both, specific elements—say the concept of a closeup and a corresponding image—are re-

lated to the conceptual system of editing and the practical instance of the
edited sequence on the timeline.

However, the students are also pursuing creative and social pleasures as
producers of new, unique texts. These pleasures express specific social interests, and these are related to the social context from which the concepts
are appropriated. The students' writing suggests the pleasure of self-
representation ("inject ourselves into the film"), of the cultural work of the
film maker ("I'm the producer of my own film"), and of different sites of
spectatorship ("I don't think I shall be able to go to the cinema . . . without
imagining"). Curiously, the one social site they do not suggest is the classroom, which perhaps implies the success of the course in connecting this
work to the cultural contexts in which the students experience film. These
contexts support the argument of Wells (1994) that Vygotsky's framework
must be extended to account for the social context of scientific concepts as
well as spontaneous concepts.

In their written work, students consolidate the understandings they have
gained. Danielle explains the grammar of a part of the first sequence:

> The camera tilts upwards on Tybalt, this is because the last shot was Romeo
> and he is on the floor and the camera was going upwards from the floor focus-
> ing on Tybalt's reaction of what Romeo has just said. This tells the audience
> that Tybalt is the one in control and gives you the sense of power.

She has picked up some formal terms in which to describe camera shots
(*tilts, reaction*), but these scientific concepts are still mixed with spontaneous terms (*the camera was going upward*). Similarly, when discussing how
meaning is made, she switches between a formal media term (*tells the audience*) and the more colloquial *gives you the sense.*

Meanwhile, Siyao describes the grammar of the sequence in a confidently precise way, using technical terms with ease:

> The first frame of the sequence is a close-up from front of Tybalt's angry and
> aggressive face, which is very frightening and involving. The next frame is a
> cut to reverse angle, over the shoulder medium shot, which allows the audi-
> ence to share Mercutio's view of what is happening and also, this rapid cutting
> to Mercutio's point of view adds to the sense of danger.

This not only uses the terminology of the continuity system, but also recognizes both the multimodal nature of film in its description of the dramatic
work of the actor (although this is described rather than fully conceptual-
ized) and the system of address at work in the film's positioning of the audience. This level of response is evidence of the potential of this kind of work,
with moving images to accelerate students' analytic thinking and writing,
prompting sophisticated, precise, and imaginative articulations of the rela-

tionships among form, meaning, and effect. Perhaps this has to do with the nature of the visual medium. Students are abstracting from visual, rather than verbal, constructs. The technical terms can be linked to mental pictures or combinations of pictures. This is not to suggest that articulating ideas about images is easier than doing so about verbal texts or less subtle, but that it motivates and prompts precise argument and careful distinction. This is true for students of all abilities, including those who might be termed *gifted and talented.* Joe, for example, perceives and explains considerable subtlety in editing decisions:

> Also, at that point when the camera tracks up, it is the first time there has been any significant movement in it. the camera has stayed still to reflect the movement of the most important character in the sequence: like Mercutio, the camera has witnessed everything, but has done nothing about it . . .

> The final shot is of a new character to the sequence: Samson. The camera is placed at an oblique angle to him. He is not an important character, he is at the side of the action. His emotion, his expression of fear and anxiety, needs to be acknowledged—not felt—by the audience. He simply watches—he does not act.

What seems to be happening here is that the analysis is exceeding the conventional descriptive apparatus of the continuity system and exploring more experimental ideas. The equation of an oblique camera angle to a meaning of social detachment is an example: similar meanings of oblique angles are proposed as an aspect of visual grammar by Kress and van Leeuwen (1996).

Already it is becoming clear, then, that whatever concepts the students inherit at the beginning of the course are by no means a fixed and undisputed set of ideas any more than the notion of a *scientific concept* is a homogeneous category. Rather, such concepts are relative (exhibiting degrees of abstractness), disputed, and subject to forms of transformation and extension by both teacher and student.

PRESENTING *PSYCHO*

In Year 9 at Parkside, 13- to 14-year-old students study Hitchcock's *Psycho* as part of an exploration of the horror genre. Our choice of *Psycho* may seem a little conservative, and it is indeed our intention to introduce students to their cinematic heritage—to the work of a valued auteur. However, they also watch and discuss numerous clips from contemporary horror and explore the way *Psycho* has influenced them. They often bring to lessons comments from older relatives who remember the original release of the film, and so they are encouraged to reflect on modern popular culture as part of a historical movement among generations. Although *Psycho* is easy to study objectively because of its historical distance, this does not seem to alienate the students, who still find it gripping and worthy of repeated viewing.

At the start of the course, students discuss issues surrounding the horror genre and explore their own relationship with it. They consider the difference between subgenres—notably *gothic* and *slasher,* which are particularly pertinent to *Psycho.* They explore the relationship between pleasure and fear, reflect on the culture of what Buckingham (1996) called *distress and delight,* and analyze how directors seek to frighten their audiences in numerous clips. In doing so, they begin to catalogue techniques, and they continue to extend their language for describing film. They are reminded that film has its own grammar, and they look for how this works in pairs of shots from *Psycho,* working out why—when placed in sequence—they promote fear or anxiety in an audience.

Although the students do produce some writing, the main assessed outcome of the course is oral. Pairs or small groups of students choose short sequences from the film and present analyses of them to the rest of the class using *PowerPoint.* The following is an extract from an oral presentation by two students, working through the sequence in which the detective Arbogast is murdered on the staircase.

Farhana: Right, here . . . if you comp . . . If you compare, sorry, compare the scene to the *Gift* scene, you can see that the door opens and the music gradually gets higher and higher until it just blares out and the woman, well, Bates comes from here and attacks him, just as the woman in the bathroom, the music blares out and she turns round.

Richard: Erm . . . the high strings, I think, adds more tension, just as the woman's just about to come out of the door.

Farhana: OK, mise-en-scene very typical—horrible, old kind of doors, and old rugs—gothic rugs . . .

Richard: The door is now fully open, and it makes you really want to know what's behind the door, but you can't tell.
They play a short clip, within the PowerPoint *presentation. Class laughter. Clip ends. More laughter.*

Farhana: Ok, erm, we kind of felt that he's just about to reach the top of the stairs, he's just about to step away from danger, but as he takes that step . . . something appears.

Richard: Erm, the bird's eye view shot is very good, Hitchcock has used it amazingly well, because you can see Arbogast just getting to

> the top of the stairs, and you can also see the attacker coming out of the door.
>
> Farhana: We've highlighted this area because we don't know what it is. It could be something, could it be the attacker, or is it some ... freaky ... towel-like thing *(Laughter)* ...

By the reference to *The Gift* (Sam Raimi, 2000), the students are relating their understanding of *Psycho* to their knowledge of popular contemporary texts. Here the comparison is within an academic discourse that the students have learned, exemplified by formal terms like *mise-en-scene* and *gothic*. However, the counterpointing informality and jokiness of the delivery, and the laughter of the class at seeing—yet again—the famous clip of the detective being stabbed, reflect social pleasures of performance, repetition, and rehearsal. This choosing and presenting of sequences by the students is like a formalization and harnessing in the classroom of a familiar teenage cultural event: the repeated watching, recounting, and anatomizing of frightening horror sequences, which recall Wood's (1993) study of how teenage boys repeatedly rewind enjoyable bits in horror videos. This begins to give some shape to the social nature of the movement from spontaneous to scientific concepts. Far from being a move into an abstract realm somehow positioned outside society, it is still firmly attached to the pleasures and discourse of popular viewing, although the possible readings, language, and identities implied by a quasi-academic discourse also have a presence in the room.

PowerPoint allows the students to quote from the film—just as they might quote from a novel—by incorporating still images and moving clips. To create these, they use *Windows Moviemaker*, on which they can view the whole of *Psycho*, chopped up into small chunks (Fig. 15.3).

This is a completely new way of viewing film. The hundreds of clips are arrayed in a frame, which the students can scan by scrolling up and down. They can play these clips individually or they can assemble them on the timeline to make longer sequences. They can easily wind backward and forward through shots and sequences, and they can easily assemble contrasting or similar shots. The students are encouraged to reflect on how this way of working with film differs from a video or DVD. Ada articulates very clearly how she is using production technology to anatomize a film text:

> Seeing the film in little clips makes it seem more like a work in progress than a finished film. You feel like you are in the editing studio choosing what clip goes where and analyzing what difference things will make. The advantages for this sort of work are that you can experiment many different ways with the clip of frame. You can change the order of sequences or flip the image to see

FIG. 15.3. Students working with Microsoft *Moviemaker 2* to explore shot
types in *Psycho*.

how it would have been done differently. Also you can compare the two shots,
looking at the contrast and similarities between them.

The verbs she uses map the complexity of this process: *choosing, analyzing, experiment, change, flip,* and *compare.* To her, the distinction between
analysis and production is blurred: "You feel like you are in the editing studio. . . ." In terms of conceptual learning, the emphasis here is on the dynamic process, rather than on the abstract concept. The verbs in effect
undo the concentrated abstraction of concepts like *edit, sequence, order,* and
inversion, remaking them as social actions. It is true that such actions must
accompany concept acquisition. Just as important, we suggest, they need to
be continually returned to if the concepts are to remain dynamic.

Ada also pointed to the pleasure of this way of working—the feeling of
"control" and ownership over the text:

> Viewing the film this way on Moviemaker, all cut up into sections, makes you
> feel in control as you can do whatever you like with the film. Whereas when
> you are watching a film you are the one who is weak, you can't change what
> you are watching.

Significantly, this has to do with both affect and agency. "You feel like you
are in the editing room" and "you feel in control" indicate the affective load
of such work, as we have noted before in relation to girls' digital editing
work (Burn & Reed, 1999). The agency is not some kind of abstract power,
but is imagined by Ada in a specific social context—the world of professional editing.

In the following extract, two girls, Hannah and Hannah, are using *Moviemaker* to choose a short clip to import to *PowerPoint* as a quotation. It gives a glimpse of how students use the two pieces of software in, as it were, dialogue—moving from one to the other on screen. They use *Moviemaker* to disassemble one text, and they use *PowerPoint* to design a different one. It shows the crucial affordance of the editing software to revise and experiment as the girls try out different lengths of clip to judge their effect.

Hannah 1:   *(Viewing clip on timeline)* Ok, let's skip . . . we don't want . . . actually, shall we have, I don't know whether that's too long, is that too long, or this . . .

Hannah 2:   How long does it go on for?

Hannah 1:   How many seconds . . . *(Peers at timeline)* oh, it's only 22 seconds . . . can that be?

Hannah 2:   *(Patiently)* Yes, that can be.

Hannah 1:   Is that . . . is that too long . . . ?

Hannah 2:   No.

Hannah 1:   So if we have all of this . . . *(Scrolls backwards and forwards along timeline, to view length of clip.)* But I don't know how we join them, how we have all of this. . . . How do we have all of this?

Hannah 2:   Well you just save it!

Hannah 1:   Well shall we see what it's like when we get rid of the bit with the woman in?

Hannah 2:   Yes.

Hannah 1:   All right. *(Uses mouse to drag end of clip on timeline.)*

Hannah 2:   The woman coming by gives more suspense and tension.

Hannah 1:   Yeah, shall we leave her then?

Hannah 2:   Yeah.

Hannah 1:   Good thinking Hannah. I'm proud.

Hannah 2:   Well, at least once you admit to my fantastic . . .

Hannah 1:   No, I've told you all the day through . . .

Hannah 2:   Yeah, yeah, yeah . . .

Hannah 1:   What shall we save it as? We'll call ourselves "Hans" . . . *(Saves clip to disc)*
Right, let's go into PowerPoint. (*"Minimises"* Moviemaker; *"Maximises"* PowerPoint)
We want it on a new slide though.

Hannah 2:   Yeah, put it on a new slide.

This dialogue also shows how, at the preparatory stage, the students are again engaged in a hybrid discourse, combining analytic talk with social chat, role-making, and humor. Again conceptual understandings of order, selection, and generic characteristics such as suspense and tension are worked through as action, exploiting the iterative nature of digital video editing, Manovich's (2001) principle of variability. As in all the activities in this project, at least two sets of semiotic tools are in play to mediate the concepts—in this case, the editing software and the accompanying speech. By contrast with Ada's writing, the conceptual understandings here are not rooted in an imaginary projection of the students' identities as future film directors, but in the language of pleasurable apprenticeship, secure in its search for technical competence, and wittily dismissive of pretension.

At times humor is explicitly satirical of the insistent search for signification that the students have been taught:

James:	It's set in a bedroom, which suggests security and . . . can't remember what it was.
Qiu Xiang:	Secrecy.
James:	Secrecy, right.
Qiu Xiang:	Cos, you don't usually get random people going into your bedroom.
James:	And, also, very strangely, she has a moustache . . .
Qiu Xiang:	(Laughs)
James:	. . . suggests something or other—we're not quite sure what . . .
Qiu Xiang:	She might be a transvestite herself . . . you never know . . .

Again, the abstraction of inferential readings of the film ("suggests security") is as accurate as any teacher might require, but located within a parodic play on such interpretive work.

A further extract from the same pair working gives a glimpse of how sophisticated this anatomizing on *Moviemaker* can be:

James:	. . . from the money to the suitcase, suggesting they're making a getaway.
Qiu Xiang:	Yes.
James:	And then . . .
Qiu Xiang:	Ok, and then that's, her—Marion's thoughts on the money, being shown by the camera inter-cutting between

close-ups, no, medium close-ups of Marion, and various shots of the money.

James: That's her agitation shown by quick, jerky movements, 'n taut expression, and always keeping one eye on the money . . .

In a largely recursive media curriculum, it is interesting to consider how the Year 9 course, in which there is more emphasis on the discovery and articulation of subtle meanings, might represent genuine progression from the Year 8 course. Qiu Xiang and James show a more secure understanding of the multimodality of moving images, analyzing the integration of camerawork, editing, acting, and sound, and a more fluent relation of editing decisions to narrative concerns. They are also engaging more confidently with scientific concepts and the terminology that represents them. At times they discuss this metalanguage explicitly:

Qiu Xiang: . . . the music is a very slow, but, tense. A mixture of high and low strings. I dunno what else to say about the music . . .

James: If you hear very closely you can hear a door in the background.

Qiu Xiang: . . . are they non-ju . . . oops, can't talk, are they diegetic or non-diegetic?

James: I think non-diegetics are sounds that only the viewer can hear. And diegetic is things that the people can hear, in the thing . . .

Qiu Xiang: Oh . . .

Interestingly, the way they talk here about the music demonstrates the problems of seeing absolute distinctions between spontaneous and scientific concepts, rather than treating them, as we want to do, more as ideational complexes, which may have greater or lesser degrees of abstraction and systematicity. Qiu Xiang's and James' terms for describing the sound are on a continuum between the everyday and technical concepts: *very slow but tense, high and low strings*, and *diegetic or nondiegetic*. Also, although *diegetic* is clearly *scientific*, a word like *slow* is less easy to categorize. Although clearly an everyday term, it also fulfills all of Vygotsky's criteria for scientific concepts here: it is general, systematic, consciously applied, and voluntarily controlled. However, the distinction between them may be better accounted for in terms of discursive genres: the former clearly belongs to the explicit and specific preoccupations of an academic community, whereas the latter does not.

Qiu Xiang's subsequent writing about this same sequence exemplifies the increased fluency and confidence of the Year 9 work. There is more sense of argument in the writing—of an effort to persuade. There is a more sophisticated sentence structure than in the Year 8 writing, reflecting more sophisticated interpretations, and evaluation is woven into explanation and analysis. Again there is a strong sense of the multimodal nature of film as the analysis of filming and editing structures is integrated with a recognition of the dramatic work of the actor, and she explicitly considers how these two signifying modes work together to create meaning:

> Throughout the sequence the camera would keep intercutting between Marion and the money, to emphasize that she is finding it really hard to refrain from stealing the money for her own use. There is also a fine balance of panning, tracking and cutting to set a pace that's just right for creating the right atmosphere: the sequence is tense but not too action packed for lots of cutting and not too relaxed for long pans and tracks.
>
> Marion's expression and body language remains more or less the same throughout the sequence, the same taut, troubled look she seems to sport throughout the film. To emphasize how hurried she was, the camera stops at a medium shot of her doing up her one-handed blouse while packing/ roughly throwing her clothes into a large trunk. Every time the camera cuts from the money to her and vice versa, she would always stop and look at the money for a good while before carrying on with whatever she's doing. This shows how much she thinks about the money and her stopping to look at the money symbolises that if faced with the dilemma, she will be willing to do whatever it takes to get the money.

To some extent, this is a function of the students' general development over time. However, students do study a greater variety of sequences, and there is in the course a culture of student autonomy and expertise, in which students choose sequences to analyze independently. Of course *PowerPoint* and *Moviemaker* represent different and powerful ways to organize and develop analytic thinking through quasi-production practices.

It is tempting to see concept acquisition as a one-way trek from the fuzzy informality of the spontaneous concept (characteristically oral) to the precise fixity of the scientific concept (characteristically written). In fact this sequence of activities shows a complex shuttling between oral and written modes (including the writing of DV editing and *PowerPoint*), in which the concepts become temporarily fixed in print, diagram, and still and moving image. Interestingly, the sequence ends with an oral presentation, in which the concepts become fluid again in talk. These forms of provisional exemplification, transformation, and oscillation between modes and social registers seem to be good examples of how concepts are built and revised.

CONCLUSION

Our argument, then, is that the technologies of production can and should be used for the digital anatomy and analysis of the moving image. If a text is something woven, from the Latin "to weave," *texere*, then this is an argument for unweaving, deciphering, and reweaving differently. Renaissance pioneers of anatomy like Michelangelo and Leonardo sliced into human musculature for artistic purposes; science and art were harder to distinguish. In these media courses, again, we can strategically blur scientific and artistic purposes, processes, and outcomes. The semiotic tools operate in two ways—first, in the Vygotskyan sense, to manipulate conceptual understandings; and second, in the artistic sense, to create a new moving image text.

Like Buckingham, then, we argue that the scientific concept needs to be understood in its social contexts. The context of this learning in the two activities considered in this chapter is social in four important ways:

1. The rehearsal of the concepts and the refinement of the edit occur through joint manipulation of the software by pairs of students and through the talk that accompanies this work. Our argument here is that the classroom is an authentically social site, characterized by hybrid discourses that mingle genres such as jokes and social chat with the formal registers of quasi-academic talk and writing.

2. The development of the concepts also emerges from student-to-teacher conversations.

3. The developing elaboration of the specific concepts in play refers backward to prior experiences of popular cinema, and moving image and media cultures more generally.

4. It also refers forward to changes in the students' sense of the pleasures of film and aspects of their identity in relation to this.

Yet in the examples in this chapter, we also want to say that we creatively transform the uses of the technology. The emphasis here is not on making for its own sake, but on forms of analytical production. The use of *Moviemaker* to analyze shots in *Psycho* is a long way from the intention of the software developers when they, like the makers of *i-movie*, decided to incorporate scene detection and split the source material into clips. But we consider this use of digital technologies to anatomize media texts to be a creative exercise and, more important, so do the students who do this work. If conceptual languages are subject to contestation and transformation, as in the move from traditional moving image grammars to a multimodal framework, for instance, then so are the semiotic tools of moving image production. These semiotic tools build on key affordances of the digital medium—in particular, the principle of variability that allows both the analytical decomposition of these film texts and the iterative editing process of new compositions.

Finally, a word about media literacy. If literacy implies the reading and writing of the media, as many have said already, then reading and writing are inextricably related and mutually reinforcing. But the reading and writing analogy can be misleading, not least because it oversimplifies the communicative and representational work at stake here. Our examples here show how young people listen, think, draw, talk, design, produce, present, and write; and how they do all these in a complex web of hybrid discourses, shuttling among the languages of their peer group and the school, the home, and the academy, the private and the public, to say what they want to say. We need to understand these multimodal processes better—how the images in a film become the words of the teacher, become the jokes of teenagers, become abstract ideas in a diagram or, differently, in a piece of writing, or become new moving images composed in Premiere. We need better understandings of how, through these hybrid, context-sensitive forms, children gain increasingly sophisticated understandings of the familiar media texts they live with, as well as the less familiar ones school can introduce to them. Kress and van Leeuwen (2000) argued that reading and interpretation is a form of design, and these students' reworkings of *Romeo and Juliet*, or re-presentations of *Psycho*, are good examples of this.

We also need to discuss what kinds of grammar of the moving image are best suited for work with school students. The well-understood notions of *mise-en-scene* and the conventions of the continuity system elaborated by Bordwell and Thompson are certainly a start and certainly what students will also move on to if they take up specialist film studies or media studies at a later stage. However, these systems do not always cope well with the multimodal complexity of film texts—of, say, the articulation of the rhythms of speech with the rhythms of music and editing (van Leeuwen, 1985), or the articulation of dramatic gesture with editing, which at least one of the students in this study is already dealing with.

These discourses and production practices, these anatomies and reassemblies, are the activities of the space between the domestic and professional spheres. The use of both the conceptual language and the digital tools locates such work in the interstitial space suggested earlier—the quasi-professional realm in which education, like amateur elites, bridges the gap between the domestic and professional spheres. In these spaces, children and young people can experiment with projected identities (Gee, 2003)—a sense of themselves as graphic artists, animators, film makers, cartoonists, and game designers. But they can also experiment with critical and analytical roles: the role of the critic, media analyst, or even the academic. But dipping a toe in these waters need not mean the loss of their ordinary uses of and pleasures in the stories, games, and fantasies of the media. This experience, this knowledge, and the anatomical and compositional skills learned in education make up the cultural capital of children and young people. It is a joint enterprise between school and the wider media culture; the two need each other, and it is our job to make the connection.

REFERENCES

Bordwell, D., & Thompson, K. (2001). *Film art: An introduction* (6th ed.). New York: McGraw-Hill.

Bruner, J. (1983). *Child's talk: Learning to use language.* New York: Norton.

Buckingham, D. (1996). *Moving images: Understanding children's emotional responses to television.* Manchester: Manchester University Press.

Buckingham, D. (2003). *Media education: Literacy, learning and contemporary culture.* Cambridge: Polity.

Buckingham, D., Grahame, J., & Sefton-Green, J. (1995). *Making media—Practical production in media education.* London: English & Media Centre.

Burn, A. (1999, Winter). Grabbing the werewolf: Digital freezeframes, the cinematic still and technologies of the social. *Convergence, 3*(4).

Burn, A. (2000, Spring). Repackaging the slasher movie: The digital unwriting of film in the secondary classroom. *English in Australia, 127,* 24–34. Available at www.aate.org.au

Burn, A., Brindley, S., Durran, J., Kelsall, C., & Sweetlove, J. (2001). The rush of images: A research report into digital editing and the moving image. *English in Education, 35,* 34–47.

Burn, A., & Durran, J. (1998, Winter). Going non-linear, with James Durran. *Trac, 2.* Available at www.mediaed.org.uk

Burn, A., & Parker, D. (2003). *Analyzing media texts.* London: Continuum.

Burn, A., & Reed, K. (1999). Digiteens: Media literacies and digital technologies in the secondary classroom, with Kate Reed. *English in Education, 33*(3), 5–20.

Eisenstein, S. M. (1968). *The film sense* (J. Layda, Trans.). London: Faber & Faber.

Gee, J. P. (2003). *What video games have to teach us about learning and literacy.* New York: Palgrave.

Kress, G., & van Leeuwen, T. (1996). *Reading images: The grammar of visual design.* London: Routledge.

Kress, G., & van Leeuwen, T. (2000). *Multimodal discourse: The modes and media of contemporary communication.* London: Arnold.

Manovich, L. (2001). *The language of new media.* Cambridge, MA: MIT Press.

Raimi, S. (2000). *The gift.* Lakeshore Entertainment.

van Leeuwen, T. (1985). Rhythmic structure of the film text. In T. van Dijk (Ed.), *Discourse and communication* (pp. 216–232). Berlin: de Gruyter.

Vygotsky, L. S. (1978). *Mind in society.* Cambridge, MA: Harvard University Press.

Vygotsky, L. S. (1986). *Thought and language* (A. Kozulin, Ed. & Trans.). Cambridge, MA: MIT Press.

Wells, G. (1994, September). *Learning and teaching "scientific concepts": Vygotsky's ideas revisited.* Paper presented at the "Vygotsky and the Human Sciences" conference, Moscow.

Williams, R. (1989). *What I came to say.* London: Hutchinson.

Wood, J. (1993). Repeatable pleasures: Notes on young people's use of video. In D. Buckingham (Ed.), *Reading audiences: Young people and the media* (pp. 184–201). Manchester: Manchester University Press.

Chapter 16

Digital Rapping in Media Productions: Intercultural Communication Through Youth Culture

Liesbeth de Block
University of London

Ingegerd Rydin
Halmstad University

The expanding array of new media offer many different ways in which young people can actively engage in media making and exchange. Although such activities might be very localized in terms of their immediate production processes and relationships, they also have the potential to create global products, both in terms of their distribution and audiences (through the Internet) as well as in the resources on which they might draw for inspiration. Youth cultures may have local references and influences, but they are also increasingly global, allowing young people from very different parts of the world to recognize, identify with, and utilize similar styles of music, fashion, graphics, and dance. These global styles are not exclusively derived from the U.S. mainstream, but include other influences and countercultures. Contemporary popular music, for example, often incorporates a range of different styles, bringing them together to create new forms. For children who have experienced migration, separation, and new settlement and who are living their everyday lives with different cultural influences, these developments are particularly significant, and they also raise several interesting questions for educators and researchers involved with youth media work. What media do young migrants and refugees draw on when making their own productions? What role can media production play in communicating the experiences of migration? How are such productions received and interpreted by other youth? Can such productions form part of research looking into the lives and experiences of young people?

What are the implications for media education, particularly in the context of intercultural exchange and learning?

To examine some of these questions, we would like to discuss the production and exchange of a series of videos made by young people participating in the European project Children in Communication About Migration (CHICAM; www.chicam.net). The project comprised six European countries: Germany, Greece, Italy, the Netherlands, Sweden, and the United Kingdom. CHICAM was an action research project funded by the European Commission (Framework 5 Program) and coordinated by the Centre for the Study of Children, Youth and Media at the Institute of Education, University of London. Six media clubs for refugee and migrant children ages 10 to 14 years were set up in the participating countries. The clubs met weekly after school over the course of a year, with some extra full days during school holidays. The clubs made videos and exchanged them on the internet. The research focused on particular themes (education, peer relations, family, and intercultural communication), and the videos made by the children were mainly on these topics. In this chapter, we look at a small set of productions within the genre of rap. We discuss two videos in some detail, focusing on how they were made, the ways in which they used global youth culture as their starting point, and their significance in the context of the young people's experiences of migration.

GLOBAL YOUTH IN PRODUCTION

Our research starts from the underlying assumption that young people are active agents in making meaning in their lives and negotiating their identities through their social interactions, in the same way as adults. Many contemporary sociocultural theories also emphasize that identity is a hybrid and dynamic concept, which is formed in the relationship and interaction between the individual and his or her sociocultural environment (Giddens, 1991; Hall, 1996). Even if children's lives are more or less framed and structured by society and its major institutions such as family and school, there is evidence that children develop their own cultural spaces separate from the adult world. According to recent work in childhood studies (e.g., James, Jenks, & Prout, 1998), children's lives involve a complex interplay between structure and agency. They refer to "the tribal child," meaning that children create play communities with specific rules and rituals. There is even evidence that quite young children, both at home and in children's institutions, develop their own countercultures—that is, a kind of resistant behavior directed against the adult authorities in their lives (e.g., Evaldsson, 1993; Hake, 2003). Of course, media play an important role in the social lives of children and in the talk and play that is part of their social and identity development

(Buckingham, 1993, 1996). Media crazes and fashions are central to many youth cultures.

In the context of migration, media also play a role in facilitating diasporic cultures and lifestyles (Morley, 2000; Naficy, 1993). Transnational TV, radio, the internet, and mobile telephones have all created ways of bringing the local and global closer together, both in the way we experience them and in the ways in which one can influence the other. The mediascapes that are created have challenged national and regional cultural boundaries, creating cross-cutting diasporic influences and new hybrid identities (Appadurai, 1996). New media technologies, in particular, have become a means for migrants and diasporic communities to be in touch with each other, to exchange experiences, and to confirm, challenge, and negotiate ethnic identities (e.g., Cunningham & Sinclair, 2000; Karim, 2003). There is, for example, increasing evidence showing the use of chatrooms (see e.g., D'Haenens, 2003; Karim, 2003), e-mails with attached digital photography, and video films among migrant and diasporic communities. As Shami (2001) stated: "Diaspora identities are constructed in motion and along different lines than nation-states. They affirm multiple attachments, deterritorialization, and cultural hybridity" (p. 222). Depending on their origins, ethnicity, religious affiliations, gender, and class, young people are therefore exposed to very diverse cultural products as well as commercial U.S.-based youth cultures. Indeed mainstream cultural products are often derived from multiple influences and may draw from countercultures and different ethnic traditions.

Many young people are therefore now growing up with hybrid identities that are subject to constant adaptation and change. The images they present of themselves in different contexts to different audiences are equally complex and draw on and represent the different influences in their sociocultural lives. Even where there are social or political restrictions, young people are able to play with, mix, and create new identities, and media consumption and production offer important platforms for this play (de Block, 2002; Gillespie, 1995). In analyzing children's media productions, therefore, we are interested in the ways in which children construct identities (e.g., in terms of religion, nationality, and ethnicity) and with how children's *heritage* of, for example, music, visual culture, and storytelling is combined with or fuses into global and local youth cultures, forming what has been labeled *hybrid* cultures (e.g., Canclini, 1995; Hannerz, 1996).

With the development of increasingly accessible camera and editing technologies, there has been a growing trend to use media production as one element in research with young people. The process of production becomes an opportunity for observation and in-depth discussion about what is being filmed or edited, and the final product becomes the focus for further interviews and textual analysis in its own right. Rather than the camera being pointed at the subject of research, as in traditional anthropological studies, it becomes a means through which to see the child's world and indeed for the child to turn the camera on the researcher. This is in line with the tradition within the "sociology of childhood," in which children are seen as co-researchers, and there have been several promising studies showing how photographs and video films can be used in the analysis of children's every-day lives (e.g., Gauntlett, 1996; Mitchell & Reid-Walsh, 2002; Rasmussen, 2004). This was the approach adopted by the CHICAM project, although by setting up the clubs and the intranet, it also became a form of action research. All the children had a wide range of media experience (CHICAM, 2004), and media played very important roles in their family and community lives as well as in their personal friendships. However, although some children were already familiar with video cameras, others, often due to their economic and family circumstances, had not had access to such technologies. Therefore, the project needed to teach them the technical skills of video production and editing and enable them to exchange the videos through the project intranet. The aim was to study the children as they planned, filmed, and edited, and to analyze their videos and observe how they received and responded to the videos made in the other media clubs.

To overcome some of the obvious language differences that such a project involves, we encouraged the children to try as far as possible to avoid the use of spoken language and to concentrate on visuals. We had not intended to focus specifically on sound. However, it soon became clear that sound and music were major points of contact between the clubs and, in many cases, also important points of access to the production process. We found that global music culture often provided a way to open up communication between clubs. One genre that seemed to be appealing to the children, and particularly to the boys, was rap music.

RAP GOES INTERNATIONAL

Hip hop and rap, as forms primarily associated with African-American youth, are often seen both as means of expression and as forms of resistance against the dominant and oppressive White culture. Rap has its roots in the South Bronx of New York City and in expressions of alienation and protest at the social situation of Black youth in that neighborhood. It was originally promoted by an ex-street gang member, Afrika Bambaataa, as a way to redirect the anger and energy of neighborhood young people away from gang fighting and into music and performance. The musical roots of rap are claimed to derive from African bardic traditions and rural southern traditions of African Americans (Keyes, 2002), although other accounts refer to the influence of Jamaican-style toasting, arguing that rather than being a purely American form, its roots have always been global and situated in the Black diaspora (Gilroy, 1992).

Most accounts of the history of rap stress its didactic nature, the ways in which particularly early rap focused on educating its audience about Black history, leaders, and resistance—thus seen as message rap. However, rap was also born out of gang life and the posturing of gang leaders—gangsta rap. Both traditions speak from local neighborhood conditions, depicting particular places and events—representing the 'hood and its inhabitants. Rappers' identity is very much connected to their posse (gang members and followers) and their need to speak of their local experiences. Forman (2000) described the ways in which rappers or rap groups hone their skills in the local neighborhood, and even once commercially successful will refer back to their home grounds to claim the required authenticity. Rap videos also stress particular neighborhoods. Keyes (2002) described the ways in which video producers go to great lengths to create a sense of the artist's locality and belonging. Yet hip hop culture also relies heavily on technology, both in the way it is produced and also in attempting to reach its audience. International forms of rap are shared and adapted by new audiences over the internet, and it is partly its technological base that appeals to young people, as we discuss later.

There are several tensions apparent in critical accounts of rap. Gilroy (1992) expressed concern that in its emphasis on the 'hood, rap (message rap) loses its ability to create dialogue across divided social territories and cultural zones and feeds into inward-looking gang-based territorial wars (gangsta rap). The more commercially successful rap and the media coverage of the artists' lives has tended to promote and highlight the misogynistic, macho, materialistic, and violent face of rap, whereas academic studies (Kellner, 1995; Mitchell, 1998; Rose, 1994) have a tendency to celebrate its countercultural elements, its sense of local belonging, and its global reach. It is the internationalization and the varied forms that rap can take in different contexts that is our focus here. One argument is that the emphasis on the local and on expressing the immediate experiences of young people living in particular neighborhoods has facilitated its popular youth appeal and global expansion, particularly among immigrant and working-class youth. The repetitive nature of the rhythm and text of the rap, which is emphasized by Simpson (1996), makes it easy to appropriate, remember, and convey to new audiences, in the same way as a nursery rhyme. Simpson claimed that rap music offers a distinctive model of self-formation: Rappers are concerned with constituting and referencing an authentic self, and therefore appropriate materials and memories from others to form, through repetition, a new meaning, and a new place from which to speak.

The global spread of rap has attracted considerable discussion. The Swedish author Sernhede (2002), for example, suggested that rap music has become a kind of symbol for the feeling of social exclusion among immigrant boys from very diverse backgrounds, as rap has been adopted by Latinos and young people from the Balkans living in ghettos and segregated areas in Sweden. There is a growing number of accounts of the ways in which rap is being used in very different settings both to assert local identities but also to claim a belonging to a global youth culture. Solomon (2005) traced the flow of rap and hip hop cultures between Turkey and Germany in an ongoing diasporic dialogue that relies on the Internet to avoid Turkish government censorship. In France, which has a very vibrant hip hop scene, there is a high proportion of rappers from West African, North African, Arab, and Mediterranean migrant origins (Mitchell, 1998). Other accounts (Bennett, 2000; Mitchell, 2001) testify to the ways in which rap is being appropriated in different ways in different settings around the globe. This argument can become overromanticized, however. Solomon's (2005) study, for example, stresses that the youth he studies in Istanbul are middle-class kids who got into rap partly because of their interest in computers and because they have the economic access to the necessary technology. Much hip hop style has now become a fashion accessory and is promoted for commercial rather than countercultural reasons. It is also very reliant on new technologies and the distribution of videos. Even so, its power as part of both local and global youth culture, and the fact that it continues to find new forms, means that it remains a vibrant and expressive form of communication.

The fact that hip hop has its roots in different musical and performance traditions (Jamaican toasting, Puerto Rican dance styles, etc.) and is therefore, even in its origins, a hybrid form perhaps means that it lends itself more easily to the development of international variations. As a form that encompasses fashion, language, dance, graffiti, videos, and technology, it provides rich resources with which meaning can be inscribed and negotiated. It lends itself to the development of genuine subcultures and a way of life (Best & Kellner, 1999) that can speak of different locales and identities and the creation of different forms of subcultural capital (Thornton, 1995). Because the local is a contested, not a fixed, space, the process of glocalization (Robertson, 1995) is not smooth, but "fraught with tensions and contradictions as young people try to reconcile issues of musical and stylistic authenticity with those of locality, identity and everyday life" (Bennett, 2000). The creation of new styles may involve elements of imitation, but the imitation acquires a new meaning as a result of the person who appropriates it and the context in which it occurs. The idea of mix or bricolage is central to rap (Simpson, 1996). The mix creates a loose structure, which can be changed and rearranged over and over again. The struggle is to reconcile issues of musical and stylistic authenticity with those of locality, identity, and everyday life (Bennett, 2000).

The visibility of the artist and the 'hood are important elements in rap videos. The performance of the artist and the scenes depicted in videos are often overly dramatic and theatrical, giving them a sense of the hyperreal. It is the performances of Black alienation and a type of violent masculinity, particularly in gangsta raps, that have caused the most controversy. Some critics are disturbed by the way in which some such depictions fall into White racist images of the Black macho and the objectification of Black womanhood (hooks, 1994), in the tradition of the blaxploitation films of the 1970s. But others, including some rappers, point to a need to view such portrayals as theatrical performance, as play rather than truth, and to the fact that many of the videos are dramatic critiques of the American dream that excludes its Black citizens (Saddick, 2003). Although there is clearly truth in this, during the 1990s, play did indeed become truth, with a spate of rap challenges and gang shootings that took the life of at least one prominent rapper—Tupac Shakur.

Tupac was a particular hero for one of the boys in the CHICAM clubs whose own rap is discussed next. Since his death, Tupac has taken on a mythic quality for many fans. His history as a talented youngster who had to struggle with poverty, relocation, family separation, and violence was all part of the rap tradition. His lyrics were a mix of romanticism and violence, speaking of his love for his mother, family, and friends, and of the injustices of society—all while he was being indicted for violent crimes. His death came as a result of gang warfare between East and West Coast gangs in the United States in 1996. His popularity continues, and there is a well-promoted myth that in fact he might still be alive. This is fueled by the fact that new or revised tracks are still being released posthumously, and by debates on dedicated Web sites.

THE PLACE TO BE

Most studies of rap culture have concentrated on older adolescents, often within street gangs. But younger children watch and learn from their older peers and shape their own street images. So it was no surprise that this genre also appeared in the CHICAM project, as the children were in their younger teens. When the clubs had been operating for more than half a year, a video production from the club in the UK called "The Place to Be" was put up on the intranet. This had arisen out of discussions about the research theme on schools and education. Work on this theme had started with fairly conventional ideas about how to represent schools. There were news-style reportages, role-plays in classrooms with authoritarian teachers, and tours of school buildings. Eventually as some of the children learned to use various production techniques, they became more comfortable and found their own ways of expressing their feelings about their lives, not least through the use of body language and music. These children had a preference for spontaneous and unplanned productions, as opposed to adult-guided productions. Communication between the children was also more easily established when the children set the agenda and spoke with their own voices, as the series of communications discussed next illustrate.

David, the author of "The Place to Be," was a 14-year-old boy from Angola who had been living in the UK for 2 years. He had arrived as an unaccompanied child asylum seeker and was living with extended family members. He never spoke about his parents or his life in Angola other than to refer to the plane journey on his own and his desire to focus on the future and adapt to new circumstances. From the start, he saw himself as a performer and was reluctant to take part in the production side of the media work. However, one afternoon, while working alone with the researcher, he began to play with making a sound track for a group production the club was completing. He began (with some encouragement) to use objects in the room to create different sound effects and lay them straight onto the video soundtrack. The afternoon ended with him conducting the others in creating overlaid voice patterns that again were immediately edited in. This experience encouraged him to participate more fully in the next sessions. Sound was clearly his entry point to production. David was also an ardent fan of Tupac Shakur and spent a lot of club time searching for Tupac web sites. He was very interested in the fan debate about whether Tupac was alive or dead. He also wrote poetry at home and said that this was his way of dealing with issues that worried him. Although he wrote privately, he did not talk publicly.

Work on the education research theme in the UK club began with a group discussion about the club members' experiences of schools, writing down key words on a large piece of paper. Many of the topics raised by the group gave a fairly negative view of their present school life. In the group, David was the only one who differed. Despite what he and his teachers had told us about his difficulties in school, he insisted on portraying a positive image. The researcher asked him to write a rap about school, and also suggested that he direct the filming and edit the piece himself. He rose to the occasion and arrived at the club the following week with a script.

THE PLACE TO BE

School fantastic the teachers are cool
I am a teen but don't take me as a fool
My mission is to study hard, be brave
Never fall apart
And dress smart

I came here to learn
Always look at where I'm gonna turn
Listen to the teacher if u wanna have a future
Try not to be an abuser
Cos if you're not qualified u a loser
Try to keep your head up
Never give up
Cos in the future u gonna pay your own bill
Starting tomorrow realise that school is for real
Cos if u turn into a gang dealing
Look at the pain u might feel
School school the place to be school
Be a man
I am trying to help you my friend
We all go through hard times
So let me hold your hand
I won't say this again

This is a very positive take on school, teachers, and educational aspirations. David states that he came to the UK to learn and improve his circumstances. He takes, and is encouraging others to take, responsibility for their lives. He states that he is young (a teenager), but not irresponsible. But he also makes it clear that there are the street temptations of drugs and gangs that he lives with and that are difficult to resist. This is a call in the didactic, message rap tradition to recognize the dangers and aspire to better values. The rap arises from his experiences as an asylum seeker, a Black youth coming to this country to make a new future, and living in the East End of London with its drug and gun problems.

It is also important to examine the visual style of the video because this is also central to the message and the form. David performed and directed the filming. He chose the locations in the school, the camera movement, and angles. He chose his clothes and also completed the editing on his own. In all the shots, he dominates the scene. It is almost as if he is alone in the school. There are no teachers and no other authority figures. He parades in the main hall and across the stage. He uses the equipment in the gymnasium. He wears a red jacket, rejecting the usual school uniform. In every way, he is in charge. In the edit, he uses reversals so that he jumps backward up onto the platform. Slow motion is used when he makes a prayer-like movement as he talks about "trying to help u my friend."

The text is a sophisticated commentary on school—the boy's thoughts about his future and his relationship with the locality in which he now lives. David was very proud of his work, but he was initially reluctant for other students to see it. He was continually struggling with his street image, in which he needed to oppose authority, and the belief that he must try to conform and have an education to fulfill his aspirations and his reason for being in the UK. He draws on the global Black music form of rap both because it allows him to identify with his hero, Tupac Shakur, and the political messages of oppression and rebellion, but also because it is a form he can play with and adapt to his own lived experience and his own expression of hope in his new locality. In addition, it offers him status in his local environment as a form that his peers have adopted. Through the rap, he is negotiating place and identity while also making a more generalized statement about education and migrant aspiration.

As in the other project videos made in the UK, the interest here is in negotiating the local youth and mainstream culture/s. David is not speaking of his culture of origin, and the other members of the club are not particularly interested in finding out about it. Both his and their interest are in connecting with where they are now and the global and local youth cultures that are visible and accessible to them, which will enable them to find an accepted place in their present neighborhood. Although the multicultural experience of the club enabled them to get different views on the mainstream culture, they were not interested in looking at each other's cultures. As we see in the Swedish rap in response to David's, where the young people in the clubs did bring aspects of their home cultures into the club work, it was to adapt and play with them, rather than present them as a direct reflection of their identity.

This also had implications for the ways in which the children engaged in intercultural communication with the other clubs. By implication, we are expecting them to represent the different cultures from which they had come, to speak for them in ways that might well oversimplify the experience of migration and cultural adaptation and change. There is a burden of representation (Hall, 1992) implicit in the way intercultural communication is conceived in educational terms. There is little reflection of the mix, play, and hybridizing that is part of everyday life in multicultural settings. These children were as yet unsure of themselves as UK residents, yet they were also unsure about their identity as representatives of where they came from. They were in the process of negotiating new multiple identities. In this situation, what image did they want to portray to the other children in the other clubs, to these people who are both known (and therefore require some investment) and unknown (thus offering the possibility of bluffing)? Given these complexities, the process of communication was unlikely to be smooth or straightforward.

David chose to use a form that is both representative of his identity in different ways (as young, as Black, as a boy, and as a refugee) and one that speaks across cultures. He chose to use this form to make a universal statement that he felt would be accepted and understood, that he felt strongly about, and that fitted the project use of the internet. He was careful to control what he said and refused to rap off script, fearing that what might come out would be inappropriate to the context in which it was being performed. He controlled and adapted the form to the immediate context of the club and its educational setting. The rap form, although generally viewed as symbolic of subcultural alienation, in this context acted as a means of communication and inclusion. Indeed it offers a relatively conventional message. Yet interestingly, this is not how it was received by the members of the other clubs, who focused on what the rap form symbolized and not on the message the text of the rap contained.

THE RECEPTION OF THE RAP

David's rap video was fast-moving, showing elaborate and expressive body language. The production immediately inspired children in the other clubs to make responses. They appreciated both the performance and the style of music. It encouraged children in the other clubs to write comments on the intranet and, perhaps most important, it encouraged them to make video productions in a similar style. We would like to track the exchanges that took place around "The Place to Be" and the response raps from the Netherlands and Sweden in particular.

"The Place to Be" was put on the project intranet quite late in the project—about 1 month before the fieldwork finished. Around the same time, David placed a question on the General Discussion Room (the intranet's open discussion forum) about the rapper, Tupac Shakur. David wanted to initiate a discussion about whether Tupac was alive or dead, but the question also indicated that he really wanted to find out how many serious followers of rap there were in the other clubs.

To David's disappointment, it took a long time before there were responses to his rap video or his query about Tupac. This coincided with David beginning to drift from the club. With the better summer weather coming, he wanted to do sports after school or hang out with his friends. He felt he knew all there was to know about video now that he had made a production he was clearly proud of and that was highly rated by the rest of the club and his friends. However, he did return to the club a few weeks later when the researcher said there were some replies to the rap.

The intranet responses were as follows. The club from Germany said: "Hi, as you know I love your video and its really good." David was pleased with this first positive response, but when he opened the following Italian reply, he was shocked at the title and refused to reply:

Fuck World
your rap is very beautiful, but we dont like the music.
I like the video but not the end
By
ARfis

He also felt that the following response from the Netherlands, about walking on the table (in fact he was walking on the stage), was inappropriate
and countered the message of the rap: "We were surprised that you can
jump backwards off the ground on the table. Did you do that with the computer? We liked the way you walked around in the school and that you were
allowed to stand on the tables" (The Netherlands).

The word *allowed* also indicated a misunderstanding of what he was doing. The overall result was that he felt the other clubs were not worth reply-
ing to. The media educators tried to explain that this rudeness (as he had
interpreted it) was not intentional, and that they were trying to be cool but
had got it wrong, but David did not agree. Despite the fact that the other
messages were all positive, he refused to reply at all. His reaction was probably compounded by the lack of response to his query about Tupac. In
Thornton's (1995) terminology, the other club members had demonstrated a lack of "subcultural capital," and so for David they had failed the
test that would qualify them for entry into his group.

David had expected commentaries on the substantive message about education. This lack of response may partly have been due to the language
barrier, although the text was also posted on the intranet and translated to
the children by the researchers. Even if David was disappointed because the
other children did not catch his text, they were impressed by his physical
and musical skills. The text spoke to the children in the other clubs, but on
a different level; body language (visual language) and rap music were
enough to evoke interest. In the Netherlands, it encouraged two boys (one
Somali, one from the Democratic Republic of the Congo) to finish a production they had started long before as a personal project. Now they felt
that it was all right to make their rap public and to include it in the project
work even though it was not directly related to any of the research themes.
In the video, one child raps in Dutch while the other accompanies by vo-
cally "beat-boxing." Again there are interesting issues about which language
is used when rapping (Bennett, 2000). Here the boys have chosen to adapt
the form into their new shared language (Dutch). They are demonstrating
an understanding of the form for their local audience. Their concern is
therefore less about imitation of an African-American style and even less
about their new audience in the other clubs, none of whom would understand what they are rapping about.

THE SWEDISH RESPONSE

The other rap response came from Sweden, and it is this rap that we wish to examine more closely. In the Swedish club, two boys grabbed a video camera directly after they had watched the UK video and went outside the school building and started to improvise. Such improvisations normally took place either in the school corridor or outside. Both boys were from refugee families, but had been living in Sweden for a long time. Mohammed, who belonged to a refugee family of Palestinian descent, was the performer, the artist, and the dancer, whereas Ibish, an Albanian boy from Kosovo, was the film crew, standing behind the camera and offering encouragement. The two boys were used to working together, and they were good friends even outside the club. But this setup was different because Mohammed normally preferred to be behind the camera, whereas Ibish did not mind being a performer. Now the roles were reversed. Mohammed's rap initially followed a global rap format, in which he is rapping the lyrics of the artist "50 Cent." His video production is a story in four distinct sections: (a) imitation of "In Da Club," (b) improvisation around a car, (c) a mainstream pop song, and (d) an Arabic dance.

The first section of the production is the rap "In Da Club" from the album *Get Rich or Die Tryin'*. The song was a hit on the radio as well as on the web. We do not present the entire lyrics, but some selected verses that give a flavor of the content of this rap:

Go, go, go, go
Go, go, go shawty
It's your birthday
We gon' party like it's yo birthday
We gon' sip Bacardi like it's your birthday
And you know we don't give a fuck
It' not your birthday!
Go, go, go, go
Move it lil' lady
[. . .]
(Chorus)
You can find me in the club, bottle full of bub
Look mami I got the X if you into taking drugs
I'm into having sex, I ain't into making love
So come give me a hug if you into getting rubbed
[. . .]
(Verse 1)
When I pull out up front, you see the Benz on dubs
When I roll 20 deep, it's 20 knives in the club
Niggas hear I fuck with Dre, now they wanna show me love

When you sell like Eminem, and the hoes they wanna fuck
[. . .]

Mohammed, who was known as a "well-behaved" boy, recited the lyrics almost verbatim in his performance. His enthusiasm is partly an effect of the provocative content of the lyrics—to perform in public what is forbidden. It has a subversive content, dealing with money, sex, drugs, booze, and so on. Mohammed's performance shows excitement and pride in his competence as a rapper, mimicking the U.S. style and using English. The gestures and body language are all within the genre, but he is clearly parodying as well. He is able to adapt and play with the form, and at one point he ironically raps in front of a very un-American small car, belonging to the CHICAM researcher, referring to it as a *limo*. In most hip hop videos, the large cars depicted are a symbol of wealth, power, and sexual appeal. Here Mohammed is playing with the contrasting style of the researcher's car. Then he takes up melodies and lyrics from other famous pop songs, now clearly within mainstream genres.

Finally, the two boys step inside the school, and Mohammed performs to a tune that has influences from Arabic music. Of course this music style has been adopted by mainstream musicians globally and can be downloaded from the Internet. Here Ibish's mobile phone provides the background music, and Mohammed finally ends his performance with a dance influenced by Arabic culture. The boys are very proud of being able to master different musical styles and being able to switch between them. They radiate self-confidence and joy. In this very moment, the boys have appropriated the schoolyard and the empty school and treat these spaces like a huge theater scene, very much like David did in his rap. In both his rapping body style and his dancing, one can imagine him practicing in front of the mirror at home in private. Yet here he has the opportunity to perform—to make visual his adaptations of his favorite global and local musical styles. This rap differs from David's in the sense that it contains a mix of Arabic music in combination with mainstream global music, reminding the audience about the ethnic origin of the rapper.

Sernhede (2002) points out that, like other cultural forms with roots in the African-American cultural heritage, hip hop (including rap) is characterized by call and response and an openness toward the recipient's reactions. With respect to rap music, such an attitude includes an openness related to many different kinds of contexts and cultures, sometimes incorporated by means of sampling. Simpson (1996) holds that rap consciously promotes derivative borrowing, changing the meaning of originality. Intertextual references to other artists and phenomena in the society are certainly apparent in Mohammed's performance. When Mohammed is performing his rap, he has a joking face. He is recontextualizing it, thereby giving it a new meaning. He moves it from the urban ghetto into a school-yard in a rural Swedish town. By combining the original text from "50 Cent" with his improvised text as well as mainstream music tunes, his perform-ance gives a fresh and somewhat benign impression. The subversive and an-tisocial content of the original text loses its meaning. In the end, when he performs an Arabic dance, global youth culture is combined with tradi-tional culture, a clear example of embodied hybrid culture (cf. Canclini, 1995). The same holds for David, with his inspiration from Tupac as a base for his own text, which is far from subversive.

At the time that David produced his rap, there had been, over the previ-ous months, a public debate in the UK about the influence of rap on violent crime. There had been calls by several artists to repudiate guns and vio-lence, and this had been voiced in popular raps. David's rap can be seen in this tradition. However, the two videos are in very different ways a mix of cultural influences that are combined together to form new expressions. David had a conscious political thought and message in his mind, which he wanted to show to children in the other CHICAM clubs. Their responses failed to catch this political message presented in the verbal mode, but they had enough understanding of visual language and music to respond any-way. What is most interesting here is that both videos (as well as the Dutch rap) in different ways repudiated the subversive and antisocial character of the popular gangsta rap form.

CONCLUSION

In this chapter, we tracked the development and exchange of two video productions made in the UK and Swedish media clubs set up by the CHICAM research project. Both were rap videos, and we discussed them in light of studies of the globalization of rap—a process in which technology is playing an increasingly significant role. Rap has become a form utilizing lyr-ics, music, and visuals that can be adapted to different local contexts, and that is often used by immigrant youth to represent their experiences of liv-ing in their local neighborhoods. The form allows them to draw on differ-ent cultural influences to create new hybrid styles. It also allows them to speak to others internationally.

The two raps discussed here are very different, but both are also narratives of migration. David's rap talks of his educational aspirations and his hope for a better life. He speaks very clearly of the dangers of his local neighborhood, but presents himself as a newcomer aiming to get the best out of his situa-tion. He follows a message rap form very carefully. Mohammed meanwhile is less interested in the spoken message, but more concerned to demonstrate that he is familiar with the form while representing the other cultural influences of his life, both in music and dance. He is pleased to be able to move fluently from one to the other, playing with the form.

The examples in this chapter illustrate some of the range of production and communication processes involving new media, as well as some potentials and problems of using visual communication in an intranet exchange. The findings indicate that the starting points of communication are not always as controllable or predictable as researchers and educators might wish. The children realized that verbal language would be a constant obstacle, and that body language and music seemed to be more effective for communication both within and between the clubs. Although some children tried hard to express themselves verbally, often in English, this was not as effective as a more visual approach. Yet many of the children had little experience within an educational setting of utilizing visual and nonlinguistic forms of communication. They were also keen to present themselves as part of a current youth culture, rather than as school children or migrants. Therefore, they needed to look elsewhere for other modes of expression, and the obvious place to turn was popular music and global youth culture.

In this case, in this set of communications, sound and particular musical forms inspired by global youth culture were the basis and facilitator of communication. This meant a turn away from strictly narrative communication about the children's immediate experiences of migration and an exploration of more indirect representations. In doing so, they used a form that derived from a source not directly connected with their past lives. Yet the results are open to different interpretations. They could be seen as avoiding communication about their personal experiences, as not authentic, or they could be rejected as a pick and mix of African-American styles that neither represents themselves nor where they are now living and that was perhaps chosen simply to appear cool to the other clubs.

The two raps we have discussed here are in different styles and, in an educational setting, would be received very differently. David's video is polished and edited, but could be seen as too derivative, as not self-expressive enough. Mohammed's might be criticized for being too playful, as too unresolved. Both use elements that we have discussed earlier as being central to rap: as an expression of the dispossessed and as bricolage, drawing from different musical and performance traditions and from their media experience. The children in the clubs saw them both as subversive (because they brought a subcultural form into an educational setting) and exciting. Pushing the boundaries of what were acceptable ways of representing and communicating aspects of their lives was an important part of the educational process of the clubs and one that was facilitated by the use of digital technologies.

REFERENCES

Appadurai, A. (1996). *Modernity at large: Cultural dimensions of globalization.* Minneapolis: University of Minnesota Press.

Bennett, A. (2000). *Popular music and youth culture: Music, identity and place.* Hampshire: Macmillan.

Best, S., & Kellner, D. (1999). Rap, Black rage and racial difference. *Enculturation, 2*(2). Retrieved October 10, 2005, from http://enculturation.gmu.edu/2_2/best-kellner.html

Buckingham, D. (1993). *Children talking television: The making of television literacy.* London: Falmer.

Buckingham, D. (1996). *Moving images: Understanding children's emotional responses to television.* Manchester: Manchester University Press.

Canclini, N. C. (1995). *Hybrid cultures: Strategies for entering and leaving modernity.* Minneapolis: University of Minnesota Press.

CHICAM. (2004). *Visions across cultures: Migrant children using visual images to communicate* (Report to the European Commission). Available at www.chicam.net

Cunningham, S., & Sinclair, J. (Eds.). (2000). *Floating lives: The media and Asian diasporas.* Oxford: Rowman & Littlefield.

de Block, L. (2002). *Television as a shared space in the intercultural lives of primary aged children.* Unpublished doctoral dissertation, Institute of Education, University of London.

D'Haenens, L. (2003). ICT in multicultural society. The Netherlands: A context for sound multiform media policy? *Gazette: The International Journal for Communication Studies, 65*(4–5), 405–421.

Evaldsson, A. C. (1993). *Play disputes and social order: Everyday life in two Swedish afterschool centres.* Linköping: Linköping University Press.

Forman, M. (2000). "Represent": Race, space and place in rap music. *Popular Music, 19*(1), 65–90.

Gauntlett, D. (1996). *Video critical: Children, the environment and media power.* Luton: Luton University Press.

Giddens, A. (1991). *Modernity and self-identity.* Cambridge: Polity.

Gillespie, M. (1995). *Television, ethnicity and cultural change.* London: Routledge.

Gilroy, P. (1992). It's a family affair. In P. Gilroy (Ed.), *Small acts: Thoughts on the politics of Black cultures* (pp. 192–207). London: Serpents Tail.

Hake, K. (2003). Five-year-olds' fascination of television: A comparative study. In I. Rydin (Ed.), *Media fascinations: Perspectives on young people's meaning making* (pp. 31–49). Gothenburg: Nordicom.

Hall, S. (1992). The question of cultural identity. In S. Hall, D. Held, & T. McGrew (Eds.), *Modernity and its futures* (pp. 273–326). Cambridge: Polity.

Hall, S. (1996). Who needs "identity"? In S. Hall & P. du Gay (Eds.), *Questions of cultural identity* (pp. 1–17). London: Sage.

Hannerz, U. (1996). *Transnational connections: Culture, people, places.* New York: Routledge.

hooks, b. (1994). *Outlaw culture: Resisting representations.* New York: Routledge.

James, A., Jenks, C., & Prout, A. (1998). *Theorizing childhood.* Cambridge: Polity.

Karim, K. H. (Ed.). (2003). *The media of diaspora.* London: Routledge.

Kellner, D. (1995). *Media culture.* London: Routledge.

Keyes, C. (2002). *Rap music and street consciousness.* Chicago: University of Illinois Press.

Mitchell, T. (1998, March 18). *Australian hip hop as a "glocal" subculture.* Paper presented at The Ultimo Series Seminar, University of Technology, Sydney.

Mitchell, T. (Ed.). (2001). *Global noise: Rap and hip hop outside the USA.* Middletown: Wesleyan University Press.

Mitchell, C., & Reid-Walsh, J. (2002). *Researching children's popular culture: The cultural spaces of childhood*. London: Routledge.

Morley, D. (2000). *Home territories: Media, mobility and identity*. London and New York: Routledge.

Naficy, H. (1993). *The making of exile cultures: Iranian television in Los Angeles*. Minneapolis: University of Minnesota Press.

Rasmussen, K. (2004). Fotografi och barndomssociologi [Photography and the sociology of childhood]. In P. Aspers, P. Fuehrer, & Å. Sverrisson (Eds.), *Bild och samhälle. Visuell analys som vetenskaplig metod* [Visual culture and society: Visual analysis as research methodology] (pp. 267–287). Lund: Studentlitteratur.

Robertson, R. (1995). Glocalization: Time–space and homogeneity–heterogeneity. In M. Featherstone, S. Lash, & R. Robertson (Eds.), *Global modernities* (pp. 25–44). London: Sage.

Rose, T. (1994). *Black noise: Rap music and Black culture in contemporary America*. London: Wesleyan University Press.

Saddick, A. (2003). Rap's unruly body: The postmodern performance of Black male identity on the American stage. *The Drama Review, 47*(4), 110–127.

Sernhede, O. (2002). *Alienation is my nation. Hiphop och unga mäns utanförskap I det nya Sverige*. Stockholm: Ordfronts förlag.

Shami, S. (2001). Prehistories of globalization: Circassian identity in motion. In A. Appadurai (Ed.), *Globalization* (pp. 220–250). Durham: Duke University Press.

Simpson, T. A. (1996). Constructions of self and other in the experience of rap music. In D. Grodin & T. R. Lindlof (Eds.), *Constructing the self in a mediated world* (pp. 107–123). London: Sage.

Solomon, T. (2005). "Living underground is tough": Authenticity and locality in the hip hop community in Istanbul, Turkey. *Popular Music, 24*(1), 1–20.

Thompson, J. (1995). *The media and modernity*. Cambridge: Polity.

Thornton, S. (1995). *Club cultures: Music, media and subcultural capital*. Cambridge: Polity.

Chapter 17

Hopeworks: Youth Identity, Youth Organization, and Technology

Carol C. Thompson
University of Pennsylvania

Jeff Putthoff
Ed Figueroa
Hopeworks

With the increasing interest in the role of digital technologies in education has come the hope, explicitly or implicitly contained in various out-of-school youth programs, that technology will both engage and "improve" disenfranchised youth. Indeed most prior research in educational technology has examined its effects on increasing rote academic skills or in preparation for the workplace. Digital technologies such as video production or Geographic Information Systems (GIS) mapping are often seen as a means to engage youth, and technologies may indeed carry a high intellectual valance and be crucial to engaging young people in activities that will stimulate their curiosity. However, digital technologies are insufficient tools for creating shifts in identity that will help disenfranchised youth.

Sustaining engagement even in activities that are initially quite attractive can be difficult unless youth are able to see their participation within an organization in relation to their own interests and aspirations. In this chapter, we argue that youth participation, enacted in various social languages (Gee, 2000–2001), enables not only sustained engagement and development, but also identity growth. If we focus only on technologies rather than the various factors that mediate participation, we will fail to understand the importance of, for example, the scaffolding and mentoring that older youth can provide to their younger counterparts in such organizations. Thus, it is useful to look at how technology and organizational practices can require collaboration and leadership in one youth organization and thereby influence the trajectory of identity development. This study uses notions of identity as enacted in activity (Holland et al., 1998; Rogoff, 2003). To understand how these different ways of participating encourage identity formation, we use Rogoff's (1990, 1995) framework of guided participation. Rogoff argued that the way newcomers enter new situations can be critical to how they will develop and change their participation once they are in them. She further noted the power of apprenticeship situations in "organizing development, . . . the use of other people in social interaction . . . and the socioculturally ordered nature of the institutional contexts, technologies, and goals of cognitive activities" (p. 39). Ragoff's framework of guided participation is helpful in analyzing how youth-to-youth mentoring in out-of-school organizations can be enacted within a realm of both interpersonal and historical practices. Youth at the training center discussed in this chapter, for example, need not be equally experienced, and collaboration need not be symmetrical; yet participants can contribute to and help constitute situations early on.

If activities, as Holland and her colleagues (1998) argued, are "traditions of apprehension which gather us up and give us form as our lives intersect them" (p. 41), identity is the trace left by participation in those activities. Identity is "improvised—in the flow of activity within specific social situations—from the cultural resources at hand" (p. 4). Identity is enacted through participation, dynamically constructed, and contingent. Lave and Wenger (1991) stressed the active nature of identity development: "Learning implies becoming a different person with respect to the possibilities enabled by systems of relations" (p. 53) that exist in communities.

This chapter first looks generally at how youth participate in the programs at one youth organization, Hopeworks, in Camden, New Jersey. It then traces the changing participation and consequent identity development of one trainee at Hopeworks, Ed Figueroa, who is one of the co-authors of this chapter. As Ed has altered his participation, he has been able to articulate his own new sense of himself, and he has looked at his participation collaboratively with the other authors. One of the country's poorest cities and its most violent (Gettleman, 2004), Camden provides its youth with few resources for constructing their senses of themselves as effective agents in their world. At Hopeworks, Ed and his peers have learned web page design or the GIS technology that has allowed them employment while in high school, and they have also proved themselves in online GIS college courses. However, it is in taking on their roles as apprentices and then as leaders, passing along the culture of Hopeworks, that the trainees discover themselves. These roles, along with many others the trainees play, are enacted in the social languages of the organization, clients, and digital media with which they are learning to work. By looking at the ways in which Ed, like others, changes his roles and participation within the organization, we are able to examine changes in opportunities for developing a new identity.

THE COLLABORATIVE STUDY

This chapter grew out of a participant observation study by the first author, Carol Thompson. Carol trained informally alongside several Camden youth as they learned GIS, a complex data-collection and mapping program. This software, which is described in more detail later, enables researchers to collect data and analyze their city by walking door to door and assessing each house or parcel of land in a given neighborhood. Such information may then be used by communities to measure, for example, the health of their housing stock. Carol accompanied one team leader on a data-collection trip and learned to use the hand-held computer and collection software. Over a 6-week period, she also learned some of the elementary protocols for map construction. Although trainees also take and pass required online college courses in GIS mapping, as discussed later, this was not part of Carol's participation.

Subsequently, Carol conducted interviews with Father Jeff Putthoff (the executive director of Hopeworks and co-author of this chapter), a previous GIS director, and three youth in leadership positions. She also conducted follow-up interviews with Ed Figueroa, one of the three youth with whom she did the GIS training. Over time, as Ed assumed a leadership role in the organization, he began to take over some of the interviewing tasks for this study, helping to frame questions to ask trainees and conducting and videotaping the interviews.

Data for this chapter include field notes, interviews, videotape of organizational practices, the organizational web site containing GIS data gathered by the mapping teams, trainees' personal web pages, and other documents. As mentioned earlier, this chapter has grown out of a participant observation study by the first author and action research by the second and third. It has thus become a truly collaborative ethnography.

HOPEWORKS AS A YOUTH ORGANIZATION

The Hopeworks Program

Out-of-school organizations have the flexibility and freedom to improvise and experiment that schools often do not, as Heath (1983), McLaughlin and Heath (1994), Cole (1996, 2001), Matusov, Bell, and Rogoff (2002), Hull and Schultz (2001), and others have noted. Cole, whose Fifth Dimen-

sion projects are well-known examples, has discussed the ways in which after-school organizations can alter the frameworks within which youth participate, "turn[ing] the usual structures on their heads" (p. 298). Brown
and Cole (2002) also emphasized the rich environments that after-school
programs may provide. Hopeworks provides both an atmosphere that encourages improvisation and the necessity for collaborative mentor/mentee
relationships among the youth. Although there is clearly a great deal of
learning taking place at Hopeworks, the organization also carefully distin-
guishes itself from school. The youth are called trainees, not students, for
example, and they may move at their own pace and enlist other trainees to
help them. Indeed "learning to use your resources" is an organizational
mantra articulated to new trainees as soon as they enter the organization.

Hopeworks is located in a city whose poverty plays a significant role in
the lives of its inhabitants. Camden's youth face uncertain futures. The Bureau of Labor Statistics web site indicates that the unemployment in Camden for December 2002 was 15.2%; and according to the *Camden County
Workforce Investment Board Report* (2000), the unemployment rate for youth is
34%. Fifty-seven percent of youth will continue to live below the poverty
level. The dropout rate at the two local high schools is estimated to be 70%.
Thus, there is a tremendous need to offer hope, in the form of real opportunities, to Camden youth.

But Hopeworks is an example of the optimism that can also be found in
some of Camden's neighborhoods. Located in an old family brownstone,
Hopework's exterior is welcoming and its interior spaces intimate. The parlor, dining room, and kitchen all lend themselves to family-like groupings
of youth—no more than 8 to 10 people can work in any given room. Desks
with late-model Dell computers line the perimeters of most rooms, and the
trainees sit close enough to each other that leaning over or back to ask a
question is easy (see Fig. 17.1). The executive director sits at a desk in the
front parlor, which also has a large easy chair, several other chairs for visitors, a small indoor wall fountain, a large calendar, and plants. The GIS director works on the second floor with the GIS trainees. Web designers are
on the third floor, along with the Youth Formation Director, a conference
room, and a room devoted to literacy studies.

One hundred seventy-five youth between the ages 14 and 23 come to
Hopeworks each year; they include middle and high school students as well
as those who have dropped out. Because trainees enter the programs on a
rolling admissions basis, there are always peers with just a bit more or just a
bit less experience with the organizational practices. Business practices
such time cards, dress codes, a chore wheel, and learning to answer the
phone and greet visitors are an important part of Hopeworks. Youth begin
their technical training by learning to design web pages, first for themselves
and then for clients in the greater Camden/Philadelphia area. To do this

FIG. 17.1. Hopeworks trainees learning the web design curriculum.

they must learn the self-paced curriculum in HTML and a series of graphics programs like Photoshop and Image Ready, Java Script, and Flash. When trainees have completed their web pages, the pages are added to the Hopeworks web site, and the trainees decide whether they want to continue with web page design or move to GIS mapping. GIS is a method for visualizing databases. A complex and sophisticated system, like MapQuest it enables viewers to uncover data in maps by zooming in. The structure of GIS enables viewers to see connections in the data from communities, which can consist of water resources, crime statistics, plant life, streetlights, among others. It is thus possible, for example, to see correlations between streetlight outages and crime statistics. Such data are useful in crime fighting, environmental analysis, and community development.

The Hopeworks GIS program has a varied client base, including small nonprofits such as community development corporations, the City of Camden, and for-profit businesses. Hopeworks holds design meetings with clients, after which individual trainees (for large projects teams of trainees) are assigned. Trainees' hourly pay is included in the price negotiations for projects. Construction of the maps requires multistaged projects in which trainees learn to collect data using hand-held computers, download the data into the GIS computer program, and then carefully construct maps (see Fig. 17.2) to the customer's specifications, often combining their data with census and other data. The data collection is done in teams, and each project has a project leader—a trainee who has progressed through the ranks. The GIS program is meant for adult project work; to be considered competent to work for clients, trainees must take and pay for online college courses. For some trainees, these courses, although quite difficult, have given them confi-

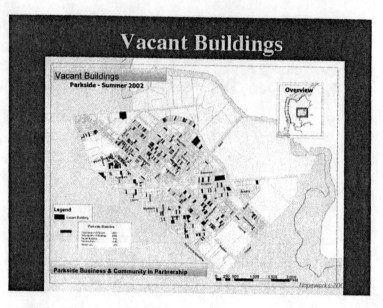

FIG. 17.2.   GIS parcel map constructed by youth indicating vacant buildings in Camden.

dence to complete their high school educations. Although trainees do not always say so, the fact that their training includes writing code for web page design or an online college course in GIS is important. Because they pay for the course out of their paychecks, the fact that they are investing in themselves is unmistakable, and earning college credit in high school certainly is evidence of one's academic capability. This credit also becomes part of the currency of the college admissions process for youth who need funding to attend college, and the youth understand its importance.

In whatever program trainees choose, there are clearly set goals and clear indicators of success in reaching them. The web site contains the work of the trainees who complete projects, and the walls in the downstairs rooms contain the photos of the trainees who have completed their web pages. Such physically prominent reminders of progress are everywhere, and they both mark the passage of the experienced trainees and offer models for participation for the new trainees who sit at the computers under the photographs.

Interactional Patterns of Participation: Collaboration and Mentoring

When youth arrive at Hopeworks, they take on the role of trainee and immediately begin learning how to design web pages. Although the curricula are easy for youth to engage with on their own, the tasks eventually present sufficient difficulty that youth must ask for help to participate. This deceptively simple act of asking for help sets in motion a number of complex interactions. First, tasks are immediately situated in language(s)—both the language of Hopeworks and the technical language of the software—and the tasks will also be situated in the language of clients. Because trainees must learn to ask, and those with even slightly longer tenure must learn to explain, the two most important roles trainees play—mentor and mentee—are verbal and set from the beginning. This mentoring framework is open rather than constrained; it is an opportunity for trainees to decide when they need help and how much help they need. This ad hoc nature of requests for help fits nicely with the notions of improvisation that the organization values. The mentoring framework is also institutional and collaborative; for example, one of the organizational mantras is that a trainee with even a day's experience can help someone new. Thus, from the first day of training, roles, language, and a collaborative organizational stance are set in motion. As Lave and Wenger (1991) suggested, we participate in communities of practice first peripherally and then more centrally as we learn the practices—a *centripetal* process. Peripherality has its compensations in allowing members new to a community of practice to understand its at-large functions before moving toward more specific activities. Hopeworks spells out the development trajectories from the beginning, affording complex kinds of participation. To understand how trainees' identity formation occurs as they begin to participate, it will be helpful to look at these also. The following section examines the ways in which various kinds of participation are enacted, how they build on each other over time, and how such notions of participation can account for the process of identity formation in Hopeworks youth.

**Identity Formation Through Participation
in a Community of Practice**

The initial problem-solving task that new trainees face, then, situates them in a new community of practice with other trainees, with a technology that they are just learning to use as a tool and with a set of expectations and goals toward which they have agreed to work. As Clases and Wehner (2002) found, there are usually triggering events that require people to work jointly. At Hopeworks, the triggering event occurs when a trainee first is stymied by a problem and turns to another trainee for help. Because all of the elements with which trainees work are socially embedded and intricately connected, trainees will collaborate, continuing to build on their first interactions. As they gain experience, they not only help each other, but also occasionally participate in finding new ways to solve small problems. Vygotsky's (1978) richly described notion of the Zone of Proximal Development (in which people can do with help things they otherwise would be unable to) is a helpful model for understanding the first, collaborative, way of working because the trainees with even slight experience can be helpful to those with none. Newer trainees work in this Zone for quite a while as they learn the web design or GIS mapping technologies, but their participation may quickly change back and forth from novice to mentor as even newer trainees arrive. Ed, whose participation and identity work are discussed later, has mentioned that even relatively new trainees often step in and out of the roles of mentor and mentee many times within a day.

Rogoff's (1990, 1995, 1997) model of participation is also helpful in conceptualizing how the complex practices of an organization like Hopeworks are enacted. Participation, she noted, takes place on three "inseparable and mutually constituting planes" (p. 140) within a realm of both interpersonal and "historical practices" (p. 147). One of those planes, guided participation, is a space in which individuals new to a situation "engage with others and with materials and arrangements collaboratively managed by themselves and others" (p. 147). This kind of participation does not require that participants be equally experienced or that their collaboration be symmetrical; and at the same time, such a notion allows for participants to contribute to and constitute situations early on, as is the case at Hopeworks.

The latter capacity for inclusion is crucial in understanding the differences between youth organizations that encourage youth to learn a skill and reproduce it without evaluation or change, and those that open the possibility of altering the mode of problem solving. As the Hopeworks trainees progress and find themselves in situations where there are no clear answers and in which problem solving requires improvisation, they begin to co-construct some problem-solving strategies. They are encouraged to do this partly because the executive director is self-taught, and because improvisatory thinking is part of the institutional practices. In addition to enabling problem solving, this kind of participation simultaneously performs another function: To be truly intellectually challenging, Hopeworks must allow participants, trainees, and staff alike to act dynamically. Rogoff (1995) noted the importance of allowing participants to "stretch . . . as they seek a common ground of understanding in order to proceed with the activities at hand" (p. 148). Such stretching thus allows for institutionalized improvisation, which enables trainees to continue to experiment with and play an increasing variety of roles. The trainees are aware that such collaborative modes of participation and problem solving are different from those they encounter at school, which places a premium on individualistic problem solving. Such individualistic problem solving tends to limit most students to their student roles. Where youth are called on to participate as mentors, leaders, and conference presenters, however, they are able to try on a variety of roles, experimenting with new kinds of identity.

ROLES

How Trainees Assemble a Repertoire of Roles

As trainees construct their expertise in collaborative problem solving and consequently their funds of knowledge, they increasingly become mentors to newer trainees. Although the role of mentor is the overarching one, whatever their specialty in terms of training, the trainees begin to add other roles to their repertoires as well. Those wishing to move into GIS mapping will first complete an elementary protocol of lessons before beginning their required online college course in GIS at the University of Montana. This subsequent kind of participation propels them into yet another role—that of college student. Such shifts into new kinds of participation and roles are not effortless, however, and trainees may falter as they learn how to enact new roles. For example, trainees need interpretation and support from more experienced adults to parse misunderstandings with contacts outside of Hopeworks. One such instance occurred within the context of the required online University of Montana course, which is structured primarily for adults and has a required chatroom. Trainees, often sophomores in high school, are unused to playing the role of college student, and in one case presented themselves inappropriately, using styles that felt too informal to their far older classmates, so much so that they lodged complaints. The trainees' style was actually one considered quite permissible in teen chatrooms and contained no objectionable language. However, the trainees had not carefully "read the room." The conflict in the University of Montana chatroom between the other adult class members and the trainees became the occasion for substantial discussions with the trainees about how they construct roles linguistically in situations where they must rely on language alone. Learning how speech alone is read without gesture or facial expression was an important lesson for the trainees, as was learning that styles may not translate well across cultures. For the trainees, the incident was a powerfully instructive example of the ways in which access to roles can be limited by inability to position oneself carefully.

As the trainees gain competence in handling their roles as college students, they begin to take on client work, and they thereby begin to enact their relation to clients as paid, skilled employees. The more experienced trainees are able to build on their GIS work and their mentoring, eventually becoming project leaders. At first they maintain their apprenticeship roles with the adult staff, but they increasingly want to take on more collegial roles. How and to what extent that should happen are subjects of continual negotiation among the adults at Hopeworks. Those who assume such leadership roles talk about the ways in which such public acknowledgment of their competence ratifies their senses of self-worth, both in and out of

Hopeworks, mentioning as one trainee did, for example, that his peers in the neighborhood look at him differently and seek his advice. But learning leadership skills is also fraught with difficulties, and youth unused to leading teams of peers may find themselves struggling to negotiate the responsibilities of carrying through tasks and being liked by their peers. When leaders have not been able to negotiate responsibilities well, the adults have stepped in. Leaders have been demoted and their pay lowered until they have been ready to reassume more responsibility.

For those GIS trainees who have attained leadership status, a linked role is that of conference presenter. Each year several trainees travel across the United States to a large conference held by the major GIS software developer (ESRI). Trainees present work at the plenary session, which is attended by thousands of other GIS users. They have also presented at smaller academic conferences, and for all of them speaking in such forums has been a profoundly affecting experience. They mention being less shy, less afraid, and more able to speak in front of groups after presenting at these conferences. As they begin to look ahead to being full-time college students, they also know that their experience in conference presentations will stand them in good stead as they prepare to assert themselves in college.

As can be seen from the diagram of Hopeworks roles (Fig. 17.3), the trainees are enacting multiple roles in relation to multiple audiences in multiple communities of practice. These audiences are linked. For example, the role of the trainee as high school student and prospective college student presupposes interaction between the high school and college as that transition is accomplished. Trainees who mentor within Hopeworks are frequently seen in the same role in their communities, and they often bring their friends to Hopeworks as well. (In fact, word of mouth is an important entry point for many trainees.) Participation in a conference at the University of Pennsylvania brought Ed into a different relation with the first author. He began to look at the multiplicity of roles he was playing and the ways in which they altered how he thought about his social positioning. He subsequently took on the role of interviewer for this chapter, and his interviews and preparation for this chapter will doubtless have an effect on his performance in college.

As trainees gain experience in collaborative problem solving and leadership, they increasingly want to contribute their own ideas to Hopeworks practices. Although, as mentioned earlier, trainees contribute from the beginning to Hopeworks practices by mentoring, leadership roles are particularly powerful ways in which trainees can have a mutually constituting effect on Hopeworks. Trainees who have become adept at collaboration are able to suggest new ways of solving problems that may be (perhaps temporarily) institutionalized. A previous GIS director used a trainee's solution in map construction, and it was afterward put into the remembered repertoire of

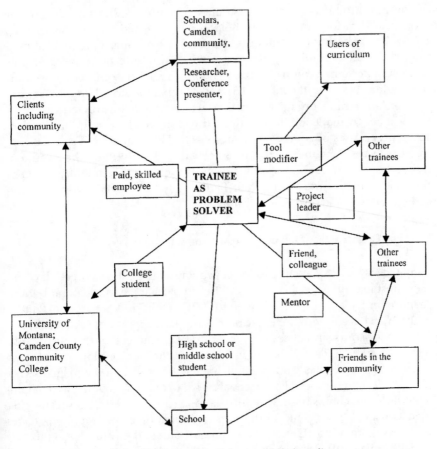

FIG. 17.3. Roles played by trainees and their audiences.

possible ways to solve such problems. Trainees, then, are not simply being asked to learn to accomplish repetitive tasks, but are intellectually engaged in dealing with evolving situations in a community of practice. The participation of trainees who stay at Hopeworks over time thus evolves along with the organization. As Rogoff (1995) noted, the earlier modes of participation enable changes later on: "This is a process of becoming, rather than acquisition . . ." (p. 142). It is impossible to look at the trainee leadership of projects without seeing that leadership as firmly implanted in the early days of "learning to use your resources."

Such new ways of being profoundly alter trainees' identities, and they require what Wenger (1998) called *reconciliation*, a process both profoundly social and "very private . . . [with] a deeply personal dimension of individuality" (p. 161). It is not difficult to see how such new ways of being within the organization can greatly alter trainees' identities. Enacting the role of project leader, for example, has helped convince trainees to stay in high school, thus altering their identity as probable dropouts. One such trainee found himself becoming a mentor to friends outside of Hopeworks and marveling at being seen by his friends both in and out of the organization as a leader. As Holland et al. (1998) and others have noted, identity is contingent, and youth organizations that are carefully constructed can offer youth a set of malleable interactions through which to temporarily construct new senses of competence and of self. The trainees are aware of the variety of ways they now have to interact with each other and their communities. Still, they remain, they say, primarily high school students, although they take pleasure in hearing their families say, as one did, "You're taking college classes? Girl, you're so young!"

Roles as Constructed Through Social Languages

Language is the primary means for enactment of the roles trainees play, and they must learn how to talk to each other to participate in the organization. As Lave and Wenger (1991), Hymes (2001), Ochs and Schieffelin (2001), and others have noted, the entry point into participation in communities is through discourse practices; to move forward, trainees must learn to use what Vygotsky (1978) saw as the fundamental tool for development. Different activities and roles come with characteristic modes of language use. As Gee (2000) noted, "social languages are used to enact, recognize, and negotiate different socially situated identities and to carry out different socially situated activities" (p. 6). The youth bring with them their own social languages and ways of knowing (Heath, 1983), but as trainees they must learn the new social languages of Hopeworks practices, the technology they are using, and their clients. They must learn the business and other insider languages of Hopeworks practices. Trainees who subsequently learn GIS will be learning a technical language to do with parcel mapping as they learn to collect data; and as they begin to construct maps with their data, they must use the complex terminology of rasters and symbology. Client languages will be yet another linguistic variety: Some clients may want maps that deal with economics, whereas others are doing environmental surveys. One of the important ways in which trainees help each other is as translators of these languages, often using synonymous terminology. Vocabulary from outside often percolates through the organization as trainees and outsiders talk with each other. Ed's discussions with Carol, for example, led to his interview questions about roles, which he successfully rephrased for the trainees he interviewed with the examples we had discussed.

Language, of course, is not only vocabulary and phrasing, and for trainers learning to use social languages effectively, a great deal of time is spent learning appropriateness. As trainees negotiate notions of appropriateness in learning particular social languages, they can see the weight stylistic differences can carry. That language has a social dimension and that it is not neutral are important lessons for youth to learn. As trainees enlarge their linguistic repertoires (Duranti, 1997), they are able to operate within a system of multiples, moving from one to another as they change roles. Their languages are also part of larger discourses (Gee, 1999), and they index the belief systems and institutions of which they are a part. They can thus pose interesting issues for youth previously disenfranchised by such institutions. There does not seem to be a conflict between these languages for the trainees interviewed for this project; instead they uniformly credit learning how to program, talk to clients, and present at conferences with making them more articulate and more assertive. They all note their newfound pleasure in speaking up, asking questions, and taking charge. These new repertoires are also an entry point into a part of the world to which they would not previously have had access, such as professional conferences mentioned earlier. The multiple social languages, which are for Rogoff (2003) "tools of thinking that channel and result from community wide ways of thinking and acting" (p. 267), thus not only structure practices and roles, they also open doors into other forms of participation in other communities of practice.

One further distinction is important. As Rogoff, Paradise, Arauz, Correa-Chavez, and Angelillo (2003) noted, it is helpful to distinguish between the kinds of talk being used and their relation to the task at hand. There is great difference between "talk [that] is used *in the service* of engaging in the activity, augmenting and guiding experiential and observational learning" and the kind of talk used "in an assembly line lesson, [where] talk is *substituted* for involvement" (p. 195; italics original). The former allows for intent participation—the beginnings of engagement prior to expertise. The latter, including, for example, I/R/E responses to quizzes and exercises unconnected to cooperative projects, requires non-negotiable roles and presents no entry point at all into either participation or identity formation.

A CASE STUDY OF PARTICIPATION, ROLES, AND IDENTITY FORMATION IN ONE YOUTH

Ed began at Hopeworks as a high school junior and rapidly acquired facility and engagement with GIS processes. After being at Hopeworks for 6 months, he described in an interview with the first author the effects that collecting data in and analyzing his own neighborhood had on him. As a resident, he saw his neighborhood as his own safe space, but collecting data with the hand-held computers provided him with the mediating eyes of a different set of social criteria. The hand-helds prompt the data collectors to analyze parcels (the lots contained within city blocks) on the basis of several questions, including whether the property is vacant, has broken windows, graffiti, peeling paint, and so on. The data are downloaded into the GIS programs; when maps are constructed from the parcels, it is possible to evaluate the health of neighborhoods.

"At first," Ed remarked at the end of his junior year in high school and his first at Hopeworks, "before the surveying I thought of my neighborhood as a place to hang out with friends. After I started surveying I looked at the conditions and began to see what could be done. I see a lot of things that need to be fixed up." Noting that "nobody pays attention to what is really going on" in Camden, he is in a particularly interesting position:

> I hear shots outside my window and I think with all the work I've done for the city of Camden that the city should work with what we have given them and fix up those areas. . . . I've played a role in collecting the information, and now it's a matter of presenting it to the city, saying to the police, "Here's what we've collected." . . . In Spring 2002 we did a presentation on safety and how the land was used; some people were looking at vacant buildings and wanted to do something that would help. The mayor—Mayor Faison—was there, and she got to see the technology we were using, and she was very impressed.

As a 16-year-old resident, Ed was thus in the role of knowledgeable advisor, both as inhabitant and as trained assessor, in the process of saving his own neighborhood. His position was particularly interesting in its illustration of what a GIS project map can and cannot do. On the one hand, GIS can be used to map urban decay, lack of lighting, and even the publicly available crime statistics; and inferences can be drawn about life in a given set of blocks and parcels. Trends can be ascertained and possibly headed off. But maps by their very nature are constrained constructions, and without Ed's intimate and interpretive knowledge of the neighborhoods, the maps are relatively mute.

As Ed moved from data collection to project leadership, he began to be aware of how other neighborhood residents now viewed him. Residents, sometimes suspicious of groups of youth holding red hand-held computers, could occasionally be confrontational. Ed began to understand how to manage situations in the field where wary residents may not welcome *outsiders* staring at their properties. By the end of his junior year, he had learned that explaining what he was doing to curious or wary residents often had unexpected yields: "People contribute ideas and information and help us out even more." By enlisting the help of the neighborhood in such a nonthreatening way, Ed was already keeping open the conversation between residents and *experts*—a sophisticated insight for a high school junior. His dual roles as assessor and resident put him squarely in the realm of action research. During his senior year—his second at Hopeworks—the first and second authors and he presented this action research at a national conference at the University of Pennsylvania, and Ed was able to teach the audience some of the data-collection techniques he used. During that same year, Ed continued to take on increasing leadership roles within Hopeworks and also began to make plans to attend college. As he began to make the mental shift toward the future, he was well equipped to analyze his time at Hopeworks and to look at the ways in which it contained the same patterns of participation as other trainees. He remarked that negotiating the roles of high school student, college student, mentor, project leader, and conference presenter had become fairly easy for him, but that he still thought of himself mostly as a high school student. As he and other trainees who present at conferences are aware, audiences also see them primarily as high school students, and they earn kudos simply for being far younger than their professional colleagues. Their role as high school students, of course, is also a comfortable home base.

By his junior year, Ed had already taken pleasure in both his participation as a trainee and, significantly, in "helping to pass along the culture of Hopeworks" to new trainees. As he made preparations for college, Ed was also aware of taking his presentation, research, and leadership skills with him. Together with the other authors, he worked to construct a list of interview questions that we hoped might indicate the extent to which trainees see their identities as changed. Ed's interviews with trainees now form the basis of some of this chapter. Not only did he learn a repertoire of roles, but he also learned a great deal about how he plays them and how they have changed his own sense of himself.

CONCLUSION

The trainees use technology, social languages, and roles to construct their identities within the practices of Hopeworks. Youth in cities like Camden, New Jersey, have grown up in harsh communities in which roles and identities are bound by poverty. For most Camden residents, the expensive condominiums and skyscrapers of Philadelphia so clearly visible across the Delaware River are another universe altogether. Although middle-class youth may, if they are fortunate, negotiate multiple communities of practice in multiple spaces, the only public institutions many Camden youth have are the streets, and perhaps school and church. Hopeworks, in its intimate family-like brownstone, offers a different universe—small, but connected to other universes as close as Camden and as far away as conferences in California. If the youth who come to Hopeworks construct their identities out of the stuff of the roles they learn to play, and if, as part of their new community of practice, such roles are also enacted within other communities of practice, then their identities are both grounded and somewhat portable. Youth who learn to do action research in their own neighborhoods can see themselves as active agents in trying to effect change. Youth who present at academic conferences can begin to imagine themselves as university students.

Portability does not, however, mean that trainees necessarily want to leave their city. They often see themselves coming back to help, linking medical research to GIS data about neighborhood environments, for example. University education, which seemed like an impossible path for one trainee who considered dropping out of high school, now seems attainable. But for him, as for some others, the present is more important. His leadership position, he says, "has given me something now; I have a skill before I've even attended college."

Much ink has been used to decry the failure of technology in the classroom. Perhaps that is because we have often endowed technology with magical properties rather than looking at it as a tool. The answer to the failure may be found not in the tool, but in the relationships that can be built around its use. Understanding how people collaborate in a community of practice is a step toward that end. For youth living in poverty, however, a community of practice must also include the kind of mentoring that allows them to try on as many roles as possible, connecting with many other communities of practice. Youth need examples and support as they try on these roles and imagine themselves as different kinds of people.

ACKNOWLEDGMENTS

Carol Thompson is grateful to the Next Generation Foundation for a grant that allowed presentation of an earlier version of this chapter at the Digital Generations Conference in London in July 2004. We also thank Lisa Bouillion for her reading and comments on this chapter.

REFERENCES

Brown, K., & Cole, M. (2002). *Cultural historical activity theory and the expansion of opportunities for learning after school.* Accessed from http://lchc.ucsd.edu/People/localz/MCole/browncole.html

Camden County Workforce Investment Board Report. (2000, March). *Camden County Workforce Investment Plan,* pp. 21–22.

Clases, C., & Wehner, T. (2002, August 9). Steps across the border: Cooperation, knowledge production and systems design. *Computer Supported Cooperative Work, 11,* 39–54.

Cole, M. (1996). *Cultural psychology: The once and future discipline.* Cambridge, MA: Belknap Press of Harvard University Press.

Cole, M. (2001, January 19–20). *Sustaining model systems of educational activity: Designing for the long haul.* Paper presented at symposium honoring the work of Ann Brown, Berkeley, CA.

Duranti, A. (1997). *Linguistic anthropology.* Cambridge, UK: Cambridge University Press.

Gee, J. P. (1999). *An introduction to discourse analysis.* New York: Routledge.

Gee, J. P. (2000). Teenagers in new times: A new literacy studies perspective. In J. Elkins & A. Luke (Eds.), *Re/mediating adolescent literacies* [Reprinted from the February 2000 *Journal of Adolescent & Adult Literacy*] (pp. 15–23). Newark, DE: International Reading Association.

Gee, J. P. (2000–2001). *Identity as an analytic lens for research in education. Review of research in education.* Washington, DC: American Educational Research Association.

Gettleman, J. (2004, December 29). Camden's streets go from mean to meanest: Life and death in a city called America's most dangerous. *The New York Times,* pp. B1, B5.

Heath, S. B. (1983). *Ways with words.* New York: Cambridge University Press.

Holland, D., Lachicotte, W., Skinner, D., & Cain, C. (1998). *Identity and agency in cultural worlds.* Cambridge, MA: Harvard University Press.

Hull, G., & Schultz, K. (2001). Literacy and learning out of school: A review of theory and research. *Review of Educational Research, 71*(4), 575–611.

Hymes, D. (2001). On communicative competence. In A. Duranti (Ed.), *Linguistic anthropology: A reader* (pp. 53–73). Malden, MA: Blackwell. (Original work published 1972)

Lave, J., & Wenger, E. (1991). *Situated learning: Legitimate peripheral participation.* Cambridge, UK: Cambridge University Press.

Matusov, E., Bell, N., & Rogoff, B. (2002). Schooling as cultural process: Working together and guidance by children from schools differing in collaborative practices. *Advances in Child Development and Behavior, 29.*

McLaughlin, M. W., & Heath, S. B. (1994). Learning for anything everyday. *Journal of Curriculum Studies, 26*(5), 471–489.

Ochs, E., & Schieffelin, B. B. (2001). Language acquisition and socialization: Three developmental stories and their implications. In A. Duranti (Ed.), *Linguistic anthropology: A reader* (pp. 263–301). Malden, MA: Blackwell. (Original work published 1984)

Rogoff, B. (1990). *Apprenticeship in thinking: Cognitive development in social context.* New York: Oxford University Press.

Rogoff, B. (1995). Observing sociocultural activity on three planes: Participatory appropriation, guided participation, and apprenticeship. In J. Wertsch (Ed.), *Sociocultural studies of mind* (pp. 139–164). New York: Cambridge University Press.

Rogoff, B. (1997). Evaluating development in the process of participation: Theory, methods, and practice building on each other. In E. Amsel & K. A. Renninger (Eds.), *Change and development: Issues of theory, method, and application* (pp. 265–285). Mahwah, NJ: Lawrence Erlbaum Associates.

Rogoff, B. (2003). *The cultural nature of human development.* New York: Oxford University Press.

Rogoff, B., Paradise, R., Arauz, R. M., Correa-Chavez, M., & Angelillo, C. (2003). Firsthand learning through intent participation. *Annual Review of Psychology, 54,* 175–203.

Vygotsky, L. S. (1978). *The mind in society: The development of higher psychological processes.* Cambridge, MA: Harvard University Press.

Wenger, E. (1998). *Communities of practice: Learning, meaning, and identity.* Cambridge: Cambridge University Press.

Author Index

Subject Index